EXECUTIVE SKILLS AND READING COMPREHENSION

Also from the Author

Literacy Processes:
Cognitive Flexibility in Learning and Teaching
Edited by Kelly B. Cartwright

Executive Skills and Reading Comprehension

A GUIDE FOR EDUCATORS

KELLY B. CARTWRIGHT

Foreword by Nell K. Duke

THE GUILFORD PRESS
New York   London

©2015 The Guilford Press
A Division of Guilford Publications, Inc.
370 Seventh Avenue, Suite 1200, New York, NY 10001
www.guilford.com

Printed in the United States of America

This book is printed on acid-free paper.

Last digit is print number: 9   8   7   6   5   4   3

Library of Congress Cataloging-in-Publication Data

Cartwright, Kelly B.
   Executive skills and reading comprehension : a guide for educators / Kelly B. Cartwright ;
foreword by Nell K. Duke.
      pages   cm
   Includes bibliographical references and index.
   ISBN 978-1-4625-2114-2 (paperback) — ISBN 978-1-4625-2116-6 (hardcover)
   1. Reading comprehension.   2. Executive ability in children.   I. Title.
   LB1573.7.C37 2015
   372.47—dc23
                                                                         2015016851

For my son, QiQi,
who likes to "think with my brain . . . because I like it!
All day long!"

About the Author

Kelly B. Cartwright, PhD, is Professor of Psychology, Neuroscience, and Teacher Preparation at Christopher Newport University, where she teaches undergraduate and graduate courses in cognitive, language, and literacy processes. Her research focuses on the development of skilled reading comprehension and the neurocognitive and affective factors that underlie comprehension processes and difficulties from preschool through adulthood. Dr. Cartwright is the editor of the book *Literacy Processes: Cognitive Flexibility in Learning and Teaching*. She regularly works with teachers in schools throughout the United States to better understand and improve comprehension instruction for struggling readers.

Foreword
The Expansion of Comprehension Instruction

In 2002 David Pearson and I published a chapter on reading comprehension instruction in the third edition of *What Research Has to Say about Reading Instruction*. We spent some space in the chapter on creating a supportive classroom context for reading comprehension instruction, but the bulk of the chapter focused on teaching reading comprehension strategies. We identified individual comprehension strategies worthy of instruction (predicting, drawing on prior knowledge, thinking aloud, attending to text structure, visualizing, using graphic organizers, questioning, and summarizing), presented a gradual release of responsibility model for teaching comprehension strategies, and described teaching the strategies individually as well as in clusters or routines, as in reciprocal teaching, for example. We had a very substantial body of research on which to draw, and positioned strategy instruction as ripe for classroom implementation.

For the fourth edition of *What Research Has to Say about Reading Instruction*, published in 2011, David and I again wrote a chapter on reading comprehension instruction, this time with colleagues Stephanie Strachan and Alison Billman. That chapter also attended to teaching reading comprehension strategies, but as a much smaller portion of the chapter and of our model for effective comprehension instruction. Specifically, strategy instruction was one of 10 elements we identified as essential to effective comprehension instruction:

1. Build disciplinary and world knowledge.
2. Provide exposure to a volume and range of texts.

3. Provide motivating texts and contexts for reading.
4. Teach strategies for comprehending.
5. Teach text structures.
6. Engage students in discussion.
7. Build vocabulary and language knowledge.
8. Integrate reading and writing.
9. Observe and assess.
10. Differentiate instruction.

The evolution in the chapters from the third to the fourth edition reflected growth in the research base and greater recognition on our part that strategy instruction alone will not begin to suffice for developing highly effective comprehenders. We were previously aware of the other recommended elements, of course, but afforded them greater prominence in this expanded account of effective comprehension instruction.

In her groundbreaking book *Executive Skills and Reading Comprehension: A Guide for Educators*, Kelly Cartwright further expands our understanding of effective comprehension instruction. In simple terms, one might say she adds an 11th element to the list: "Develop executive skills." But she does much more than that. Kelly helps us understand how executive skills actually undergird and are intertwined with many of these elements of effective comprehension instruction. For example, in the Epilogue (which might be my favorite part of the book, and that's saying something, as I love every section of this book), Kelly explains how these executive skills are integrally related to traditional comprehension strategies. In fact, if you are well versed in comprehension strategy instruction, you might want to start by reading the Epilogue, and then return to it again after reading the full text. Whatever order you read the book, I believe you will leave it convinced of the fundamental importance of executive skills to comprehension strategy use and reading comprehension more broadly.

Another major contribution of this book is to help us understand how executive skills undergird attainment of many Common Core State Standards (and other rigorous standards). Take this second-grade standard from the Reading Standards for Informational Text K–5: "Identify the main purpose of a text, including what the author wants to answer, explain, or describe." This standard requires that the young student be able to think about the thinking of another, in this case the author, essentially getting inside the author's head. This ability is known in the literature as *theory of mind*, but it is relatively rarely discussed in relation to reading comprehension, and quite rarely discussed in a way that provides actionable instructional strategies for teachers, as Kelly does in her chapter on social understanding. I believe you will leave this book with a deepened appreciation of what the Common Core State Standards require of students and how to help them meet those requirements.

It is quite fitting that Kelly demonstrates her own highly developed executive skills in the writing of this book. Chapter 2 is on planning and goals; Kelly's plans and goals for the text are crystal clear (from before Chapter 2, in fact). Chapter 3 is on organization; the entire text is beautifully organized, with a consistent and logical structure for each chapter and plenty of roadmapping. Chapter 4 regards the ability to simultaneously attend to multiple aspects of reading. Kelly considers many aspects of comprehension and of reading more broadly, including how executive skills fit into the complex cognitive dance between attention to letters and sounds and attention to word meaning. Chapter 5 deals with working memory; it was not lost on me that Kelly incorporates a number of devices, such as summaries and tables, to support the reader's processing of the text. And Chapter 7 deals with social understanding. I think you will find that Kelly has gotten into our minds as educators, answering questions from how we actually put particular findings into practice to what constitute important directions for future research. You might notice that I left out Chapter 6: "Inhibition and Impulse Control: Resisting Distractions to Support Comprehension." I don't doubt that Kelly enacted this executive skill as a writer, but you may find it difficult to do the same as a reader. As I read, I found myself making so many connections—what does this mean for a curriculum unit I just wrote, what does this suggest about the length of text students read, how do I use this to get my easily distracted son ready for bed?—some of which admittedly took me a bit off track. I hope and expect that you, too, will find that this text enriches your thinking on a wide variety of fronts.

It must have been a herculean task to pull together all of this theory and research and make it as practical as this. I am enormously grateful to Kelly for doing so, and I believe you will be, too.

NELL K. DUKE, EdD
University of Michigan

Preface

The 1990s were called the "decade of the brain" (Library of Congress, 2000). That label may have been premature, because within the last 3 years the brain and its executive functions have made it to center stage on a national scale. President Obama launched the BRAIN Initiative in April 2013, which brought the brain and its executive functions into central national focus, and the National Institutes of Health and the National Science Foundation are partnering to implement the initiative (Insel, Landis, & Collins, 2013; White House Press Release, April 2013). The Centers for Disease Control and Prevention launched a Healthy Brain Initiative in 2013 to target healthy brain development and executive functioning in our aging population (Alzheimer's Association & Centers for Disease Control and Prevention, 2013). And prestigious universities like Harvard and Johns Hopkins recently launched programs aimed at identifying the ways that the neurosciences can help us better understand educational processes. (See *www.gse.harvard.edu/masters/mbe* for more information on Harvard University's Mind, Brain, and Education Program, and see *education.jhu.edu/research/nei* for more on Johns Hopkins University's Neuro Education Initiative.)

Despite the national focus on the brain and its executive processes, and the amazing advances we have gained since the decade of the brain in the 1990s, insights from this work have not yet made it into the front lines of teaching reading. For example, recently I had a conversation with a reading specialist colleague who was lamenting a young reader who didn't seem to have the memory skills to understand text. I was deep into writing this text at the time, and I mentioned that the student might have difficulty with executive skills. My colleague told me she hadn't heard of those. Yet knowledge of executive skills may be just what she needs, and what we all need, to help our struggling comprehenders engage in the kinds of processing we observe in their more skilled counterparts.

You may be like my colleague. Although resources on improving executive skills for students with special educational needs, such as those with attention-deficit/hyperactivity disorder (ADHD) or those on the autism spectrum, abound, the field has just recently begun to focus on the ways that executive skills may serve typical educational processes like reading or math. What the research is showing is that when students have age-appropriate, fluent decoding abilities that should support comprehension, the differences between good and poor comprehenders can quite often be attributed to problems with executive skills (e.g., Borella, Carretti, & Pelegrina, 2010; Cain, 2006; Locascio, Mahone, Eason, & Cutting, 2010). This knowledge has the potential to change the way we teach these students. And that's why I wrote this book.

My goal in these chapters is to provide practitioners and researchers with an understanding of executive skills and how they are related to reading comprehension and comprehension instruction. In Chapter 1, I define executive skills, describe their development, explain why they would be important for reading comprehension, and provide a brief history of the recent surge in attention to the connection between reading comprehension and executive skills. Additionally, I provide a description of a subset of struggling readers for whom executive skills may be a key difficulty, those whom researchers call "poor comprehenders" because they have limited reading comprehension skill, despite having age-appropriate fluent decoding abilities (Duke, Cartwright, & Hilden, 2014). Finally, to support understanding of how neighboring and overlapping brain regions serve the various executive skills involved in reading comprehension, I provide a brief overview of brain structure and development. Chapter 1 concludes with a description of the common structure of the subsequent chapters, each of which focuses on a particular executive skill important for reading comprehension, so that you know what to expect as you make your way through the book.

I provide greater depth of information on the executive skills that have emerged as important in the reading comprehension process but that have received comparatively less attention in professional work on reading comprehension than familiar skills like monitoring and self-regulated strategy use (e.g., Harvey & Goudvis, 2007; Keene & Zimmerman, 2007). Consistent with recent trends in research on executive skills (e.g., Ardila, 2013; Peterson & Welsh, 2014; Zelazo & Carlson, 2012), I include attention to *cool*—purely cognitive—executive skills and *hot* executive skills that include a social–emotional or motivational component. Finally, as much as possible, I have attempted to present executive skills in the order in which they might be recruited in the reading comprehension process.

Because skilled comprehenders approach reading tasks with a plan to understand texts for particular purposes (Pressley & Afflerbach, 1995; Pressley &

Lundeberg, 2008), I begin with *planning*, a cool executive skill, in Chapter 2. You will find that planning is associated with successful reading comprehension, and students with comprehension difficulties, despite adequate decoding abilities, exhibit significantly poorer planning than their peers with better reading comprehension (Locascio et al., 2010). Because planning also requires an organized approach to reading tasks, including attention to texts' organizational structures, I address another cool skill, *organization*, in Chapter 3. You will see that readers' own organizational abilities, as well as their awareness of language and text organizational structures, are significantly related to their reading comprehension (Cain, 1996; Gaux & Gombert, 1999; Nation & Snowling, 2000; Williams, 2003).

Chapters 4, 5, and 6 address the three core executive skills in turn: *cognitive flexibility, working memory,* and *inhibition,* respectively. In Chapter 4, you will learn that *cognitive flexibility,* a cool skill, involves the ability to hold multiple elements of a task in mind and actively switch between them, which plays a significant role in readers' abilities to manage decoding alongside meaning-making processes across the lifespan; teaching cognitive flexibility improves reading comprehension on school-based and standardized measures (Cartwright, 2015). In Chapter 5, you will find that *working memory,* another cool executive skill, involves the ability to hold information in mind while working with part of that information, which plays an important role in processes that support readers' construction of mental models of text meaning, such as inference making, resolution of ambiguity, and integration processes (Gernsbacher & Faust, 1991; Nation, Adams, Bowyer-Crane, & Snowling, 1999; Seigneuric & Ehrlich, 2005). Chapter 6 focuses on *inhibition,* which has both hot and cool components. The cool component involves the ability to suppress or ignore irrelevant information so that it does not intrude on meaning construction during comprehension, whereas the hot component involves suppressing responses that may detract from comprehension processes; both contribute in important ways to reading comprehension (Andersson, 2008; Arrington, Kulesz, Francis, Fletcher, & Barnes, 2014; Borella et al., 2010).

Finally, Chapter 7 focuses on *social understanding,* a hot executive skill that is understudied with respect to reading comprehension but that is critical to developing nuanced understandings of the causal chains of events in texts that describe characters' actions and interactions, whether fictional or expository. These kinds of social inferences are essential to the kinds of close reading we expect of students, yet elementary students have significant difficulty understanding characters' internal motives (Shannon, Kame'enui, & Baumann, 1988), focusing instead on characters' actions, which may yield only a superficial understanding of texts' content (McConaughy, Fitzhenry-Coor, & Howell, 1983). I close with a brief Epilogue that is designed to relate the executive skills that may be relatively new to you, described in Chapters 2 through 7, to more familiar comprehension skills and strategies (e.g., making predictions), as well as to illustrate how all of these skills work together to produce skilled reading comprehension.

In sum, after reading this book, I want you to take away (1) new information about executive skills and what they look like in young readers, (2) an understanding of why executive skills are essential to successful reading comprehension and comprehension instruction, (3) intervention strategies that can improve students' executive skills and reading comprehension, and (4) a sense of what we know now and what we need to know to take best advantage of what the neurosciences have to offer for our understanding of teaching and learning reading comprehension.

Acknowledgments

Many people make a project like this possible. I am indebted to the classroom teachers, reading teachers, colleagues, and students whose feedback has helped me better understand the many ways executive skills support reading comprehension. I owe a huge debt of thanks to Jesse Spencer, the very best interlibrary loan librarian that a researcher could hope to have in her corner. Thank you, Jesse, for the "same-day service"—without you, the writing of this book would not have been possible. I am most grateful, too, to Craig Thomas, Senior Editor for Education at The Guilford Press, for his vision, enthusiasm, and support for this project from start to finish. Last, but certainly not least, many thanks are (over)due to my family for sharing me with this book for so many, many hours and days.

Contents

Purchasers can download and print
larger versions of select materials from
www.guilford.com/cartwright2-forms.

CHAPTER 1

Executive Skills

What Are They, and Why Are They Important for Developing Thinking Readers?

And so, to completely understand what we do when we read would almost be the acme of a psychologist's achievements, for it would be to describe very many of the most intricate workings of the human mind, as well as to unravel the tangled story of the most remarkable specific performance that civilization has learned in all its history.
—EDMUND BURKE HUEY (1908, p. 6)

Huey was on to something back in 1908. Skilled reading is remarkably complex and requires readers to juggle actively multiple sources of information in text, integrate that information with what they already know, and consciously monitor their own understanding to produce nuanced interpretations of text content. In short, reading is thinking, very active and incredibly complex thinking! Yet we often find that our students seem to lack the thinking skills, such as memory, the ability to plan ahead, and the ability to shift focus when necessary, that seem natural to us as skilled comprehenders.

Consider your own reading of a text: you must translate the letters on the page into sounds and words, link those words to their appropriate meanings, and weave those meanings together to make sense of sentences, paragraphs, and the text as a whole. When reading fiction, you make inferences about characters' emotions from information about their behavior, and you also anticipate characters' future actions based on inferences about their thoughts, feelings, and intentions. When reading fictional and informational texts, you use your knowledge about different kinds of text structures to construct your interpretations of texts, and you make connections between your own knowledge and the information you encounter as you read. Not only that, you somehow manage to hold all of this information in mind while continuing to work your way through the text, and you shift your focus when necessary to ensure that you understand what you read.

These processes are just the tip of the iceberg in skilled reading. These cognitive feats are indeed impressive, and they are also difficult to teach! The trouble for teachers (who are also skilled readers) is that the thinking processes we use when we read are so well practiced that they often occur below the level of conscious awareness (Duffy, 2014). That is, they occur automatically, which makes it difficult for us to reflect on them in ways that help us explain them to our students. Much like riding a bicycle, we know we can do it, but explaining how it happens is another story entirely! Contemporary neuroscience perspectives have much to say about the kinds of higher order thinking skills necessary for academic success (Blair et al., 2007; Guare, 2014; Katzir & Paré-Blagoev, 2006; Liew, 2012; Meltzoff, Kuhl, Movellan, & Sejnowski, 2009) and for the development of reading comprehension in particular (Cartwright, 2012; Cartwright & Guajardo, 2015; Fuhs, Nesbitt, Farran, & Dong, 2014; Sesma, Mahone, Levine, Eason, & Cutting, 2009). These higher order skills, called executive skills (or executive functions), also have important implications for instruction.

If you've opened any education professional book catalogues recently, you've probably seen a host of new texts on executive skills and learning problems, executive skills and ADHD, "smart but scattered" students, or some other such topic (e.g., Dawson & Guare, 2009, 2010, 2012; Guare, Dawson, & Guare, 2012; Kaufman, 2010; McCloskey, Perkins, & Van Divner, 2009; Meltzer, 2010; Solanto, 2013). The burgeoning market for texts with these popular themes may lead us to believe that knowledge of executive skills is particularly important for special education teachers, but that executive skills are not necessarily relevant for teachers in regular education classrooms or for literacy coaches and reading specialists who support implementation of the reading curriculum for all students.

As it turns out, executive skills are important not only for understanding learning *problems*, but they are also important for understanding learning *successes* across the curriculum (Guare, 2014; Meltzer, 2010). What's more, new research is revealing that executive skills play important roles in literacy learning, with particularly critical roles in successful reading comprehension (see Cartwright, 2012, 2015; Kieffer, Vukovic, & Berry, 2013; Sesma et al., 2009). Furthermore, as you might expect, children who have difficulties with reading comprehension, despite having age-appropriate word reading skills, have lower levels of executive skills than their peers with better comprehension (Borella, Carretti, & Pelegrina, 2010; Cain, 2006; Locascio, Mahone, Eason, & Cutting, 2010). These discoveries are important for all educators because reading comprehension is the foundation for all other learning in school: students cannot understand, enjoy, or respond to literature without effective reading comprehension; likewise, students cannot gather new information from science, math, or social studies texts when they don't understand what they read. Fortunately for reading educators and for our students, executive skills can be taught, providing us additional ways to convey the complex thinking processes involved in skilled reading to our students, and yielding improvements in executive skills and reading comprehension to support our students' current—and future— academic success (e.g., Cartwright, 2002; García-Madruga et al., 2013).

Or, perhaps the term *executive skills* is new to you; without any background knowledge, this term may sound a bit like the kinds of managerial skills required of a CEO. You may be like one of my reading specialist colleagues who recently lamented that one of her students did not seem to have the memory skills necessary to comprehend a text. As our conversation continued and I mentioned executive skills, she shared that she had never heard of them and wondered what they were. Like my colleague, you may be asking what exactly are these skills, how do they support reading comprehension, and how can we incorporate them into classroom instruction in ways that promote better reading comprehension in students who struggle? This text is designed to answer those questions. I have two main goals in writing this text:

1. To provide practitioners and scholars with new information about executive skills and why they're essential to successful reading comprehension and comprehension instruction.
2. To provide executive skill-based intervention strategies that can be used to improve students' executive skills and reading comprehension, and thus their future academic success.

Because this research area is so new, most studies to date have focused on the various contributions of different kinds of executive skills to reading comprehension, with promising results. I review these findings in the chapters that follow. Many interesting questions remain to be investigated, and comparatively fewer studies have been done to explore ways to improve students' executive skills for better reading comprehension. The results that are emerging in this area are exciting and have the potential to revolutionize the ways we teach reading comprehension, especially for students who struggle in this area.

In addition, some research on comprehension interventions, though not originally focused on executive skills per se, has utilized methods that target children's executive functioning to improve reading comprehension. I will also share information about these promising interventions to support your comprehension instructional practices, especially for students who struggle with reading comprehension. All of the interventions I will present can be integrated into a differentiated literacy instruction framework, such as the response-to-intervention (RTI) framework

(Fuchs & Fuchs, 2009; Fuchs, Fuchs, & Vaughn, 2008; Fuchs & Vaughn, 2012) to support readers at all levels of instructional need. Furthermore, comprehension interventions that target executive skills have been designed for both narrative and informational (expository) texts; thus, they address two important strands of the reading standards in the Common Core State Standards Initiative (CCSS; 2014), as well as other components of the CCSS. When appropriate, I note connections of executive skills and instructional techniques to the College and Career Readiness Anchor Standards (CCR) of the CCSS to facilitate the alignment of your instruction with these important standards. Look for the CCSS margin notes throughout this text. I use the CCSS notation system in these notes: R.CCR.1, for example, stands for Reading—College and Career Readiness Anchor Standard 1.

Overview of This Chapter

In this introductory chapter I define executive skills, explain why executive skills would be related to reading comprehension, describe how these skills develop and relate to underlying brain structures, and provide a history "mini-lesson" to describe the recent surge in attention to the connection between reading comprehension and executive skills. After briefly addressing executive skills assessment (and referring you to useful resources), I will describe a subset of readers (about 10–30% of struggling readers; Aaron, Joshi, & Williams, 1999; Applegate, Applegate, & Modla, 2009; Buly & Valencia, 2002; Catts, Hogan, & Fey, 2003; Shankweiler et al., 1999; Torppa et al., 2007; see Cartwright, 2010, for a review) who struggle with reading comprehension despite having adequate decoding skills. These students, who teachers commonly call "word callers" because they read aloud fluently without any apparent understanding of what they are reading (Cartwright, 2010; Dolch, 1960), have specific reading comprehension difficulties (RCD); they emerge in most classrooms, don't respond to typical evidence-based comprehension instruction, and puzzle their teachers and parents because they sound like good readers (Applegate et al., 2009). Additionally, and important for our discussion, these students typically have weak executive skills (e.g., Borella et al., 2010; Cain, 2006; Locascio et al., 2010). Thus, students with RCD are particularly likely to benefit from reading comprehension interventions that target executive skills. I close the chapter with an overview of the remainder of the book.

Before we embark on a discussion of formal definitions of executive skills, however, I thought we should begin with a definition of reading comprehension to frame our discussion for the remainder of the book. Additionally, I want to provide an example of a struggling comprehender whose reading behaviors will help you better understand the operation of executive skills in reading comprehension processes and to whom you can relate our future discussions of particular executive skills.

What Is Reading Comprehension?

The RAND Reading Study Group (RRSG; 2002, p. xiii) defined reading comprehension "as the process of simultaneously extracting and constructing meaning through interaction and involvement with written language. It consists of three elements: the reader, the text, and the activity or purpose for reading." See Figure 1.1 for a visual representation of these three types of factors that interact to produce successful reading comprehension. The operation of executive skills in reading comprehension cuts across all three of these areas. Executive skills are reader factors that influence the comprehension process, and the ways we deploy our executive skills depend on the type and structure of texts that we are reading as well as our purposes in reading tasks. I will continue to refer to this model of reading comprehension throughout the book.

Consider Brittany, Who Has Specific RCD

Brittany is a phenomenal reader (or, perhaps I should say phenomenal *decoder*) who just entered your third-grade class at a fifth-grade reading level. Brittany can already read all of the third-grade sight words, and she's rarely stumped by a new word when reading aloud during small-group instruction. During the beginning-of-year assessments, as you take a running record on Brittany, you find that her reading accuracy is high, and she reads with appropriate rate and expression. (No surprise there!) You are so pleased to have such a good reader in your class and expect that she'll be an "easy" student this year. And then, as you continue your assessment, you ask Brittany to retell a story she just read aloud (flawlessly, of course), and she's stumped. Her retelling misses several key story events, she confuses important story details, she seems to have misunderstood the protagonist's goals in the narrative, and she completely omits one of the main characters entirely. These behaviors don't align with everything else you know about Brittany, and

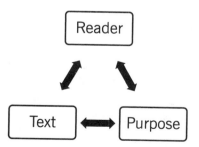

FIGURE 1.1. The three factors that interact to produce successful reading comprehension, according to the RAND Reading Study Group (2002).

you wonder what might be going on. She has the requisite skills to be a successful comprehender, according to the National Reading Panel (2000; good phonemic awareness and phonics knowledge, wonderful fluency [both rate and expression], and good oral and sight word vocabularies). But, clearly, something is missing!

For Brittany and students like her, "what's missing" is often executive skills. Many times, students like Brittany are unable to remember and integrate story details, or they have difficulty staying focused on relevant aspects of the text, attending to irrelevant information instead. These students may lack the ability to focus on multiple aspects of a text while reading (e.g., thinking about meaning while they are also focusing on decoding), or they may not understand that they should approach a text with the intention of making meaning. They may lack the planning ability to preview and attend to text features that support understanding or lack the monitoring ability to realize that they do not actually understand what they are reading. These students may also have trouble inferring an author's intentions or making inferences about characters' actions, based on the characters' beliefs or feelings. Finally, these students may lack comprehension strategy knowledge, or—even if they have knowledge of comprehension strategies—they may be unable to deploy those strategies to support understanding.

By now, you have probably identified several Brittanys in your class or school. And, if you are like other teachers with whom I have worked, you have probably struggled to find interventions that help these students achieve better comprehension because they just don't respond to your regular comprehension instruction the way that your other students do. Understanding what will work for them requires understanding the kinds of thinking processes that may be missing for these students beyond the skills we typically consider important for reading comprehension (e.g., vocabulary and decoding skills like phonemic awareness, phonics, and fluency). The next sections describe executive skills, the higher order thinking processes quite often missing for struggling comprehenders, so that you have a foundation on which to base your understanding of effective interventions for these students.

What Are Executive Skills?

Think of the term executive skills as an umbrella term that refers to a set of mental tools we use to manage tasks and achieve goals (Anderson, 2002; Dawson & Guare, 2010; Goldstein & Naglieri, 2014; Meltzer, 2010). Thus, the notion of goal-directed activity is essential to the definition of executive skills. Just as a chief executive of a company sets goals for the company and manages that company's operations to achieve those goals, our executive skills are what we use to engage in self-regulated, goal-directed behavior in any area of life, from planning and executing a trip to the grocery store to reading and understanding a complex journal article. Other words used to describe executive skills are *executive control processes* and *executive functions*, and these terms are used interchangeably in the literature on this topic.

As you might expect, executive skills emerge early in life (Bell, 2012; Cuevas & Bell, 2014; Fuhs & Day, 2011; Morasch & Bell, 2011) and develop across childhood and beyond (Anderson, Anderson, Northam, Jacobs, & Catroppa, 2001; Cartwright, Isaac, & Dandy, 2006; Davidson, Amso, Anderson, & Diamond, 2006; Fuhs & Day, 2011; Guare, 2014; Peterson & Welsh, 2014). Even in very young students, executive skills enable the self-control that is necessary to remember classroom routines, pay attention to the teacher's directions (and not to the fidgety classmates nearby), and inhibit inappropriate behaviors like the impulse to grab the colorful toys on the shelf when one is supposed to be sitting criss-cross-applesauce and listening to the teacher during circle time (Blair et al., 2007; Liew, 2012; Zhou, Chen, & Main, 2012; Zelazo, 2013).

Because research on executive skills is relatively new, there is wide variation in definitions for this set of skills. In addition, beyond three core skills (cognitive flexibility, working memory, and inhibition, described below), the numbers of thinking processes that fall under the executive skills umbrella vary depending on whose work you're reading. However, common among all of the varied definitions is the notion that executive skills involve regulating one's own thinking to achieve desired goals (Guare, 2014). For our purposes in this text, I will provide information on the executive skills that have emerged as important in the reading comprehension process but that have received comparatively less attention in professional work on reading comprehension than familiar skills like self-regulated strategy use (Harvey & Goudvis, 2007; Keene & Zimmerman, 2007). Thus, this text will include chapters on the three core skills I listed above as well as other, more complex executive skills that depend on the core skills and are also essential to the meaning-making process.

The development of executive skills is significantly related to children's oral language and vocabulary (Allan & Lonigan, 2011; Astington & Jenkins, 1999; Fuhs & Day, 2011), thus it is no surprise that executive skills would also be related to reading comprehension. In the traditions of Vygotsky and Luria, Bodrova and colleagues (Bodrova, Leong, & Akhutina, 2011) suggested that executive skills are voluntary behaviors over which students gain increasing control by using language to guide themselves through tasks. In other words, children develop increased control over their executive skills through verbal regulation of their own thinking (Kray & Ferdinand, 2013). Talking about their own thinking helps children regulate their behavior because it causes them to reflect on their performance, become more aware of their thinking, and ignore other distracting information (Cragg & Nation, 2010; Marcovitch, Jacques, Boseovski, & Zelazo, 2008). Indeed, even in preschoolers, children's developing vocabulary is related to their executive skills (see Cartwright & Guajardo, 2015, for a review). And preschoolers' self-regulatory speech is also related to cognitive flexibility, one of the core executive skills (Alarcón-Rubio, Sánchez-Medina, & Prieto-García, 2014).

Core Executive Skills

There is fairly wide agreement that the core, or most basic, executive skills are cognitive flexibility, working memory, and inhibition (Best & Miller, 2010; Diamond, 2013; Miyake, Friedman, Emerson, Witzki, & Howerter, 2000). Cognitive flexibility is the ability to shift attention from one activity to another or to actively switch back and forth between important components of a task. Students must shift attention during classroom transitions, such as when shifting from recess to math. Likewise, when reading, skilled comprehenders actively shift focus between many things, such as word and text meanings, letter–sound information, and syntactic information.

Working memory is the child's capacity for holding information in mind while working with part of that information, such as when a child remembers the steps involved in the classroom's morning routine while engaging in each of those steps (e.g., put my backpack in the cubby, sit in my assigned seat, get my journal out of my desk, find the next clean journal page, and respond to the writing prompt my teacher has put on the board). Similarly, when building a mental model of a text's meaning (what Kintsch, 1994, calls a situation model), a good comprehender must keep in mind the various text ideas presented, note the causal links between them, and update the model as he or she encounters new ideas in text.

Finally, inhibition involves the ability to resist engaging in a habitual response as well as the ability to ignore distracting information. In other words, inhibition requires one to think before acting (Diamond, 2013). You might think of this as stifling a gut reaction, such as when the preschool child at circle time (described above) resists her impulse to grab an attractive toy nearby. Similarly, good comprehenders must inhibit activation of inappropriate word meanings, such as ignoring ideas about financial institutions when reading about the *banks* of a river, or irrelevant connections to ideas encountered in texts. These three core skills underlie more complex executive skills, such as planning and organization (Diamond, 2013).

More Complex Executive Skills

Other, more complex executive skills also contribute to reading comprehension. For example, planning involves setting and working toward a goal, and organization involves ordering and sequencing information or subtasks in ways that support completion of a goal. Thus, these two executive skills work hand-in-hand to support reading comprehension. As an example, consider what you do when you need to go shopping for various items. A shopping trip requires planning, such as choosing a route and making a shopping list, as well as organization, such as remembering the elements of your route in the correct order and arranging the items on your shopping list by the stops along your route (or even by the sections in the store, such as when you list all produce items together so that you can collect them all when you visit the produce section of the grocery store). You cannot reach your goal without a plan, and you can do so most effectively if you are aware of the steps you need to take, in the proper order, to ensure that your goal is met.

For the purposes of this text (and for most teachers and reading researchers I know), the overarching goal in reading tasks is to understand the text, and good readers approach text with a plan to do just that. For example, even before they read, good readers do particular things intentionally to ensure that they understand a text, such as activating their prior knowledge, attending to text structure, or previewing the text (Pressley & Afflerbach, 1995; Pressley & Lundeberg, 2008; Wyatt et al., 1993). That is, they begin reading with a plan to understand. Readers may also have a specific type of comprehension goal in mind when they read, which affects how they organize their approaches to reading. Students can generate goals themselves, such as when one reads an informational text to learn about the feeding and nesting patterns of an interesting bird at the classroom bird feeder. Alternatively, specific comprehension goals can be assigned by a teacher to support students' comprehension of texts, such as when we ask our students to identify the characters and problem in a story. Regardless of the comprehension goal, we know that good readers begin with goals in mind, and engage in particular activities to reach those goals (Pressley & Afflerbach, 1995; Pressley & Lundeberg, 2008; Wyatt et al., 1993). Organization supports planning because it helps the reader systematically manage his or her reading activities and track the order of incoming text information, noting text structure (Armbruster, Anderson, & Ostertag, 1987; Cain, 1996; Gersten, Fuchs, Williams, & Baker, 2001; Meyer, Brandt, & Bluth, 1980; Taylor, 1982; Williams, 2005) and causal relations between text elements (Graesser, Singer, & Trabasso, 1994; van den Broek, 1989), which directly support comprehension.

The Distinction between Hot and Cool Executive Skills

In addition to varying in complexity, executive skills also vary in the degree to which they involve students' motivational or social–emotional processes. Consider the students in your class who adapt well to classroom routines and are able effectively to manage and control their own behavior. These students are able to regulate thinking and learning, and they are also able to regulate their emotional processes. In addition, they have good peer relations, and they have strong self-regulation skills. By contrast, other students are impulsive and emotionally reactive, they have difficulty controlling their own behavior, interacting with peers, and sticking to classroom routines. And these students may also have problems focusing on tasks and ignoring irrelevant information. The differences you see in these children are both cognitive and social–emotional, and both kinds of differences reflect variations in executive skills.

Although executive skills have traditionally been viewed as purely cognitive activities involved in regulating one's own thinking and behavior, such as planning, inhibition, cognitive flexibility, and working memory (abilities known as "cool skills"), new research suggests executive skills also include processes with a social, emotional, or motivational component, often called effortful control processes, such as self-regulation, impulse control, and social understanding (abilities known as "hot skills"; Blair et al., 2007; Brock, Rimm-Kaufman, Nathanson, & Grimm, 2009; Peterson & Welsh, 2014; Zelazo & Carlson, 2012; Zelazo & Müller, 2002; Zelazo, Qu, & Müller, 2005; Zhou et al., 2012; also see Dawson & Guare, 2010, and Kaufman, 2010, for more on emotional control and self-regulation). The distinction between cool and hot executive skills is not as important to reading comprehension as the fact that *all* of these skills contribute meaningfully to readers' comprehension processes; thus, I include attention to both types of executive skills in this book to expand our focus beyond just the cool, purely cognitive skills that have been traditionally viewed as important to reading comprehension processes.

Hot and cool executive skills are related in preschool (Carlson, Moses, & Claxton, 2004; Drayton, Turley-Ames, & Guajardo, 2011; Frye, Zelazo, & Palfai, 1995; Fuhs & Day, 2011; Guajardo, Parker, & Turley-Ames, 2009), elementary school (Bock, Gallaway, & Hund, 2014; Guajardo & Cartwright, 2015), and in adulthood (Saxe, Schulz, & Jiang, 2006). Additionally, although scholars have debated whether hot executive skills precede cool ones in development (or vice versa; e.g., see Perner & Lang, 1999), evidence suggests these skills reflect the same kinds of self-regulation abilities, just expressed in different areas of development (Miller & Marcovitch, 2012; Zelazo et al., 2005; Zhou et al., 2012). Because both hot and cool skills reflect the same kinds of underlying thinking processes, scholars argue that we should integrate work on hot and cool skills in order to have a more complete understanding of the executive processes necessary for academic success, including success in reading comprehension (Cartwright & Guajardo, 2015; Liew, 2012; Zhou et al., 2012). Thus, I have included attention to both types of skills in this book.

The following findings point to the important overlap between hot and cool executive skills. These two varieties of executive skills:

- Develop in parallel (Fuhs & Day, 2011; Hongwanishkul, Happeney, Lee, & Zelazo, 2005; Miller & Marcovitch, 2012).
- Predict one another in development; that is, hot skills assessed in infancy and toddlerhood predict cool skills in childhood and adolescence (Friedman, Miyake, Robinson, & Hewitt, 2011; Ursasche, Blair, Stifter, Voegtline, & The Family Life Project Investigators, 2013); and cool skills in the

early preschool years predict hot skills later (Benson, Sabbagh, Carlson, & Zelazo, 2012; Blankson et al., 2013; Hughes & Ensor, 2007).

- Contribute to the same underlying complex thinking abilities (rather than emerging as separate constructs), especially in younger students (e.g., Allan & Lonigan, 2011; Fuhs & Day, 2011; Prencipe et al., 2011; see Rueda, Posner, & Rothbart, 2005, for a review).
- Are served by adjacent and overlapping brain regions: cool skills are typically associated with dorsolateral prefrontal cortex (around the top and sides of the frontal lobes), hot skills are typically associated with orbitofrontal cortex (around the bottom and front of the frontal lobes, closer to the eyes), and ventral and medial areas of the prefrontal cortex (near the bottom and sides of the frontal lobes) are associated with both hot and cool skills (Ardilla, 2013; Aron, Robbins, & Poldrack, 2004; Blakemore & Choudhury, 2006; Fletcher & Henson, 2001; Rueda et al., 2005; Saxe et al., 2006; Stone, Baron-Cohen, & Knight, 1998; Zelazo et al., 2005; Zelazo & Carlson, 2012); you will read more about these topics later in this chapter.
- Are impaired in individuals on the autism spectrum (Ozonoff, Pennington, & Rogers, 1991; Pellicano, 2007; see Cartwright & Guajardo, 2015, for a review).
- Play important roles in academic tasks and academic success (Blair et al., 2007; Liew, 2012).

Although self-regulation is probably the most widely cited hot executive skill (Dawson & Guare, 2010; Kaufman, 2010), social understanding, also called *theory of mind*, is another hot executive skill that is significantly related to reading comprehension. Theory of mind involves a child's ability to understand her own and others' mental states, intentions, beliefs, perspectives, and desires (Astingtin, Harris, & Olson, 1988; Miller, 2012). Of particular importance for teachers, social understanding can be taught with positive effects on reading comprehension (e.g., Guajardo & Watson, 2002; Lysaker, Tonge, Gauson, & Miller, 2011)! This makes sense, because students must understand others' thoughts to comprehend an author's purpose or to make inferences about characters' motivations and intentions from their behaviors; and, social understanding also facilitates readers' understanding of their own reading processes (i.e., metacognition; Lecce, Zocchi, Pagnin, Palladino, & Taumoepeau, 2010).

A related aspect of social understanding is counterfactual reasoning, which involves making inferences about alternative outcomes to one's own or others' behavior. For example, when reading *Alexander and the Terrible, Horrible, No Good, Very Bad Day* (Viorst, 1972), a reader might ask him- or herself, "How might Alexander have had a better day?" (Guajardo & Turley-Ames, 2004; Guajardo et al., 2009; Hutto, 2007; Roese, 1997). Counterfactual reasoning in preschoolers predicts success in reading comprehension in the elementary years

(Cartwright & Guajardo, 2011), and counterfactual reasoning in adults is also related to reading comprehension skill (Trabasso & Bartolone, 2003). Thus, this aspect of hot executive functioning also contributes positively to the development of reading comprehension.

Because both cool and hot executive skills are related to reading comprehension and can be taught, I have included chapters in this text that focus on traditional, cool skills like planning, organization, cognitive flexibility, and working memory. Other chapters will focus on hot skills such as inhibition (which has both cool and hot components) and social understanding, and all chapters will include implications of these cool and hot executive skills for improving your students' reading comprehension (see Table 1.1 for a list of executive skills and their definitions as well as additional examples of ways these skills support comprehension processes).

The Development of Executive Skills

As noted above, the development of executive skills begins early in life (Bell, 2012; Cuevas & Bell, 2014; Fuhs & Day, 2011; Hoehl, Reid, Mooney, & Striano, 2008; Morasch & Bell, 2011) and is associated with the development of oral language skills (Allan & Lonigan, 2011; Astington & Jenkins, 1999; Fuhs & Day, 2011), especially the self-regulatory language that children use to talk themselves through tasks (Alarcón-Rubio et al., 2014; Bodrova et al., 2011; Cragg & Nation, 2010; Kray & Ferdinand, 2013; Marcovitch et al., 2008). In fact, one of the important ways researchers have learned about the processes necessary for skilled reading comprehension is to ask skilled comprehenders to think—and talk—aloud as they comprehend texts, voicing aloud the self-regulatory thinking that supports their comprehension (Pressley & Afflerbach, 1995; Pressley & Lundeberg, 2008; Wyatt et al., 1993).

A recurring theme in studies of executive skills is that there is both unity and diversity in these skills; that is, each executive skill has unique features and makes unique contributions to development in other areas (like reading), but these skills are also closely related (Miyake et al., 2000). For example, children can already demonstrate working memory, cognitive flexibility, and inhibition by 3 years of age (Hughes, 1998), and these three skills overlap considerably in the preschool years and become more differentiated with age (Lee, Bull, & Ho, 2013). Of these three core skills, inhibition improves most dramatically across the preschool period (Best & Miller, 2010; Montgomery & Koeltzow, 2010), and continues to develop more gradually across the elementary school years (Altemeier, Abbott, & Berninger, 2008). Consistent with these findings, I have recently observed striking improvements in my 4-year-old son's inhibition skills with the emergence of inhibition-related self-regulatory language, which he even uses to remind me to "Wait!" and "Be patient!"

TABLE 1.1. Processes Typically Included in the Umbrella of Executive Skills That Support Reading Comprehension

Process	Definition and example(s)
Cognitive flexibility	The ability to consider multiple bits of information or ideas at one time and actively switch between them when engaging in a task; this is related to *switching* or *shifting*, which involves the ability to change focus from one aspect of a task to another; also called *attentional control* (see Zhou, Chen, & Main, 2012). Note that tasks that require single shifts (such as sorting by beginning sound, and then changing the sorting rule to sort along another dimension) are less challenging than tasks that require continual shifting back and forth between multiple elements of a task (such as sorting a group of words by their beginning sound and number of syllables at the same time). *The ability to think about multiple aspects of print simultaneously, such as thinking of words as composed of sounds but also as representations of meaning, requires cognitive flexibility. Additionally, the ability to focus on a character's perspective and then change focus to consider the author's purpose in writing a story in a particular way requires the shifting (or switching) aspect of cognitive flexibility.*
Inhibition	The ability to restrain one's normal or habitual responses as well as the ability to ignore or suppress irrelevant or distracting information; sometimes called *inhibitory control* or *impulse control*. *Maintaining focus on constructing meaning from text and resisting the temptation to daydream requires inhibition. Likewise, ignoring irrelevant word meanings or text connections, while focusing on the meanings and connections that aid meaning construction, also requires inhibition.*
Monitoring	The ability to take a step back and reflect on one's own thoughts, perspectives, and mental processes and assess their effectiveness. This is an aspect of *metacognition* or thinking about one's own thinking. *Readers show monitoring skills when they actively track their own understanding while they read; such monitoring often results in the choice to engage in self-regulatory behaviors to ensure that comprehension takes place (see below).*
Organization	The ability to impose order on information and objects, create systems for managing information or objects, and recognize such orders and systems so that one can use them successfully to complete tasks *The awareness of structures for different types of texts enables readers to organize text details in ways that make sense and support meaning construction; for example, knowing typical story structure or the patterns and features found in informational text permits readers to organize incoming information in ways that support comprehension of those types of texts.*

(continued)

TABLE 1.1. *(continued)*

Process	Definition and example(s)
Planning	The ability to decide what tasks are necessary to complete a goal, including understanding which ones are most important to goal attainment and the order in which those tasks should be completed to most effectively reach the goal.
	Planning necessarily involves a goal orientation, which can support comprehension in a number of ways. Readers who approach reading tasks with a plan to understand the text for a particular purpose can engage in specific goal-directed behaviors that are executed with that overarching comprehension goal in mind. For example, when reading the book Wolf, *by Becky Bloom (1999), students who have the goal of understanding the wolf's motivation in the story, perhaps in comparison to other wolves in children's books with which they are familiar, will be better able to recognize the wolf's desire to be accepted by a group of literate barnyard animals and better able to remember the various attempts the wolf makes to become a successful reader during the course of the narrative.*
Social understanding	The ability to consider or infer one's own and others' mental and emotional states, such as thoughts, feelings, desires, motives, or intentions, and use those to make predictions and generate explanations for others' behavior; also called *theory of mind* or *social imagination*.
	A reader shows good social understanding when he knows characters' emotional states and intentions play a causal role in characters' actions and can use that information to make predictions about story outcomes. Similarly, when readers can infer an author's purpose for writing a text and then use that information to better understand the text, they are benefiting from the application of social understanding.
Switching or shifting	The ability to change one's attentional focus from an initial idea to a new one (this is related to *cognitive flexibility* and *attentional control*; see above).
Working memory	The ability to hold information in mind to support completion of tasks while working with part of that information and updating it as needed; working memory includes a storage component and a processing component.
	Working memory is necessary to hold story details in mind to construct a coherent representation of a text's meaning while continuing to add new details one discovers while reading.

Note. Italics indicate examples of how executive skills support comprehension processes. Adapted from Cartwright (2012). Copyright 2012 by Taylor & Francis. Adapted by permission.

In a study of 4- to 13-year-olds, Davidson and colleagues found that working memory and inhibition develop earlier than cognitive flexibility, which continues to develop into adolescence and beyond (Davidson et al., 2006; also see Cartwright et al., 2006, who showed that cognitive flexibility develops into adulthood). Yeniad et al. (2014) found that cognitive flexibility develops across the transition from kindergarten to first grade (when students were 5 to 6 years of age), with much room for continued improvement after first grade. Best, Miller, and Jones (2009) similarly observed that the development of working memory and cognitive flexibility occurs after age 5 (i.e., after the preschool years), and like cognitive flexibility, the development of working memory continues into adulthood (Huizinga, Dolan, & van der Molen, 2006). More complex cool executive skills, such as planning, improve across the elementary school years and beyond (Best et al., 2009). Hot skills, such as theory of mind, follow a similar developmental pattern, showing much improvement across the preschool years (Wellman & Liu, 2004), with continued development of more sophisticated versions of these skills into adolescence and adulthood (Miller, 2012; Lovett & Pillow, 2010; Pillow & Lovett, 1998). Because reading comprehension also develops considerably across the elementary school years and into adulthood, it makes sense that the development of executive skills would impact reading comprehension development in important ways.

You may be wondering what kinds of factors influence the development of executive skills in your students, as you undoubtedly observe differences in these skills, even among students at the same grade level. As is typical of any academic skill, children from homes with lower socioeconomic status or those who experience poverty and financial hardship usually have lower executive skills than their peers with more material resources (Raver, Blair, Willoughby, & The Family Life Project Key Investigators, 2013). Additionally, the quality and types of family interactions children experience are related to the development of executive skills. For example, children with siblings have higher levels of social understanding than peers without siblings (Perner, Ruffman, & Leekam, 1994). But it's having older (not younger) siblings that seems to foster social understanding (Ruffman, Perner, Naito, Parkin, & Clements, 1998), probably because younger siblings must learn quickly how to infer older siblings' intentions in order to avoid unpleasant situations!

With respect to parents, infants whose mothers are sensitive to their needs, express positive regard, and exhibit animation in interactions have higher levels of executive skills in preschool than infants whose mothers are more detached, who impose their own interests (rather than being sensitive to infants' needs), and show negative regard (Rhoades, Greenberg, Lanza, & Blair, 2011; also see Fay-Stammbach, Hawes, & Meredith, 2014, for a review). Furthermore, when mothers of 3-year-olds exhibit positive parenting qualities, such as responsiveness and sensitivity to children's needs, positive regard, and provision of cognitive stimulation for children, the children show more growth in cool executive skills from 3 to 5 years of age (Blair, Raver, Berry, & Family Life Project Investigators, 2014). Consistent with these findings, Aram, Fine, and Ziv (2013) observed that parents' references to characters' mental and emotional states during book reading fostered higher social understanding in their preschool children. The relation between parenting quality and executive skill development appears to be bidirectional in the preschool years: the levels of children's executive skills at age 3 also predict changes in parenting quality from 3 to 5 years of age, with higher child executive skills related to (and possibly eliciting) better parenting quality (Blair et al., 2014). Finally, Cuevas and colleagues (2014) recently examined whether mothers' own levels of executive skills, in addition to parenting quality, contributed to the development of child executive skills from infancy to age 4 years. As you might expect, mothers' executive skills contributed positively to children's executive skills, whereas mothers' negative care-giving behaviors were negatively related to children's executive skills. A recent review summarized research on parental influences on the development of executive skills, finding that parental scaffolding of children's thinking, including elaboration, praise, redirection, and autonomy support; provision of cognitive stimulation; and parental warmth, sensitivity, and lack of hostility were all related to the development of children's executive skills (Fay-Stammbach et al., 2014).

On the whole, although research on family and contextual influences on executive skill development is relatively new, we now know that children tend to develop better executive skills when they:

- Have access to more material resources (i.e., come from homes of higher socioeconomic status).
- Experience better quality, more positive, supportive parenting.
- Experience fewer negative, hostile parenting practices.
- Experience cognitively stimulating activities like conversations about characters' mental and emotional states during shared book reading.
- Experience scaffolding in interactions with adults, such as elaboration, praise, redirection of attention, and autonomy support.
- Have older siblings.
- Have parents with better executive skills.

Similarly, maternal positive responsiveness, children's home literacy environments, and children's early home literacy experiences are associated with better reading comprehension in grade 3 (Sénéchal & LeFevre, 2002; Taylor, Anthony, Aghara, Smith, & Landry, 2008).

In the next section, I review research on brain development to illustrate the kinds of physical changes that underlie the development of executive skills. Developmental changes in brain structures occur at particular ages and are thought to be associated with corresponding developments in children's thinking and executive function. What we know about brain development also highlights the importance of children's experiences in developing the executive skills necessary for success in reading comprehension.

How Does Brain Development Relate to the Development of Executive Skills?

The outer layer of the brain, the cerebral cortex (typically just called the cortex), is responsible for our higher order cognitive functions, including executive skills. The cortex has two parallel halves, or hemispheres, on each side of our head, joined by a wide band of fibers called the corpus callosum. Each of our hemispheres is divided into four sections, called lobes, which are associated with different functions. The occipital lobes at the back of your head, for example, are associated with visual processing. The temporal lobes, just above your ears and near your temples, are associated with hearing. The frontal lobes, which are just behind your forehead, are associated with executive skills in children and adults (see Figure 1.2; Bunge & Wright, 2007; Dawson & Guare, 2010; Eslinger, Biddle, Pennington, & Page, 1999; Kane & Engle, 2002; Montgomery & Koeltzow, 2010; Zelazo & Müller, 2002).

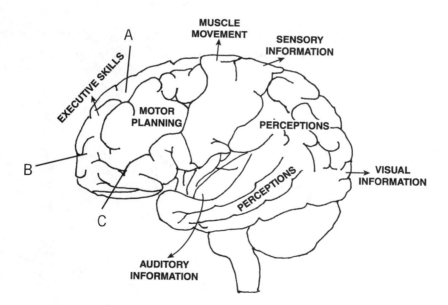

FIGURE 1.2. The human brain, with the approximate locations of major functions. *A,* dorsolateral prefrontal cortex; *B,* orbitofrontal cortex; *C,* ventrolateral, ventromedial, and medial prefrontal cortex. Adapted from Dawson and Guare (2010). Copyright 2010 by The Guilford Press. Adapted by permission.

As noted above, different regions of the frontal lobes are related to different kinds of executive skills: the parts at the top and sides (dorsolateral prefrontal cortex—A in Figure 1.2) are related to cool executive skills; the parts at the front and bottom near the eyes (orbitofrontal cortex—B in Figure 1.2) are related to hot executive skills; and the parts on the bottom and sides (the ventral and medial parts, such as ventrolateral prefrontal cortex, ventromedial prefrontal cortex, and medial prefrontal cortex—C in Figure 1.2) are active in both hot and cool executive skills tasks (Ardilla, 2013; Aron et al., 2004; Blakemore & Choudhury, 2006; Otero & Barker, 2014; Rueda et al., 2005; Saxe et al., 2006; Stone et al., 1998; Vogeley et al., 2001; Zelazo et al., 2005; Zelazo & Carlson, 2012). I will refer briefly to these parts throughout the book as we discuss various executive skills, so I have provided a primer here for your reference as you encounter these words in the text.

BRAIN PARTS VOCABULARY PRIMER

dorso: top (like the word *dorsal*)
frontal: front
lateral: side
medial: middle
orbito: near the eyes
ventro: bottom (like the word *ventral*)
DLPFC (dorsolateral prefrontal cortex): near the top and sides of the frontal lobes
MPFC (medial prefrontal cortex): area in the middle of the frontal lobes
OFC (orbitofrontal cortex): area in the front of the frontal lobes, near the eyes
VLPFC (ventrolateral prefrontal cortex): bottom and sides of the frontal lobes
VMPFC (ventromedial prefrontal cortex): middle and sides of the frontal lobes

To understand how brain development is related to the development of executive skills, it will be helpful for you to know about the basic building blocks of the brain and how they change. The brain is made up of neurons (see Figure 1.3), or nerve cells, and the majority of our neurons are produced before birth, which means we are born with all of the neurons we will have throughout our lives

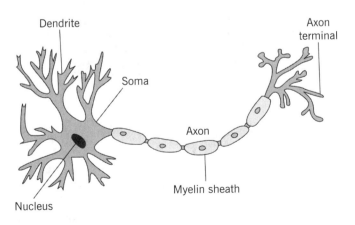

FIGURE 1.3. A neuron or nerve cell. Image by Quasar Jarosz (public domain).

(Bjorklund, 2012; Johnson, 2011). Nevertheless, the brain grows rapidly through the preschool years, and brain weight nearly triples by age 5 (Bjorklund, 2012; Dawson & Guare, 2010)! These changes in brain weight reflect important physical brain developments that occur throughout the cortex; the changes in the frontal lobes in particular are related to the development of executive skills (Anderson & Spencer-Smith, 2013).

Because we generally do not add new neurons in development, the tremendous increases in brain weight across the preschool period reflect changes in our existing neurons that facilitate processing of information. For example, dendrites, or the branching parts of neurons that receive incoming information from other neurons (see Figure 1.3), increase in number and size. And axons, the long parts of neurons that send outgoing messages, get longer and thicker, and they grow more terminal branches. Each of these changes produces more places for neurons to connect and communicate with one another, providing junctions called synapses. You should note, however, that neurons do not actually touch one another—they lie very close together and pass chemical signals through the microscopic spaces around them. You might have heard people refer to the building of "connections" in the brain; these connections are synapses (sometimes called synaptic connections), which increase rapidly in the preschool years to produce the raw connections necessary to support learning (see Bjorklund, 2012; Cartwright, 2012; Dawson & Guare, 2010; and Johnson, 2011, for reviews of brain development). After the brain over-produces synapses in this way, it begins pruning away the ones that are not used. When children have experiences that require the use of particular synapses, those synapses (connections) are strengthened. But if children do not experience activities that activate connections between their neurons, those connections will be lost and not replaced.

A good example to illustrate this use-it-or-lose-it concept comes from language acquisition. In the course of prenatal brain development, we all develop synapses that support the learning of all languages around the world, and babies are thus able to distinguish all sounds (or phonemes) in all spoken languages in early infancy (Werker & Tees, 1984). However, the set of phoneme-related synapses we keep depends on the language(s) that we hear and experience. If we grow up hearing English, for example, we do not need to understand or produce the sounds that are uniquely characteristic of other languages, such as the rolled *R* in spoken Spanish. Thus, we lose the synapses associated with the ability to hear and produce that sound. As a result, many late learners of Spanish find it quite difficult to produce rolled *R*'s in high school Spanish class! In contrast, even hearing Spanish spoken around you during childhood (even if you didn't speak the language yourself) will help you retain the ability to learn and pronounce those Spanish sounds later in life (Knightly, Jun, Oh, & Au, 2003).

One other brain development that produces increases in brain weight and that is important to the acquisition of executive skills is the addition of a fatty sheath—the myelin sheath—around the axons of some neurons (see Figure 1.3). The myelin sheath is much like the insulating rubber coating on electrical wires, and it improves the speed and efficiency of communication for those neurons that it covers (Bjorklund, 2012; Cartwright, 2012; Dawson & Guare, 2010; Johnson, 2011). Myelin is added to different areas of the brain at different times in development in ways that support children's developmental needs (Bjorklund, 2012; Sowell et al., 2004). For example, the parts of the cortex that control our sensory systems acquire myelin before birth, as infants need efficient sensory systems to gather information about their world once they are born. Areas that control movement, on the other hand, generally receive myelin across the first year after birth, supporting infants' developing locomotor abilities. The frontal lobes do not acquire myelin until later in development, when executive skills become more important to developmental success (Anderson & Spencer-Smith, 2013; Gotgay et al., 2004; Sowell et al., 2004).

You may have heard the terms *gray matter* and *white matter* in reference to the brain. These terms reflect the fact that the bodies of neurons appear gray, whereas myelinated axons appear white. Thus, the actual color of these different types of brain tissues has led to the labels gray matter and white matter, respectively. As you might expect, the volume and proportion of white matter increases across development as more myelin is added, whereas the proportion and volume of gray matter decreases due to the addition of myelin and the pruning of unused neurons and synapses. So, babies have more gray matter than white, and teenagers and adults show the opposite pattern (Amso & Casey, 2006; Gotgay et al., 2004; Sowell et al., 2006).

In the frontal lobes, these processes work together to support the development of executive skills (Anderson & Spencer-Smith, 2013; Gotgay et al., 2004; Sowell et al., 2006; Zelazo & Müller, 2002). In the first 3 years of life, the number of synapses in the frontal lobes increases dramatically to produce the raw connections necessary for successful development, and preschoolers actually have more synapses than adults (Bjorklund, 2012; Dawson & Guare, 2010; Johnson, 2011). Then, at about age 4 or 5, synaptic pruning begins, which refines the connections and makes processing more efficient. These changes are related to the rapid increase in executive skills we see across the preschool period. From ages 7 to 9, there is a surge in the addition of myelin in children's frontal lobes with a second surge in myelination from 10 to 12 years of age. I think it is interesting—but perhaps not surprising— that these age ranges correspond roughly to the points in development when Piaget (Piaget & Inhelder, 1969) observed important advancements in children's thinking (i.e., the onset of concrete logical thinking around age 7 and the onset of abstract logical thinking at the beginning of adolescence). Perhaps increases in myelination provide the improvements in processing efficiency necessary for these important advances in children's thinking. Finally, in adolescence and early adulthood we see shifts in the proportions of gray to white matter due to the parallel processes of continued pruning and myelination, with increases in amounts of white matter and decreases in amounts of gray matter (Anderson & Spencer-Smith, 2013). These changes serve to support advancements and improved efficiency in the development of executive skills across the lifespan, permitting the increased use of executive skills in support of the development of reading comprehension.

My purpose in including this section on brain development is to help you see the neurological basis for executive skills in your students. Brain-based learning is a popular term in education circles. And executive skills are cognitive functions that are linked to developments in the frontal lobes of the brain. Strategic reading comprehension and learning from text are associated with activity in the frontal lobes in regions typically associated with executive skills (Moss, Schunn, Schneider, McNamara, & VanLehn, 2011; Moss, Schunn, Schneider, & McNamara, 2013; see Baker, Zeliger-Kandasamy, & DeWyngaert, 2014, for a review). However, students with reading difficulties actually show atypical patterns of frontal lobe activity, which vary with different kinds of reading problems. Patterns of brain activity for students with reading comprehension difficulties suggest they have problems accessing the meaning-focused aspects of the words that they are reading, whereas students with dyslexia have difficulty with the phonological, or sound-related, aspects of words (Cutting et al., 2013). Consistent with this notion, Henderson, Snowling, and Clarke (2013) recently showed that children with specific reading comprehension difficulties have problems accessing less common word meanings for homonyms (words with the same spelling but different meanings); for example, for the word *bank*, students with reading comprehension difficulties would not have trouble accessing the common definition *financial institution*, but they would have difficulty accessing the less common definition, *the land on either side of a river*.

Furthermore, although relatively few studies have examined the neurological changes associated with reading interventions, a recent review of this work provided evidence that reading interventions literally change the brain by producing increases in activation in the frontal lobes as well as other areas to levels of activity that more closely match those seen in typical readers (Barquero, Davis, & Cutting, 2014). Although these results are promising, a limitation of this review is that the studies varied considerably in their definitions of reading disability, so specific conclusions about the effects of interventions for specific reading comprehension difficulties cannot be drawn at this time. I expect we will see much more work in this area in the near future.

Children with Specific RCD

As I noted earlier in the chapter, there is a particular group of students you may encounter in your classroom who have difficulties with reading comprehension despite having intact (and quite skilled) word decoding abilities (Duke, Cartwright, & Hilden, 2014). These students exhibit wonderfully fluent oral reading of texts and thus sound like good readers (Applegate et al., 2009; see Cartwright, 2010, for a review), yet they are at risk for lower educational attainment in comparison to their peers with better reading comprehension (Ricketts, Sperring, & Nation, 2014). Many times, we do not detect these students' comprehension difficulties in early elementary grades because our assessments in those grades often focus on decoding processes rather than on comprehension. However, when we ask these students to remember information from texts they've just read or to retell a story, we discover their primary reading problem: they are just not getting the meaning of the texts that they are reading! These students have specific RCD, which are distinct from word recognition difficulties (WRD) and have distinctly different underlying problems (Cutting et al., 2013; Locascio et al., 2010).

As you might expect, these students also have problems with oral language comprehension (Nation, Cocksey, Taylor, & Bishop, 2010; Nation & Snowling, 2004; Stothard & Hulme, 1992) and processes that support oral language comprehension, such as determining semantic relations among words (Nation & Snowling, 1999), making inferences (Bowyer-Crane & Snowling, 2005; Cain & Oakhill, 1999), understanding appropriate syntax (Nation & Snowling, 2000) and grammar (Nation et al. 2010), resolving ambiguity in language (Oakhill & Yuill, 1986; Yuill & Oakhill, 1988), and understanding and awareness of narrative structure (Cain, 2003; Cain & Oakhill, 1996). Narrative comprehension development is also supported by executive skills (see Cartwright & Guajardo, 2015, for a review), and students with RCD have significantly lower executive skills than their peers with better comprehension, which may contribute to their global (oral and print) comprehension problems. For example, students with RCD have significantly lower working memory (Carretti, Borella, Cornoldi, & De Beni, 2009; Carretti, Cornoldi, De Beni, & Romanò, 2005; Oakhill, Hartt, & Samols, 2005), inhibition (Borella et al., 2010; Cain, 2006; Kieffer et al., 2013), planning (Cutting, Materek, Cole, Levine, & Mahone, 2009; Locascio et al., 2010), and cognitive flexibility (Cartwright & Coppage, 2009; Cartwright, Coppage, Guiffré, & Strube, 2008; see Cartwright, 2015, for a review) than typically developing readers. In other words, what the research is showing is that when students have age-appropriate, fluent decoding abilities that should support comprehension, the differences between good and poor comprehenders can quite often be attributed to problems with executive skills. These differences suggest important targets for intervention, which we will discuss in subsequent chapters in this book.

A Brief History of Executive Skills and Reading Comprehension

Now that you know what executive skills do for thinkers and a bit about how they develop, you understand how these skills would support successful reading comprehension and many other academic and everyday tasks. At this point you may be asking yourself why you haven't seen information on executive skills before now, given their potential for transforming the ways your students approach texts as well as your comprehension instruction. As is the case in many academic areas, practice often lags behind research. This section traces the emergence of attention to executive skills in research on reading comprehension so that you know where the field stands with respect to these important discoveries.

Across the last decade, research on the role of executive skills in education has flourished. Although executive skills have traditionally been studied from a neuropsychological perspective to better understand processing deficits associated with illness or brain injury, recent decades have seen a remarkable increase in research on broader applications of executive skills, especially in education and development (see Zelazo & Müller, 2002, for a review; also see Zelazo & Carlson, 2012). Much of this research has focused on the ways that executive skill deficits contribute to learning disabilities such as ADHD (Barkley, 1997; Berlin, Bohlin, & Rydell, 2003) or mathematics learning difficulties (Mazzocco & Kover, 2007; McLean & Hitch, 1999; Toll, Van der Ven, Kroesbergen, & Van Luit, 2011). At the time of this writing, the Guilford Press catalog alone includes 25 titles published since 2005 that focus on executive skills, and consistent with trends in the field, most of these are based on the assumptions that (1) deficits in executive skills underlie a host of learning problems and (2) executive skills interventions will improve academic performance.

I wrote this book because, although recent research indicates executive skills underlie successful reading comprehension and that executive skill deficits underlie reading comprehension problems in children and adults (e.g., Borella et al., 2010; Cartwright, 2002, 2007, 2012; Cartwright & Coppage, 2009; Cartwright et al., 2008; Cartwright, Marshall, Dandy, & Isaac, 2010; Cutting et al., 2009; Locascio et al., 2010; Sesma et al., 2009), there are no published texts available that focus on the relation between executive skills and reading comprehension. Further, much new research on the relation between executive skills and reading comprehension has occurred quite recently and has not been included in existing professional books on executive skills in the classroom (e.g., Dawson & Guare, 2010; Kaufman, 2010; Meltzer, 2010). Thus, the primary purposes of this text are to provide an updated research base for individuals and schools interested in the role of executive skills in reading comprehension as well as to provide practical guidance on executive skills interventions for reading comprehension difficulties.

As I noted above, there are no practitioner-oriented texts on the market that focus exclusively on the role of executive skills in reading comprehension; in fact, there are not even scholarly texts on this topic! Existing practitioner texts focus on executive skills more generally, with limited attention paid to specific applications of executive skills for improving performance in particular academic subjects such as math or reading. Further, although the role of working memory—probably the most well-known executive skill—has been the focus of reading comprehension research for decades, scholarly texts are just recently beginning to include attention to a full range of executive skills (e.g., planning, organization, inhibition, cognitive flexibility, and self-regulation, to name a few), consistent with trends in the field. A brief summary of significant milestones in the development of resources on executive functions and reading comprehension follows.

One of the earliest texts to focus on the relation between executive skills and reading processes was Britton and Glynn's (1987) edited collection of chapters entitled *Executive Control Processes in Reading*, of which only Wagner and Sternberg's chapter focused exclusively on reading comprehension. At that point in history the study of executive skills was in its infancy. As Wagner and Sternberg noted (p. 2) there was "as yet little, if any, consensus about what executive control [was], or even what it [was] not." They reported findings of a study that focused on a particular aspect of the reading comprehension process: how readers manage their time and effort in reading tasks, depending on the difficulty and purpose of a text. However, given the state of the field at that time, the chapter provided scholars and practitioners little guidance regarding the breadth of influence of various executive skills on reading comprehension and even less guidance on how these might impact reading comprehension instruction.

Six years later Dawson and Guare (2003) published the first edition of their practitioner-oriented text on executive skills in children and adolescents. The updated second edition (2010) provides a thorough overview of executive skill assessment techniques, makes recommendations for identifying executive skill deficits in students, and provides guidance for designing individual executive skill intervention plans. The bulk of Dawson and Guare's text provides recommendations for teaching executive skills in classroom routines throughout the school day. Thus, Dawson and Guare's (2010) widely used text is applicable to education more generally but not reading comprehension specifically, as evidenced by the fact that the terms *reading comprehension, reading*, and *comprehension* do not even appear in the index of that text. Similarly, a more recent text on executive skills, *Executive Functions: What They Are, How They Work, and Why They Evolved* (Barkley, 2012), includes no table of contents or index references to *reading comprehension, reading*, or *comprehension*.

After Dawson and Guare published the first edition of their text (2003) that offered classroom applications of executive skills research, texts with applications to specific academic subjects began to emerge. For example, Lynn Meltzer published two texts: *Executive Function in Education* (Meltzer, 2007), which is an edited collection of chapters by leading scholars in the field, including one on reading comprehension (Gaskins, Satlow, & Pressley, 2007), with recommendations for classroom practice; and *Executive Function in the Classroom* (Meltzer, 2010), which is organized into chapters that each focus on a particular executive skill. While reading comprehension is mentioned briefly in several chapters in

Meltzer's 2010 text, her focus is on teaching executive skills to support struggling learners more generally, across academic subjects. (See also Kaufman's [2010] practitioner-focused text, *Executive Function in the Classroom*, which has a similar focus.)

My 2008 text, *Literacy Processes: Cognitive Flexibility in Learning and Teaching*, presented an edited collection of chapters from leading scholars in the field that focused on the role of one executive skill, cognitive flexibility, in literacy processes; however, that text was not practitioner-oriented, and its focus was on various aspects of literacy teaching and learning, not reading comprehension specifically. Additionally, the only practitioner-oriented text on the market that focuses solely on reading comprehension with attention to executive skills is my 2010 practitioner-oriented text: *Word Callers: Small Group and One-to-One Interventions for Children Who "Read" but Don't Comprehend*. However, this text's primary focus is on interventions that improve comprehension for children with RCD and includes only a brief review of work in executive skills. In fact, many contemporary studies of the role of executive skills in reading comprehension had not yet been completed or published when I wrote that text (e.g., Borella et al., 2010; Cartwright & Coppage, 2009; Cartwright et al., 2010; Cutting et al., 2009; García-Madruga et al., 2013; Kieffer et al., 2013; Locascio et al., 2010; Sesma et al., 2009).

It is not surprising that practitioner-oriented texts have not yet emerged that focus exclusively on the role of executive skills in reading comprehension because, as noted above, no scholarly texts even exist at this intersection. Contemporary neuropsychological research on the role of various executive skills in reading comprehension is just beginning to appear in scholarly books (e.g., Cutting, Eason, Young, & Alberstadt, 2009, and Eason & Cutting, 2009). Even scholarly handbooks have lagged in this area. For example, although executive skills have been studied from the perspective of learning disabilities for quite some time, the *Handbook of Reading Disability Research* (McGill-Franzen & Allington, 2011) includes no mention of executive skills in chapter titles, in headings, or in the index; furthermore, even the chapter on neuropsychological perspectives on reading disabilities does not include attention to executive skills. I should note, however, that *The Handbook of Language and Literacy: Development and Disorders* (Stone, Silliman, Ehren, & Wallach, 2014) includes a chapter on reading comprehension difficulties that attends to the role of executive skills in reading comprehension (Duke et al., 2014).

In summary, although we have known about the important role of executive skills in reading comprehension processes for some time, this is the first text that examines this relation. Work in executive skills has important implications for understanding skilled reading comprehension processes as well as reading comprehension difficulties. Furthermore, incorporating instructional approaches that enhance students' executive skills in service of their comprehension can enrich classroom reading comprehension instruction. Thus, I wrote this text to meet those needs in the field.

Can We Assess Executive Skills?

In short, yes! Dawson and Guare (2010; see Chapter 2) provide a thorough overview of existing assessments for the majority of the executive skills that we will discuss in this text. Additionally, they provide rubrics to guide your observations of students' behaviors in the classroom so that you can note various levels of executive skills among your students. Furthermore, they provide guides that help you determine how executive skill difficulties may appear in testing, classroom, and home contexts, with suggested assessments for each type of executive skill. Finally, they also include teacher and student forms of an executive skills assessment that you can use to determine your students' strengths and weaknesses. The remainder of their text is focused on classroom routines and other interventions to promote students' executive skills across the school day.

When students have problems with executive skills, those problems impact behavioral and academic functioning across a wide range of activities, not just reading comprehension. Thus, Dawson and Guare's (2010) text provides a broader view to help you identify executive skills difficulties in your students across multiple contexts. In the current text, I provide specific information on the impact of executive skills on reading comprehension with recommendations for instruction and intervention. In the course of doing these things I will refer you to assessments when appropriate. However, assessment is not a primary focus of this text. I highly recommend the Dawson and Guare (2010) text if you want to learn more about executive skills assessment and about how to link the results of those assessments to instruction across the curriculum. In addition, to assist you in determining whether your students might be exhibiting weaknesses in executive skills in the context of reading comprehension tasks, I have developed a rubric that you can use to informally assess executive skills in observations of your students' reading behavior (see Appendix A on pp. 237–239).

Structure for the Book

The majority of the remaining chapters in this text will focus on a particular executive skill or set of related skills (e.g., shifting and cognitive flexibility are related executive skills) and how each skill contributes to reading comprehension. Chapters are organized chronologically with respect to their operation in the reading comprehension process as much as possible. For example, planning occurs before inference and integration in working memory when one comprehends a text, so planning will be described in Chapter 2. Chapters will share a common structure to facilitate your comprehension and use of the text, including the following sections.

- *What Is the Skill and How Is It Typically Assessed?* This section will provide a definition of the skill that is the focus of the chapter, and I will describe how the skill is typically assessed in research on executive skills so that you better understand the kinds of behaviors that are associated with the skill. Additionally, I will link each executive skill to your knowledge of children's games, because such games typically require the kinds of reasoning involved in executive skills (Hessels-Schlatter, 2010; Kulman et al., 2010; Larner, 2009). Although research in this area is relatively new, there is emerging evidence that executive skills are actually improved by game play (Kim et al., 2014; Hessels-Schlatter, 2010), and children's games best teach cognitive skills when game demands are aligned with the skills to be learned (Laski & Siegler, 2014). Because most of us have knowledge of common children's games, these serve as good examples to illustrate the behaviors associated with particular executive skills by building on our shared background knowledge about familiar activities. Therefore, in addition to providing a formal definition for each executive skill in this book and describing the typical ways each skill is assessed, I will also provide examples from common children's games to connect these skills to your prior knowledge. (See Appendix B on pp. 240–241 for a list of games that require behaviors related to the executive skills described in this book.)

- *Why Is the Skill Important to Reading Comprehension?* This section will provide an explanation to illustrate how the skill(s) would be important for reading comprehension.

- *What Does the Skill Look Like in Real Readers?* This section will provide practical examples to illustrate how that chapter's executive skill would look in successful and unsuccessful reading comprehension.

- *What Does the Research Say?* This section will provide a brief treatment of the research base on the relation of the skill(s) to reading comprehension with attention to comprehension of various types of texts (e.g., fictional vs. informational) when supported by the research base.

- *How Can I Apply This Knowledge to Classroom Practice?* This section will provide recommendations and applications for classroom practice, including descriptions of specific, research-based interventions (when available) that target that particular skill to improve reading comprehension.

- *What Do We Still Need to Know about This Skill?* In many cases, because this text covers a relatively new area in research and practice, there will be issues and topics that deserve future research, and this section will highlight those needs and directions for future work.

In sum, after reading this text, I intend for you to have (1) new information about executive skills, what they are, and what they look like in young readers; (2) an understanding of why executive skills are essential to successful reading comprehension and comprehension instruction; (3) knowledge of instructional techniques and intervention strategies you can use to improve your students' executive skills and reading comprehension; and (4) a sense of what we know about particular executive skills and reading comprehension now and what we need to know in the future in order to take full advantage of what the neurosciences have to offer to support the teaching and learning of reading comprehension.

CHAPTER 2

Plans and Goals
Getting Ready to Read

People with goals succeed because they know where they're going.
            —attributed to EARL NIGHTINGALE (*brainyquote.com*)

Recently, Best and colleagues suggested that "the pinnacle of executive functioning is the ability to plan" (Best et al., 2009, p. 188). If the pinnacle of executive skill is planning, you may be wondering why we are beginning with something that sounds like it should be a culminating activity! As I noted in Chapter 1, I have elected to present the executive skills that support reading comprehension in the order in which they occur in the reading comprehension process. Thus, even though planning may be considered to be the pinnacle of executive skill (Best et al., 2009), planning and goal setting are where successful reading comprehension begins.

As you discovered in Chapter 1, goal setting is central to the definition of executive skills (a set of mental tools we use to manage tasks and achieve goals; Anderson, 2002; Dawson & Guare, 2010; Meltzer, 2010). In fact, the ability to hold goals in mind is important for the successful application of multiple executive skills across contexts (Blaye & Chevalier, 2011). Additionally, the relations between young children's performance on various executive skill tasks, such as inhibition, working memory, and cognitive flexibility, are driven by the ability to hold goals in mind (Chevalier et al., 2012). Similarly, successful comprehenders set out to read texts with particular comprehension goals in mind. And they are aware of the actions they need to take, in the appropriate order, to reach their comprehension goals (Pressley & Afflerbach, 1995; Pressley & Lundeberg, 2008; Wyatt et al.,

1993). However, poor comprehenders are less able to hold purposes for reading in mind, and consequently they adjust their reading behaviors to reading purposes less often than good comprehenders (Smith, 1967). Thus, planning and goal setting seem to be the glue that holds our complex thinking together.

In preparing to write this chapter I read a wonderful quote about planning, attributed to Yogi Berra (*www.goodreads.com/quotes/tag/planning*), "If you don't know where you're going, you'll end up someplace else!" Certainly this applies to many of our everyday activities, such as driving to a new bookstore in an unfamiliar area without a map or GPS. But this quote applies equally well to the reading comprehension process. I'm sure you have seen students who work their way through a text without any advance thought for why they are reading it. Even college students do this! A few years ago, I asked a class of first-year college students what they did to prepare to read their textbooks. When they gave me blank stares, I rephrased the question this way: Before you read your text, do you do anything to help you understand the text better, or do you just open the book and plow through it? Sheepishly, my students muttered, "Plow through!" Upon further probing, they also admitted that this really wasn't an effective approach for remembering text content, which provided a wonderful opportunity for a discussion of planning and goal setting for reading.

What Is Planning and How Is It Typically Assessed?

So, what exactly is planning? In Chapter 1 we defined executive skills as mental tools we use to manage tasks and achieve goals, and in the literature on executive skills, planning is considered an essential component of goal-directed activity (Anderson, 2002; Best et al., 2009) that involves the ability to "formulate actions in advance and to approach a task in an organized, strategic and efficient manner" (Best et al., 2009, p. 188). Key to this definition of planning is the notion of a proactive rather than a reactive approach to a task or goal. Rather than using trial and error to see what behaviors might get one closer to a desired goal, planning involves the advance generation of a sequence of steps that are logically connected in order to get one closer to a desired goal. Planning is intentional and purposeful. In addition, good planners are able to evaluate their proposed sequence of steps to a goal and change course if necessary to ensure that their goal is met.

Planning: the ability to decide what tasks are necessary to complete a goal, including understanding which ones are most important and the order in which tasks should be completed to most effectively reach the goal.

Consider, for example, the kinds of mental abilities necessary for success in a game of checkers. (See Appendix B on pp. 240–241 for a list of games that require behaviors related to the executive skills described in this book.) In order to get one's checkers pieces to the opposite (winning) side of a checkerboard, a player must consider more than just her next move. She must consider her opponent's probable responses for each of her own possible moves. Additionally, she must consider whether each of her possible moves will leave her checkers pieces at risk of being "jumped" and taken by her opponent or whether they will enable her to safely move her checkers pieces closer to the other side of the board. Skilled checkers players are able to think about many successive moves in advance, both their own and their opponent's, in order to achieve their goal. And they can change course if necessary to ensure that their goal is met. (My great-grandfather was one of those multistep checkers thinkers and was quite the checkers champion in our family!)

Assessments of planning require the same kind of step-by-step thinking as a game of checkers. The most common assessment of planning used in research on executive skills is called a tower task, which involves manipulating disks on a series of pegs to build towers. Performance on tower tasks is associated with frontal lobe activity, specifically in the DLPFC, which is associated with cool executive processing (Morris, Ahmed, Syed, & Toone, 1993). Furthermore, injury in the frontal lobes is associated with deficits in planning (Karnath, Wallesch, & Zimmerman, 1991; Owen, Downes, Sahakian, Polkey, & Robbins, 1990). The Tower of Hanoi (Simon, 1975), the Tower of London (Shallice, 1982), the NEPSY Tower task (Korkman, Kirk, & Kemp, 1998), and the Delis–Kaplan Executive Function System (D-KEFS; Delis, Kaplan, & Kramer, 2001) Tower Task are all common indicators of planning ability, and they are administered and scored in a similar manner. The towers are typically made of wood and are similar to children's stacking toys (think of the familiar Fisher-Price Rock-a-Stack plastic stacking toy for infants and toddlers, just with more pegs on which to place the disks). Students are provided the disks, arranged in a prescribed starting position on the wooden pegs (see example in Figure 2.1a), and they are shown a picture of a goal tower (see Figure 2.1b). The tower task requires students to move the wooden disks to reach the goal in as few moves as possible, moving only one disk at a time, using only one hand, and without placing larger disks on top of smaller ones. The towers begin with simple arrangements, using few disks, and they progress to more difficult arrangements, using all of the disks, such as the one depicted in Figure 2.1.

Designers of the tower assessments originally thought that presenting the towers in order of increasing difficulty would support performance by enabling individuals to rely on their knowledge of solutions for simpler towers to help solve more complex ones. However, other researchers have found that students' own internal strategy use influences performance on tower tasks to a much greater extent than tower problem presentation order (Welsh & Huizinga, 2005). As you can imagine, similar to the thinking required for a game of checkers, students must consider more than just one move in order to solve each tower problem at hand. They must consider the effects of each possible disk move on subsequent moves of

(a) Starting arrangement

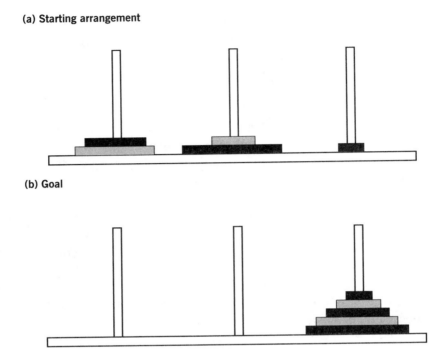

(b) Goal

FIGURE 2.1. Example of a tower task that is used to assess planning.

that disk as well as the other disks in the array. Tower tasks are typically scored using several metrics, such as:

- Number of correctly built towers, which indicates greater proficiency in planning because the towers increase in difficulty.
- Time it takes students to build the towers, which indicates the amount of time the students need to correctly negotiate all steps and build the tower; typically, slower times indicate less efficient planning.
- Time before a student's first move, which indicates the time used to think about (i.e., plan) that move and subsequent moves before beginning the task.
- Number of total moves a student makes because more moves may indicate inefficiency and poor planning; this is sometimes scored as excess moves beyond the known number required to build the tower, and more excess moves indicates poorer planning.
- Number of errors, where making more errors indicates poorer planning.

Klahr and Robinson (1981; also see Welsh, 1991) modified the original Tower of Hanoi task (Simon, 1975) and added a narrative to support young children's comprehension of the task procedure and rules. In the modified version, fewer disks were used (either three or four, depending on age), and the children were told that they were going to play a game in which they needed to help monkeys climb trees. When introducing the tower apparatus, the researcher told the children that the pegs (see Figure 2.1) were trees, the disks were monkeys, and the tabletop on which the apparatus was displayed was water. Finally, to convey the task rules, the researcher told the children that the big monkeys could not sit on top of the little ones in the trees, or they would squash them; and, the monkeys could not be placed in the water (on the table). The narrative supported even 3-year-olds' understanding of and performance on the tower task, though performance still increased with age from 3 to 12 years (Welsh, 1991).

In addition to the tower task, other tasks have been used to assess younger children's planning, and these have also included a narrative component to make them more understandable and engaging for young students (see Carlson et al. 2004, for a review of these tasks). For example, Fabricius (1988) used a route-planning task in which children had to retrieve baby animals from a number of buckets and deliver them to a mama animal. They were told to go the "quick way" in order that they would avoid backtracking, which would indicate an inefficient plan. Similarly, Fagot and Gauvain (1997) used a mail delivery task in which children had to use a toy mail truck to deliver color-coded invitations to various houses of matching colors arranged around a block, and they were instructed that they could only pass around the block one time. Thus, successful performance on the task required that they place the colored invitations into the mail truck in the correct order to ensure they made only one pass around the route.

Recently, Goldin et al. (2013) presented promising evidence that planning can be taught in third-grade students using a brief, computerized version of a planning task like the ones I just described. In the computerized task, the students have to help a cat, dog, and mouse get to their "homes" in as few moves as possible, with rules similar to those that govern other planning tasks. Intervention students outperformed control students on the cat-dog-mouse task, and these effects transferred to other tasks, such as the Tower of Hanoi, and a measure of nonverbal intelligence. These results are exciting because they show that the effects of planning interventions can transfer to other kinds of tasks. Furthermore, given that planning is related to reading comprehension and teaching other executive skills results in improved reading comprehension (Cartwright, 2002; Dahlin, 2011), future work may confirm that improvements in planning also transfer to reading comprehension.

Although these tasks do not involve reading per se, it certainly makes sense that performance on the tasks with narrative components, such as the modified tower task that involved monkeys and trees (Klahr & Robinson, 1981; Welsh, 1991), the baby animal delivery task (Fabricius, 1988), and the mail delivery task (Fagot & Gauvain, 1997), would be related to children's oral comprehension of narrative. However, I know of no studies that have tested that relation directly, and vocabulary was not related to planning in the studies that assessed it (Carlson et al. 2004; Fagot & Gauvain, 1997). What we do know is that performance on planning tasks is significantly related to reading comprehension (see review of research, below), and in the next sections I describe why this may be the case.

Why Is Planning Important to Reading Comprehension?

The step-by-step reasoning required for typical planning tasks is important for many activities in daily life. Applied to the domain of reading, planning involves choosing the behaviors necessary to achieve the goal of understanding a text. Additionally, planning "involves the allocation of time and effort in order to optimize task solutions. The good reader, like the good problem solver, selects reasonable goals and generates suitable means to accomplish them" (Paris, Cross, & Lipson, 1984, p. 1241). So, skilled reading comprehension requires selection of appropriate comprehension goals for reading tasks as well as the ability to plan the behaviors necessary to achieve those goals. Clearly, my first-year students who claimed to "plow through" their textbooks were not making time—and were perhaps not even aware that they needed to make time—for planning and goal setting activities that support comprehension.

Recall that the RRSG (2002) suggested there are three types of factors that interact to produce successful reading comprehension: reader factors, text factors, and the purpose for reading (see Figure 1.1). Planning, as an executive skill, is a reader factor, and individual readers differ in their planning abilities, as you will see in the review of research below. But the type of text and reading purpose (the other two factors identified by the RRSG as important to reading comprehension) also influence the nature of the planning process. For example, if one is reading a fictional text, such as *There Is a Bird on Your Head!* (Willems, 2007), to find the characters, setting, and story problem (characters are Gerald the Elephant and Piggie, setting is outside, and the problem is that birds build a nest on Gerald's head),

R.CCR.2 the activities to support this purpose are different than those needed to support the goal of learning about the solar system when reading an informational text on this topic, such as *There's No Place Like Space! All about Our Solar System* (Rabe, 2009; from The Cat in the Hat's Learning Library). Additionally,

R.CCR.1 the approach to reading a text on the solar system may differ too, depending on one's purpose, such as reading to expand knowledge of the structure of the solar system versus reading to gather information about a particular planet and its characteristics.

Hence, in the sections that follow, we will discuss the nature of the planning process itself as well as the role of text type, reader goals, and reading purpose in supporting reading comprehension.

What Does Planning Look Like in Real Readers?

Brittany, a Student with RCD

Remember Brittany, whom I discussed in Chapter 1? Like other students with poor comprehension, Brittany is not aware that she can engage in behaviors to support understanding even before beginning to read a text. So, when she is assigned a new text on the solar system (e.g., *National Geographic Little Kids First Big Book of Space*; Hughes, 2012) to learn more about the structure and function of the system, Brittany doesn't seem to approach the text with any clear plan in mind. Rather, she picks up the text and begins reading on the first page without even previewing the text. When she encounters new information on the shape of the Earth's orbit around the Sun, she doesn't link it to what she had already learned about this topic, by expanding on the introduction that her teacher provided with a model, read-aloud, and class discussion the day before. Additionally, Brittany doesn't seem to pay attention to the organizational features that highlight important points in the text, such as bolded glossary terms, headings and subheadings, diagrams, and labels. When she finishes her reading of the text, her summary of the content lacks structure, and she misses important details that should have been apparent because of their position in the text and their relation to the previous day's lesson. Brittany could benefit from some instruction in planning for reading!

Gabriela, a Good Comprehender

Now consider Gabriela, who received the same assignment to read a new text on the solar system to expand her knowledge of its structure and function. Before she begins reading the text she thinks about what she has already learned about the solar system in yesterday's class discussion and read-aloud (there are several planets in the solar system that revolve around the Sun), and she decides that she needs to see if the new text offers any additional information to add to what she already knows. That is, Gabriela asks herself what she already knows about the topic and sets a goal for her reading.

Next, Gabriela flips through the pages of the text and notices that there are headings to denote five subsections: *Looking Up from Earth*; *Earth's Neighborhood*; *Earth's Other Neighbors*; *Far, Far Away*; and *Exploring Space* (Hughes, 2012). Additionally, she notes that there are several bolded terms in each subsection to highlight important new vocabulary words. Gabriela wonders whether there are other things in the solar system besides the planets and Sun that she learned about yesterday, and she also wonders what the fourth subheading, *Far, Far Away*, is talking about. Gabriela thinks about what she already knows about the solar system. She knows that the Sun and the other planets in the solar system are very far away, so the fourth section might be talking about that. But the picture next to the second section's title, *Earth's Other Neighbors*, shows the Sun and the other planets. So, she predicts that the fourth section probably will focus on things other than the Sun and planets that are also far, far away from us on Earth. After setting a goal, checking her prior knowledge, and previewing the text, Gabriela feels like she is ready to begin reading the text her teacher assigned.

What Does the Research Say?

Research on Planning from an Executive Skills Perspective

Of all the cool executive skills, planning is one that has received relatively little attention in the research literature on reading comprehension. Scholars in this area have only very recently turned their attention to this important executive skill. Laurie Cutting and her colleagues have done the most prominent work in this area; their studies have revealed that planning, assessed with tower tasks, plays an important role in reading comprehension in children and adolescents, aged 9 to 15 years (Cutting, Materek, Cole, Levine, & Mahone, 2009; Locascio et al., 2010; Sesma et al., 2009). Specifically, these researchers have found that planning and working memory both make independent contributions to reading comprehension, even when inattention and decoding skills are controlled. However, neither planning nor working memory contributes to word reading ability (Sesma et al., 2009).

A few studies have assessed longitudinal relations between planning and reading comprehension in students ranging in age from 4 to 15 years. For example, Bull, Espy, and Wiebe (2008) found that planning, assessed with the Tower of London task, was associated with reading achievement in preschool, first grade, and third grade, using the PIPS (Performance Indicators in Primary Schools; Centre for Evaluation and Monitoring, 2014) assessment of reading achievement that included measures of vocabulary; letter, word, and sentence recognition; and reading comprehension. Similarly, Clark, Pritchard, and Woodward (2010) found that Tower of Hanoi performance at age 4 was significantly related to reading comprehension performance at age 6. Finally, in a study of 5- to 17-year olds, Best, Miller, and Naglieri (2011) found significant relations between planning and reading comprehension at every age, using different assessments of planning that required students to systematically match codes or make connections between items in an array of numbers or letters; each of these tasks required making, holding in mind, and carrying out a plan of action. Planning was also related to math achievement in this study, and the authors noted, "Matching Numbers, a task that consists solely of finding identical numbers (i.e., no letters) correlated as strongly with reading as with math, suggesting that the ability to generate and apply a plan, monitor its effectiveness, and self-correct as necessary is similarly relevant to both domains" (Best et al., 2011, p. 334).

You may be wondering about children with reading comprehension problems. As I noted in Chapter 1, children with RCD, despite good decoding, are notorious for treating reading as a decoding task, with the goal of ensuring accurate word reading (Gaskins & Gaskins, 1997; Gaskins et al., 2007; Yuill & Oakhill, 1991). Thus, when these students finish reading, they end up drawing very different information from texts than skilled comprehenders. That is, because they don't have an appropriate plan or goal for comprehension, they "end up someplace else," to reference the quote from Yogi Berra with which I opened the chapter. When students with RCD were compared to students with general reading difficulties (GRD; difficulty with both word reading and comprehension) and typically developing students, students with RCD were significantly lower on planning, assessed with excess moves on the tower task (Cutting, Materek, et al., 2009). Additionally, in a comparison with students who have specific word reading difficulties (WRD) and typically developing students, students with RCD were significantly lower on planning, but not on inhibition and working memory (Locascio et al., 2010). Finally, Mahapatra, Das, Stack-Cutler, and Parilla (2010) compared ESL students in fourth grade who were good and poor in reading comprehension on planning tasks that involved matching items and making connections (the same tasks that were used by Best et al., 2011, described above), finding that poor comprehenders were significantly lower on planning than peers with better comprehension. But teaching these types of tasks improved reading comprehension and planning for poor comprehenders (Mahapatra et al., 2010), indicating planning can be taught.

Few other studies have examined the relation of planning to reading comprehension using traditional assessments, such as the tower task. However, an important recent study by Crook and Evans (2014) that examined the role of poverty in reading and math achievement, did so using Tower of Hanoi scores from the National Institute of Child Health and Human Development (NICHD) Study of Early Child Care and Youth Development (Griffin & Friedman, 2007). As noted in Chapter 1, children of higher socioeconomic status (SES) tend to have better executive skills than peers who come from homes with fewer resources. Children's SES was assessed with an income-to-needs ratio in infancy; planning was assessed with the Tower of Hanoi in third grade, and reading and math achievement were assessed with the Woodcock–Johnson Psycho-Educational Battery—Revised (WJ-R; Woodcock, Johnson, & Mather, 1989). They found that planning, in particular, appears to account for a significant portion of the income-related achievement gaps in math and reading achievement in fifth grade, even when IQ was controlled. These results make sense, given what we know about the relation of executive skills to SES. I should note, though, that the WJ-R measure of reading achievement combined measures of word reading and reading comprehension into an overall score, so we must be cautious in interpreting these results. However, because planning does not contribute to word reading (Locascio et al., 2010;

Sesma et al., 2009), I suspect planning would actually account for more of the relation between SES and reading had they used only a measure of reading comprehension to assess reading achievement.

Finally, one additional study that used traditional measures of planning deserves mention. Altemeier, Jones, Abbott, and Berninger (2006) examined the contribution of executive skills to children's ability to integrate reading and writing tasks, and they used the NEPSY Tower subtest (Korkman et al., 1998) to assess planning. Planning contributed significantly to third graders' ability to use notes they had taken from a science text for the purpose of writing a paper. Although this study involved note taking, because the task also involved reading and comprehending a text for a specific purpose, it seems particularly relevant to our discussion.

W.CCR.9

Taken together, these findings suggest planning, assessed with tower tasks and other nonreading step-by-step planning tasks, plays a significant role in the development of reading comprehension.

Research on Planning from a Reading Perspective

Although these findings are exciting, traditional assessments of planning, such as tower tasks, do not relate explicitly to reading processes in ways that may support instruction. Thus, you may be wondering what we know about reading-specific planning. Reading scholars have long recognized the importance of students' awareness of their own reading processes, also called their metacognitive awareness of reading processes, to successful reading comprehension. Such awareness necessarily begins with actions readers take before they begin to read to ensure comprehension proceeds smoothly. That is, such awareness begins with planning (Duke & Pearson, 2002; Israel, Block, Kinnucan-Welsch, & Bauserman, 2005; Paris et al., 1984). Even early investigations of metacognition and reading comprehension (Jacobs & Paris, 1987; Paris et al., 1984; Paris & Jacobs, 1984) recognized the importance of planning for successful comprehension because "skilled readers often engage in deliberate activities that require planful thinking" (Paris & Jacobs, 1984, p. 2083).

To assess readers' awareness of their own reading processes before, during, and after reading, Jacobs and Paris (1987) developed an Index of Reading Awareness that included a planning subscale (see Jacobs & Paris, 1987, for planning items and scoring criteria), which targeted what readers would do under particular reading circumstances, such as:

- What sentences they would read in a passage if they were in a hurry.
- What text features they would highlight when telling others about what they read.

- What they would do if instructed to read to remember the gist of a text.
- What plans they make to support their reading.
- Which words in a text they would read if they had to read quickly.

Although Jacobs and Paris (1987) did not examine separately the relation of planning to reading comprehension, they did find that good comprehenders scored significantly higher than poor comprehenders on reading awareness at pretest, and metacognitive awareness training improved reading comprehension for all students, regardless of initial comprehension level (low, medium, or high). These findings suggest that reading-specific planning is important for successful reading comprehension, though more research is needed to determine the precise relation between awareness of planning processes and reading comprehension.

Self-reports of behaviors do not always match one's actual behaviors, and children are not as aware of their own behaviors as adults. Thus, Dermitzaki, Andreou, and Paraskeva (2008; also see Dermitzaki, 2005) set out to investigate the relations of various metacognitive skills, including planning, to reading comprehension in third-grade students, using observations of children's behavior rather than children's self-reports of their own behavior. They pretested reading comprehension, and selected students low and high in reading comprehension. Then they used an observation checklist (developed by Dermitzaki, 2005) to record students' behaviors during reading comprehension tasks (see Table 2.1 for the criteria they used to assess planning in observations of students' behavior). As you might expect, students low in reading comprehension were significantly worse at planning than their peers with high reading comprehension. Additionally, regardless of the students' initial reading comprehension levels (low or high), reading comprehension scores were significantly and highly correlated with planning scores. These results suggest that planning does, indeed, play an important role in reading comprehension. But, what specific things might be involved in the planning process for good comprehenders?

TABLE 2.1. Criteria for Assessing Planning in Observations of Students' Behavior

Criterion[a]	Description of behavior
1	Approaching the task as trial and error, waste of time
2	Working with a plan only occasionally, usually wasting time
3	Building in gradual steps; however, a clear plan is not always apparent
4	Working with a clear plan, using time effectively

Note. From Dermitzaki (2005). Copyright 2005 by Ammons Scientific, Ltd. Reprinted by permission.
[a]Higher numbers indicate better planning.

Research on Elements of Planning
for Reading Comprehension

Fortunately, we know a bit about the kinds of things good comprehenders do before beginning to read to ensure they understand texts, and these activities are consistent with what we know about executive skills. Good planning for reading comprehension requires that readers are aware of, and can execute, the various actions required to reach a comprehension goal. As you will see in the paragraphs that follow, the actions necessary for successful comprehension vary depending on the type of comprehension goal a reader is seeking to accomplish. You may have even taught some of these things as reading strategies (e.g., predicting), but you may not have thought of these—or taught these—as parts of a good reader's plan to understand a text. These planning behaviors can be taught to support better comprehension.

Setting a Goal or Purpose for Reading

As I noted in the beginning of this chapter, planning involves setting goals and generating a series of actions necessary to achieve the goals one sets (Dawson & Guare, 2010; Meltzer, 2010). We know that skilled comprehenders approach texts with particular goals for reading, or a plan to understand the text in a certain way for a particular purpose, whereas poor comprehenders are less likely to read in goal-directed ways (Duke & Pearson, 2002; Graesser et al., 1994; Pressley & Afflerbach, 1995; Pressley & Lundeberg, 2008). For example, high school students with good reading comprehension are significantly better able than peers with poor comprehension to adjust their reading behaviors for different purposes, such as reading more slowly and closely to gather details from texts or reading more quickly to get a general overview of texts; poor comprehenders, on the other hand, make few adjustments in reading behaviors to read for these different purposes (Smith, 1967). In fact, poor comprehenders are significantly less able than good comprehenders to hold a purpose for reading in mind, which may account for their failure to adjust their reading processes for varied purposes (Smith, 1967).

R.CCR.1

The type of reading goal determines what information readers gather from texts (Mills, Diehl, Birkmire, & Mou, 1995). Further, the type of reading goal interacts with readers' working memory, which also makes a difference for comprehension. For example, when college students who are either high or low in working memory read for the goal of entertainment, they do not differ in comprehension; however, when their goal is to read for studying (e.g., to remember information for a test), students high in working memory demonstrate better comprehension than their peers with lower working memory (Linderholm, 2006; Linderholm & van den Broek, 2002). These results point to the strong relations between executive skills that I mentioned in Chapter 1, such as planning and working memory. Students' memory skills affect their abilities to implement plans and achieve reading goals, and those with lower working memory skills may even have difficulty holding goals in mind while reading. However, developing comprehenders are capable of adjusting their performance to meet different kinds of reading goals. For example, when middle and high school students are asked to read to get details from a text or to read to get an overview, they can adjust their reading rate for those particular goals, reading faster for the purpose of getting an overview and reading more slowly when they need to get details from text. But their ability to make these adjustments is affected by text difficulty. Middle and high school students, just like adults (Pressley & Afflerbach, 1995), must read more slowly to understand more difficult texts, and adjustments for different goals are less likely to occur on difficult texts (DiStefano, Noe, & Valencia, 1981).

Instructional support can foster successful goal setting and progress toward goals. When teachers work with students in goal-setting conferences that involve explicit discussions of goals and means to achieve them, students' goals are more realistic and result in greater academic achievement in reading and content-area learning (Gaa, 1973, 1979). Teacher-guided goal setting also has positive effects on developing comprehenders' understanding of text. Fuchs, Fuchs, and Deno (1985) assessed the effects of teacher-set goals on the reading achievement of students identified as needing special educational services. They found that ambitiousness of reading goals positively impacted reading comprehension, whereas goal mastery did not.

For students with RCD, setting concrete goals can make a positive difference in comprehension. However, some types of goals are better than others. Schunk and Rice (1989, 1991) assessed the effects of goal setting on reading comprehension for students with RCD (those who had poor reading comprehension whose teachers indicated they had no decoding problems). Schunk and Rice distinguished between product goals, which focus on the knowledge that should be gained from reading a text, such as reading in order to answer comprehension questions; and process goals, which focus on the means by which students learn information from text, such as reading with the purpose of finding the main idea in text so that one can answer comprehension questions after reading.

These different goals reflect two different instructional purposes. The first, reading in order to answer questions, reflects the instructional purpose of comprehension assessment, or determining whether students have understood a text or have gleaned the appropriate information from it. However, product goals do not help

Product goals focus on the end results of reading comprehension, such as knowledge students should have acquired after reading a text.

Process goals focus on the specific actions taken in order to understand a text, such as the particular steps students take to achieve a comprehension goal.

students understand the actual means by which they can comprehend a text. Unfortunately, however, comprehension instruction typically reflects product goals, with comprehension questions (that assess students' comprehension) constituting the most frequent instructional move for teachers for many decades (Durkin, 1978; Pressley & Allington, 2014; Pressley, Wharton-McDonald, Mistretta-Hampston, & Echevarria, 1998); even within the last 5 years, data indicate comprehension questions constitute the predominant instructional move in elementary (Joint Legislative Audit and Review Commission [JLARC], 2011; Ness, 2011a) and secondary content-area (Ness, 2008, 2009) classrooms. Process goals, on the other hand, such as reading in order to accomplish a specific meaning-getting task like finding a text's main idea, reflect the instructional goal of teaching students how to comprehend a text using a particular strategy that they can generalize to new reading situations (Durkin, 1978; JLARC, 2011; Ness, 2008, 2009, 2011a; Pressley & Allington, 2014; Pressley et al., 1998).

R.CCR.1, R.CCR.2

In Schunk and Rice's studies (1989, 1991), process goal students were provided a specific, five-step plan for finding the main idea in text in order to answer questions about it, introduced with the following instructions: "While you're working, it helps to keep in mind what you're trying to do. You'll be trying to learn how to use the steps to answer questions about what you've read" (Schunk & Rice, 1991, p. 358; see Table 2.2 for the five steps). Additionally, the five steps students were expected to complete in order to achieve the goal were displayed prominently under the heading "What do I have to do?" (Schunk & Rice, 1991, p. 357; see Table 2.2).

R.CCR.2

As students were working toward their goals, the instructor provided explicit feedback on the students' progress toward the goals. Students in the product goal condition were simply told, "While you're working, it helps to keep in mind what you're trying to do. You'll be trying to answer questions about what you've read"

TABLE 2.2. Steps in the Plan for Process Goal Completion: Getting the Main Idea of Text in Order to Answer Questions about the Text

Step	What do I have to do? (tasks)
1	Read the questions.
2	Read the passage to find out what it's mostly about.
3	Think about what the details have in common.
4	Think about what would make a good title.
5	Reread the story if I don't know the answer to a question.

Note. From Schunk and Rice (1991). Copyright 1991 by Sage Publications. Reprinted by permission.

(Schunk & Rice, 1991, p. 358). The process goal students were given an end goal, but they were also provided an explicit plan for the steps necessary to help them achieve that goal.

Finally, consistent with what is known about effective reading comprehension instruction, the instructor used the gradual release of responsibility model (Duke & Pearson, 2002; Duke, Pearson, Strachen, & Billman, 2011; Pearson & Gallagher, 1983) to teach the process goal students by explicitly explaining and modeling the five-step process, supporting the students in implementing it, and providing opportunities for independent practice. The texts in these studies were predominantly informational, though about 10% of texts in the second study were narrative texts in order to maintain students' interest (Schunk & Rice, 1989, 1991). As you would expect, the process goal students showed significantly greater improvement in reading comprehension after the intervention than the students in the product goal condition. That is, the students who were provided a specific, R.CCR.1, multistep plan for achieving the goal of getting meaning from text were R.CCR.2 more effective at actually getting meaning from the text!

As Schunk and Rice (1989, 1991) demonstrated, process goals are more effective than product goals when comprehending informational texts. Other researchers have shown that this is the case for narrative texts as well. For example, Levin (1973) also demonstrated the effectiveness of process goals for students with poor comprehension, using researcher-constructed narrative texts. Some students were told that they were going to "see some sentences that told a story," and that they should "look at them carefully" because they would be asked questions about the story (a product goal). Other students were provided the same instructions but were also given a process goal for their reading of the story: they were R.CCR.2 taught to construct a mental image of each of the sentences in the story as they read them. Thus, because there were multiple sentences, the image construction activity constituted a multistep process for imagining the content of the story.

Students with good and poor reading comprehension with age-appropriate vocabulary were compared, and the imagery process goal resulted in significant improvement for the poor comprehenders over the product goal condition. In the product (reading only) condition, good comprehenders answered 81% of comprehension questions correctly, whereas poor comprehenders answered only 60% of comprehension questions correctly. In contrast, when provided the process goal of creating images of sentences, good comprehenders answered 95% of comprehension questions correctly, and poor comprehenders answered 86% of questions correctly—an increase of 26% over their performance without the imagery process! And, when pursuing the process goal, the poor comprehenders' performance was similar to the performance of good comprehenders on text alone.

In a similar study with authentic texts, Michael Pressley (1976) taught students to pause and construct mental images after each page of text in order to remember the stories better (a process goal), and instruction occurred in authentic, small-group settings. The students in the control condition, on the other hand, were told to do whatever was necessary to remember the stories for later (a product goal without a specific action plan for completion). Students were divided according to the school's third-grade reading achievement scores into two groups: (1) good readers and (2) average and poor readers because there were not enough poor readers to constitute their own group. (I should note that although Pressley did not indicate whether the school's reading achievement scores reflected word reading or comprehension, I assume that they were based on reading comprehension ability, given his research focus.) Consistent with Levin's (1973) results, the students who received the imagery process instruction answered significantly more comprehension questions correctly than the students in the product goal condition, regardless of ability level. Further, and similar to Levin's results, the average and poor readers who received the imagery process goal instruction performed at levels similar to the good readers in the control (product goal) condition. Thus, process goals **R.CCR.10** improve reading comprehension for struggling comprehenders on narrative (Levin, 1973; Pressley, 1976) and informational (Schunk & Rice, 1989, 1991) texts, bringing their performance in line with good comprehenders under typical, product goal conditions.

The goals in the studies reviewed so far have focused on getting the gist or main idea of texts, whether they are informational or narrative, which may not fit all reading purposes. Often, in reading informational texts, rather than reading to get the gist or main idea, a reader's goal might be to search for specific information. This type of goal reminds me of the popular educational television program, *Super Why*, that introduces literacy skills to preschoolers. (My 4-year-old son loves this show, so I have seen it quite a bit in recent months.) The opening lyrics for *Super Why* go something like this: "Who's got the power, the power to read? Who looks into books for the answers we need?" (PBS Kids, 2014). The main theme in this show is that when a character has a problem, the Super Readers look in a book to find the solution. Thus, this television program is introducing the concept of information search goals to preschoolers even before reading begins! This is exciting because information search is one of the primary and most frequent reading purposes in adulthood (Kirsch & Guthrie, 1984), which may explain why informational texts are by far the most read texts for adults (White, Chen, & Forsyth, 2010). Although adults choose to read informational texts more often than fictional texts, I should note that there are distinct executive skill benefits of reading fictional texts, even for adults, which we will review in Chapter 7. These findings **R.CCR.7,** regarding frequency of informational text reading suggest that although we **R.CCR.10** do not spend much time teaching with informational texts (Duke, 2000; Ness, 2011b), we should do so, including teaching children how to understand the graphics and other visual devices embedded in informational texts (Duke et al., 2013; Roberts et al., 2013), an instructional practice emphasized in the CCSS to support comprehension of informational texts.

Let's consider an example of an information search goal. Suppose a teacher assigns a student the task of learning more about the planet Saturn when reading the books on space mentioned earlier in this chapter (*There's No Place Like Space! All about Our Solar System*, Rabe, 2009; and *National Geographic Little Kids First Big Book of Space*; Hughes, 2012). Armbruster and Armstrong (1993) reviewed research on searching for information in texts and suggested a four-step process necessary to enable readers to meet the goal of information search in reading informational texts: goal formation, or setting one's particular information search goal; text selection, or choosing appropriate texts (or sections of texts) in which to search for information; information extraction and integration; and evaluation. Dreher (1992, 1993; Dreher & Brown, 1993; Dreher & Guthrie, 1990; Dreher & Sammons, 1994), however, suggested that information extraction and integration (Armbruster & Armstrong's Step 3) are actually two separate activities that support the goal of locating information in texts.

I tend to agree with Dreher, because obtaining appropriately relevant information from different texts or sections of texts seems to require a separate type of cognitive process than integrating the information derived from those various sources. Students may be quite good at extracting relevant information from separate texts, yet they may not yet be able to link that information together in meaningful, integrated ways. Dreher and colleagues found that when given planning prompts for search tasks, such as asking students what they are supposed to be doing (i.e., asking them about their goal), what elements of the text they will use to accomplish that task (e.g., table of contents, headings, or index), and what specific pieces of information they will look for (e.g., particular vocabulary words or glossary terms), improves college students' (Dreher & Brown, 1993) and elementary students' (Dreher & Sammons, 1994) abilities to gather appropriate information from texts to meet their goals. Thus, planning and goal setting facilitate comprehension of informational texts for one of the most frequent uses of those texts, locating information, which becomes a predominant focus of reading activities in adulthood (Dreher & Guthrie, 1990; Kirsch & Guthrie, 1984; White et al., 2010). **R.CCR.1, R.CCR.10**

Certainly, setting a goal or purpose for reading is important for planning to understand a text. But there are also other things that good readers do to prepare themselves to understand texts before reading begins, and these are things that you can teach your students. So, what other elements are parts of good readers' plans to understand texts?

Previewing the Text

One of the first things skilled readers do before reading is to preview the text to get an overview of the text's content and structure (Duke et al., 2011; Klingner & Vaughn, 1999; Pressley, 2002a; Pressley & Afflerbach, 1995; Pressley &

Lundeberg, 2008; Wyatt et al., 1993). I will say more about how text structure supports reading comprehension when we talk about organization, another important executive skill for reading comprehension, in Chapter 3.

R.CCR.5

As far as planning goes, knowing about the content of a text before reading begins enables readers to tailor their reading subgoals to that particular text in order to support overall comprehension. For example, previewing an informational text allows readers to plan to spend more time on text sections that are most relevant to their comprehension goals, such as when a student seeking information on classifications of reptiles for a school report previews a table of contents and decides to focus more of her attention on a section entitled "Many Kinds of Reptiles" in the informational text *Reptiles of All Kinds* (MacAulay & Kalman, 2005).

Considering What One Already Knows about the Text's Topic

When good comprehenders set out to read a text, not only do they preview the text's content, they also think about what they already know about the text's topic (Afflerbach & Pressley, 1995; Pressley & Allington, 2014; Wyatt et al., 1993). As Elbro and Buch-Iversen (2013, p. 435) noted, "Texts cannot be understood without contributions from readers." Prior knowledge, which is organized into schemas (networks of related information) in readers' heads, plays a critically important role in reading comprehension (Anderson & Pearson, 1984; Pearson, Hansen, & Gordon, 1979; Priebe, Keenan, & Miller, 2012). And the deliberate activation of prior knowledge in this way enables readers to connect newly encountered information in text with concepts already stored in their memory, linking the new information to their already existing knowledge. Because our long-term memory is organized according to meaning, connecting new information to already-stored information increases the likelihood that one will be able to remember the new information over a longer period (Bjorklund, 2012).

Not surprisingly, students with reading comprehension difficulties are less good at activating their prior knowledge than peers with better comprehension (Elbro & Buch-Iversen, 2013). However, when students with reading comprehension difficulties are taught to activate their background knowledge and link it to texts, their reading comprehension improves significantly (Elbro & Buch-Iversen, 2013; Hansen, 1981; Hansen & Pearson, 1983; also see Gersten et al., 2001, and Pressley, Johnson, Symons, McGoldrick, & Kurita, 1989, for a review). One of the reasons activating prior knowledge is effective for supporting reading comprehension is that it facilitates inference making as students read (Elbro & Buch-Iversen, 2013), by helping them fill gaps in the information presented in texts with their own prior knowledge; that is, activation of prior knowledge when planning to read enables readers to make gap-filling inferences during reading. This planning activity is effective for supporting comprehension of both narrative text (Hansen, 1981; Hansen & Pearson, 1983) and informational text (Carr, Dewitz, & Patberg, 1983; Dewitz, Carr, & Patberg, 1987). Additionally, prior knowledge facilitates other prereading planning activities, such as self-questioning and making predictions.

Asking Oneself Questions about the Text

Studies of expert comprehenders show that once they have previewed the text content and checked their own prior knowledge, they ask themselves questions about a text before they even read it (Afflerbach & Pressley, 1995; Pressley & Lundeberg, 2008; Wyatt et al., 1993). A reader's prior knowledge informs his or her self-directed questions. For example, when reading *The True Story of the Three Little Pigs* (Scieszka, 1996), a reader might consider his knowledge of the classic story of the three little pigs and then ask himself how this new version might differ from the three pigs story he already knows. Self-directed questions, such as this one, serve to guide subsequent reading because they provide subtasks to support the intentional, goal-directed reading of text. Looking for the answers to one's self-directed questions, then, is part of a skilled comprehender's plan for under- R.CCR.10 standing text.

We also know that when poor comprehenders are taught to ask themselves questions about text, their comprehension improves (Davey & McBride, 1986; Palincsar & Brown, 1984, 1986; see Pressley et al., 1989, for a review). Because question generation instruction produces improvements in poor comprehenders' reading comprehension but not in typical readers' comprehension (Wong & Jones, 1982), such instruction seems to enable poor comprehenders to plan to seek particular text information at levels comparable to their peers with better comprehension. This effect is magnified when poor comprehenders are taught to focus on a subtask—underlining parts of text they think will be important for later assessment—that supports their overarching comprehension goal (Wong & Jones, 1982). In addition, students can be taught to ask better quality questions that are more closely tied to the meaningful ideas in text. Wong and Jones (1982) had teachers identify the most important idea units in passages and assessed the quality of the questions generated by the students trained on self-questioning, using the following rubric. Questions received:

- One point if the student's question simply replicated an idea in the text.
- Two points if the student's question restated a text idea in the student's own words.
- Three points if the student's question asked the student to provide an example from the text.

After question-generation instruction, Wong and Jones (1982) found that the poor comprehenders' reading comprehension improved. Additionally, in contrast to students who did not receive question generation instruction, intervention students became better at generating more good-quality questions that were tied to particular meaning-focused ideas in text across the four instructional days. I should note that their poor comprehenders were of average IQ and were 3 to 4 years below their current grade level on the Nelson Reading Skills Test (Hanna, Schell, & Schreiner, 1977, as cited in Wong & Jones, 1982), which assessed both reading comprehension and vocabulary knowledge (Mather, 1985). Thus, it seems that the poor comprehenders in the Wong and Jones (1982) study had specific comprehension problems, but decoding skills were not assessed; so, we cannot determine if they fit the profile for students with RCD.

Taken together, these findings indicate that students' generation of specific questions about texts before reading is an important component of the construction of an overall plan for understanding text. Self-generated questions provide specific subtasks to accomplish along the route to text comprehension, and can serve to keep students on-task and focused on the meaning of a passage to be read. As Cain, Oakhill, and Bryant (2004, p. 33) noted, "Children's reading comprehension benefits when children are trained to generate questions to promote the interpretation of text and to facilitate prediction from text." Students' self-directed questions provide the springboard from which to engage in another important prereading planning task, making predictions, which is described in the next section.

Making Predictions about What One Will Encounter in the Text

Once skilled comprehenders have previewed a text, figured out what they already know about it, and have asked themselves questions about it, they make specific predictions about what they think they might encounter in a text (Afflerbach & Pressley, 1995; Pressley & Lundeberg, 2008; Wyatt et al., 1993). And when poor comprehenders are taught to make predictions, their comprehension improves (Palincsar & Brown, 1984, 1986). Predicting goes hand-in-hand with self-questioning, because one's predictions may be possible answers to self-directed questions. Thus, the student I mentioned in the previous section who asks himself how *The True Story of the Three Little Pigs* (Scieszka, 1996) may differ from the classic three pigs story he already knows can use his question to make a specific prediction about what he might encounter in the new text. For example, he may predict that because the classic story is written from the perspective of the pigs that claim to be mistreated by a big, bad wolf, perhaps the new version is written from an opposing perspective, in which the wolf claims to have been mistreated by the pigs. (And, in this case, the student's prediction would be supported as he reads the text.) Just like self-questions, these kinds of predictions serve as subgoals in a reader's plan to work toward their overall comprehension goal (Pressley et al., 1989).

Recently, Hong-Nam, Leavell, and Maher (2014) examined the relation of predicting (and other reading strategies) to reading comprehension performance in ninth- to twelvth-grade students. They administered the Metacognitive Awareness of Reading Strategies Inventory and found that four clusters of strategies emerged. One of those clusters, which they described as "predicting strategies," included readers' self-reported activities involved in planning for reading comprehension, such as:

- Guessing what text is about.
- Deciding which parts of text to read carefully and which ones to skip.
- Guessing meanings of unfamiliar words.
- Checking to see whether guesses are right or wrong.
- Using text features like bold, italic, or underlining to find important information in text.
- Changing reading rate, based on the reading task.

Predicting was significantly related to students' reading comprehension performance, measured with the state-mandated comprehension assessment, and students who scored in the "commended" range were significantly more likely to use predicting strategies than students scoring in "standard" or "below standard" ranges; likewise, students scoring in the standard range were more likely to use predicting strategies than their counterparts who scored in the below standard range (Hong-Nam et al., 2014). A similar pattern of results emerged for students' self-perceptions of reading competence, and use of predicting strategies increased with grade level from nine to 12 (Hong-Nam et al., 2014). Taken together, these findings confirm the importance of predicting to successful reading compre- R.CCR.10
hension, and they point to specific student behaviors, like those we have been discussing, that can be taught to help your students better plan for understanding texts.

Furthermore, just as working memory interacts with the goal-setting and goal-pursuit aspects of planning (Linderholm, 2006; Linderholm & van den Broek, 2002), working memory also supports the ability to make predictions (Pérez, Paolieri, Macizo, & Bajo, 2014). This makes sense because predictions require that readers hold many things in mind, such as their own prior knowledge, their questions about the text, and text information they may have gleaned from previewing the text, while continuing to work with those sources of information to make a sensible prediction. This is consistent with the definition of working memory that we discussed in Chapter 1: *the ability to hold information in mind to support completion of tasks while working with part of that information and updating it as needed; working memory includes a storage component and a processing component.* (see Table 1.1).

How Can I Apply This Knowledge to Classroom Practice?

Before I describe specific recommendations for teaching planning abilities to support your students' reading comprehension, I want to talk a bit about the nature of successful comprehension instruction more generally. Many decades of research show that the best way to teach reading comprehension, and the thinking processes that underlie successful reading comprehension, is the gradual release of responsibility model (Duffy, 2014; Duke & Pearson, 2002; Duke et al., 2011; Pearson & Gallagher, 1983). You are likely very familiar with this model for comprehension instruction that involves

- *Providing an explicit explanation* of a skill or strategy, including information about when and why good readers use it.
- *Behavioral and mental modeling* of the skill or strategy, using real texts, with accompanying explanation of the behaviors and the thinking involved.
- *Shared use* of the skill or strategy in which the teacher supports students' involvement in using the skill or strategy, beginning with the teacher's own use (this is where responsibility begins to shift to the student).
- *Guided, supported practice* in using the skill or strategy with continued teacher support (note that responsibility is still shared here).
- *Independent practice* in using the skill or strategy on new texts.

This model provides a blueprint for successful comprehension instruction that I will continue to reference throughout this book. Forgive me a metacognitive moment, but this is actually a good example of the kind of planning that is supportive of good readers' comprehension. We have just activated our shared background knowledge about the gradual release of responsibility model, and you have probably thought about what you already know or remember about how the gradual release model works in your own teaching. You may wonder how the gradual release model will apply to executive skills, the new thinking processes you will encounter in this book (thus, you may be engaging in self-questioning). Finally, you may have already made some prediction about how I might use this framework in future chapters to talk about teaching executive skills for better reading comprehension. In doing these things, you are already engaging in planning behaviors to support your comprehension of this text!

The preceding review of research demonstrated that although there are few studies of the role of planning in reading comprehension in which planning was assessed with traditional executive skills-based measures (like the tower task), we actually know quite a bit about the things skilled comprehenders do as they make a plan to understand text. As we noted in Chapter 1, planning involves "the ability to decide what tasks are necessary to complete a goal, including understanding which ones are most important to goal attainment and the order in which those tasks should be completed to most effectively reach the goal."

The first step in helping your students understand and implement planning for understanding is to provide explicit instruction about this important executive skill: what it is, when good readers do it, and how it helps support good readers' understanding of texts. You may introduce planning during whole-group instruction, but goal-setting conferences and guided practice of prereading planning activities are more effectively presented in small-group instruction or one-to-one conferences. To introduce planning to your students, begin with an explanation like this:

EXPLICITLY EXPLAINING PLANNING

"Good readers are good planners. This means that before good readers start reading, they do lots of things to help themselves understand what they read. They start with a plan to understand! The first thing good readers do is to set a goal for reading. This means that good readers know why they're reading. They make a plan to understand the text in a certain way or for a certain reason. Then, to help themselves reach the goal, they take steps to get there, like preview the text and think about what they already know. The steps in your plan depend on your goal. To be a good planner, remember to always think about *why* you are reading. Keeping your goal in mind while you read will help you understand and remember what you read."

Central to effective instruction in reading comprehension is talk about the thinking that good readers do (Duffy, 2014). So, you should talk explicitly about how good readers are good planners and return to that idea again and again throughout the instructional day, whether you are in your language arts, science, or social studies block. Planning supports comprehension of all texts. As Schunk and Rice (1989, 1991) demonstrated, students benefit from explicit reminders of their goals. So, you should remind your students that good readers know why they are reading, and they keep their goal in mind as they progress through a text. Provide your students cues to help them remember to maintain their goals in mind, "Remember, think about why you are reading; what is your goal? Keeping your goal in mind will help you remember what you read." Figure 2.2 provides a concrete cue, My Plan to Understand, which you can print as a handout that your students can use to guide their planning activities. Additionally, you can enlarge the Plan to Understand and hang it in the classroom so that your students have a visual cue they can use to remember to plan for understanding texts.

My Plan to Understand

First ask: Why am I reading? What is my goal?

Then, with my goal in mind . . .

- Preview: Looking through the book, what do I see to help me get there?
- Should I pay more attention to some parts and slow down for others?
- Connect: What do I already know about this topic that will help me reach the goal?
- Question: What goal-related question(s) can I ask myself?
- Predict: What do I guess will be in this book?
- What other steps can I take to reach my goal?
- What will I know when I'm done?

FIGURE 2.2. A planning guide for your students.

From *Executive Skills and Reading Comprehension: A Guide for Educators* by Kelly B. Cartwright. Copyright 2015 by The Guilford Press. Permission to photocopy this figure is granted to purchasers of this book for personal use only (see copyright page for details). Purchasers can download a larger version of this figure from *www.guilford.com/cartwright2-forms*.

Setting a Goal for Reading: Knowing Why You're Reading

Goal setting is the first step in planning for reading comprehension, yet students may have difficulty setting goals for reading. Gaa (1973, 1979) and Fuchs et al. (1985) demonstrated that teacher-directed goal setting helps students set, remember, and achieve goals. Typically, this might occur in individual conferences or in small-group instruction, providing students explicit knowledge of the thinking activity they are learning so that they can transfer the new goal-setting behavior to other texts with less support from you. So, you might introduce goal setting this way:

> "Remember, good readers are good planners. Today I'm going to help you learn the first step in making a good plan to understand what you read, and that is setting a goal! Setting a goal means deciding *why* you are reading so that you can do things while you read to make sure your goal is met. For example, sometimes you might want to remember details of a story you read, sometimes you may want to learn something new to connect to a topic you are studying, or sometimes you may want to answer a question or find a particular kind of information."

Ask your students why they think they're reading a text, and lead them to an appropriate goal for that type of text or for the assignment at hand. The following questions can guide your goal setting discussions with your students.

R.CCR.1,
R.CCR.2,
R.CCR.10

Questions to Guide Goal-Setting Discussions

- Why are you reading this text?
- What kind of a text is it, a story or an informational text (fiction or nonfiction)?
- What do you need to know when you are done?
- Do you need to remember details of a story, or are you reading to learn information about a new topic?
- Are you reading to answer questions?
- Are you reading to find a particular kind of information?
- Are you reading for fun?

Have your students write down their goal on their Plan to Understand (Figure 2.2). This action reinforces the goal in memory and provides them with a concrete reminder of their goal to which they can refer as they continue to think about and read the text.

Steps to Reach Reading Comprehension Goals: Knowing How You'll Get There

After students have a particular goal in mind, they need steps in a process to reach that goal. Recall that process goals, those with particular actions students can take, are more effective than product goals, which focus only on the end result of the goal, such as answering questions or remembering a story (Levin, 1973; Pressley, 1976; Schunk & Rice, 1989, 1991). Thus, your students need particular actions they can use to help them accomplish their goals. The student guide in Figure 2.2 lists prompts to help students remember the most common steps in a good reader's plan to understand a text. These steps include the pre-reading activities typical of skilled comprehenders, such as connecting text to one's prior knowledge or making predictions about the text (e.g., Pressley & Afflerbach, 1995; Pressley & Lundeberg, 2008; Wyatt et al., 1993). However, rather than teaching these actions as isolated strategies, as often occurs in instruction aligned with basal readers (Dewitz, Jones, & Leahy, 2009), these actions are presented as steps in an overall plan to help students reach a reading goal. Each of these processes is helpful, regardless of a student's reading goal or the type of text being read (narrative or expository). However, there are other steps students can take to help them with particular kinds of goals; I will turn R.CCR.10

to these in the next section. The steps in the My Plan to Understand student guide that are pertinent to all reading goals are reprinted here to facilitate our discussion.

My Plan to Understand: Steps in the Plan
- Preview: "Looking through the book, what do I see to help me get there?"
- "Should I pay more attention to some parts and slow down for others?"
- Connect: "What do I already know about this topic that will help me reach the goal?"
- Question: "What goal-related question(s) can I ask myself?"
- Predict: "What do I guess will be in this book?"
- "What other steps can I take to reach my goal?"
- "What will I know when I'm done?"

After you have taught goal setting, your students need to be provided explicit instruction in the steps readers take to achieve their goals. Some of these may be familiar to your students, as comprehension strategies such as these are pervasive in reading curricula. However, understanding how they fit into an executive skills framework, particularly with respect to planning for comprehension, is probably new to you and your students. So, what might you say to your students to help them understand how these steps form the backbone of a plan to comprehend a text? I suggest the following introduction to the most common steps in a good reader's plan to understand. Then, I provide suggested explanations for each of the steps below. Consistent with best practices, these explanations focus on the thinking processes involved in planning to understand a text (Duffy, 2014; Duke & Pearson, 2002; Duke et al., 2011; Pearson & Gallagher, 1983).

How to Introduce Steps in the Plan to Understand

"Remember when we talked about how good readers are good planners and set goals? Well, any good plan has a number of steps in it to help you reach your goal. Today we're going to talk about the most common steps (or whichever steps you have chosen for that day) that good readers take to make sure they understand a text."

Schunk and Rice (1991, p. 358) used explicit reminders to help students keep goals in mind and stick to the steps in their plans for understanding texts, such as "You're learning to use the steps. You're using the steps to answer the questions. You're getting good at using the steps. You got it right because you followed the steps in order." Also, "While you're working, it helps to keep in mind what you're trying to do. You'll be trying to learn how to use the steps to answer questions about what you've read" (Schunk & Rice, 1991, p. 358). These kinds of reminders are essential as your students are learning to plan for understanding texts. As they work their way through their plans for understanding texts, applying the steps depicted in Figure 2.2, your explicit reminders of the planning process will support the development of their planning skills, whether they are reading during small-group reading instruction or whether they are reading texts for science, social studies, or math. You might use the following explicit reminders to support planning while your students are reading:

Explicit Reminders to Support the Development of Your Students' Planning

- "Don't forget to follow the steps in your Plan to Understand."
- "While you're reading, it helps to keep your goal in mind."
- "Remember what you're trying to do; remember why you're reading this text."
- "Use your steps to help you _____ (fill in the goal)."
- "Good job! You remembered what this text was about [or wrote a good summary, or found the information you were looking for, etc.] because you followed your Plan to Understand."

In addition to explicitly explaining the planning process for your students, you will need to explain each of the steps in the plan, making sure to help your students understand that they are engaging in an overall planning process. The following sample explanations are provided to support you in this task. For example, to introduce previewing the text and connect it with the overall plan, you might say this:

How to Introduce Previewing the Text

"You already know that good readers start with a goal in mind. Once they know why they are reading, they preview the text to get an idea of the things they'll find when they read, like different sections, headings, or vocabulary words that might relate to their goal; even pictures and diagrams help readers understand better what they are going to encounter in text. That way, you know what parts you may want to read more slowly or pay more attention to, and which parts you may want to read more quickly. Previewing the text also reminds you of what you already know, which will help you do the next step in a good reader's plan to understand." **R.CCR.5**

You might use language such as the following to explain connecting:

How to Introduce Connecting

"The next step in good readers' plans to understand is to think about what they already know about the topic of the text and the topic of their goal. Linking things we read to knowledge we already have helps it to stay in our minds longer. It helps it to stick, so that we can use it later. Thinking about what you already know about a text's topic will also help you to do the next step in a good reader's plan, asking yourself questions about the text."

To introduce self-questioning and link it to the overall planning process, you might say something like this.

How to Introduce Questioning

"After you've set your goal, previewed the text, and thought about what you already know, you probably have a question or two in mind. Thinking about questions related to reading goals helps good readers stay focused on their reason for reading. Questions are better when they are related to your goal. You may have a question about something you saw when you previewed the text. Or, if you're reading to learn more about a topic, you may have a question about how the text information adds to what you already know. Write your questions down on your Plan to Understand and see if you can answer them while you read."

Finally, good readers make predictions about what they will encounter in text. Often, their predictions arise out of the questions they have generated in the previous step. Your students may be quite familiar with predicting, but they may not connect it to an overall plan for understanding text. Thus, you may want to introduce predicting in the context of their Plan to Understand by linking it to the previous steps in their plan, as follows.

How to Introduce Predicting

"OK, remember how we're learning that good readers make a plan to understand? They set a goal for reading, preview the text, think about what they already know, and they ask questions about the text that help them keep their goals in mind. The next thing good readers do is something you've done before, and that's make predictions about what they are going to find in text! When you ask yourself a question about a text, that question can naturally lead to a prediction. If you are getting ready to read a story called *A Big Guy Took My Ball!* [Willems, 2013], then you may ask yourself why the big guy took the ball. When you make a prediction about a book, you guess what you're going to find in the book; and, guessing the answer to your question is a way to make that kind of prediction. [Engage your students in a discussion of possible answers to the question.] See how the steps in your plan naturally lead to predictions? As you read, thinking about whether your predictions are right or not will help you stay focused on your goal, understand, and remember the text."

Last Step: Reinforcing the Goal by Asking, "What Will I Know When I'm Done?"

Sometimes, these steps are sufficient to help your students plan for understanding the text for a particular purpose. Other times, your students may need additional supports for creating plans to understand the text; I describe some of these below. If your students need these additional supports, they can be noted in their Plan to Understand under "What other steps can I take to reach my goal?" Otherwise, after your students have worked through the steps in their Plan to Understand, have them return to the goal by answering the question "What will I know when I'm done?" This question helps to bookend the planning process with the comprehension goal. Your students begin by formulating the goal, they perform steps to help them focus on meaning related to the comprehension goal, and they end the planning process by returning to the purpose of the goal—they're going to know something more than when they started.

What Other Steps Can Readers Take to Plan for Understanding Texts?

Sometimes students need extra support for planning, tailored to their goals, to help them understand text. The following supports focus on connecting, self-questioning, attending to the main idea of text, and finding information in text.

More Steps to Support Connecting

Connecting one's own knowledge to a text is often called a gap-filling inference because readers use their own knowledge to supplement what the author has provided in order to better understand text (Baker & Stein, 1981; Cain & Oakhill, 1999). I explain this process to students by telling them that authors write down a lot of things, but they cannot provide all of the information we need to understand a text. So, authors expect us to use what we know to fill in the missing parts (Cartwright, 2010). I will expand on this comprehension skill when we discuss working memory in Chapter 5.

R.CCR.1

NARRATIVE TEXT

Hansen (1981; Hansen & Pearson, 1983) devised an intervention to support students' gap-filling inferences by teaching them to connect their lives to stories. I will return to this technique in our discussion of inference making and working memory in Chapter 5.

These lessons occur across at least 2 days and include the following steps:

• First, the teacher engages students in a discussion of the benefits of connecting their prior experiences to things that they read. Explain that making these connections helps students better understand what they read.

• Begin a discussion with students about an "important idea" relevant to a text that you will read with them on a subsequent day. For example, if you are reading *Ferry Tail* (Kenah, 2014) about a dog that lives on a ferry and takes a detour to an island where he is lost for a day, you might explain that an important idea is that life on a boat is very different from life on land. You might ask if they have ever been on a ferry or a boat, ask what that feels like, and have them share experiences that you note for the next day's discussion. Another important idea relevant to this text is getting lost; thus, you can engage your students in a discussion of their feelings if they were ever lost (or ask them to predict how they would feel if they haven't had that experience before). Jotting down notes about your students' comments will help you support their connections later.

• Then, when reading the selected text on a subsequent day, support students in making explicit connections between their lives and the story. Draw from the experiences they shared to help them understand how to make those connections.

EXPOSITORY TEXT

Elbro and Buch-Iversen (2013) recently developed an intervention to support gap-filling inference-making with expository texts. Students who lack relevant background knowledge or who have inaccurate background knowledge are less able to make appropriate connections to support comprehension (Kendeou & van den Broek, 2007). Elbro and Buch-Iversen (2013) used a graphic organizer to help students visualize the gaps in the information provided in texts and show how the students' own knowledge contributes to their understanding of text. To teach these steps, select short texts for which students must make connections to their own knowledge to ensure comprehension. I will return to discussion of this technique in Chapter 5 when we discuss inference making and working memory. See Figure 2.3 for examples of how one might use graphic organizers to support gap-filling inference making. In these examples, students should supply general knowledge that the poles are colder than other places on Earth in order to make

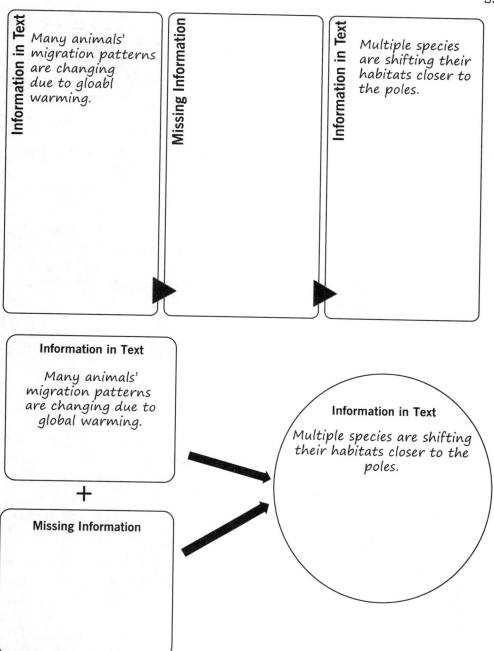

FIGURE 2.3. Examples of graphic organizers to support gap-filling inferences in expository text. (Students should supply general knowledge that the poles typically have colder temperatures than other places.)

an explanatory inference about the text idea that some species are moving their habitats closer to the poles. Figure 2.4 provides blank organizers for your use with your students.

Find relevant pieces of information from the text for which students must supply their own knowledge.

- Write the relevant text pieces in the graphic organizer in the "Information in Text" boxes. For example, when reading a science text about global warming, you may find the following statements that require a connection.
  - "Many animals' migration patterns are changing due to global warming."
  - "Multiple species are shifting their habitats closer to the poles."

- To understand the text, students must draw from their basic knowledge to fill the gap between the two text statements. Thus, in our example, students must supply the information that the poles are colder, so being closer to the poles means having a cooler habitat. Students should write that information in the "Missing Information" box in the graphic organizer.

Using the graphic organizer helps students see the gaps in the information provided in text and visualize how connecting their own knowledge to texts can help fill gaps in support of comprehension.

More Steps to Support Question Generation

There are at least two reasons why self-questioning might be beneficial as students prepare to read a text (Davey & McBride, 1986): generating and answering questions requires readers to process the meaning of text more deeply, and this process also makes them more aware of whether they understand a text.

NARRATIVE AND EXPOSITORY TEXT

Indeed, Wong and Jones (1982) showed that teaching poor comprehenders to engage in question generation improved their awareness of important text information as well as their reading comprehension. Their self-questioning process included five steps, which you can use with your students on both narrative and expository texts, adapted for their comprehension goals. Your students should:

- Determine why they are reading a particular text (e.g., so that they can answer questions after they read, so they can find a particular kind of information); in other words, they should restate their goal.
- Underline the main idea in the passage when they preview the text; this can be adapted for their particular goal.

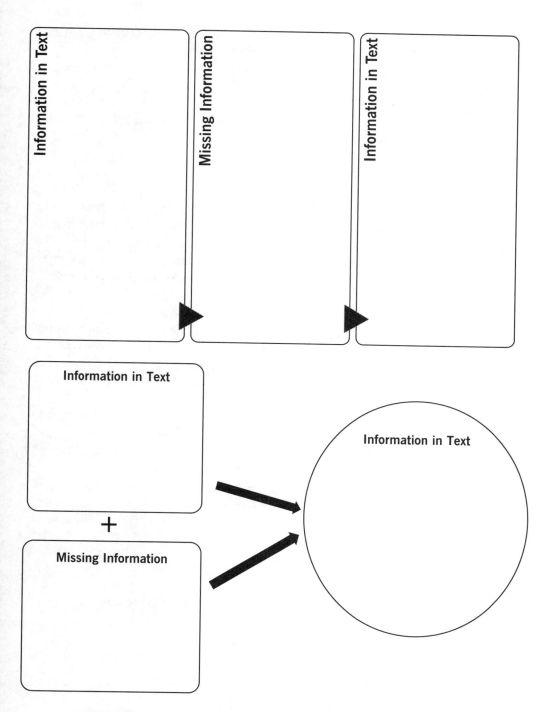

FIGURE 2.4. Blank graphic organizers to support gap-filling inferences.

- Come up with a question about the main idea and write it down; again, this can be adapted for their goal.
- Find out the answer to the question while reading, and write it down.
- Look back at questions and answers to see how questions help knowledge grow while reading.

R.CCR.2

EXPOSITORY TEXT

Davey and McBride (1986) taught question-generation for expository texts, using the gradual release of responsibility model. They taught sixth graders how to generate questions in five 40-minute lessons across 2 weeks and to evaluate their own performance, using the following steps. After the intervention, students were more aware of whether they understood what they were reading, and their comprehension improved.

- The instructors explicitly explained that making one's own questions about texts helps readers remember important information in texts, know whether they need to reread a text, and predict test questions that they'll see after they read.
- The students were taught to distinguish between "think" and "locate" questions; "think" questions focus on the important information in a text, and "locate" questions link ideas in a text.
- Instructors modeled finding important ideas in text and writing "think" and "locate" questions, depending on the students' purpose.
- Students were given opportunities to practice writing "think" and "locate" questions on their own, using new passages.
- Students evaluated their own performance with the questions presented in Table 2.3.

TABLE 2.3. Student Self-Check of Self-Generated Questions

A Likert-type check was provided for the following items:
- How well did I identify important information?
- How well did I link information together?
- How well could I answer my question?

A yes–no checklist was used for the following items:
- Did my "think" question use different language from the text?
- Did I use good signal words?

Note. Adapted from Davey and McBride (1986). Copyright 1986 by the American Psychological Association (APA). Adapted by permission. The use of APA information does not imply endorsement by APA.

More Steps to Support Information Search Goals

As I noted in the review of research on planning and reading comprehension, sometimes a reader's goal is more specific than finding the main idea of a passage. Instead, students may read a text in order to find a particular type of information for a report or to answer comprehension questions. Searching for information is one of the most common reasons for reading in adulthood (Dreher & Guthrie, 1990; Kirsch & Guthrie, 1984; White et al., 2010).

EXPOSITORY TEXT

As noted earlier in the review of research, Dreher (1992, 1993; Dreher & Brown, 1993; Dreher & Guthrie, 1990; Dreher & Sammons, 1994) has investigated a multistep process for efficiently accomplishing information search goals in expository text that is effective for elementary, high school, and college students. These steps can also be incorporated into your students' Plans to Understand to provide additional support for students' information search goals.

- Goal formation. This step involves setting one's particular information search goal. In this step, students review their comprehension goals, which they should have already formulated when they began completing their Plan to Understand.

- Text selection. This step involves choosing appropriate texts (or sections of texts) in which to search for information. In this step, you should model for your students the ways that good readers search for information. For example, if a student is searching for information on the digestive system for a science report, she should be able to locate texts in the library, and use the texts' table of contents, index terms, and subheadings to help her locate the information she needs.   **R.CCR.1, R.CCR.10**

- Information extraction. In this step, students should focus on gathering information that is relevant to their specific information search goal. Thus, if a student's goal is to better understand motility in the digestive system, she should focus on those aspects of the texts she chooses rather than on the structure of the digestive system.

- Integration. This step involves pulling the various bits of relevant information, gathered from different sources, into a unified whole.   **R.CCR.7, R.CCR.9**

- Evaluation. In this step, students examine the information they have gathered and integrated to determine whether they have accomplished their information search goal and located appropriate information. If they find that their response is incomplete, Dreher suggests that students recycle these steps to continue to increase the breadth of their answer.

NARRATIVE AND EXPOSITORY TEXT

Finally, when looking for information in texts, sometimes students need to be reminded that information in text can come from a variety of sources. Graham and Wong (1993) provided students a mnemonic to help them plan their information search, the three-H strategy, for remembering the various potential sources of information in text.

The Three-H Strategy

- Sometimes information is obvious and is explicitly stated in text. That is, the information is "here."
- Other times, information is implied in text and requires that readers make connections between various parts of text; that is, the information is "hidden."
- Finally, sometimes readers need to supply information from their own prior knowledge to supplement text information; that is, the information is in the reader's "head."

R.CCR.1,
R.CCR.10

Students who used the three-H strategy were more efficient at locating information in text to answer comprehension questions, and they also had significantly better awareness of their own reading processes (Graham & Wong, 1993).

What We Know and What We Still Need to Know about Planning

Planning contributes in important ways to successful reading comprehension. And research has demonstrated this connection with traditional, executive skills-based measures of planning (like tower tasks), as well as with reading-specific assessments of planning. We know that skilled comprehenders complete a series of tasks before they ever begin reading a text that supports their later reading comprehension. These plans for understanding can be made explicit to support developing comprehenders' awareness of the necessity to plan their own steps to understanding.

The research conducted to date is promising, but there are still many gaps in our knowledge. The following questions deserve research attention to provide a more nuanced understanding of the role of planning in reading comprehension as well as to inform instruction in this area.

- Does teaching planning using traditional tasks improve reading comprehension? We know that planning, assessed with traditional measures, such as tower tasks, contributes significantly to reading comprehension. However, no work has examined whether teaching these tasks produces improvements in reading comprehension.

• Does self-reported planning relate to reading comprehension? Jacobs and Paris (1987) assessed readers' self-reported planning behaviors as a subscale in their metacognitive reading inventory. However, they used only total scores and did not examine readers' performance on the planning subscale alone and its relation to reading comprehension. Additionally, no work has examined whether self-reported planning is related to objective measures of planning behavior, either traditional or reading-specific. More work is needed in this area to help us determine whether self-reported planning would be a useful assessment in instructional contexts.

• Do reading-specific measures of planning relate to traditional assessments of planning, like the tower tasks? Dermitzaki et al. (2008) assessed planning in reading comprehension with a behavioral observation rubric (see Table 2.1); however, no work has examined whether such observations are related to traditional assessments of planning or to the reading-specific planning behaviors used by good comprehenders (goal setting, connecting, questioning, etc.).

• How can we incorporate awareness of planning into comprehension instruction curricula? As noted earlier, although we frequently teach strategies like predicting and connecting in reading comprehension instruction, these behaviors and others are not typically presented in an executive skills framework as steps in a good reader's overall plan to understand a text. Research reviewed in this chapter demonstrates that planning is essential to skilled comprehension, and teaching about the planning process can provide a useful means for helping students remember all of the important steps in skilled comprehenders' prereading behaviors.

CHAPTER 3

Organization
Why Text and Reader Organization Matter

Organization is what you do before you do something,
so that when you do it, it's not all mixed up.
—attributed to A. A. MILNE
(*www.goodreads.com/quotes*)

Winnie the Pooh's creator described well the importance of organization, another executive skill that supports reading comprehension: without it, readers are all mixed up! This chapter focuses on readers' abilities to keep things in order, mentally, either by imposing order on information through application of self-generated organizational processes or by noticing and using the organizational structures inherent in text that convey meaning and support comprehension. Our brains are built to detect patterns and similarities in information we encounter in the world and then extract organizational principles that will help guide future learning (Carpenter & Grossberg, 1987; Medin, Goldstone, & Gentner, 1993; Medin & Schaffer, 1978; Pulvermüller & Knoblauch, 2009). However, children who struggle with reading comprehension are significantly less likely to exhibit such organizational skills and are less sensitive to language and text structures (e.g., Cain, 1996; Meyer et al.,1980; Nation & Snowling, 2000; Oakhill & Yuill, 1996).

Just think about the way language itself is structured. We know what sentences mean because of the way they are organized. For example, the sentence *Store the please to milk go buy to* makes no sense because it lacks organization.

On the other hand, *Please go to the store to buy milk* makes much more sense (and will make your raisin bran go down more easily tomorrow morning) because it is better organized. Linguists call this organization syntax.

Sensitivity to organizational patterns, such as syntactic patterns, is an important contributor to reading comprehension (Gaux & Gombert, 1999; Mokhtari & Thompson, 2006; Weaver, 1979), even beyond vocabulary knowledge (Mokhtari & Niederhauser, 2010; Shiotsu & Weir, 2007). In a more general sense, organization is often thought to be a contributor to planning, which occurs before a task begins. For example, when previewing a text, good comprehenders note texts' organizational features that will support their comprehension while reading, by providing them a means to keep track of text information and events (Gaskins et al., 2007; Pressley & Afflerbach, 1995; Pressley & Lundeberg, 2008). However, as with all executive skills, individuals vary in their abilities to recognize and generate organizational structures to support reading comprehension.

SL.CCR.4, SL.CCR.6

R.CCR.5

What Is Organization and How Is It Typically Assessed?

Organization is the ability to impose order on information and objects, create systems for managing information or objects, and recognize such orders and systems so that one can use them successfully to complete tasks (see Table 1.1 in Chapter 1; Dawson & Guare, 2010; Meltzer, 2007, 2010). Like other cool executive skills, organization processes are associated with DLPFC functioning (Fletcher & Henson, 2001), and injury to the frontal lobes results in deficiencies in verbal organizational skills, like those required for reading (Gershberg & Shimamura, 1995; Stuss et al., 1994). In the contemporary executive skills literature, organization is most often discussed as a component of planning, and far less research exists on organization than on other executive skills, such as working memory, inhibition, cognitive flexibility, or planning. However, without organization, planning and other executive skills are difficult to manage. Imagine planning the shopping trip I mentioned in Chapter 2 without any means of organizing your route through the store; much like shopping in an unfamiliar store, a disorganized route would undermine the success of your plan and add a great deal of time to your shopping trip!

Consider the game I Spy. The object of the game is to find an item with a particular type of feature in the surrounding environment. I used to play this game with my daughter when we were waiting in line at a store or

Organization: the ability to impose order on information and objects, create systems for managing information or objects, and recognize such orders and systems so that one can use them successfully to complete tasks.

waiting at the doctor's office. To begin the game I would identify an item (say, a yellow flower in a painting on the wall) and say, "I spy something yellow!" She would guess items with that feature until she identified my target item. To be successful at this task, a student must recognize the target feature in various objects and ask questions systematically in order to eliminate possibilities and narrow down to the target item. If my daughter had approached the task in a haphazard or disorganized manner by randomly selecting objects about the room, she may not have found the target item. Instead, she used the structure of the room to help her organize her questions, looking first at all objects on one wall in the room, then moving to the next wall, and so on. In this game, students can use the structure of the physical environment to organize responses. Likewise, in the game Twenty Questions, which has a similar objective, students must use information from their mental conceptual structures and gradually narrow down to the target item (e.g., by asking "Is it living or nonliving?," then "Is it an animal or plant?," and so on), using twenty questions or fewer. Whereas I Spy requires recognizing and using an existing structure, Twenty Questions requires imposing one's own conceptual structures to reach a successful outcome, and both of these skills are important to reading comprehension.

Assessments of organization may be nonverbal or verbal, and they may also reflect other executive skills that support or are supported by organizational abilities. For example, Cutting, Materek, et al. (2009) used the Elithorn Perceptual Maze Test (Benton, Elithorn, Fogel, & Kerr, 1963), a nonverbal task, to assess planning, organization, and monitoring abilities in their study, which was significantly related to reading comprehension. According to Cutting, Materek, et al. (2009, p. 40), the Elithorn Perceptual Maze Test "requires choosing a single path that passes through circles within a 'lattice' of lines in an inverted triangular structure without backtracking." Such a task, however, makes it difficult to tease the effect of organizational abilities apart from other skills.

I know of one standardized nonverbal, nonnarrative assessment of organizational ability, the Leiter International Performance Scale Sequential Order subtest (Roid, Miller, Pomplun, & Koch, 2013), which requires students to order pictures of objects (e.g., shapes of varying size) along a dimension, such as size. A similar assessment of organizational ability with which you may be familiar is Piaget's seriation task. Piaget's work was published in the United States in the 1960s, prior to the steep rise in attention to executive skills seen in recent decades, yet he studied extensively children's control of their own thinking (i.e., he studied executive skills). He was certainly ahead of his time! As part of this work, Piaget devised seriation tasks to assess children's organizational abilities that required students to arrange items into arrays that increased in graded quantity, like weight or length (Inhelder & Piaget, 1964). See Figure 3.1 for an example of a seriation task.

As noted in the research review that follows, seriation is related to reading comprehension. However, Pasnak and colleagues (Hendricks et al., 1999; Hendricks,

(a) Starting array for seriation task

(b) Correct solution for seriation task

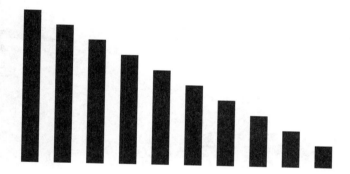

FIGURE 3.1. Example of a seriation task to assess children's organizational abilities; given a random array of rods (a), the child's is asked to arrange them in order by length (b).

Trueblood, & Pasnak, 2006; Kidd et al., 2013, 2014) noted that the organizational skill required for a seriation task is typically one-dimensional, and may not be sufficiently difficult to capture the kinds of organizational abilities necessary for successful reading performance as children continue to progress through school. Thus, these scholars have focused on assessing an organizational ability they call patterning, which involves recognizing and imposing organizational schemes that include more than one dimension (Hendricks et al., 1999; Hendricks, Trueblood, & Pasnak, 2006; Kidd et al., 2013, 2014). Patterning is typically taught in elementary schools (e.g., Domnauer, 2012; Ganske, 2006) and involves "the ability to recognize an ordering of numbers, letters, shapes, symbols, objects, or events according to some rule of progression" (Hendricks et al., 2006, p. 83). For example, in an array of shapes that includes a red square, two yellow giraffes, a red square, two yellow giraffes, and a red square, students should recognize that the next shapes in the pattern should be two yellow giraffes. The educational television program Sesame Street frequently engages children in these kinds of patterning activities, as well. An example of one such patterning activity excerpted from a Sesame Street program can be found on YouTube at: *http://www.youtube.com/watch?v=pO9b7BTOIOU* or by searching online for "Sesame Street—Guess What's Next." Pasnak and colleagues taught patterns involving such things as numerical sequences counted by 1s, 2s, 3s, 5s, or 10s; different colors, shapes, and types of objects; and clock faces. (See Figure 3.2 for examples of patterning problems.) Finally, other researchers have used rhythm patterns to assess children's ability to recognize and recall patterns across sensory modalities (Rudnick, Sterritt, & Flax, 1967; Sterritt & Rudnick, 1966). For example, a rhythm pattern may be presented in auditory mode (e.g., a series of two hand claps, a pause, and then

Problem 1

Possible Solutions (correct answer is c)

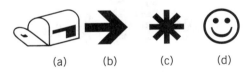

(a)   (b)   (c)   (d)

Problem 2

Possible Solutions (correct answer is b)

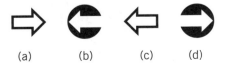

(a)   (b)   (c)   (d)

FIGURE 3.2. Example of items in a patterning task.

three hand claps) and then students must recognize the pattern in visual mode (e.g., by choosing the appropriate series of dots that corresponds to the auditory pattern from these three options: [a] ... .., [b] .. ..., [c] .. .. ..; option [b] corresponds to the series of two claps then three claps mentioned above).

Other nonverbal assessments of organization require students to recognize categorical or narrative relationships in order to perform successfully. For example, the Picture Concepts subscale of the Wechsler Intelligence Scale for Children requires that children recognize objects from an array that go together because they have a categorical relationship (e.g., in an array of pictures of a bird, squirrel, umbrella, and crayon, a child would indicate that the squirrel and bird go together because they are both animals). This test does not require a verbal response (Pearson Education, 2014) and reflects a student's conceptual organizational abilities. Picture arrangement tasks that require individuals to order story events in causal sequence have also been used to assess students' sensitivity to causal organization in narrative. Although the Wechsler Intelligence Scale for Children no longer includes a picture arrangement subtest (Pearson Education, 2014), these can be created quite easily by cutting apart multiframe graphic sequences from comic books or graphic novels, even with primary students (Chase, Son, & Styner, 2014), to assess their narrative sequencing ability and sensitivity to story organization. Furthermore, a simple Google images search on "story sequence pictures" turns up a host of line drawings that can be used for teaching and assessing students' sensitivity to narrative structure.

Finally, another indicator of students' conceptual organization is the DKEFS Twenty Questions subtest, which is much like the game I described earlier. This subtest requires that students identify an object by asking questions that narrow down the category to which the object belongs until they determine the identity of the specific object (Delis et al., 2001). The correct answers are chosen specifically because they are members of a category hierarchy (e.g., a zebra is a living thing, an animal, and a mammal, and each of these categories is nested within a larger category). Students' questions reflect the organization of their conceptual knowledge as well as their ability to apply that organization to the creation of appropriate questions in order to arrive at a correct response, using as few questions as possible.

Why Is Organization Important to Reading Comprehension?

The abilities to recognize structures and organizational schemes and to devise and implement such schemes oneself are important for many activities in everyday life, from storing and indexing journal articles by topic to arranging items in closets or cabinets so that one can find and use them later. Likewise, organizational structures are inherent in language and texts, and readers need structured means to store information gathered while reading text as well as to integrate text information with their existing knowledge. Readers can deal with these tasks by using existing organizational structures (e.g., text structures) to organize incoming text information, or they may impose their own organizational schemes to manage new information that they encounter in texts. Regardless of the approach, organization is essential for skilled reading comprehension.

With respect to the RRSG (2002) framework for reading comprehension (see Figure 1.1), organization is a reader feature, as readers vary in their abilities to organize information and to notice organizational schemes in information they encounter. As noted earlier, syntax provides language organization, and readers vary in their syntactic awareness, or their awareness of the organization of language, which affects reading comprehension (Gaux & Gombert, 1999; Mokhtari & Thompson, 2006; Nation & Snowling, 2000; Weaver, 1979). Additionally, organization can be considered a text feature to be used by readers for successful comprehension. Some texts contain many cues to their organizational structures, whereas other texts contain few organizational cues. Differences in texts' organizational cues interact with reader characteristics, such as motivation, to affect
R.CCR.5   reading comprehension: readers with high motivation show equivalent comprehension regardless of texts' organizational cues, but readers with low motivation show significantly lower reading comprehension without explicit cues to texts' structure, indicating that they are less able to use texts' organizational structures without support (Kardash & Noel, 2000).

Furthermore, different genres of text, such as expository or narrative texts, have different kinds of structures (Williams, 2003, 2005). Even within genres, there are different types of organizational structures (e.g., Anderson & Armbruster, 1984, suggested six different types of expository text structures), and a single expository text may even contain more than one of these structures (Williams, 2003)! The ability to recognize and utilize these various structures in texts to organize incoming text information is essential to skilled reading comprehension.

What Does Organization Look Like in Real Readers?

Brittany, a Student with RCD

As you learned in Chapter 2, when Brittany picks up a new text, she dives right in without a plan for ways to understand it. In addition, she seems to be less aware of proper word order and sentence structure than her peers, as evidenced by her production of sentences in speaking and writing, and in her understanding of sentences in listening and reading. Furthermore, Brittany's entries in her writing journal and retellings of stories at small-group time lack a coherent structure, suggesting that she isn't as aware of the typical organization of narratives as her peers. Finally, in science and social studies, and when reading expository texts during the language arts block, Brittany doesn't seem to pay attention to the organizational features that highlight important points in the text, such as bolded glossary terms, headings and subheadings, diagrams, and labels. Moreover, she doesn't even appear to understand that the organizational features of expository text can help her understand it better or connect new information in text to her existing knowledge structures. As with her retellings of narratives, when Brittany finishes her reading of the text, her summary of the content lacks organization, and she misses important details that should have been apparent because of their position in the text's structure.

Gabriela, a Skilled Comprehender

In contrast, Gabriela seems to have a knack for language structure, producing and understanding complex and correctly formed sentences in her speaking, reading, and writing. She has a clear sense of narrative structure, as evidenced by her well-organized retellings of stories during small-group instruction that preserve causal relationships between story elements; her entries in her writing journal preserve narrative structure as well. Gabriela seems to be well aware of the organization of her conceptual knowledge, making connections from her prior knowledge to new concepts encountered in text, which facilitates her memory for new information. Furthermore, Gabriela seems to have a good grasp of the organizational cues in expository text, using features like headings and bolded words to guide her interpretation of the meanings and importance of expository text information.

What Does the Research Say?

Consistent with our plan for this book, this section will provide a brief treatment of the research base on the relation of organization to reading comprehension with attention to comprehension of various types of texts (e.g., narrative or expository) when supported by the research base. As I mentioned earlier in the chapter, organization has received little attention in the executive skills research literature in comparison to its better-studied counterparts, cognitive flexibility, inhibition, and working memory; these core skills, however, likely contribute to individuals' organizational abilities. For example, working memory probably enables readers to keep a text's organizational scheme in mind while reading, inhibition likely enables readers to ignore irrelevant text features and attend to those important for tracking a text's organizational scheme, and cognitive flexibility probably enables readers to shift focus from one level of organization to another while reading, such as shifting focus between one's conceptual organization of new academic vocabulary and a text's organizational features when reading an informational text on a new topic. However, these suggested relations are speculative; more research is necessary to understand the precise contribution of core executive skills to more complex skills like organization.

As was the case with the research on planning, some studies of the relation of organization to reading comprehension use nonreading measures of organizational ability (i.e., measures of general cognitive processes, rather than reading-specific ones). Other studies target processes that support reading in a more direct way, such as studies of text structure. Thus, I will present research on general, nonreading organizational processes first and then move on to reading-specific organizational processes in the review that follows.

Research on Organization from an Executive Skills Perspective

Sequencing

One of the simplest forms of organization is sequencing, or arranging items in a logical order based on a particular feature. Children begin learning to order items along gradations of size, such as length, width, or diameter, as early as infancy. Think about the nested stacking cups or stacking rings found in most infant playrooms: those toys teach children how to attend to relations between objects and to order those objects according to an overall organizational scheme. Piaget's seriation task (Inhelder & Piaget, 1964) assesses this kind of sequencing skill, as does the Sequential Ordering subtest of the Leiter International Performance Scale (Roid et al., 2013). (See Figure 3.1 for an example of a seriation task.) Watson (1979) found a strong correlation between seriation ability and reading comprehension in fourth-grade students that was independent of their general intellectual ability. Additionally, Webster and Ammon (1994) demonstrated that seriation correlated significantly with the ability to understand and use narrative sequences in reading and writing tasks in fifth-grade students. They noted that "it appears that for children to write a highly organized composition, or to recall a passage in an organized fashion, they must possess a certain level of the relevant cognitive ability" (Webster & Ammon, 1994, p. 104).

SL.CCR.4

Similar results have emerged for prereading students. For example, seriation and classification instruction produced increases in verbal comprehension in kindergarten students that persisted for 3 months but did not persist into first grade, probably because the intervention students had caught up with their peers (Pasnak, Madden, Malabonga, Holt, & Martin, 1996). Finally, Zampini and colleagues demonstrated significant relations between nonverbal sequential ordering and preschool children's comprehension of narrative sequences (Zampini, Suttora, D'Odorico, & Zanchi, 2013).

Not only are poor comprehenders worse than typically developing peers at ordering objects sequentially by size, they are also significantly worse at remembering sequences presented in different sensory modalities (Tyrrell, 1980). For example, Tyrrell administered several sequential memory tasks to good and poor readers in second, fourth, and sixth grades. She used a variety of tasks, such as aurally and visually presented digits that had to be recalled in order; memory for rhythm patterns recalled in order; and sequential memory for a series of finger taps (i.e., the researcher tapped the children's fingers, and children had to recall the sequence of taps in order). The poor readers performed significantly worse on all of the sequential memory tasks at all ages tested, supporting the prediction that these students have specific difficulties remembering organized sequences of information. This makes sense, when one considers that poor comprehenders also have difficulty remembering sequences of events in stories; their underlying difficulty with remembering organized sequences, in general, seems to contribute to their comprehension problems.

Patterning and Rhythm

Reading comprehension involves understanding organization at many levels (e.g., syntax, sentence, paragraph, and text meaning), yet seriation involves organizing items along only one dimension. Thus, Pasnak and colleagues suggested that more complex organizational schemes, in which students must order items along multiple dimensions, or recognize which items come next in such multidimensional patterns, would be a strong predictor of successful reading and general academic performance (Hendricks et al., 1999; Hendricks et al., 2006; Kidd et al., 2013, 2014). Consistent with their predictions, patterning ability was related to reading ability, including comprehension in first graders; and patterning was also significantly related to cognitive flexibility (Bock et al., 2015). Furthermore, patterning instruction improved first-grade students' total academic achievement scores and IQ (Hendricks et al., 1999), mathematics achievement (Hendricks et al., 2006), mathematics concepts (Kidd et al., 2013), written language (Hendricks et al., 2006), and reading comprehension (Kidd et al., 2014).

Along similar lines, because oral language is organized into auditory patterns that must be converted to visual patterns for reading (e.g., the sounds /d/ /o/ and /g/ are heard in a sequential pattern that corresponds to the letters *d*, *o*, and *g*), researchers have studied whether students' abilities to process auditory rhythms correlates with reading skill. Although most of this work has focused on word reading, two studies demonstrated elementary students' abilities to recognize the organization of rhythm patterns is related to reading comprehension, even when intelligence is controlled (Rudnick et al., 1967; Sterritt & Rudnick, 1966). In those studies, researchers presented rhythm patterns in one sensory modality (e.g., children heard a series of sounds, such as tones or claps, in a particular pattern), and then students had to recognize those patterns in a different sensory modality (e.g., presented as an array of symbols or dots, as described earlier). In more recent, similar work, Tallal and colleagues have demonstrated that children's abilities to process rapidly presented auditory patterns is related to language comprehension (Tallal, 2004; Tallal & Gaab, 2006), and infants' abilities to process rapidly presented auditory patterns predicts later language comprehension (Benasich & Tallal, 2002). Finally, promising recent work has demonstrated that a rhythmical music intervention with poor readers improves their word reading skill as much as a phonological awareness intervention (Bhide, Power, & Goswami, 2013); however, no research has examined the effects of musical rhythm training on reading comprehension.

Conceptual Organization

Another way organizational skill supports reading comprehension is in the way that readers' knowledge is organized. Decades of work in cognitive science have revealed that individuals' stored knowledge is organized hierarchically into networks of related concepts called semantic networks or schemas (Collins & Loftus, 1975; Quillian, 1967), and these play a significant role in reading comprehension (Adams & Collins, 1977; Anderson & Pearson, 1984). Many children readily infer and use their conceptual organization to support their understanding of texts. (See Figure 3.3 for an example of a schema's structure, which is often called a concept map or semantic map in instructional contexts.) Well-structured background knowledge is particularly important for understanding expository texts in comparison to narrative texts (Best, Floyd, & McNamara, 2008), because expository texts are typically dense with content-specific vocabulary that, if not known, must be integrated into children's existing schemas. However, for children who are less able to infer and use conceptual organizational structures, reading comprehension problems occur.

As you might expect, the richness of students' schemas affects their ability to comprehend texts. Students with more extensive, better-organized background knowledge are significantly better at understanding and recalling information from texts (Recht & Leslie, 1988). Additionally, although the richness and organization of students' schemas do not have as much of an impact on information that is stated explicitly in text, students with richer schematic knowledge are better at inferring information that is not explicitly stated in text (Pearson et al., 1979). Furthermore, students' awareness of the hierarchical structure of their conceptual knowledge is significantly related to their reading comprehension; that is, children who are more aware of the ways their knowledge is organized are more successful comprehenders (Gillett & Richards, 1979). Taken together, these findings point to the potential importance of teaching students to organize their knowledge and to

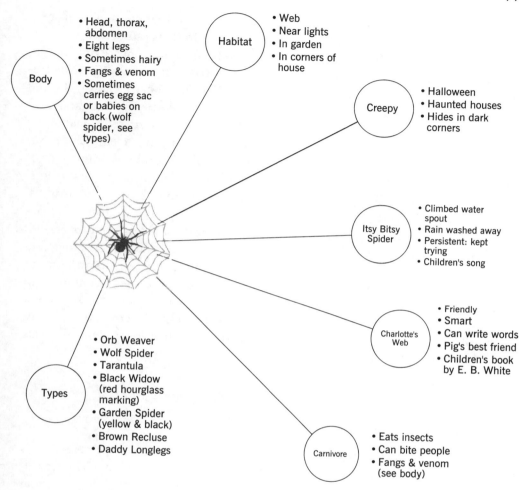

FIGURE 3.3. An example of a schema's structure.

become aware of the organization of their knowledge in order to support reading comprehension.

Consistent with this notion, two recent reviews of research in this area demonstrated positive effects on reading comprehension of teaching students to organize their knowledge. For example, Nesbit and Adesope (2006) conducted a meta-analysis of concept mapping studies that included fourth graders to college students and found such interventions significantly improved memory for text content across ages; furthermore, concept mapping was more effective than having students make lists of concepts or outlines of texts. (I wish that my high school teachers who required textbook outlining had known this!) Additionally, Kim, **R.CCR.4** Vaughn, Wanzek, and Wei (2004) synthesized the research on using various types of concept maps with struggling readers and found that concept maps produced significant increases in reading comprehension for these students.

Not only do concept maps enable students to become more aware of the organization of their knowledge, they provide distinct instructional advantages over traditional instruction. For example, Guastello, Beasley, and Sinatra (2000) showed that having seventh-grade struggling comprehenders read science texts and then make concept maps improved comprehension significantly over traditional "read and discuss" methods. Additionally, Johnson, Pittelman, and Heimlich (1986) demonstrated that organizing concepts is a wonderful pre- and postreading strategy that enables teachers to see, simply by looking at concept maps, if students' knowledge has changed. However, concept maps are best used in particular ways. For example, Oliver (2009) showed that concept mapping is more effective for science texts when students are provided the superordinate (broadest) concepts rather than having to come up with the entire maps on their own. And Chang, Sung, and Chen (2002) showed that having fifth-grade students correct errors in concept maps after reading expository texts improved reading comprehension more than scaffolding their map construction or having them generate maps on their own. Thus, scaffolding conceptual organization, consistent with the gradual release of responsibility model of instruction, produces better outcomes for students in terms of reading comprehension.

Research on Organization from a Reading Perspective

Awareness of Language Structure

As I noted at the beginning of the chapter, awareness of language structure is critical to reading comprehension. Students' ability to organize language according to syntactic rules contributes in significant ways to reading comprehension in children and adults (Chik et al., 2012; Gaux & Gombert, 1999; Guo, Roehrig, & Williams, 2011; Mokhtari & Niederhauser, 2010; Mokhtari & Thompson, 2006; Shiotsu & Weir, 2007; Tong, Tong, Shu, Chan, & McBride-Chang, 2014). Thus, not surprisingly, teaching sentence organization strategies improves students' reading comprehension (Weaver, 1979). For example, Weaver taught sentence organization by first teaching students to find the action in sentences and then group remaining words into phrase chunks according to their relation to the action in 14 to 19 individual lessons that lasted approximately 15 minutes each. Lessons resulted in significant improvements in syntactic awareness and reading comprehension. You may be familiar with the highly effective Reading Recovery intervention for struggling beginning readers that involves (among other activities) having children dictate a sentence in each lesson, which is written on a sentence strip and then cut apart (Pinnell, Fried, & Estice, 1990). The child's task is to reassemble the sentence, which requires accurate decoding but also attention to the syntactic structure of the sentence, promoting students' attention to language organization. Students who experience the Reading Recovery intervention demonstrate significant gains in reading comprehension beyond typically developing peers that persist up to 4 years later (Moore & Wade, 1998). These findings should be interpreted with caution, however, as Reading Recovery involves more than just sentence organization instruction.

Awareness of Text Organization

In addition to the syntactic organization inherent in language, texts have specific organizational features and structures that good comprehenders extract and use to help themselves understand and track incoming information as they read. These structures are different, depending on text genre. Thus, I will review what we know about narrative and expository text organization separately in this section.

R.CCR.5

NARRATIVE TEXTS

Narrative text is taught most frequently in elementary classrooms (Duke, 2000; Ness, 2011b) and is organized in particular ways. Readers can use typical organizational components of narrative structure to track information in text, resulting in better comprehension. For example, events in narratives are typically causally related; additionally, narratives have particular components that appear across stories and contribute to readers' developing story schemas. I will review what we know about each of these organizational features in the sections that follow.

Causal Connections in Narrative. One aspect of text organization that supports successful reading comprehension is the causal relatedness between events in narratives. Characters' goals serve organizing roles in narratives (Trabasso & Magliano, 1996; Wenner, 2004), creating causal connections between elements of stories. College students (Trabasso & Magliano, 1996) and even preschoolers are sensitive to the causal structure of stories, with greater numbers of causal connections leading to better recall of story content (Wenner, 2004).

To illustrate the importance of causal connections to the organization and understanding of narratives, consider the classic story *The Little Engine That Could* (Piper, 1976). In this familiar book the plot centers on a group of toys that ask several train engines to pull them over a mountain because their own engine has broken down. Students who understand that the initiating event (a broken train engine) precipitated the subsequent character actions (asking several other engines for help, resulting in varying consequences and ending with a successful request) will have a better, more integrated understanding of the story and a better memory for those events.

R.CCR.3

In fact, fifth- to eighth-grade students recognize and recall events that are causally related to stories' structures significantly better than events not causally related to stories' structures; this holds for students with learning disabilities and typical levels of intelligence, students with intellectual delays, and typically developing students (Wolman, van den Broek, & Lorch, 1997). Thus, causal organization supports reading comprehension for students of varying ability levels. However, children's understanding of the importance of causal connections in stories varies according to connection type, such as connections between elements of a story episode versus connections across story episodes. Additionally, for a given statement from a story, there may be more or fewer connections to the causal structure of the narrative. For example, van den Broek (1989) had 8-, 11-, 14-, and 18-year-old students judge the importance of story statements that varied in type and number of causal connections. All ages showed sensitivity to number of connections, judging statements with more connections to the narratives' causal structure to be more important. However not until age 11 did children show sensitivity to the type of causal connections, understanding that cross-episode connections were more important.

That said, even 3- to 5-year-olds are sensitive to the causal organization in narratives (Walker, Gopnik, & Ganea, 2015), and they can explain both psychological and physical causes for events—understandings that are required for making inferences that support reading comprehension (Trabasso, Stein, & Johnson, 1981). (We will discuss psychological causes—and the social inferences that readers must make about them—in more depth in Chapter 7.) Preschoolers' understanding of the causal organizational structure of narratives is also related to their developing executive skills. In fact, all three core executive skills (inhibition, working memory, and cognitive flexibility) contribute to preschoolers' recall of causally related story events, but only working memory contributes to recall of separate (unrelated) story events (Strasser & del Río, 2014).

As you would expect, 3-year-olds' awareness of causal connections in narratives contributes significantly to their narrative comprehension (Zampini et al., 2013). Zampini and colleagues assessed children's sensitivity to causal relations between narrative events with a picture-sequencing task involving narrative events consisting of three, four, and five pictures that had to be arranged into proper causal sequence, which contributed to narrative comprehension beyond age, cognitive flexibility, and nonverbal reasoning. These findings point to the importance of picture sequencing as an assessment of students' sensitivity to the causal organization of narratives, but also as a potential teaching tool. Indeed, Chase and colleagues showed that teaching causal sequencing can be done quite easily using graphic novels for primary students (Chase et al., 2014). Unfortunately, Chase and colleagues did not assess reading comprehension in their study, but they did provide anecdotal reports of improved motivation and sequencing ability. I would assume that improved sequencing ability would reflect a greater awareness of causal connections in narratives, which would, in turn, transfer to comprehension. Along similar lines, older students' awareness of the causal organization of narratives can be assessed with a scrambled stories task in which they must rearrange sentences from stories into a better organized narrative that makes sense; like picture sequencing, teaching students to reorder scrambled stories in meaningful ways significantly improves upper elementary students' reading comprehension (Fitzgerald & Spiegel, 1983).

Another way to assess sensitivity to the causal organization of narratives is to examine readers' retellings of stories for uses of connective words that denote causal relationships between events. Poor comprehenders are significantly less likely than better comprehenders to use words that refer to causal connections in their retellings of narratives (Cain, 2003; Weaver & Dickinson, 1982). Connective words link ideas in text and vary in the type of connection they denote. For example, text ideas may be independent of one another, they may be dependent on one another, and they may be related because they follow one another in time (Cain, 2003; also see Trabasso et al., 1981). Examples of connecting words or phrases that denote these relations are provided below in the *How Can I Apply This Knowledge to Classroom Practice?* section. Of particular interest is that good and poor comprehenders sometimes differ little in recall of elements of story structure that we regularly target in comprehension instruction, such as main character or setting (Weaver & Dickinson, 1982). Causal language thus may be a more accurate way to assess readers' awareness of the causal organization of narrative texts. When assessed with a picture sequencing task, such as the one described above, not only do elementary school-age poor comprehenders use fewer causal connecting words in their narratives, they tend to describe each picture as an independent event rather than part of an integrated whole. That is, instead of expressing stories as overall narratives, these students seem to provide "running commentaries," picture by picture (Oakhill & Yuill, 1996, p. 75).

Adults with learning disabilities show a similar pattern, producing significantly fewer causal words to describe connections between events than typically developing adults, and using significantly more "then" connectives, as though narrating a list of unrelated actions (Roth & Spekman, 1994). Finally, poor comprehenders also exhibit less coherence in the structure of narratives produced in response to a story title (similar to children who treat pictures in a story sequence as independent events). In other words, the events in their narratives do not relate to one another in causal ways, independent of the language used to describe them (Cain, 2003). In sum, struggling comprehenders seem unaware of the causal organization in narratives, even into adulthood, and are not able to use information about causal relations to produce an organized story structure.

Story Schemas: Organization of Narrative Texts. Teachers often introduce children to organizational principles of narrative text structure by teaching students to think about the beginning, middle, and end of stories. (See sample "simple story map templates" that illustrate this structure on the Reading Rockets website at *www.readingrockets.org/strategies/story_maps*; Reading Rockets, 2014) However, little research supports the effectiveness of teaching this simple beginning–middle–end structure. What we do know is that, beginning early in life, individuals learn the organizational principles of narrative structure because stories have common elements, which shape readers' (and listeners') story schemas (Mandler & DeForest, 1979; Mandler & Goodman, 1982; Mandler & Johnson, 1977; Stein & Glenn, 1975). Story schemas provide a mental framework of general knowledge about stories that enables readers and listeners to organize new story information along familiar lines. Even prereaders' retellings of stories exhibit structural elements of story schemas, and practice with retelling stories enhances prereaders' abilities to recall these elements (Morrow, 1985). However, students with learning disabilities are less good at extracting the common organizational features of stories, resulting in underdeveloped story schemas and significantly lower reading comprehension (Montague, Maddux, & Dereshiwsky, 1990).

R.CCR.5,
R.CCR.10

Story schemas are also called story grammars because they guide the way that stories are organized, just as linguistic grammar guides the way language is organized (Mandler & DeForest, 1979; Mandler & Goodman, 1982; Mandler & Johnson, 1977; Stein & Glenn, 1975). In a nutshell, story schemas include two main types of information: setting and episodes (Stein & Glenn, 1975). The setting introduces the main character(s) and story context (e.g., place, time), and episodes relay information about the main events that comprise the story, which usually include the following (see Mandler & Goodman, 1982; Short & Ryan, 1979; Stein & Glenn, 1975):

- The beginning event, which produces some change that initiates the story.
- The internal reaction of the main character, which may include thoughts and feelings, as well as goals that emerge in response to the beginning event.
- The attempt, which involves the character's actions intended to reach his or her goals.
- The outcome of the character's attempt to reach his or her goal.
- The conclusion of the episode, which includes the reaction of the character to the outcome and any lasting consequences.

Several events may be strung together in a coherent narrative, such as the several attempts the toys make to secure a new engine for their train in *The Little Engine That Could* (Piper, 1976). Readers vary in their abilities to extract and use the organizational principles inherent in story structures to support reading comprehension. For example, Cain (1996) demonstrated that 7- to 8-year-old poor comprehenders were significantly less sensitive to the organizational components of story structure than their peers with better comprehension. More recently, in a longitudinal study, Oakhill and Cain (2012) showed that knowledge and use of story structure predicted significant, unique variance in sixth-grade reading comprehension even when third-grade reading comprehension was controlled.

These findings suggest that poor comprehenders are at a distinct disadvantage because they lack awareness of the organizational features of stories and are thus unable to use those organizational features to support comprehension. However, when poor comprehenders are taught to monitor and use story structure, their reading comprehension improves to a level not distinguishable from typically developing peers. For example, Short and Ryan (1984) taught fourth-grade poor comprehenders to answer five questions designed to support awareness of particular elements of story structure: main character, time and place, action, consequence, and reaction. After story structure instruction, the initially poor comprehenders did not differ from their peers with better comprehension on recall R.CCR.1, of story elements or the ability to use story schemas to support their reading R.CCR.5 comprehension.

Similarly, when provided verbal or visual cues to story organization (integrative titles or pictures, respectively), Yuill and Joscelyne (1988) showed 7- to 8-year-old poor comprehenders' reading comprehension performance did not differ from the performance of their peers with better reading comprehension. Furthermore, poor comprehenders who were taught to look for clues to stories' organizational structures exhibited reading comprehension performance that was indistinguishable from their peers with better comprehension (Yuill & Joscelyne, 1988).

In a sample of older elementary students, Johnson, Graham, and Harris (1997) taught a story structure strategy to fourth-, fifth-, and sixth-grade students with school-identified learning disabilities, average intelligence, and school-based reading achievement scores at the second to third-grade level. Specifically, they taught students to list eight elements of a story, incorporate them into a story map, SL.CCR.4, and explicitly explained that the story structure strategy would help the SL.CCR.5, students understand and remember stories better. And, in fact, they did R.CCR.1, recall stories better! Story retellings of the students with learning disabili- R.CCR.5 ties did not differ from typically developing controls after the intervention. Furthermore, intervention students' gains were sustained over a month, and they generalized to other activities in the classroom.

Idol (1987; Idol & Croll, 1987) administered a similar intervention (listing story elements and completing a story map) to third-, fourth-, and fifth-grade struggling comprehenders in a group setting, yielding significant improvements in reading comprehension that were sustained, even when students were no longer using the strategy. Thus, for students who struggle with comprehension, explicitly explaining the organizational structure of stories and providing concrete strategies to aid students' awareness of stories' structures seem to be powerful strategies to improve narrative comprehension.

Although typically developing students seem to automatically infer the organizational components of story structure over time as they are exposed to numerous stories with similar elements (Mandler & Goodman, 1982), explicit teaching of the organization of story structures also provides typically developing children with important organizational tools they need to support their comprehension. Even kindergarten students can benefit from explicit instruction in story structure elements! Stevens, Van Meter, and Warcholak (2010) explicitly taught kindergarten students several story structure elements, one at a time, "beginning with the main character and progressing through setting, problem, solution, and attempted (but failed) solution" (Stevens et al., 2010, p. 169). After instruction, these young students had better recall of story content and better awareness of elements of story structure than their peers who did not receive explicit story structure instruction.

R.CCR.2   Finally, one of the more abstract aspects of story organization, theme, is not always included in descriptions of basic story schemas. However, story themes provide important ways that stories can connect to students' existing knowledge structures and provide life lessons that will generalize to new situations (Dymock, 2007; Williams, 2005). Williams and colleagues (2002) taught story themes to second and third graders in a program that highlighted the more concrete aspects of story schemas described above, and then provided explicit instruction in finding and generalizing the theme. Students who received theme instruction successfully generalized knowledge to new texts but not necessarily new themes (Williams et al., 2002).

EXPOSITORY TEXTS

Although narrative texts are used most frequently in elementary classrooms, expository texts—also called informational texts—are gaining ground. I will use these terms, expository text and informational text, interchangeably in this book. In 2000, Duke reported that first-grade teachers used informational text in instruction an average of 3.6 minutes per day, and only 9.8% of books in first-grade classroom libraries were comprised of informational text. More recently in a study of K–5 informational text use, Ness (2011b) indicated that first-grade teachers in her study used informational text for instruction an average of 18.36 minutes per day with 27.81% of books in first-grade classroom libraries comprised of informational text. I should note here that Duke (2000) used direct observation of classrooms, whereas Ness (2011b) used teachers' self-reports to estimate the contents of classroom libraries, which could have inflated the percentages. If these findings represent consistent trends in elementary literacy instruction, our students are getting more exposure to expository texts than in past decades. However, this trend poses unique instructional challenges for teachers (and executive skill challenges for learners) because—with the exception of the causal structure—expository texts' organizational structures are markedly different from the organizational structures found in narrative texts (e.g., see Williams, 2003). These challenges are magnified when we consider that children typically come to the task of comprehending expository texts with a dearth of experience in this genre; thus, their schemas for understanding expository text structures are less well organized than their schemas for narrative text structures. That said, even very young children can learn about the features of different genres (see Duke, 2000, for a review). So, for expository text, students need experience in that genre to ensure they build the knowledge base and rich schemas necessary to utilize the organizational information available in expository texts to support comprehension. However, as you might expect, students with learning disabilities are less sensitive to expository text structure and are less likely to utilize structural information to support comprehension (Englert & Thomas, 1987); thus, these students may need explicit instruction in the organization of expository text structures in order to support their comprehension of these kinds of texts. In the sections that follow, R.CCR.5 I will review information on two different kinds of organizational cues available in expository texts: organizational signals and expository text structures.

Organizational Signals. Authors of expository texts use different types of signals or markers to cue readers' attention to important features of the structural organization of expository texts. These common writing devices "emphasize aspects of a text's content or structure without adding to the content of the text" (Lorch, 1989, p. 209) and often include the following items (Fisher, Frey, & Lapp, 2008; Hall, Sabey, & McClellan, 2005; Kardash & Noel, 2000; Lorch, 1989; Lorch & Lorch, 1996): titles, subtitles, previews and overviews (introductory overview of content), headings, subheadings, clue words that highlight texts' organization (e.g., *alike, both, same, similar, but, different, however, in contrast*), bold or italic words, and ending summaries. Organizational signals direct attention to important information in text (Lemarié, Lorch, Eyrolle, & Virbel, 2008), help readers track the organizational structure of the text (Lorch, Lemarié, & Grant, 2011), facilitate recall of text content (Lorch & Lorch, 1996; Spyridakis & Standal, 1987), and support readers' comprehension when motivation is low (Kardash & Noel, 2000). Other features that aid in comprehension of expository text include graphics, such as charts, tables, graphs, flowcharts, maps, timelines, or diagrams; illustrations; captions; the table of contents; glossary; and index (Duke R.CCR.7 et al., 2013; Fisher et al., 2008; Roberts et al., 2013).

Finally, although research indicates organizational signals support memory for text content, little research has investigated whether teaching organizational signals improves comprehension. The one recent study that did so with college students provided some evidence that explicit teaching about organizational signals improves reading comprehension (Kara, 2013). However, much more research is needed in this area.

Structural Organization of Expository Texts. The purposes of expository text are different from those of narrative text, and thus they have different organizational structures. This may be obvious to us as skilled comprehenders, but to our students this may be new, important information! Expository texts are intended primarily to share information in ways that readers can learn something new. The common structures for expository text, therefore, convey information in particular formats to achieve different information-sharing purposes. Meyer and Freedle (1984) suggest collection, description, problem–solution, causation, and comparison are the most common structures, and the amount of organization inherent in these structures varies, with description and collection structures typically comprised of less organized lists of information, whereas problem–solution, comparison, and causation structures have more inherent organization. Similarly, Anderson and Armbruster (1984) identified six types of expository text structures, listed here roughly in terms of inherent organization: description, explanation, definition-example, problem–solution, temporal sequences, and compare–contrast. (See Anderson & Armbruster, 1984, for key words associated with each of these expository text types.) Meyer and Freedle (1984) confirmed their prediction regarding more and less tightly organized structures' effects on recall: causation and comparison structures facilitated memory for text content better than collections or descriptions, and problem–solution structures fell somewhere in between. I should note here that narrative typically has a causal structure, which provides a fairly organized framework to facilitate memory for information in narrative text, and not surprisingly, comprehension of narrative is usually better than comprehension of expository text (Best et al., 2008). Thus, it is not surprising that causal organization in expository text would facilitate better recall too (Meyer & Freedle, 1984) because students have typically had more experience with causal structures than other expository text structures due to their greater experience with causal structures in narrative texts. The main point here is that structures with more organizational features provide more ways for new bits of information to be related together as well as to readers' existing schemas, making the new information easier to recall in the future. See Table 3.1 for a list of expository text structures, arranged roughly according to their inherent organizational structure from least to most organized.

R.CCR.5,
R.CCR.10

Although using an author's intended structure enables good comprehenders to retain and recall information from texts, ninth-grade poor comprehenders do not spontaneously do so (Meyer et al., 1980). Likewise, children with learning disabilities have difficulty extracting and using information about expository texts' organizational structures to facilitate their reading comprehension (Taylor & Williams, 1983; Wong & Wilson, 1984). The use of organizational structures in expository texts can be taught, however, with positive effects on comprehension, even in adults. For example, Meyer and Poon (2001) taught younger and older adults to find a text's structure, use it to organize incoming information, and then use the

TABLE 3.1. Types of Organizational Structures in Expository Texts, Arranged Roughly by the Organizational Principles Inherent in Each Structure (from Less to More Organization)

Expository Text Structure	Purpose
Collection	Collects information about a topic in one place; typically arranged as a list of facts, which makes information more difficult to recall than when it is presented in a structure with links between subparts
Description	Describes an item or topic; like collection, this structure is often arranged as a list of features about a topic, which makes information more difficult to recall than when it is presented in a structure with links between subparts
Explanation	Explains reasons for the mechanism of a particular concept (e.g., why the Sun appears to rise and set); expands information in a reader's schemas about the topic, which may have little inherent organizational structure, similar to the collection and description structures; may link to a reader's existing schemas, which facilitates recall of information
Definition–example	Defines a concept or event and provides an example to illustrate it; definition and example are linked and also may provide connections to prior knowledge, which facilitate recall of information
Problem–solution	Describes a problem and then describes a solution (or multiple solutions) to that problem; these are necessarily linked, which provides a means for later recall
Compare–contrast	Presents concepts or ideas that have both similarities and differences; the compare–contrast structure links concepts, which facilitates readers' abilities to identify similarities and differences in concepts as well as addition of those concepts to readers' schemas
Temporal sequence	Describe a process, procedure, or historical events that occur in sequence over time; temporal sequence provides a linked linear structure that can be used to recall information
Causation	Highlights reasons for actions or events, such as predisposing events, feelings, or actions; the cause–effect structure provides a framework that links concepts, which can be used to recall information

same structure to recall information from text—a strategy they called the "choose it, use it, or lose it" strategy—which improved their reading comprehension over control conditions. These studies show that awareness of the organizational principles in texts' structures promotes successful comprehension of expository texts, and such awareness can be taught, at least to adults, with positive effects on expository text comprehension.

Explicitly teaching elementary grades students to attend to and use expository text structures improves their reading comprehension too. Evidence exists for teaching the various structures listed in Table 3.1 with positive effects on comprehension.

• *Collection, description, explanation, and definition–example.* Textbooks are often dense with diverse information that must be conveyed to students, which means that the information in some textbooks may not be readily organized into overall frameworks. Thus, the collection, description, explanation, and definition–example structures are well suited to the type of information delivery found in such texts. Taylor (1982), for example, showed that teaching fifth graders an expository text structure strategy (hierarchical summarization) with passages from a health textbook resulted in better recall of text information than a typical instructional technique of answering questions after reading. However, a second study showed that the effectiveness of the structure strategy depended upon the students' understanding of the strategy, which certainly makes sense. Students cannot use and learn from a strategy they do not understand.

• *Problem–solution.* Armbruster et al. (1987) taught problem–solution text structure with social studies texts to fifth-grade students. In comparison to students who experienced traditional "read and discuss" instruction, students who received problem–solution structure instruction demonstrated significantly better comprehension and recall of main ideas and structure in expository text.

• *Compare–contrast.* Williams (2003, 2005; Williams, Stafford, Lauer, & Pollini, 2009) taught second-grade students to use compare–contrast text structure to attend to text content, which improved their recall of information for the instructional texts but also transferred to new texts with compare–contrast structures and different content. (Also see Hall et al., 2005, who taught cause–effect structures to second graders, with positive effects on comprehension.)

• *Temporal sequence.* Reutzel, Read, and Fawson (2009) taught third graders to use the organizational structure inherent in temporal sequences, explaining that some expository texts present information in an order or sequence, and that readers can use the sequential order structure to remember information from texts. In comparison to students who received traditional read-and-discuss instruction, structure instruction students showed significantly higher reading comprehension.

- *Causation.* Williams et al. (2014) taught second-grade students to attend to cause–effect structure in social studies texts, which improved reading comprehension more than focusing on the same content without the text structure instruction. Similarly, Gaskins, Nehring, and Solic (2013) taught fifth- and sixth-grade students to recognize action cycles in social studies texts. These authors defined an action cycle as one in which human needs produce actions, actions produce consequences, consequences affect the context, and the newly changed context produces new needs. Students demonstrated better comprehension of text themes, justification of answers with evidence, and reported that the action cycle helped them to "organize their thinking about texts."

Not only does explicit teaching of individual expository text structures improve comprehension for elementary students, but integrating those structures into one instructional framework is effective, as well. For example, Wijekumar, Meyer, and Lei (2012) developed a program for teaching structure strategy to fourth graders to improve comprehension of informational text. The program provided explicit instruction about how the organization in text structures can aid recall. They created a web-based tutoring system, which had students identify clue words, main idea, and the type of text structure for various expository passages. Students who received multiple structure instruction showed significant increases in expository text comprehension in comparison to a nonintervention control group.

How Can I Apply This Knowledge to Classroom Practice?

As with all cognitive skills and strategies that support comprehension, executive skills like organization should be taught in ways consistent with the gradual release of responsibility model in which responsibility gradually shifts from the teacher to the students through intentional instruction that requires increasing involvement from students (Duffy, 2014; Duke & Pearson, 2002; Duke et al., 2011; Pearson & Gallagher, 1983). In this model teachers should provide the following for students (see Chapter 2 for descriptions of these): an explicit explanation of the skill or strategy; behavioral and mental modeling; opportunities for shared use of the skill or strategy with the teacher; opportunities for guided, supported practice; and opportunities for independent practice.

The first step in quality instruction about organization is thus to provide an explicit explanation of this executive skill that includes information about what it is, when good readers do it, and how it helps support good readers' understanding of texts. You may introduce organization during whole-group instruction, but guided practice may be more effectively implemented in small-group instruction or one-to-one conferences. To introduce organization to your students, you might begin with an explanation like this:

EXPLICITLY EXPLAINING ORGANIZATION

"Remember how we talked about good readers being good planners? One of the reasons good readers make good plans for reading is because they are organized thinkers. Do you know what organized means? [Engage students in a discussion of organization, so that you can use their prior knowledge about this skill to link new information about organization to their existing schemas.] When I say good readers are organized thinkers, this means that they are good at noticing patterns and sequences in things, and using those patterns and sequences to better understand text. Sometimes, good readers pay attention to the patterns in stories to help them remember information from stories they read. Other times, good readers notice the different kinds of patterns in informational texts—books that are written to give us information—and use those patterns to understand texts better. Good readers are also good at arranging information in their heads so that it's easier to remember and use later, such as when you remember the various characteristics of the different kinds of animals you know about, like habitat, food preferences, behaviors, and physical attributes. We are going to be talking about many different kinds of patterns and sequences that will help you be better organizers of information that you read so that you understand it better and can remember it later."

As I noted in Chapter 2, quality comprehension instruction requires explicit talk about the thinking involved in good comprehension. Thus, in addition to reminding students of their goals and plans for reading, you should also continually remind students that good readers are organized thinkers. Remind them, for example, to notice patterns in texts that will help them understand and remember text information later, to think about the various expository text structures you've taught them and identify them in texts, or to think about how new ideas encountered in texts fit into the concept maps already in their heads (thus, explicitly reminding them to attend to conceptual organization). Specific recommendations for organization instruction follow, based on the research reviewed in this chapter.

Sequencing, Patterning, and Rhythm

Students who are better able to sequence items along a particular dimension like length (see Figure 3.1), recognize and complete patterns (like those depicted in Figure 3.2), remember sequences of items in order, and recognize and repeat rhythms across sensory modalities demonstrate better reading comprehension than students without these skills. More research is necessary to determine exactly why these skills are related to reading comprehension. However, when one considers the patterns and sequences inherent in text, it is not surprising that general sequencing and patterning ability, even with nontext items, would be related to reading comprehension skill.

How to Introduce Sequencing, Patterning, and Rhythm Activities

"Remember how we talked about good readers being organized thinkers? Well, we are going to practice being organized thinkers today. Good readers notice sequences (or orders) and patterns in everything that they see, such as patterns of objects, numbers or shapes, and patterns in text. Today we're going to work with shape patterns [or rhythm patterns, or number patterns, etc.] to give you practice creating, recognizing, and remembering patterns. This will help you be a more organized thinker!"

The research reviewed in this chapter indicates sequencing and patterning can be taught, resulting in improvements in reading comprehension. Additionally, sequencing, seriation, sequential memory, patterning, and rhythm tasks may provide useful assessments of your students' organizational abilities. You could

- Have students order items by length, weight, or other dimension to assess their sensitivity to sequential order.
- Provide lists of words, numbers, pictures, or sound patterns and assess your students' ability to recall the items in exact sequential order.
- Provide students patterns of varying complexity, such as those depicted in Figure 3.2, and assess your students' skill at recognizing and completing the patterns.
- Teach your students to recognize and complete patterns of increasing complexity using various stimuli, such as numbers counted by 1s, 2s, 3s, 5s, or 10s; various shapes or types of items; clock faces arranged according to number patterns (e.g., given a row of clock faces depicting 2:00, 4:00, _____, and 8:00, your students should recognize that 6:00 should complete the pattern).
- Present sequences of images (e.g., dots and dashes or circles and squares) to see whether students can translate those to auditory rhythms; for example, in the following sequence, dots could represent a short clap, and dashes could represent a longer, louder clap; thus, •• — ••— would translate to this clapping pattern: clap, clap, CLAP, clap, clap, CLAP.

The following are resources that may be useful in planning lessons on sequencing, patterning, and rhythm. These kinds of activities might be a good daily opening activity when students come into the classroom, or they might be a good transitional activity in the school day.

- Cleary, B. T. (2012). *A-B-A-B-A A book of pattern play.* Mills Press Trade.
- Domnauer, T. (2012). *Patterns and sequence: Stick kids workbook.* Grade K. Creative Teaching Press. (There is also a preK version.)

- Scholastic, Inc. (2010). *Scholastic teacher's friend: Patterns learning mats.* Scholastic, Inc.
- Swan, P. (2003). *Patterns in mathematics, grades 3–6: Investigating patterns in number relationships.* Didax Educational Resources.
- Pattern Matcher game for preschool and kindergarten students: *www. pbs.org/parents/education/math/games/preschool-kindergarten/pattern-matcher*

Conceptual Organization

Our brains are designed to detect patterns in the environment and organize our stored information according to similarity. Thus, our conceptual knowledge is organized into hierarchical structures of related concepts or schemas. (As an example, see the spider schema depicted in Figure 3.3; a blank concept map is provided for your use in Figure 3.4.) Students with richer, better-organized schemas and students who are aware of the organization of their schemas have better reading comprehension. You can teach students to be more aware of their conceptual organization, and you can help students better organize their conceptual knowledge. To introduce conceptual organization, you might say the following:

How to Introduce Conceptual Organization

"Remember how we talked about good readers being organized thinkers? One way good readers organize their thinking is in the way they arrange their knowledge in their heads. The things we know are stored in our heads so that related ideas are connected and stored together. That way, when we learn something new, we can easily add it to our existing knowledge. Because our brains are set up to automatically organize information for us, we might not even be aware of it, sort of like when we are not aware of how to explain other automatic things that we do, such as ride a bike. We are going to practice thinking about how our knowledge is organized. That way, when you read, it will be easier for you to connect new knowledge to things you already know."

To assess and teach conceptual organization, you can:

- Explicitly teach concept mapping, which improves students' conceptual organization as well as their awareness of their conceptual structures, enabling them to better integrate new information encountered in text with their existing knowledge.
- Assess your students' conceptual (schema) organization using concept maps **SL.CCR.5** (also called semantic maps), such as the one in Figure 3.4.

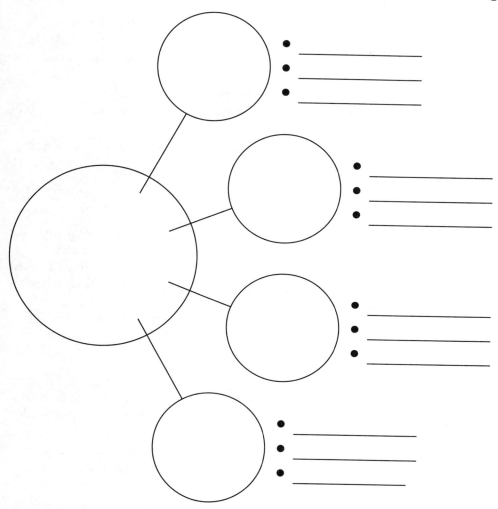

FIGURE 3.4. A blank concept map.

- Use pre- and postreading concept maps to track whether and how students' knowledge structures have changed as a result of reading a particular text, allowing you to determine whether students successfully integrated new information into their existing schemas.
- For struggling learners, especially, scaffold concept mapping by providing superordinate (broader) terms in maps prior to asking your students to complete them.
- Assess your students' awareness of conceptual organization by having them correct errors in concept maps.

Language Organization (Syntax)

Not only is knowledge organization important for reading comprehension, but language organization is important as well. Students' awareness of the organizational structure of language (or syntax) makes significant contributions to their reading comprehension, and teaching language organization improves reading comprehension (e.g., Weaver, 1979).

SL.CCR.6

To explicitly explain language organization, you might say the following:

How to Introduce Language Organization

"Remember when we talked about how good readers are organized thinkers? Well, today we're going to talk about another way they organize information in their heads to help them understand what they read better. Good readers are really good at figuring out the order words should be in to make the most sense. Look at these words. [Write a sentence anagram on the board, such as 'like dogs I' and query your students.] Do they make sense? How can we rearrange them to make a sentence that makes sense? [Work with your students to rearrange the words.] We are going to practice our word-organizing abilities today!" [Here, you can launch into one of the activities described below.]

To incorporate these kinds of activities into your classroom routines you could:

- Assess awareness of language organization by giving students sentence anagrams (sentences in which the words have been arranged randomly; you might call these *scrambled sentences* for students) and asking students to rearrange the words into sentences that make sense. This can be done in written form where students simply write out the correct versions of the sentences. For example, the following sentence anagram could be rewritten as "I am going to walk the dog."

going dog I to walk am the

- You can also present these activities in manipulative form, which is especially important for primary grades students and students who struggle with awareness of language organization, by cutting up printed sentences and having students physically rearrange the actual pieces of the cut-up-sentences into meaningful sentences again.

• Use a pocket chart and present cut-up sentences at whole-group time to engage students in shared work on language organization; to integrate this task with writing, you could use sentences written through shared writing for this activity.

• Have students write sentences on index cards (for older students) or sentence strips (for primary grades students), and then draw from those sentences to create sentence anagrams for whole-group or small-group activities.

• Begin each day with a sentence anagram on the board, which students rewrite in a daily language journal while waiting for the day's activities to begin.

• Assess primary grades students' awareness of language organization in small groups by watching your individual students as they each attempt to rearrange cut-up sentences into correct forms; you will be able to see, quite easily, who struggles and who does not (provided that you give each student a different sentence so that they cannot rely on one another's responses); see Figure 3.5 for sample sentences for primary grades students. **W.CCR.4**

like dogs I	_____
have cats fur	_____
fast run horses very	_____
books fun reading is	_____
I apple the red eat	_____
school ride I the bus to	_____

FIGURE 3.5. Sample sentences to assess primary students' awareness of language organization (syntax).

• To incorporate writing into the small-group activity, you may even start by having all of the students in the group write sentences on strips; then collect the sentences, cut them up, and distribute the sentences to students who did not author them; the students will appreciate that their own sentences are being used for others' group work.

• To assess upper elementary and secondary students' awareness of language organization, provide worksheets with five- to ten-sentence anagrams to be completed in a particular time frame (say 5 minutes—you may want to check average completion time with a few students before you set a time limit); students' accuracy and the number they can complete in the allotted time will tell you about their levels of awareness of language organization; see Figure 3.6 for sample sentences for upper elementary students.

• If your students struggle with awareness of language organization, following Weaver (1979), you can teach a word-grouping strategy that hinges on finding the action in the sentence first; once your students have the action word, then have them group the remaining words according to how they relate to the action; use cueing questions to guide them in this activity (e.g., Who did it? Where did they do it? How did they do it? When did they do it? To whom or what did they do it?); see Figure 3.7 for a rubric to guide the word-grouping activity.

---

1. walks he school to   _____

2. green ate she apple the   _____

3. pile he leaves a of raked   _____

4. the washed bathtub dog in they the   _____

5. kite park a flew they the in   _____

6. going bus I to ride am the   _____

7. into the she garage car drove the   _____

8. shells beach up he the on picked   _____

9. store the please to milk go buy to   _____

10. cream summer the like ice I eating in   _____

(continued)

FIGURE 3.6. Sample sentences to assess upper elementary students' awareness of language organization (syntax).

```
Answer Key:

  1. He walks to school.

  2. She ate the green apple.

  3. He raked a pile of leaves.

  4. They washed the dog in the bathtub.

  5. They flew a kite in the park.

  6. I am going to ride the bus.

  7. She drove the car into the garage.

  8. He picked up shells on the beach.

  9. Please go to the store to buy milk.

 10. I like eating ice cream in summer.
```

FIGURE 3.6. *(continued)*

Causal Organization in Narrative

As with the other organizational features of text we have discussed thus far, students' understanding of the causal organization of narrative texts is important for successful reading comprehension. Meaningful mental models of stories are based on the fact that stories are strung together in ways that make sense. Unrelated events are remembered far less well than events tied together because they are part of a story's causal sequence (Strasser & del Río, 2014). But, if a student is unaware of the importance of causal connections in narrative, he or she has a harder time comprehending stories (Fitzgerald & Spiegel, 1983)! Fortunately, we can assess and teach these abilities. You might introduce this skill as follows:

R.CCR.3,
R.CCR.5

How to Introduce Causal Organization of Narrative

"Remember when we talked about how good readers are organized thinkers? Today we are going to talk about one important way that stories are organized, which can help you remember stories better. The events and actions in stories happen in a particular order because certain things cause others to happen. [Provide an example from a text with which your students are familiar; I provide a sample example here.] For example, in the story *The Little Engine That Could*, the train's engine broke down, and that first event caused other things to happen in the story: the toys were sad, so they asked a bunch

First: Which word is the action word?

Next: Group the rest of the words by answering these questions:

1. Who did it? (The answer to this question usually goes before the action word.)

2. How did they do it? (The answer to this question usually goes right before the action word.)

3. To whom or what did they do it? (The answer to this usually goes after the action word.)

4. Where did they do it? (The answer to this usually goes at the end of the sentence.)

Sentence: _____

Example: quickly backyard cat the she in brushed the	
Action word:	brushed
Who did it?	she
How did she do it?	quickly
To whom or what did she do it?	the cat
Where did she do it?	in the backyard

Sentence: She quickly brushed the cat in the backyard.

FIGURE 3.7. Rubric for word grouping activity to teach language organization (syntax).

of other engines to help pull them over the mountain, and finally a little, blue engine said yes, solved their problem, and made the toys happy. If these events were rearranged, such as if the toys asked several engines for help *before* their engine broke down, the story wouldn't make any sense! The train's engine has to break first, to cause the other story parts to happen, and each of those happens in turn. Today we're going to practice organizing scrambled stories by causal order because it helps us understand and remember stories better."

To incorporate these kinds of activities into your classroom, you could:

- Assess sensitivity to the causal organization of narrative by having your students organize pictures from graphic sequences in proper, causal order; this is an especially useful technique for beginning readers; a Google image search on "story sequence pictures" will provide many narratives from which to choose.

- Along similar lines, you can have older students organize scrambled paragraphs or sentences from stories into causal order to assess their sensitivity to causal organization of narrative; a variation of this technique used by Fitzgerald and Spiegel (1983; also see Spiegel & Fitzgerald, 1986) involves providing initiating events as prompts and having students tell or write endings, which you can assess for causal relations to the initiating event prompt.

- You can assess the amount of causal language in your students' descriptions of graphic sequences, retellings of narratives, or writings of narratives (Cain, 2003; Trabasso et al., 1981) because students' use of connecting words or phrases can indicate their levels of understanding of the causal organization of narratives; students who treat picture sequences as unrelated events or who relay oral narratives, such as retellings, as a sequence of unrelated events have significantly lower comprehension than students who understand the causal connections between components of narratives or the reasons why characters take particular actions (Cain, 2003; Oakhill & Yuill, 1996). See below for examples of the kinds of connecting words your students might use to indicate causal organization in narratives or retellings.

  ○ **Independence between ideas:** *and, additionally, now, as well, also, in addition.*
  ○ **Dependence (connection) between ideas:** *if, but, because, so, so that, in order to, however, in contrast,* as (when used as a synonym for *because*), since (when used as a synonym for *because*), *or else, instead of, by* (when used to explain the manner in which a character takes an action, e.g., *She rinsed the sand off of the car by parking it next to the sprinkler*).
  ○ **Time sequence:** *later, first, next, since, and then, when, before, as* (when used to denote an event happening at the same time as another in a sequence of events).

(a) A blank map for your use

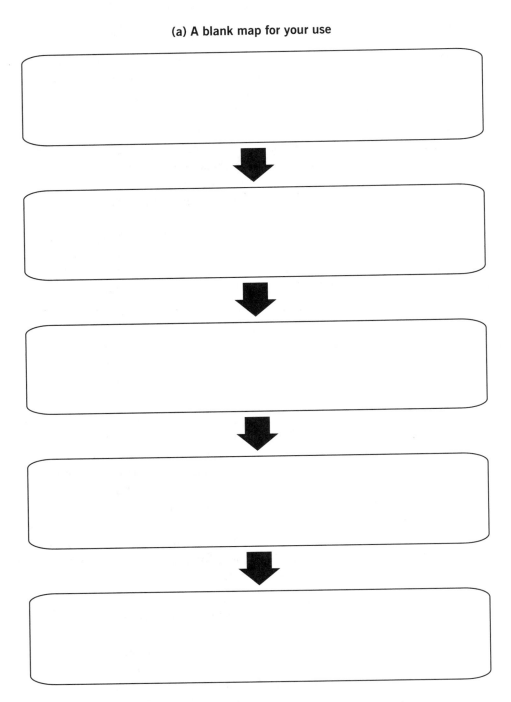

FIGURE 3.8. A sample map of the causal organization of stories.

(b) A completed map of the causal organization of *The Little Engine That Could* (Piper, 1976)

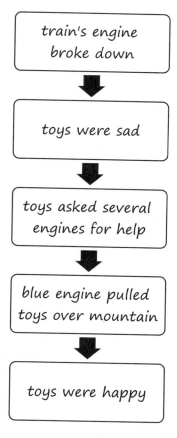

FIGURE 3.8. *(continued)*

• To assist your students in finding causal connections in existing narratives or creating connected narratives, you can provide your students a blank map of the causal organization of narratives to help them visualize the various causal links in the story's structure; see Figure 3.8 for (a) a sample map you can use and (b) a completed map as an example (this structure will facilitate narrative structure instruction, which is described in the following section). **SL.CCR.4, SL.CCR.5, R.CCR.5**

• Finally, for students who struggle with causal sequencing in narratives, you can teach causal sequence using graphic novels, following the procedure used by Chase et al. (2014); they engaged first and second graders in several activities that increased their independent sequencing ability. First they explained the features of graphic novels, such as word bubbles, thought bubbles, and dialogue. And then, they had students:

- Put frames of a graphic narrative sequence in the correct order.
- Create "dialogue, transition words, and sound effects" for wordless comics.
- Fill in empty word and thought bubbles in graphic narratives.
- Produce retellings in a graphic format.
- Create their own graphic narratives.

Story Schemas: Organization of Narrative

Sensitivity to the causal organization of narratives facilitates students' acquisition of story schemas (also called story grammar) that provide the basic organizational framework for stories (Mandler & DeForest, 1979; Mandler & Goodman, 1982; Mandler & Johnson, 1977; Stein & Glenn, 1975). A typical story schema usually includes information about the setting (e.g., character or characters and place), an initiating event, the characters' internal responses (reaction and goal), attempt(s) to reach the goal, the outcome, and the characters' reaction. To teach awareness of the components of story schemas, you can build on your students' understanding of the causal organization of stories. The various events in a story's causal chain (see Figure 3.8) typically correspond to the various parts of the story schema. If you have taught students to attend to the causal connections in stories, as described above, they already have the beginnings of story schemas. Now, you can build on those fledgling schemas by labeling the various parts of them. To introduce these kinds of activities, you might say the following:

R.CCR.2,
R.CCR.3,
R.CCR.5

How to Introduce the Organization of Story Schemas

"Remember when we talked about how good readers are organized thinkers, and they recognize how the parts of a story are organized in a causal way? Today we're going to add to your story knowledge, and we're going to talk about the names for the different parts of stories to help you remember them better. Knowing the parts of a story and how they are organized to make stories make sense will help you understand and remember what you read, and this knowledge may even help you tell and write better stories because they will be better organized!"

To teach the organization of story schemas, you can try the following activities:

- Following Idol (1987; Idol & Croll, 1987; also see Dymock, 2007), you can explicitly teach the parts of story schemas, using the causal chain map provided in Figure 3.8 so that students relate the parts of story schemas to a familiar framework; see Figure 3.9 for an adaptation of the causal chain map for teaching story schemas—the story schema components listed in the boxes in Figure 3.9 correspond to the events listed in Figure 3.8b; the story schema components are listed and described below:

- *Character(s) and setting*: the individuals with important roles in the story and the time and place in which the story occurred.
- *Beginning event*: the occurrence that initiated the story sequence; the beginning event sometimes involves a problem that must be solved.
- *Response / goal*: the characters' internal response to the beginning event; this may involve thoughts, feelings, and/or setting a goal to solve the problem that occurred at the beginning of the story.
- *Attempt(s)*: the actions the characters take to solve the problem in the story.
- *Outcome*: the consequences of the characters' actions.
- *Reaction*: the characters' internal and behavioral responses to the outcome.

• Following Short and Ryan (1984), you can provide cueing questions or prompts to guide students' identification of each of the organizational components of story schemas listed above (see Figure 3.10 for cueing questions that you can use with your students); these prompts can be used in combination with story maps for students who need extra support in learning story organization (following Idol, 1987; Idol & Croll, 1987).

• Once your students are able to identify and recall the more concrete elements of story organization listed above, you can teach theme (Williams, 2005; Williams et al., 2002; also see Dymock, 2007); over a series of several lessons, engage your students in the following activities: **R.CCR.2**

- Prereading discussions in which you introduce a text's theme (e.g., persistence, loyalty, sharing) and lead students to connect that idea to their existing knowledge (schemas).
- A read-aloud of the target text.
- A postreading discussion in which you ask questions to guide students to the identification of the basic elements of story structure (like those in Figure 3.10) and then questions to guide students to identify the theme, such as the ones that follow (adapted from Williams, 2005):
  - Tell me about what happened in the story. Was it good or bad? Why?
  - What did the main character learn he or she should do?
  - So, we should _____. Explain.
- Then, to help your students generalize the theme to new situations, you can ask:
- When would it be a good idea to _____?
- What would make it easy or hard to _____?

Story: _____

Characters: _____ Setting: _____

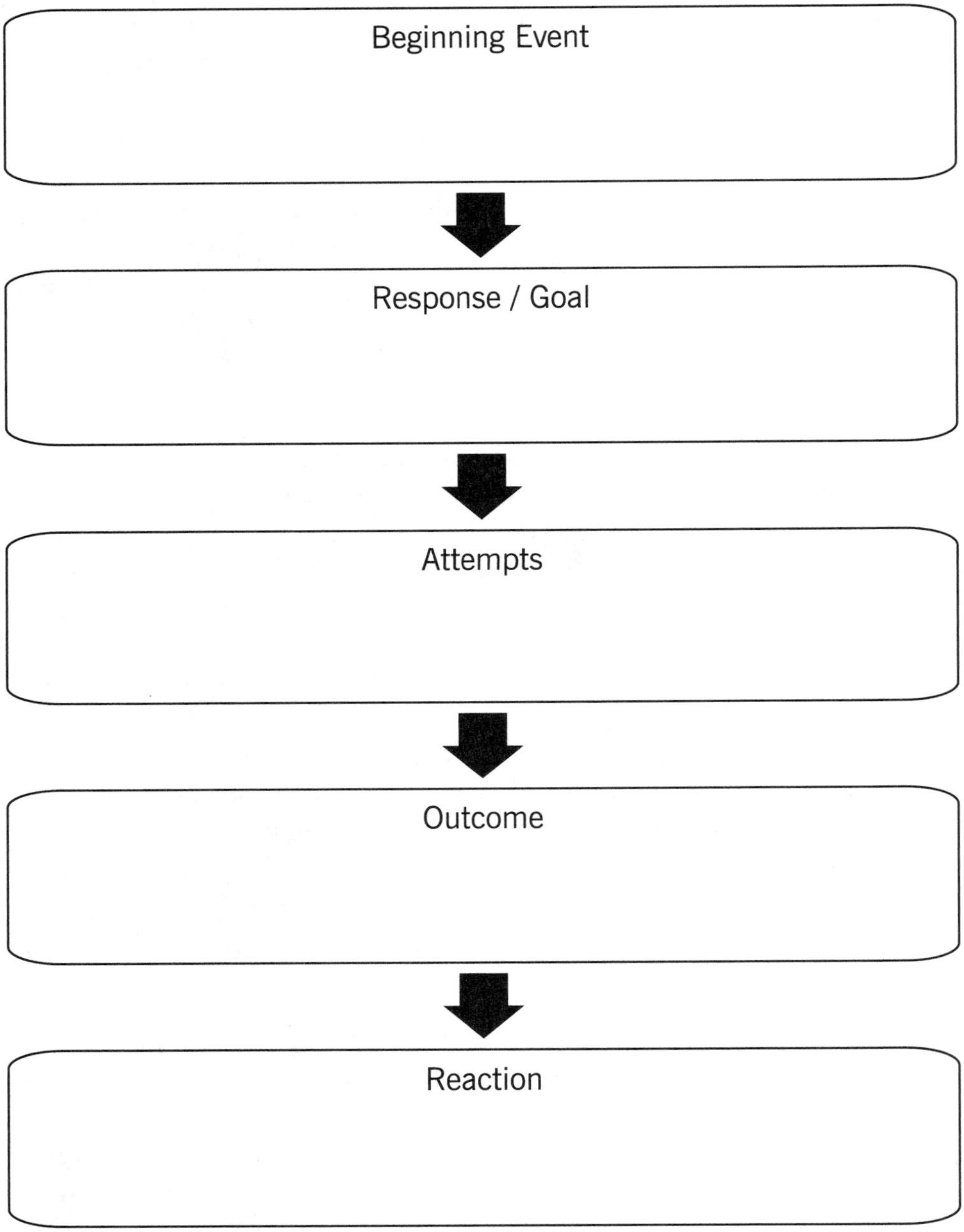

```
╭─────────────────────────────────────────────────────╮
│                  Beginning Event                     │
│                                                       │
│                                                       │
╰─────────────────────────────────────────────────────╯
                          ▼
╭─────────────────────────────────────────────────────╮
│                  Response / Goal                     │
│                                                       │
│                                                       │
╰─────────────────────────────────────────────────────╯
                          ▼
╭─────────────────────────────────────────────────────╮
│                     Attempts                         │
│                                                       │
│                                                       │
╰─────────────────────────────────────────────────────╯
                          ▼
╭─────────────────────────────────────────────────────╮
│                     Outcome                          │
│                                                       │
│                                                       │
╰─────────────────────────────────────────────────────╯
                          ▼
╭─────────────────────────────────────────────────────╮
│                     Reaction                         │
│                                                       │
│                                                       │
╰─────────────────────────────────────────────────────╯
```

FIGURE 3.9. Mapping parts of story schemas.

From *Executive Skills and Reading Comprehension: A Guide for Educators* by Kelly B. Cartwright. Copyright 2015 by The Guilford Press. Permission to photocopy this figure is granted to purchasers of this book for personal use only (see copyright page for details). Purchasers can download a larger version of this figure from *www.guilford.com/cartwright2-forms*.

1. **Character(s):** Who is the main character (or characters)?

2. **Setting:** Where and when did the story take place?

3. **Beginning Event:** How did the story begin? (What was the big event or problem that started the story?)

4. **Reaction/Goal:** How did the character(s) react? What goal did they set?

5. **Attempts:** What did the characters do to try to reach their goal(s) or solve the problem?

6. **Outcome:** What was the outcome? How did the story end?

7. **Reaction:** How did the characters react? (What did they think, feel, and do?)

FIGURE 3.10. Cueing questions to support learning and identification of the organizational components of story schemas.

- After you have introduced theme, you can help your students incorporate theme into their developing schemas for story organization (and relate story organization to what they know about their knowledge organization from your work with concept maps) by introducing the story map provided in Figure 3.11, using the guiding questions presented in this section to help your students complete the map; your students should recognize the components of their existing story schemas in the plot section.

Organizational Signals in Expository Text

You can explicitly teach the kinds of organizational signals that appear in expository texts so that your students attend to them and use them to support compre-

R.CCR.1, hension. Although there is limited intervention work in this area, we do
R.CCR.5 know that readers' knowledge and use of organizational signals is positively related to reading comprehension.

How to Introduce Organizational Signals

"Remember when we talked about how good readers are organized thinkers? One of the ways that good readers stay organized is to notice the clues in text that tell them how texts are already organized. Information texts are written to provide information, and authors of those texts use many kinds of signals to help us see how the text is organized. You can use these to help you connect information in text to your own knowledge, to figure out how texts are already organized, and to remember information in text better."

To teach organizational signals, you can explicitly explain how each of the following items provides information about the ways in which a text is organized. There are many concepts in this list; therefore, they should be taught over a series of lessons, rather than all at once. Your students may already know how to use titles and subtitles to get information about texts because of your previous work with predictions; therefore you might review those, and then start with explaining headings and subheadings. You might have students highlight these items in various texts to get a feel for how they are used, explain what each item tells readers about a particular text or texts, compare use of organizational signals across different texts, or write previews, overviews, or summaries of texts that do not have them. Understanding how these cues signal organization of texts will help your students better grasp text organization, connect text information to their existing knowledge, and support their reading comprehension.

- Titles
- Subtitles

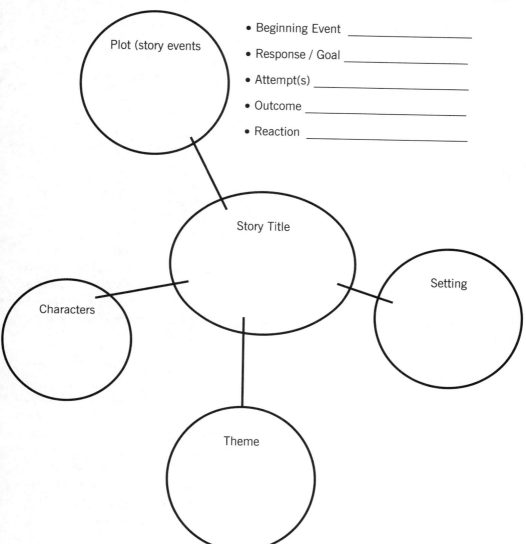

- Beginning Event _____
- Response / Goal _____
- Attempt(s) _____
- Outcome _____
- Reaction _____

Plot (story events

Story Title

Characters

Setting

Theme

FIGURE 3.11. A blank story map that includes theme.

- Previews and overviews (introductory overview of content)
- Headings
- Subheadings
- Clue words that highlight texts' organization (e.g., *alike, both, same, similar, but, different, however, in contrast*)
- Bold or italic words
- Ending summaries

Expository Text Organizational Structures

Expository texts can be written in several different kinds of organizational structures, and one text may even include multiple structure types. But the underlying purpose of all expository texts is the same: to convey information. Your students may be overwhelmed with the variation in expository text structures in comparison to narrative structure, which tends to vary far less. Thus, you need to explicitly explain that expository texts all have a common purpose of information delivery and that authors choose different text organizations, depending on the type and R.CCR.5, purpose of information to be conveyed. You might introduce expository R.CCR.8 text organization this way, holding up an expository text as an example.

How to Introduce Expository Text Structures

"This is an expository text, or informational text. This kind of text is written to convey information to readers. Remember when we talked about how good readers are organized thinkers? Well, expository texts can be organized in a bunch of different ways, depending on the kind of information we are supposed to learn from them. So, it's our job as organized thinkers about texts to figure out which kind of organization a text has so that we can use it to better understand and get information from the text. Think of the different kinds of text structures as tools you can use to help you remember what you read."

To teach expository text organizational structures, you might do the following. (See Akhondi, Malayeri, & Samad, 2011, and Hall & Sabey, 2007, for additional suggestions on teaching expository text structure.)

- Consider that your students may have difficulty with expository texts because they lack the vocabulary (and the concepts labeled by vocabulary words) found in those texts; you may wish to have prereading discussions of concepts and R.CCR.1, words to be found in a text to enhance your students' developing concep- R.CCR.4 tual organization in the area of the text's topic before reading begins as well as to fill gaps in students' existing conceptual structures.

- Start with structures that feature more organization, rather than less, as those with more organizational features better support reading comprehension (Meyer & Freedle, 1984); see Table 3.1 for text structure types.

- You might consider beginning with causal structures (e.g., those typically found in history or social studies texts) because causal structures are more familiar to students due to students' greater exposure to narrative texts and their causal structure.

- Teach one structure at a time until your students have mastered each of them, then begin helping your students learn to determine what kind of structure is in a given text so that they can use the structures as organizational tools to better understand and remember text content; integrating knowledge of expository text structures in this way enables your students to think more flexibly about them and improves reading comprehension (Wijekumar et al., 2012).

- Use graphic organizers to help your students visualize the structures as you teach them, then provide a reminder guide (e.g., as a handout, as posters on the wall of the classroom) depicting the most common structures found in expository texts that your students can use as a prompt when they begin learning to distinguish different structures on their own; see Figure 3.12 for a handout you can use for this purpose. **SL.CCR.4, SL.CCR.5**

What We Know and What We Still Need to Know about Organization

As I noted at the introduction to this chapter, organization is one of the least well studied executive skills; though, as you've seen in this chapter, many lines of research in language and reading point to the importance of the awareness and use of organization to facilitate reading comprehension. Basic cognitive organizational abilities such as sequencing, patterning, and rhythm recognition and matching across modalities (e.g., matching auditory to visual rhythm patterns) relate significantly to reading comprehension. In addition, there is some evidence that teaching these kinds of skills may improve reading comprehension, but much more work needs to be done in this area. Furthermore, we don't yet know which core executive skills (i.e., inhibition, working memory, and cognitive flexibility) contribute to basic organizational abilities; thus we need more work in this area, as well.

We have considerably more evidence that the organization of readers' own conceptual knowledge (i.e., schemas) and their awareness of their knowledge organization contribute to reading comprehension, as do knowledge and awareness of language organization like syntax. Finally, reading-specific elements of organization, like awareness of the causal organization of narrative, assessed with

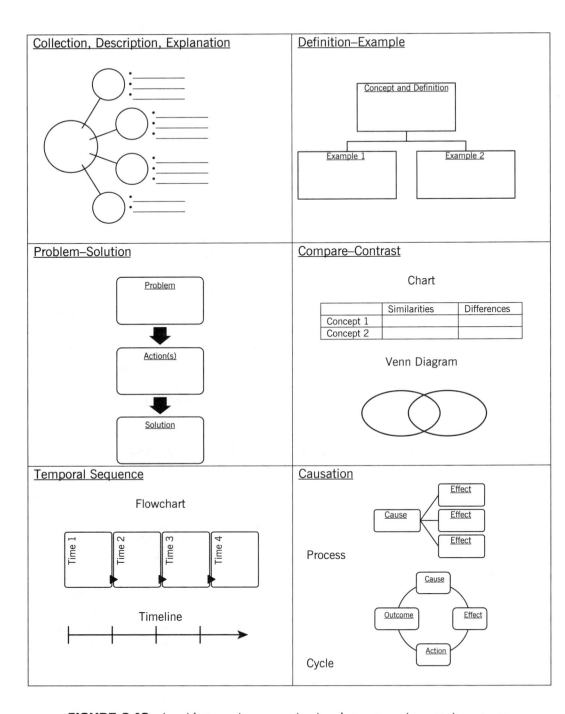

FIGURE 3.12. A guide to various organizational structures in expository texts.

picture-sequencing tasks, print-sequencing tasks, and readers' use of causal language in retellings and writings of narratives, contributes to reading comprehension. And teaching these skills improves reading comprehension. Furthermore, knowledge of narrative and expository text structures is related to reading comprehension, and text-structure instruction improves reading comprehension. Finally, readers' knowledge of the organizational signals in expository texts is related to reading comprehension, and there is limited evidence that teaching these signals can improve reading comprehension, though we need more work in this area.

It seems that we actually know quite a bit about ways that organization contributes to reading comprehension, but we do have room to learn more. For example we need to

- Develop reading-specific assessments of organizational ability.
- Determine whether we can use sequencing or patterning measures as quick indicators of students' organizational abilities as well as whether picture and print narrative sequencing tasks can be used in a similar way.
- Examine relation of cognitive measures of organization to language- and reading-specific assessments of organization; although these tasks all seem to tap the same kinds of abilities (and recent evidence suggests this is the case; see Zampini et al., 2013), we still have very little research evidence to support this assumption.
- Examine effects of sequencing, patterning, and music rhythm instruction on reading comprehension, with attention to ways these can be incorporated into classroom instruction.
- Conduct more studies of the effectiveness of teaching organizational signals on reading comprehension.
- Conduct more studies of the effectiveness of teaching specific expository text structures to elementary students; in particular, we need more work on integrating knowledge of different text structures so that students can apply this knowledge flexibly when they encounter new expository texts.

CHAPTER 4

Cognitive Flexibility
Juggling Multiple Aspects of Reading

The test of a first-rate intelligence is the ability to hold two opposed ideas in mind at the same time, and still retain the ability to function.
—F. SCOTT FITZGERALD (1964, p. 69)

Our lives are incredibly busy in this fast-paced information age. We are inundated with information; some may even argue that we are *saturated* with information (Gergen, 2000), which places great demands on our mental resources. If you're like me, you are all too familiar with the mental multitasking that characterizes much of what we do. There are days when I am quite capable of switching my focus between the many things I'm juggling at any particular moment, but there are other times when I probably would be better off doing one thing at a time! This R.CCR.7 chapter is about the kind of mental flexibility necessary to switch back and forth between and integrate ideas, tasks, or different aspects of a task, which is essential for success in many areas of our lives, including skilled reading comprehension.

In the last two chapters we discussed the planning and organization processes that underlie skilled reading comprehension. An assumption inherent in these chapters was that our students could actually focus on meaning when they pick up a text. However, for some students, a more basic challenge to reading comprehension is that they cannot see reading as more than a word-decoding task. Even when they have mastered decoding processes, they still seem unable to expand their focus to include meaning. In fact, their inflexible focus on words' features seems to prevent them from focusing on meaning at all (Cartwright, 2010; Chall, 1996; Dewitz & Dewitz, 2003; Yuill & Oakhill, 1991). Skilled comprehenders, on the other hand, display remarkable flexibility and have no trouble wrapping their minds around the decoding and meaning-making processes simultaneously, flexibly handling both of them when engaged with texts. Fitzgerald (1964, p. 69) described this feat aptly: skilled comprehenders are somehow able to "hold two opposed ideas in mind at the same time, and still retain the ability to function."

Think about the various aspects of print that we must process in order to comprehend a text: letters, the letters' sounds, the identities of words, word parts (like prefixes, suffixes, and roots), variations on word meanings, sentence meanings, our goals and strategies for reading, the structure of the text, and more. And all of these things must be done in tandem, while weaving together some semblance of meaning of the text as a whole. Skilled reading comprehension requires a tremendous amount of flexibility in handling all of these many different elements. However, you may have noticed that some of your students seem to lack flexibility, or that they focus on certain aspects of text to the exclusion of others. I am reminded here of Marie Clay's observations that skilled readers show remarkable flexibility, drawing on multiple cueing systems—meaning cues (semantics), visual cues (graphophonological, letter–sound information), and structural cues (syntax)—to understand text, whereas less skilled readers draw on far fewer cues in their attempts to understand text (Clay, 2001). Another way to think about this is that skilled readers easily monitor and integrate a variety of text features in their interpretations of text, whereas less-skilled readers cannot achieve the same kind of flexible integration and seem to be unable to monitor more than one type of text feature at a time.

R.CCR.7

Most often, I see students who are champion decoders, producing fabulous oral readings of text, but who don't seem to understand a bit of what they read. Teachers commonly call these children *word callers* (Cartwright, 2010; Dolch, 1960) because these students call out words from a page with no apparent comprehension of the text at all. One of my favorite article titles quotes a teacher as saying, "She's my best reader; she just can't comprehend" (Applegate et al., 2009, p. 512). I would argue that this teacher's student is, perhaps, her best decoder, but certainly not the teacher's best reader! Reading requires comprehension. And even when such students have vocabulary knowledge that is comparable to peers with better comprehension, they still struggle with reading comprehension (Cartwright, 2005). Students like these are puzzling to many teachers because they seem to have the first four pillars identified by the National Reading Panel as essential to skilled reading (phonemic awareness, phonics, fluency, and vocabulary; NRP, 2000), but they still lack the ability to comprehend text (NRP Pillar 5). Clearly, something else is amiss for these students, and problems with executive skills have emerged as an important contributor to these children's difficulties. As you will see in this chapter, cognitive flexibility plays a critical role in helping readers juggle word-level and meaning-focused aspects of text, which seems to be a major hurdle for some students.

What Is Cognitive Flexibility and How Is It Typically Assessed?

Cognitive flexibility is the ability to consider multiple bits of information or ideas at one time and actively switch between them when engaging in a task. This is related to *switching* or *shifting*, which involves the ability to change focus from one aspect of a task to another, also called *attentional control* (see Zhou et al., 2012). Like other cool executive skills, cognitive flexibility is associated with DLPFC activity (Eslinger & Grattan, 1993), and frontal lobe injury, particularly to the DLPFC, is associated with impairments in cognitive flexibility (Eslinger et al., 1999; Grattan, Bloomer, Archambault, & Eslinger, 1994). Let's consider the act of juggling as an analogy for the kind of mental maneuvering involved in cognitive flexibility. In this analogy, the act of juggling represents a cognitive feat, such as reading, and the three balls being juggled represent different types of information involved in the task, such as letter–sound information, syntax, and meaning. Just as a good juggler must keep all of the balls in the air and actively go between them while juggling, skilled comprehenders must hold multiple aspects of a text in mind and actively go between them while reading.

Cognitive flexibility: the ability to consider multiple bits of information or ideas at one time and actively switch between them when engaging in a task; this is related to *switching* or *shifting*, which involves the ability to change focus from one aspect of a task to another; also called *attentional control* (see Zhou et al., 2012).

A familiar game that taps individuals' cognitive flexibility is the card game "UNO," which requires that one think about two aspects of the deck of cards, color and number, and actively switch between those features while playing the game. In this game, players are dealt seven cards each, and the remaining cards comprise the draw pile. The top card of the draw pile is flipped over and begins a second pile: the discard pile. The object of the game is to be the first player to discard all of the cards in his or her hand. To do so, players take turns discarding single cards from their hands by matching a card to the top card in the discard pile by either color or number. Play proceeds in a rapid fashion; thus, players must rapidly switch back and forth between considering color and number as they try to match the cards in their hands to the ever-changing top card in the discard pile. Further, when a player has only one card remaining in his or her hand, he or she must yell, "UNO"; however, if another player catches that player before "UNO" is yelled, the player with one card must draw two more cards. This means that players not only have to monitor the multiple features of their own cards and the cards in the discard pile, they also have to monitor the number of cards in their own hand and others' hands. To be a skilled "UNO" player, one must actively and flexibly switch back and forth between all of these elements! See *www.unorules. com* for more information on the rules of "UNO."

Another game that may be less familiar to you but that captures well the demands of cognitive flexibility is "Set." "Set" is also a card game that can be played with a specially designed deck of cards, or it can be played online at the following link: *www.setgame.com/set/daily_puzzle*. The cards in "Set" have different items printed on them that vary along four dimensions: number (one, two, or three items), color (red, purple, or green), shape (oval, diamond, or squiggle), and shading (solid, striped, or none). The object of the game is to find sets of three items in which each dimension is the same across all three cards or different across all three cards. Thus, a correct set could include three cards that depict red items, but then the three cards would have to differ on number, shape, and shading. To perform well in this game, players must be able to switch back and forth between all four dimensions as they choose sets of cards that conform to the game's rules.

As you might infer from these examples, cognitive flexibility is typically assessed with sorting tasks that require individuals to group individual items along multiple dimensions. In simpler versions of these tasks, sorting is sequential. Individuals must sort along a single dimension and then switch sorting rules, continuing to sort objects along a new, single dimension; this kind of cognitive flexibility is thus called *shifting* or *switching*. The Dimensional Change Card Sort (DCCS) is an example of this kind of task (Zelazo, 2006). In the DCCS, children are asked to sort pictures of objects along one dimension (e.g., color) and then they are asked to switch sorting rules and continue sorting the objects along a different dimension (e.g., shape). Children's performance on this task improves across the preschool years, but even adults vary on this task when scoring incorporates both sorting accuracy and sorting speed (Diamond & Kirkham, 2005; Zelazo, Müller, Frye, & Marcovitch, 2003). A similar task commonly used to assess cognitive flexibility in adults is the Wisconsin Card Sorting Task (Berg, 1948).

As I noted above, these tasks require sequential shifts. That is, they require individuals to attend to one dimension of objects and then shift their focus and attend to a different, single dimension of the same kinds of objects. Additionally, the new sorting rule requires that individuals sort subsequent objects in ways that are opposite those required by the first sorting rule, which slows them down or causes them to make sorting errors. These negative effects of the switch are called switching costs. For example, when sorting a set of gray and white circles and stars as depicted in Figure 4.1, children might be asked to sort these into two piles first by color (gray and white) and then shift focus and sort instead by shape (circles and stars). A child affected by switching costs might make an error and place the white star on top of the white circle (on the right) rather than placing the white star on the gray star (on the left); an adult is more likely to sort more slowly after the switch. Although this kind of switching is demanding for students, these tasks do

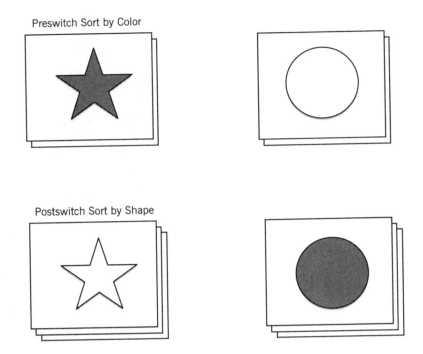

FIGURE 4.1. Initial preswitch sort by color and postswitch sort by shape.

not assess the kind of continual, online switching back and forth between multiple task elements that characterizes skilled reading comprehension.

On the other hand, multiple classification tasks that require individuals to sort objects along two or more dimensions simultaneously require continual switching between dimensions in order to sort successfully (Bigler & Liben, 1992; Cartwright, 2002, 2006, 2007, 2010; Inhelder & Piaget, 1964). And "processing of dimensions simultaneously is regarded as more complex than switching between dimensions" in cognitive flexibility tasks (Colé, Duncan, & Blaye, 2014, p. 2). For example, if one is sorting several pictures of stars and circles into piles of gray and white objects in a 2 × 2 matrix (see Figure 4.2), one must continually attend to color (gray or white) and type (circle or star) to sort each of the pictures correctly. This task has been adapted successfully to assess the flexibility with which students can consider information about social categories (e.g., that both women and men can be doctors or nurses or that members of different races can have similar or different characteristics; Bigler & Liben, 1992, 1993).

I adapted this task to assess the flexibility with which students can think about the letter–sound information and meanings associated with printed words, targeting those features that many struggling comprehenders fail to consider together.

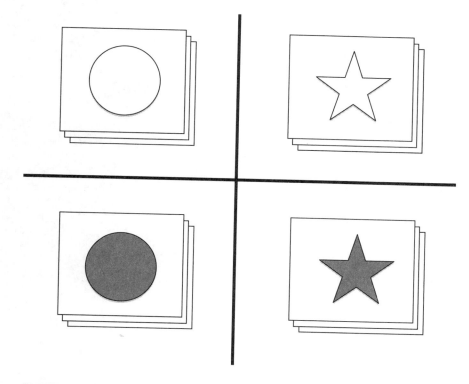

FIGURE 4.2. A multiple classification task that assesses cognitive flexibility.

And, this sound–meaning (graphophonological–semantic) cognitive flexibility contributes to skilled reading comprehension in beginning readers (Cartwright et al., 2010), older elementary students (Cartwright, 2002; Colé et al., 2014), and adults (Cartwright, 2007). You will learn more about this research later in this chapter. See Figure 4.3 for an example of a correct sort on a sound–meaning cognitive flexibility assessment; in this example the student has sorted the following list of 12 words by meaning (clothing or household items) and beginning sound (/b/ or /s/).

socks, skirt, sweater, sponge, soap, scissors
boots, bib, belt, bucket, broom, brush

Materials and directions for administering the assessment can be found in my 2010 book, *Word Callers: Small Group and One-to-One Interventions for Children Who "Read" but Don't Comprehend*. Finally, I should note that even though tasks that require single shifts like the DCCS (Zelazo, 2006) or Wisconsin Card Sorting Task (Berg, 1948) assess a simpler type of cognitive flexibility than the

FIGURE 4.3. Example of a correct sort on the Sound–Meaning (Graphophonological–Semantic) Cognitive Flexibility Task that assesses flexibility in considering the sounds and meanings of printed words.

multiple classification task (Bigler & Liben, 1992; Cartwright, 2002; Inhelder & Piaget, 1964), elementary-age students' performance on the DCCS and multiple classification tasks is significantly correlated, indicating that these tasks tap a similar ability in students (Bock et al., 2014).

Regardless of whether the assessment requires a sequential or simultaneous sort, both accuracy and speed are important in scoring cognitive flexibility assessments. In childhood, sorting accuracy develops early, and sorting speed develops later (Yeniad et al., 2014). Both scoring components are essential for lifespan comparisons of cognitive flexibility skills (Cartwright et al., 2006; Cragg & Chevalier, 2012), especially because adults and older children are often at ceiling on accuracy (i.e., they typically demonstrate uniformly high, near perfect accuracy scores); thus, speed allows you to detect additional variability in performance in these individuals (Cartwright et al., 2006; Cragg & Chevalier, 2012; Diamond & Kirkham, 2005). Even when two students demonstrate perfect accuracy, the slower of the two students would be considered less flexible because he or she required more time to produce the accurate sort.

Why Is Cognitive Flexibility Important to Reading Comprehension?

As noted above, skilled reading comprehension requires individuals to handle multiple features of texts simultaneously and fluidly for successful reading comprehension. Inability to shift focus to any particular type of feature and integrate that information into one's text interpretation, whether it is meaning, sound, **R.CCR.7** syntax, or some other text feature, prevents important components of text processing.

Sometimes, readers have trouble handling word-level, letter and sound information alongside meaning construction. Other times, readers have difficulty focusing on multiple meanings in text, or they can't shift focus from a common **R.CCR.4** word meaning to a less common but more appropriate meaning, as indicated by text context (e.g., these readers might think of the word *ball* as a type of sporting equipment and have trouble interpreting *ball* as a formal event that involves dancing).

Each of these examples of inflexibility undermines the comprehension process. However, skilled reading "is massively flexible, from before beginning to read a text to long after reading a text has concluded" (Pressley & Lundeberg, 2008, p. 165). That is, cognitive flexibility is a hallmark feature of skilled readers' processing of texts. Thus, with respect to the RRSG (2002) framework for reading comprehension (see Figure 1.1), cognitive flexibility is certainly a reader feature, as you will discover in the research review below. And cognitive flexibility may also be considered a text feature because texts that require readers to consider multiple meanings simultaneously to support understanding may be more demanding of readers' cognitive flexibility (e.g., the Amelia Bedelia book series requires readers to understand multiple meanings for homophones to understand Amelia Bedelia's frequent mistakes; Zipke, Ehri, & Cairns, 2009). Finally, although little work has explored the relation of cognitive flexibility to reading purpose, we do know that skilled comprehenders are able to adjust flexibly their reading behaviors to ensure that their reading goals are met (Cartwright, 2009; Pressley & Lundeberg, 2008); thus more demanding or complex purposes may require greater cognitive flexibility from readers in order to support comprehension.

What Does Cognitive Flexibility Look Like in Real Readers?

Brittany, a Student with RCD

Brittany, the struggling comprehender whom you met in previous chapters, displays classic signs of a student who struggles with cognitive flexibility. Her decoding skills are slightly above grade level, and her oral reading fluency is on track too. At the beginning of the year when you conducted initial assessments, these aspects of Brittany's reading ability led you to believe that she was one of the better readers in your class. Yet, once you began to ask her to retell stories, you noticed quite a discrepancy. Her word reading skills were on target, but her comprehension was surprisingly low. Once you realized that she was not really processing texts' meanings, you began to notice other things in her behavior. For example, Brittany gets stuck on particular interpretations of text and can't change her perspective to incorporate new ideas. Words with multiple meanings give her trouble too. During a read-aloud of *Amelia Bedelia, Bookworm* (Parrish, 2003) in class, you noted that Brittany didn't seem to understand the humor in Amelia's mistakes. For example, when the librarian told Amelia Bedelia that several books needed jackets, Amelia set about sewing or knitting jackets for each of them, but Brittany didn't seem to understand the play on word meaning that provided the foundation for Amelia's humorous actions. Moreover, Brittany doesn't seem to "get" any humorous jokes or riddles that rely on multiple interpretations for their humor. On a class field trip to an aquarium recently, another student told a joke about a shark:

Q: Why was the shark laughing?

A: Because it ate a clown fish!

But Brittany didn't seem to get that humor either. Finally, in a more general sense, you've noticed that Brittany just doesn't seem to transition between tasks very well. She seems fairly inflexible and unable to switch perspectives or focus when necessary to ensure understanding or to follow the routines of the school day. Clearly, Brittany lacks the kind of flexible thinking that underlies good reading comprehension.

Gabriela, a Good Comprehender

In contrast, Gabriela, our good comprehender who appeared in earlier chapters, seems to display much more flexibility than Brittany. Like Brittany, Gabriela is a skilled decoder whose fluency is appropriate for grade level; however, Gabriela's comprehension skills are vastly superior to Brittany's. For example, Gabriela can easily read aloud a story and then retell it, preserving the causal chain of events and remembering details critical to the plot. In other words, Gabriela has no difficulty processing simultaneously the word-level and meaning-focused features of texts. In addition, Gabriela makes connections across texts, flexibly considering how things she is reading now relate to other texts she has read and integrating information across texts when appropriate.

R.CCR.3,
R.CCR.7

With respect to puns and other humor that is based on words' multiple meanings, Gabriela has no difficulty. In fact, as is typical of students at her grade level,

Gabriela loves books of jokes and riddles and has even begun to attempt to write them on her own. Finally, Gabriela has no difficulty changing focus and transitioning between tasks during the school day.

What Does the Research Say?

As we discussed in Chapter 1, cognitive flexibility is one of the three core executive skills that underlie other more complex skills, such as planning and organization (Diamond, 2013). However, compared to other core skills, such as working memory, cognitive flexibility has received far less research attention. We do know that cognitive flexibility develops slowly across childhood and into adolescence (Best & Miller, 2010; Davidson et al., 2006; Zelazo et al., 2003), and some evidence suggests it continues to develop, varying across individuals, even into adulthood (Cartwright et al., 2006; Diamond & Kirkham, 2005). Like other executive skills, cognitive flexibility seems to have its roots in the development of language (Jacques & Zelazo, 2005). Recall that language serves self-regulatory functions that enable children to practice and strengthen their goal-directed executive skills, including cognitive flexibility, as they talk themselves through tasks (Bodrova et al., 2011; Cragg & Nation, 2010, Marcovitch et al., 2008). Verbal regulation supports switching, even in adults (Kray & Ferdinand, 2013); and verbal labeling supports even 3-year-olds' cognitive flexibility performance, enabling them to be successful at much greater rates than is typical for their age (Ramscar, Dye, Gustafson, & Klein, 2013). Further, learning that words can have multiple meanings, for example, or that multiple words can refer to the same objects, requires that children be flexible in their thinking about words and the world. These relations of cognitive flexibility to oral language make it no surprise that cognitive flexibility is also related to reading comprehension. As in previous chapters, I will divide our review of research on this relation into two sections, one that focuses on studies that employed more traditional, executive skill-based assessments of cognitive flexibility and a second that reviews studies that employed reading-specific assessments of cognitive flexibility.

Research on Cognitive Flexibility from an Executive Skills Perspective

Although cognitive inflexibility appears to play an important role in struggling comprehenders' difficulties, evidenced by their singular focus on letter–sound features of print (Cartwright, 2010; Dewitz & Dewitz, 2003; Yuill & Oakhill, 1991), cognitive flexibility is perhaps the least well studied of all the cool executive skills. What we do know is that across a wide variety of tasks, cognitive flexibility appears to make significant contributions to skilled reading comprehension.

For example, Wolf (1986) used a rapid automatic switching task to assess cognitive flexibility that required students to name items belonging to different sets, presented in alternating patterns (e.g., naming items from these categories: *letter, number, color, letter, number, color*). In other words, the task required students to switch back and forth between thinking about each of these kinds of items. Students were assessed three times across 3 years: when they were in kindergarten, first grade, and second grade. Rapid automatic switching was related to reading comprehension at all three time points. Additionally, children with RCD were slower than typical children at switching between letters and numbers, but not between these items and colors, indicating that their switching problems were particular to reading. Altemeier et al. (2008) assessed cognitive flexibility with a similar task that required switching between reading printed words and naming double-digit numbers, and switching made significant contributions to second to fifth graders' reading comprehension, as well.

Conners (2009), on the other hand, assessed switching (which he called attentional control) in 8-year-old students using the Star Counting Task (Das-Smaal, de Jong, & Koopmans, 1993; de Jong & Das-Smaal, 1990, 1995). The Star Counting Task presented stars, plus symbols, and minus symbols in arrays on a page and, as you probably guessed, required that students count stars in a forward direction until they reached a sign (a plus or minus sign) that indicated they had to switch and count in reverse order. The plus and minus symbols represented different directions (forward or reverse), and they had opposite roles in Parts 1 and 2 of the test, respectively, which thus required students to complete an additional switch when they moved from Part 1 to Part 2 of the test. Accuracy on this task indicated students' flexibility, which accounted for 10% of unique variance in reading comprehension beyond nonword decoding ability and language comprehension assessed independently. More recently, Kieffer et al. (2013) found similar contributions of switching to reading comprehension in fourth-grade students, using the Wisconsin Card Sorting Task, described above. Finally, Yeniad, Malda, Mesman, van IJzendoorn, and Pieper (2013) recently published a review of research investigating the role of cognitive flexibility in reading and math performance in children from preschool to middle school, and their findings confirmed the significant relationship between switching and reading comprehension across development (see Yeniad et al., 2013, for a review of those studies).

With respect to more complex assessments of cognitive flexibility using multiple classification tasks, we know that general color–shape cognitive flexibility, described earlier (see Figure 4.2 for an example), is significantly related to reading comprehension in beginning readers (Cartwright et al., 2010), second to fourth graders (Cartwright, 2002, Study 1), and adults (Cartwright, 2007). Furthermore, this relation has been demonstrated across cultures: Yan and Yu (2006) found that color–shape cognitive flexibility was significantly related to reading comprehension in fourth- to sixth-grade Chinese children. And, consistent with executive skill problems observed in poor comprehenders in other studies (e.g., Borella et al., 2010; Locascio et al., 2010; Sesma et al., 2009), struggling readers were significantly lower in cognitive flexibility than their typically developing peers (Yan & Yu, 2006). Finally, colleagues and I recently found that the relation of cognitive flexibility to comprehension emerges early in development in a sample of 3- to 5-year-old prereaders (Cartwright, DeBruin-Parecki, Vaughn, Badalis, & Orelski, 2014); moreover, cognitive flexibility predicted the students' responsiveness to inferential comprehension instruction. Specifically, we found that preschoolers with higher levels of cognitive flexibility assessed with a color–shape multiple classification task, demonstrated significant growth in narrative comprehension in response to inferential comprehension instruction, whereas children low in cognitive flexibility showed no significant comprehension growth in response to such instruction.

Research on Cognitive Flexibility from a Reading Perspective

The studies reviewed in the last section suggest cognitive flexibility plays an important role in comprehension development (narrative comprehension in prereaders and reading comprehension in readers) from preschool through adulthood. However, all the assessments of cognitive flexibility used in these studies were general measures without an explicit connection to the demands of reading. In a review of multiple studies, Melby-Lervåg and Hulme (2013) recently found that executive skill interventions that are tailored to the demands of particular tasks, like reading, are more effective for teaching task-specific executive skills; and, by extension, task-specific assessments of executive skills should also be better measures of the thinking processes involved in particular kinds of tasks. Additionally, they suggested that we should analyze task features so that we can tailor executive skills assessments and interventions to particular task demands, in order to tap the specific kinds of executive skills required by those tasks. Although their findings had not yet been published, these are just the kinds of concerns I addressed when I developed a reading-specific assessment of cognitive flexibility, described in the next section.

Reading-Specific Cognitive Flexibility Assessment and Intervention

Because poor comprehenders have difficulty integrating flexibly the letter–sound and meaning-focused features of print, I designed a reading-specific cognitive flexibility task (see Figure 4.3) to assess readers' abilities to consider simultaneously these features of printed words. In this assessment, individuals sort four sets of 12 word cards by beginning sound and word meaning into a 2×2 matrix, and the assessment is scored with a composite of speed and accuracy (Cartwright, 2010). Consistent with Melby-Lervåg and Hulme's (2013) recommendations, I've found that reading-specific cognitive flexibility is, indeed, a better predictor of reading comprehension than domain-general (color–shape) cognitive flexibility in typically developing readers across the lifespan (Cartwright, 2002, 2007; Cartwright et al., 2006; Cartwright et al., 2010).

Since the development of that task, we have discovered that sound–meaning cognitive flexibility (also called graphophonological–semantic cognitive flexibility), the ability to actively switch back and forth between sounds and meanings of printed words, contributes significantly to reading comprehension in typically developing beginning readers (Cartwright et al., 2010), second to fourth graders (Cartwright, 2002, Study 1), and adults (Cartwright, 2007), beyond students' phonological decoding (sound) and semantic (meaning) processing, assessed independently. These findings have recently been replicated in a sample of French-speaking third-grade students (Colé et al., 2014), indicating that the important role of sound–meaning cognitive flexibility in reading comprehension is cross-cultural and exists regardless of readers' native language.

In early elementary school, children tend to focus primarily on letter–sound information in words, and they gradually shift their focus to incorporate meaning across the elementary years (Bialystok & Niccols, 1989; Cartwright, 2011). Sound–meaning cognitive flexibility continues to develop across the lifespan and varies considerably in adults; in fact, adults sometimes exhibit lower levels of sound–meaning cognitive flexibility than some elementary school students (Cartwright et al., 2006). With respect to its relation to other executive skills, sound–meaning cognitive flexibility is significantly correlated with other executive skills, such as inhibition, working memory, and planning, and it contributes to reading comprehension beyond these other executive skills, even when word reading and verbal ability (assessed with an expressive vocabulary task) are controlled (Cartwright & DeWyngaert, 2014). Finally, consistent with research on other executive skills, first- to fourth-grade students with RCD show significantly lower sound–meaning cognitive flexibility than their peers with better reading comprehension (Cartwright & Coppage, 2009). And we have observed similar patterns in college students with and without RCD (Cartwright & DeWyngaert, 2014; Cartwright, Coppage, Guiffré, & Strube, 2008). See Cartwright (2015) for a review of these studies.

In one of our studies investigating the role of reading-specific cognitive flexibility in college students with poor reading comprehension, we also developed an assessment of semantic–syntactic cognitive flexibility, which tapped individuals' abilities to actively switch between syntactic and meaning-focused features of print. In this assessment, students sorted four sets of 12 target words, underlined in 12 printed sentences, by the meaning and syntactic role of the target words. For example, the following sentences can be sorted by the target words' meanings (instruments or vehicles) and syntactic role (subject or object). See Figure 4.4 for an example of a correct sort on this kind of task.

The <u>car</u> stopped.
The <u>boat</u> floats.
The <u>train</u> roared.
The <u>piano</u> played.
The <u>horn</u> honked.
The <u>trumpet</u> sounded.

Board the <u>train</u>.
Drive the <u>car</u>.
Row your <u>boat</u>.
Honk the <u>horn</u>.
Sound the <u>trumpet</u>.
Play the <u>piano</u>.

This new kind of reading-specific cognitive flexibility also contributed significantly to reading comprehension in college students; and college students with RCD were significantly lower on semantic–syntactic cognitive flexibility than their peers with better comprehension (Cartwright et al., 2008). These findings indicate that flexibility considering a variety of aspects of print—not just sounds and meanings—contributes to skilled reading comprehension. However, much more work is needed in this area before we will have a more complete understanding of the many ways that cognitive flexibility may impact reading comprehension.

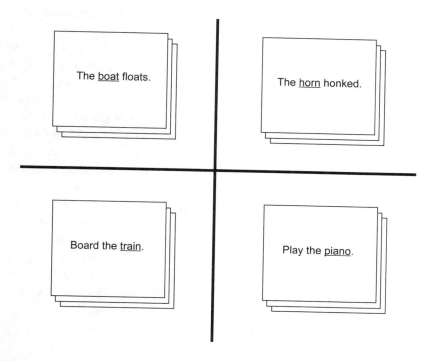

FIGURE 4.4. Example of a correct sort on the Semantic–Syntactic Cognitive Flexibility Task that assesses flexibility in considering the syntactic and meaning-focused aspects of print.

With respect to reading-specific cognitive flexibility interventions, we have found that sound–meaning cognitive flexibility can be taught across 5 days with the same sets of word cards used for the assessment, resulting in significant improvements in reading comprehension on standardized measures for typically developing students (Cartwright, 2002, Study 2; Cartwright, 2006; see Cartwright, 2010, for additional directions and materials). However, teaching general, color–shape cognitive flexibility did not improve reading comprehension, again confirming Melby-Lervåg and Hulme's (2013) argument that task-specific executive skill interventions are more effective than general ones. The sound–meaning cognitive flexibility intervention involved two kinds of sorting on each of the five instructional days, with a new set of word cards for each of the 5 days. First, students sorted along each dimension individually (i.e., they sorted word cards into two piles by meaning and then switched and resorted them into two piles by sound; see Figure 4.5a). Virtually all of the students were able to sort this way and to switch sorting rules on that second step. Then, I had students complete 2×2 sorts by placing three cards in the 2×2 matrix and then having students choose a card to complete a sound–meaning sort from the remaining cards in the set; we repeated this activity with three new cards from the same set of 12, varying the location of the empty spot, until students could complete four consecutive, correct sorts. See Figure 4.5b for an example and Cartwright (2010) for additional directions and materials.

When I taught reading teachers to administer the sound–meaning cognitive flexibility intervention to second- to fifth-grade teacher-identified struggling readers in small-group instruction, we observed significant improvements in reading comprehension on school-based and standardized measures; and we also noted that these improvements transferred to students' performance on a general color–shape cognitive flexibility task (Cartwright, Guiffré, Bock, & Coppage, 2011). These findings were exciting and suggested that we might be able to use the sound–meaning cognitive flexibility intervention as a Tier 2 intervention in a response-to-intervention framework (Fuchs & Fuchs, 2009) to support the development of reading comprehension in students with RCD. To test this possibility, I recently worked with third-grade teachers to identify students who had intact decoding skills, appropriate for grade level, but who were at least a year behind in their reading comprehension in comparison with their typically developing peers. We observed little growth in reading comprehension for students with RCD in response to Tier 1, regular classroom instruction in the fall semester. However, in the spring, after they had received 5 days of one-to-one sound–meaning cognitive flexibility intervention, these students' comprehension growth more than doubled, and their reading comprehension scores were on grade level (Cartwright, Lane, & Singleton, 2012). Teachers have asked me how skill on such a task might transfer to reading comprehension; I suggest that the skill doesn't transfer, per se. Rather, these interventions enable students to consider sound and meaning

R.CCR.7,
R.CCR.10

(a) Switching between single sorts

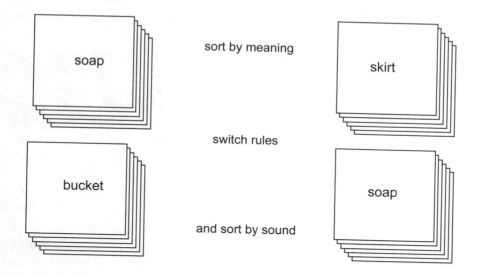

sort by meaning

switch rules

and sort by sound

(b) Completing 2 × 2 sorts (Students repeated this activity until they achieved four correct consecutive completions.)

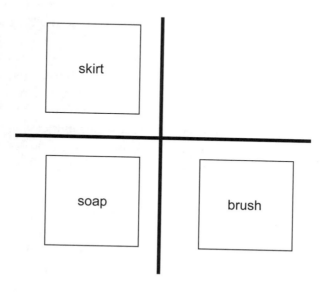

FIGURE 4.5. The two kinds of sorting activities involved in the sound–meaning cognitive flexibility intervention.

simultaneously and flexibly, enabling readers to better integrate these features of print when reading a text. In other words, the interventions provide readers an executive skill that they lack but that is necessary for skilled reading comprehension.

Few other studies have attempted to teach reading-specific cognitive flexibility. But two are worth mentioning here. For example, Yuill and colleagues adapted my sound–meaning cognitive flexibility task for computerized administration in a collaborative learning situation in which students shared control of the computer screen on which they were sorting words by word-level features and meaning. To sort correctly, students had to discuss and explain choices to their partners. As a result, students' cognitive flexibility improved, and observations of student conversations indicated comprehension might have been positively impacted, as well; however, reading comprehension growth was not assessed (Yuill et al., 2008). These findings suggest we should explore computerized cognitive flexibility interventions designed to support and improve reading comprehension. Additionally, providing students opportunities to discuss and explain multidimensional sorts of printed stimuli may improve their abilities to integrate those diverse features.

SL.CCR.1,
SL.CCR.2,
SL.CCR.3

Finally, in a recent intervention study, García-Madruga et al. (2013) taught third-grade students several reading-related tasks they believed tapped the switching aspect of cognitive flexibility, such as analogies, inference making, resolving inconsistencies and anaphora in texts, and integrating knowledge, along with other tasks that tapped additional executive skills like inhibition and working memory. Although their training program produced improvements in reading comprehension for initially poor comprehenders, these researchers did not assess relations of their switching-specific reading tasks to other measures of cognitive flexibility, nor were they able to tease apart effects of training in specific executive skills because multiple executive skills were taught in combination in the intervention. We will discuss inference, integration, inconsistency detection, and anaphora resolution in Chapter 5 when we talk about working memory. Given the sparse work in cognitive flexibility interventions and our limited understanding of reading-specific tasks that require and foster cognitive flexibility, much more work is needed in these areas.

R.CCR.1,
R.CCR.7,
R.CCR.10

Research on Other Reading-Specific Tasks That May Tap Cognitive Flexibility

Cognitive flexibility exerts its influence on reading comprehension in many ways. For example, some reading-related tasks require flexibility in considering multiple meanings in text, rather than meanings and sounds. Remember the description of Brittany from earlier in this chapter? She had difficulty determining the appropriate meanings of ambiguous words in text, and she had trouble understanding jokes and riddles that rely on lexical ambiguity; that is, ambiguity that is caused by words having more than one possible meaning. Not coincidentally, recent brain imaging work indicates these kinds of ambiguities in word meaning produce activity in the frontal lobes as readers seek to understand them (Mason & Just, 2007); recall that the frontal lobes are associated with executive skills (see Chapter 1). Although many instances of lexical ambiguity require that readers suppress one meaning in favor of considering an alternative meaning to preserve comprehension (Mason & Just, 2007), some activities require readers to hold multiple meanings in mind and actively switch between them, in order for comprehension to occur, such as understanding riddles like the clown fish riddle, above. In order to understand this riddle and discover the source of its humor, readers (or listeners) must hold in mind the two meanings of *clown* (i.e., a type of fish versus a comical entertainer) and actively switch from the first meaning (type of fish) to the second (comical entertainer). If either meaning in the pair is suppressed or absent, the source of the riddle's humor is not apparent to the reader. We will return to the notion of ambiguity in word or text meanings in later chapters, because such ambiguities also place demands on readers' inhibition and working memory skills.

Difficulty switching between multiple, possible meanings in text has negative effects on reading comprehension across the lifespan, in children, adolescents, and adults (Gernsbacher & Robertson, 1995; Yuill, 1996, 2007; Zipke, 2007). But we can teach our students to handle flexibly the multiple meanings in texts, using activities that require them to switch between meanings, resulting in improved reading comprehension (Yuill, 1996, 2007, 2009; Zipke, 2008; Zipke, Ehri, & Cairns, 2009). For example, Yuill (1996) taught 7- to 8-year-old British poor comprehenders to identify and explain multiple meanings in a variety of forms, such as in homophones or in riddles like the clown fish riddle, above, for 30 min- **R.CCR.4,** utes, once per week, for 7 weeks. After the intervention, the initially poor **SL.CCR.1,** comprehenders were much better able to switch between multiple mean- **SL.CCR.2,** ings and had reading comprehension scores that were comparable to their **SL.CCR.3** peers with better comprehension.

Furthermore, when Yuill (2007, 2009) assessed the effects of peer discussion of ambiguous forms presented on a computer, these activities still improved children's reading comprehension, suggesting that this kind of intervention might be effective in paired reading situations in literacy centers. In the United States, Zipke (2008; Zipke et al., 2009) provided a similar intervention to low-income third graders that also incorporated identification of ambiguous words' meanings in texts, such as those in the *Amelia Bedelia* book series, which improved **R.CCR.1,** their ability to switch flexibly between words' meanings and resulted in **R.CCR.4** significant improvements in students' reading comprehension.

Finally, I would be remiss if I did not mention idioms, phrases that have multiple meanings, which require the reader to consider both literal and figurative meanings to understand them. Thus, idioms require the same kind of flexibility that we have been discussing: the ability to consider flexibly two meanings associated with text. Idioms require that one understand a surface form, or literal meaning, as well as a deeper meaning. For example, as adults, we know that the idiom *break the ice* does not literally mean to break ice. Rather, it means that one engage in an activity that breaks barriers between oneself and another, unfamiliar person. Cain, Oakhill, and Lemmon (2005) found that students with comprehension difficulties were significantly worse at interpreting opaque idioms than peers with better comprehension. Additionally, Levorato, Roch, and Nesi (2007) demonstrated that children's understanding of idioms was, not surprisingly, significantly related to their reading comprehension; furthermore, poor comprehenders who improved in idiom comprehension from age 6.5 years to age 7.5 years also improved in reading comprehension. Finally, Lundblom and Woods (2012) showed that idiom comprehension can be taught effectively, using peer tutoring, like comprehension of multiple word meanings, described above.

Taken together, these findings suggest that students' abilities to hold in mind and actively switch between multiple text elements, whether sounds, meanings, or syntactic roles, plays a powerful role in reading comprehension. In the next section I provide recommendations for incorporating activities into your instruction that will strengthen your students' cognitive flexibility and, in turn, improve their reading comprehension.

How Can I Apply This Knowledge to Classroom Practice?

Just as you would with any process important for reading comprehension, you should introduce cognitive flexibility to your students in ways that are consistent with the gradual release of responsibility model (Duke & Pearson, 2002; Duke et al., 2011; Pearson & Gallagher, 1983). That is, you should provide your students an explicit explanation of this important executive skill while modeling how it's done, involve your students in cognitive flexibility activities while sharing the responsibility for this new way of thinking, provide opportunities for your students to practice under your guidance and support, and then finally provide opportunities for independent practice. You might consider explaining cognitive flexibility as follows:

EXPLICITLY EXPLAINING COGNITIVE FLEXIBILITY

"Today I'm going to tell you about another way that you can think like good readers. We already talked about how good readers are good planners, and that good readers are organized thinkers. Well, good readers are also flexible thinkers. Does anyone know what *flexible* means? [Engage students in a discussion of flexibility, drawing on their prior knowledge to construct a definition; incorporate their suggestions into the explanation that follows.] Yes, that's right! *Flexible* means that someone can bend or stretch really well. When good readers read, they don't just think about texts and words in one way or stretch their minds a little bit. Instead, they are able to bend or stretch their thinking so that they can juggle lots of aspects of the words they're reading at the same time! Have any of you ever seen someone juggle? What does that look like? [Allow students to respond.] Yes, juggling involves tossing many items at once, alternating between them. Good readers can do this in their heads with information from the texts that they read! And, they hold these things in their heads at the same time!

"Let's try something. Have you ever tried to pat your head and rub your tummy? Let's start with the head; everyone pat your head. Now, stop patting, and with your other hand, rub your tummy in circles like this. Were those hard? No, doing one thing at a time is pretty easy. Now, let's put them together. Pat your head with one hand, and rub your tummy with the other, at the same time! Was this harder? Why? [Allow students to respond.] Good reading is like this activity. Good readers can think about the letters and sounds that make up words. That's one way to think about what we read. But they are also able to think about what the words mean too! They can think about both aspects of the texts they're reading and do both things at the same time. Words may even have more than one meaning, and good readers can be flexible about those too. So, they can think about letter–sound information, while also thinking about more than one meaning for words. That's a lot of information to juggle in your head at the same time! Sometimes, it's hard for readers to think about all of the important parts of text at the same time, but this is something we can practice. And, when we do, we get even better at understanding what we read."

Practice and Assess General (Nonreading) Cognitive Flexibility

Your students may need practice with general, nonreading cognitive flexibility tasks before you begin assessing and teaching reading-specific cognitive flexibility. In my first study of cognitive flexibility and reading (Cartwright, 1997), I assessed students' general cognitive flexibility using pictures that could be sorted by color and type simultaneously into a 2 × 2 matrix, like those depicted in Figure 4.2; and I assessed sound–meaning cognitive flexibility using words that could be sorted by initial sound and word meaning into a 2 × 2 matrix, like those depicted in Figure 4.3. Half of the second to fourth graders in the study completed the general, color–shape cognitive flexibility task first, and the other half of the students completed the sound–meaning cognitive flexibility task first. I found that the children who completed the general task first were significantly better at sorting the sound–meaning word cards than their peers who received the sound–meaning cognitive flexibility task first. What this means for your students is that they may find it easier to understand general cognitive flexibility tasks, such as sorting objects by color and shape. Then, after practicing cognitive flexibility with a simpler task, they will be able to transfer these skills to the sound–meaning word sorts, which are typically more difficult for students (e.g., Cartwright et al., 2010). You might try these general cognitive flexibility activities, which could be used as transitional activities during the school day, at a center where students work in pairs and check each other's work, or in Tier 2 or Tier 3 interventions for children who struggle with cognitive flexibility.

• Create arrays of items from varying categories for your students to name rapidly, like Wolf's (1986) rapid automatic switching task; you could use letters, numbers, colors, or pictures of items, and present them in arrays that require your students to switch back and forth between categories as they name the items (see Figure 4.6 for examples).

• Create a more complex rapid automatic switching task, following Altemeier et al. (2008), who presented alternating words and double-digit numbers to be read rapidly by students.

• Like the Star Counting Task described above, you could create arrays of items to be counted in a forward direction until students reach a signal that indicates that they should change directions and count in reverse order until they reach a signal indicating that they should switch again; like Conners (2009), you could present the task in two parts, so that the signals reverse roles in the second part. See Figure 4.7 for an example of a triangle counting task; in this example, plus signs (+) indicate forward counting and minus signs (-) indicate a switch to reverse counting.

• Give your students sets of pictures that can be sorted two ways, by color and shape, and use them to practice switching; first have your students sort the cards along one dimension and then have them reshuffle the cards and sort them along the other dimension (see Figure 4.1 for an example).

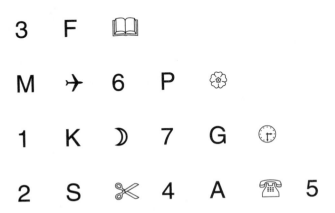

FIGURE 4.6. Examples of arrays of items that could be used for rapid automatic switching practice arranged in an alternating pattern of number, letter, object.

△ △ △ △ - △ △ + △ △ △ △ △ - △ △ + △ △ △ △ △

1 2 3 4　3 2　　3 4 5 6 7　　6 5　　6 7 8 9 10

FIGURE 4.7. A sample array to assess switching following Conners (2009), who used a star counting task; plus signs (+) indicate forward counting, and minus signs (-) indicate reverse counting. (A correct count of these items is listed below the array.)

- Have students sort pictures two ways at the same time, by color and shape into a 2 × 2 matrix (see Figure 4.2); use this task to assess general cognitive flexibility, as in prior work (Cartwright, 2002, 2007; Cartwright et al., 2006, 2010) by recording accuracy and speed of sorting (Cartwright, 2010, includes five sets of picture cards that can be used for this purpose and for the color–shape switching task, described above).

Practice and Assess Reading-Specific Cognitive Flexibility

Word sorting is something that is quite familiar to teachers and students in today's literacy classrooms. Two texts come to mind that may be familiar to you and were written to support this kind of activity to help students learn the important features of words: *The Reading Teacher's Book of Lists* (Fry & Kress, 2006) and *Word Sorts and More* (Ganske, 2006). These kinds of activities, though, typically focus on one aspect of print, such as sorting words by beginning sound, or sorting words by shared ending sounds. Thus, they do a great job of helping students think about one aspect of print at a time; however, this may promote inflexibility in thinking about words. Consider this: even if students are sorting a group of words into piles of three different word families (e.g., -*ark* words, -*at* words, and –*an* words), that sort focuses students on one aspect of those words, ending chunks of words, without consideration of meaning. The word sorting tasks described in this chapter provide students practice in thinking flexibly about more than one **R.CCR.7,** aspect of print at the same time, such as meaning, sounds, or syntactic role. **SL.CCR.2** Thus, they go beyond our typical word sorts. To incorporate these kinds of activities into your instruction, you might consider the following activities.

- When you talk about similarities or differences in words during your language arts block, highlight multiple dimensions of words, such as mean- **R.CCR.4,** ings, sounds, and spellings, to help your students think about words in **SL.CCR.2** more than one way on a regular basis.
- Give your students sets of words that can be sorted two ways, by meaning and sound; have them sort them along one dimension (e.g., meaning) and

then have them reshuffle the cards and sort them along the other dimension (e.g., sound) to practice switching between these dimensions of print (see Figure 4.5a for an example; nine sets of preprinted word cards are available with, or without, my 2010 book, *Word Callers: Small Group and One-to-One Interventions for Children Who "Read" but Don't Comprehend*).

• Have your students create sets of words that can be sorted by sound and meaning, which you could use in small groups or at a literacy center to support the development of sound–meaning cognitive flexibility; if this activity is beyond the level of some of your students, consider creating such lists as shared work in whole-group or small-group instruction to provide guided support for your students in thinking about words in multiple ways.

• Teach and assess sound–meaning cognitive flexibility (see Figure 4.3 for an example of a correct sort in a sound–meaning flexibility assessment). Track your students' progress across the academic year. Additionally, you can assess their sound–meaning cognitive flexibility before and after you administer flexibility interventions to determine whether your students' flexible thinking skills have improved.

• Similarly, teach and assess semantic–syntactic cognitive flexibility using short sentences with highlighted words like those I presented earlier in this chapter (see Figure 4.4 for a correct sort on this task). Additionally, as I suggested for sound–meaning cognitive flexibility word lists, you can have your students help you develop sets of sentences to be used for semantic–syntactic sorts.

R.CCR.4, W.CCR.4

• If you suspect that you have a student or students who struggle with flexible integration of letter–sound information and meaning when reading, or if your assessment of their flexible thinking indicates they struggle with this skill, you can try the sound–meaning flexible thinking intervention to help them improve their reading-specific cognitive flexibility; see Figure 4.5 for depictions of the two activities involved in this intervention, switching between single sorts and completing sound–meaning sorts, which can be administered in small groups (a Tier 2 intervention in an RTI framework) or individually (a Tier 3 intervention in an RTI framework); refer to Cartwright (2010) for directions and materials for administering small-group and one-to-one sound–meaning cognitive flexibility interventions.

• Once your students understand how to complete sound–meaning sorts, you might consider creating a center where students can help each other practice these skills in paired work. I have found that when students observe one another's sorts in a small group sound–meaning sorting lesson, they become even more aware of the sound and meaning dimensions of words; monitoring one another and practicing these skills will support and strengthen your students' developing sound–meaning cognitive flexibility.

SL.CCR.1, SL.CCR.3, SL.CCR.4, SL.CCR.6

- Yuill and Zipke, whose work is reviewed above, engaged students in various ambiguous language activities to support their ability to consider flexibly the multiple meanings of words; activities you might try with your students follow:

  o You might have students generate and define words with multiple meanings (e.g., homonyms and homophones, such as *fork, ball, jam, bear/bare*, and *hair/hare* provide opportunities for students to practice these skills); they can draw pictures to illustrate the meanings, use the words in sentences, or incorporate both forms and meanings in journal writing.

  o Similarly, you can have students explain the different meanings in ambiguous sentences (e.g., *I saw a person in a tree with binoculars*—this sentence could mean that I or the other person was using binoculars). Advanced students can create sentences that can be interpreted in multiple ways.

  o You can have students generate definitions for compound words, based on the meanings of the individual words in the compounds. Although the meanings students generate will likely differ from the real definitions, they will enjoy creating funny definitions (e.g., *butterfly* could be imagined to be a stick of butter with wings) and will gain practice in coordinating flexibly multiple word meanings.

  o You can have students generate jokes or riddles that rely on the multiple meanings in some words, such as the clown fish riddle described earlier; the trick to doing this well is to have your students identify a word or words that sound the same but have different meanings. Then teach your students to ask a question that makes the listener think of one of those meanings, but create an answer that refers to the other meaning (e.g., *What did the shark say when he ate a clownfish?* makes readers think of one definition of clown, and *That tasted funny!* is a funny answer, which makes readers think of the other meaning).

  o You can utilize texts that highlight multiple meanings to provide opportunities to discuss these with your students. Once they have developed some skill at this task, you might ask them to read texts, identify the ambiguous words, and explain what the multiple meanings do in those texts; the following texts might be useful for this purpose: **SL.CCR.4, R.CCR.1, R.CCR.4**

    - Any *Amelia Bedelia* text by Peggy Parrish or Herman Parrish
    - *Parts, More Parts,* and *Even More Parts* by Tedd Arnold
    - *In a Pickle and Other Funny Idioms* by Marvin Terban
    - *You're Toast* by Nancy Loewen
    - *Dear Deer* by Gene Barretta
    - *A Little Pigeon Toad* and other books by Fred Gwynne
    - Riddle and joke books that rely on verbal ambiguity to create humor, such as *Eight Ate, a Feast of Homonym Riddles* by Marvin Terban

• Yuill demonstrated that peer discussion of ambiguous forms of words improved children's reading comprehension, suggesting that these kinds of activities might also be effective in paired learning situations in literacy centers.

• Similarly, Lundblom and Woods (2012) demonstrated that peer tutoring of the multiple meanings of idioms is effective for improving idiom comprehension; this might be another activity you could implement at literacy centers. Idioms that could be used for this purpose are listed below:

SL.CCR.1,
SL.CCR.3,
SL.CCR.4,
SL.CCR.6

break the ice	hold your horses
cry over spilled milk	hold your tongue
drop in the bucket	lose your mind
fall to pieces	sharp as a tack
give me a hand	spill the beans

What We Know and What We Still Need to Know about Cognitive Flexibility

As I noted above, research on the role of cognitive flexibility in reading comprehension is still in its infancy. By comparison to other cool executive skills, there is still much we need to know about how cognitive flexibility supports reading comprehension and how flexibility assessment and instruction can be incorporated into daily practice in schools. However, we do know that inflexibility characterizes the thinking of struggling comprehenders, especially with respect to their inability to integrate flexibly the letter–sound and meaningful aspects of print (Applegate et al., 2009; Cartwright, 2010; Dewitz & Dewitz, 2003; Yuill & Oakhill, 1991).

R.CCR.7,
R.CCR.10

We also know that skilled comprehenders are "massively flexible" (Pressley & Lundeberg, 2008, p. 165), and that from elementary school to adulthood skilled comprehenders have no difficulty handling words' letter–sound information and meaning simultaneously and flexibly (Cartwright, 2002, 2006, 2007; Cartwright et al., 2010). Furthermore, we know that cognitive flexibility, assessed with a wide variety of general and reading-specific measures, is significantly associated with reading comprehension through the lifespan, from preschool to adulthood (see the research review above for relevant citations); and sound–meaning cognitive flexibility contributes uniquely to reading comprehension beyond other executive skills in adults (Cartwright & DeWyngaert, 2014). In addition, children and adults with RCD are significantly less flexible in reading-specific cognitive flexibility than their counterparts with better reading comprehension (Cartwright, 2015; Cartwright & Coppage, 2009; Cartwright & DeWyngaert, 2014; Cartwright et al., 2008). Fortunately, teaching sound–meaning cognitive flexibility can improve struggling comprehenders' cognitive flexibility and reading comprehension across a variety of measures (Cartwright, 2002; Cartwright et al., 2011; Cartwright et al., 2012). Taken together, these findings suggest that anything we can do to move our struggling comprehenders toward more flexible thinking about text should improve their reading comprehension.

These findings are encouraging and suggest that cognitive flexibility is an executive skill that is critical for successful reading comprehension. Further, they indicate that flexibility considering a variety of aspects of print—not just sounds and meanings—contributes to skilled reading comprehension. However, much more work is needed in this area before we will have a more complete understanding of the many ways that cognitive flexibility may impact reading comprehension. Simply put, we have much more to learn.

- Although we know that various measures of cognitive flexibility, general and reading-specific, are related to reading comprehension, there are few intervention studies to determine whether and how teaching these skills positively impacts reading comprehension.

- Further, we need to know which aspects of reading comprehension relate to cognitive flexibility and to other executive skills. García-Madruga and colleagues (2013) developed a reading-specific executive skills intervention that involved several reading comprehension subtasks, such as inference making, integrating knowledge, analogies, anaphora, tracking information in changing stories, finding main ideas, arranging sentences and vignettes in order, and resolving inconsistencies in text. And, although they suggested that different subsets of these tasks tapped particular executive skills (e.g., they suggested analogies, anaphora, resolving inconsistencies, making inferences, and integrating knowledge all tapped students' cognitive flexibility), no studies have determined whether students' performance on these reading comprehension subtasks is actually correlated with performance on existing executive skill assessments of the target skills. In order to devise reading-specific executive skill interventions, we need to know which aspects of reading comprehension are related to particular executive skills.

- We have a good bit of evidence that sound–meaning cognitive flexibility is significantly related to reading comprehension across the lifespan and that semantic–syntactic cognitive flexibility contributes to reading comprehension in adults; but these may be just the tip of the iceberg with respect to the wide array of text features that skilled comprehenders must consider flexibly to understand texts.

- Furthermore, we know that my sound–meaning cognitive flexibility intervention results in improvements in reading comprehension for elementary students, but we don't know whether this intervention is effective for older students, for struggling adult learners, or whether a text-free version (i.e., one that requires prereaders to sort pictures by sound and meaning) would foster comprehension development in prereaders.

• Yuill and colleagues have demonstrated that computerized interventions are useful in fostering reading-specific cognitive flexibility in students, using multiple classification and ambiguous language activities. We need additional research to test whether these might be useful for individual student interventions at a computer station in the classroom, which could serve as a Tier 3 individual intervention in an RTI framework.

• Likewise, Yuill and colleagues demonstrated that collaborative work, in which students must explain cognitive flexibility sorts or ambiguous language to one another, may be a useful intervention technique in the classroom, but more research is needed to determine the conditions under which such collaborative work is effective for improving cognitive flexibility and reading comprehension.

• Further, Lundblom and Woods (2012) showed that peer tutoring of idioms improved idiom comprehension in middle school students, but no work has assessed whether teaching the multiple meanings associated with idioms improves reading comprehension the same way that teaching words' multiple meanings does (Yuill, 2007, 2009; Zipke, 2008; Zipke et al., 2009).

• Moreover, we know that ambiguous language activities, such as those investigated by Yuill and Zipke, can improve reading comprehension, and we assume those improvements are related to readers' improved awareness of and flexibility in processing multiple meanings of ambiguous words and phrases, but no work has assessed whether cognitive flexibility is indeed related to these tasks.

• Finally, a colleague has suggested to me that poetry may require cognitive flexibility because it requires attention to both meaning and sound (e.g., for poetry that rhymes). This suggestion has merit. And poetry instruction that improves students' flexible attention to both meaning and sound may foster sound–meaning cognitive flexibility in students. However, research has yet to examine the relation between poetry and cognitive flexibility in students of any age.

CHAPTER 5

Working Memory
Holding and Linking Ideas in Mind While Reading

I am an omnivorous reader with a strangely retentive memory for trifles.

—SHERLOCK HOLMES (Doyle, 1986, p. 692)

Wouldn't it be nice if all of our students had the memory of Sherlock Holmes? In Chapter 1 I shared the lament of one of my reading specialist colleagues who felt that one of her students just didn't have the memory skills to support successful reading comprehension. Although she didn't realize she was talking about an executive skill, she was highlighting a problem that is common for children who struggle with reading comprehension: working memory issues. These students just don't seem to be able to hold as much information in mind at one time, or for as long a time, as their peers with better comprehension (Hua & Keenan, 2014). Or, they may remember things, but they remember the wrong things! Because our goal in reading is to remember the important parts of what we read, working memory problems can pose significant difficulties for learners and for teachers. If you have a student who struggles with working memory, you may see evidence for that student's memory problems in other areas of their behavior too. (Consider that if students are not able to remember relevant information from text, they are also likely to be unable to remember all of the steps in multistep directions, or remember to do their homework, or bring their lunch to school, or get their field trip permission form signed; I'm sure you've had students who have forgotten at least one of these.) This chapter will focus on the role of working memory in reading comprehension.

In contrast to the relatively understudied executive skills I have discussed thus far, working memory has a long history in the reading comprehension research literature, with foundational work in this area dating back to the 1970s!

What Is Working Memory and How Is It Typically Assessed?

Working memory is the ability to hold information in mind to support completion of tasks while working with part of that information and updating it as needed. (See Table 1.1 in Chapter 1.) In other words, working memory requires individuals to be capable of storing information while processing part of it. Like other cool executive skills, working memory is associated with activity in the frontal lobes (Prabhakaran, Narayanan, Zhao, & Gabrieli, 2000), with simple maintenance working memory tasks associated with VLPFC activity, which is typically associated with hot and cool executive processing, while complex working memory tasks involving manipulation are associated with DLPFC activity, which is typically associated with cool tasks (Fletcher & Henson, 2001; Reuter-Lorenz et al., 2000). Additionally, frontal lobe damage is related to impairments in working memory (Owen et al., 1990). Of all of the executive skills discussed in this book, working memory has received the most attention in the reading comprehension research literature over the past four decades, with seminal papers in this area cited thousands of times across that period (e.g., Daneman & Carpenter, 1980; LaBerge & Samuels, 1974). The relation of working memory to other executive skills has been viewed two ways, depending on disciplinary perspective. In experimental psychology, executive skills such as inhibition or cognitive flexibility have been viewed as parts of the overall working memory system (e.g., García-Madruga et al., 2013; Swanson, Howard, & Sáez, 2006); however, cotemporary neuropsychological perspectives view working memory as one of many, separable executive skills that we can employ to enable us to achieve our goals (e.g., Guare, 2014; Schneider, Schumann-Hengsteler, & Sodian, 2005). I take the latter perspective in this book and treat working memory as one of an array of mental tools readers can use in service of reading comprehension. The research supports this perspective because working memory is related to, but independent of, other executive skills such as cognitive flexibility and inhibition (Garon, Bryson, & Smith, 2008; Guajardo et al., 2009; Hughes, 1998; Unsworth & Engle, 2008).

Working memory: the ability to hold information in mind to support completion of tasks while working with part of that information and updating it as needed; working memory includes a storage component and a processing component.

When I was a child, my mother, sister, and I played a game that required, and perhaps fostered, good working memory skills. We called this game Johnny Has an Apple in His Pocket, and it was a useful alternative for passing the time on lengthy car trips or other long waits. The object of the game was to come up with items that might be in someone's pocket and recall, in order, all of the things previous players had mentioned. If a player could not remember all of the items in order or come up with a new item that conformed to the game's rules, then that player was out of the game. Often, we would introduce an interesting twist in which we would have to come up with items that began with each letter in the alphabet, in order. That version of the game might begin this way:

MOM: Johnny has an *apple* in his pocket.

ME: Johnny has an *apple* and a *ball* in his pocket.

SISTER: Johnny has an *apple*, a *ball*, and a *carrot* in his pocket.

MOM: Johnny has an *apple*, a *ball*, a *carrot*, and a *dragon* in his pocket.

ME: Johnny has an *apple*, a *ball*, a *carrot*, a *dragon*, and an *elephant* . . .

The game continued in this manner until there was one person left who had not made any errors. If we were able to continue through the whole alphabet, we started adding items beginning with the letter A again, and proceeded through the alphabet a second time. This game is much like The Name Game that one might play as an introductory activity on the first day of class. In The Name Game, which is designed as a get-acquainted activity, students are required to introduce themselves by sharing their name and something they like. Each student, in turn, must recall the name of each classmate who has gone before them, as well as the item each classmate likes, and then add his or her own name and liked item to the list. In both games, individuals must engage in storage and processing activities: they must store an entire list of items (or pairs of items in the case of The Name Game) and also process part of that information by coming up with new items that conform to the rules of the game.

Similarly, working memory is typically assessed with tasks that require individuals to remember an array of information (the storage component of working memory) while working with part of it (the processing component of working memory). Let's return to our juggling analogy from Chapter 4 in which the act of juggling represents a cognitive feat and the three balls being juggled represent pieces of information. Remember that cognitive flexibility involved keeping all three balls in the air and actively going between them while juggling, analogous to holding multiple aspects of a task in mind and actively going between them while engaging in the task. A variation of this analogy can also help us better understand working memory. Typically, juggling requires that one keep all three balls moving. However, working memory does not necessarily require that one keep all three balls in the air, so to speak; rather, it requires that an individual hold two of the balls in one hand (storage) while tossing the third ball with the other hand (processing) so that none are dropped.

Working memory assessments target memory for a variety of kinds of information, such as verbal or visual material (Gathercole, Pickering, Ambridge, & Wearing, 2004). A simple visual task, for example, would require students to watch the assessment administrator tap an array of wooden blocks in a random order and then repeat the pattern of taps; a simple verbal task would require students to recall a list of numbers, letters, or words in exact order (Gathercole et al., 2004). A third type of assessment, called a complex task, places increased processing demands on students, such as recalling strings of digits or letters in reverse order (Gathercole et al., 2004). For example, in a *letters backward* working memory assessment, such as the one in the Test of Memory and Learning–2 (TOMAL-2; Reynolds & Voress, 2007), students would have to recall arrays of letters of increasing length, read aloud by the assessment administrator, one list at a time, in reverse order. Hence, correct responses for the following two lists of letters would be L M X P Q and N S C R Z, respectively.

Q P X M L
Z R C S N

Gathercole and colleagues (2004) found that verbal, visual, and complex working memory are differentiated in students as young as 6 years of age, and performance on all three types of working memory tasks increases gradually across childhood and into adolescence. Thus, you should see improvements in your students' working memory skills across elementary school and into middle and high school.

As I noted in Chapter 2, working memory is also related to planning: adults with better working memory are better able to adjust their reading behavior to achieve goals (Linderholm, 2006; Linderholm & van den Broek, 2002). In fact, children's ability to recall sequences of items in simple working memory tasks, such as recalling a list of animal names, is related to planning as well. In a study of 3- to 10-year olds and young adults, Chevalier and colleagues recently showed that by age 7, children already exhibit the same kind of proactive planning as adults when attempting to remember lists of items by taking more time before responding at older ages, indicating more planning before responding (Chevalier, James, Wiebe, Nelson, & Espy, 2014). Important for our purposes, complex working memory tasks appear to be more closely related to reading comprehension than simple working memory tasks (Oakhill, Yuill, & Parkin, 1986; Yuill, Oakhill, & Parkin, 1989). This finding makes sense, because reading comprehension requires more than just remembering sequences. At the very least, good comprehenders must decode print, choose between multiple potential meanings for words, employ comprehension strategies, and access prior knowledge, all while building and holding a mental model of text meaning. Weaving all of these tasks together is certainly a complex feat!

In one of the earliest tests of the relation of working memory to reading comprehension, Daneman and Carpenter (1980) devised a complex working memory task they called a *reading span task* to assess readers' working memory, and variations of this task have continued to be used in the field. College students in Daneman and Carpenter's study had to read sentences and then recall the last word from each sentence. (That is, they were required to hold all of the sentences' final words in mind while reading only one sentence at a time.) So, if we were to use the sentence with which I began the chapter in a reading span task,

I am an omnivorous reader with a strangely retentive memory for trifles,

the reader would have to remember the word *trifles* while reading additional sentences and also storing final words from each of those. After reading all of the sentences (the processing component of working memory), the reader would then have to recall each of the final words from all of the sentences that were read (reflecting the storage component of working memory).

The reading span task has been adapted successfully for use with children. For example, Cain et al., (2004) assessed working memory with a reading span task by having children read sentences that were each missing the last word. Children had to come up with words to correctly fill the blanks in each of the sentences and remember the final words for all of the sentences when reading was complete. So, for the following sentence, children might supply the word *meadow, field, or street.*

The horse galloped gracefully across the _____.

After completing several such sentences in this manner (the processing component of working memory), children had to recall all of the child-supplied words (the storage component). See Figure 5.1 for sample sentences that you can use to briefly assess your students' complex verbal working memory. Nation, Adams, Bowyer-Crane, and Snowling (1999) used a similar task with children, except that they had children judge the truth or falsity of sentences (e.g., *Cars have four tires*, which should be judged as true; the processing component) and then recall the last word from each of the sentences (the storage component). Yuill et al. (1989) developed a numerical version of the reading span task, in which they had students read several arrays of numbers aloud (the processing component) and recall the final number from each array (the storage component). Thus, for the following arrays of numbers, students would read the arrays aloud and then recall the numbers 7 and 4.

6 4 3 2 7
5 9 8 1 4

Item	Sentences to Be Completed	Typical Words to Be Recalled
1	I use a tissue to blow my _____.	Nose
	Cows and horses live on a _____.	Farm
2	I put my shoes on my _____.	Feet
	Apples grow on _____.	Trees
	Today I have a peanut butter sandwich in my _____.	Lunch
3	The zoo has all kinds of _____.	Animals
	A boat floats in the _____.	Water
	We love to build sand castles at the _____.	Beach
	Monkeys love to eat _____.	Bananas
4	At bedtime, I turn off the _____.	Light
	When I ride my bike, I wear a helmet on my _____.	Head
	I love going to the library to get a new _____.	Book
	The dentist tells me to brush my _____.	Teeth
	We wear seat belts when we ride in the _____.	Car
5	A bicycle has two _____.	Wheels
	When I have a question in school, I raise my _____.	Hand
	Please pour some more juice in my _____.	Cup
	The train chugged along the _____.	Tracks
	It is safer to walk on the sidewalk than on the _____.	Street
	A delicious, cold summer treat is _____.	Ice cream

FIGURE 5.1. Sentences to assess complex working memory. Students may provide different words to fill these blanks; if they do, assess their ability to recall the actual words they supplied.

Poor comprehenders performed more poorly on this task, as expected, leading Yuill and colleagues to conclude that poor comprehenders seem to have a general, rather than a reading-specific, difficulty with complex working memory tasks (Yuill et al., 1989). However, on a completely nonlinguistic spatial span task, in which children had to choose odd shapes from arrays of geometric figures (processing) and then point to the locations of each of the previously selected odd shapes (storage), poor comprehenders performed as well as their peers with better comprehension (Nation et al., 1999). Because Yuill and colleagues' (1989) number span task required oral reading of numerals that represented words, it is likely that this task placed more language demands on children then they had anticipated. In sum, poor comprehenders seem to struggle with complex, verbal working memory tasks, but their nonverbal working memory is similar to that of their peers.

Finally, I should note one other kind of working memory assessment that is related to reading comprehension: an updating task. Updating is the ability to keep track of ever-changing information in working memory while continuing to process new information.

One way updating is assessed is by having students recall the last three items in lists of varying lengths, presented slowly, one list at a time. In this

> *Updating*: the ability to keep track of ever-changing information in working memory while continuing to process new information.

kind of task, students are not told how long the lists are, so they must continuously rehearse the last three items presented, and then update those three items, by discarding the least recently presented item and adding a new one, as new list items are read aloud by the assessor (e.g., St Clair-Thompson & Gathercole, 2006). In this kind of assessment, if I were to present the list A G Q R N orally to a student, reading the letters aloud slowly at a rate of one letter every 2 seconds, and asking the student to remember the last three items presented, the student would have to rehearse A G Q, then update to G Q R, then finally update to Q R N (St Clair-Thompson & Gathercole, 2006; also see van der Sluis, de Jong, & van der Leij, 2007), discarding the A and G as I presented new information. This task captures something important that is typical of reading comprehension: the idea that we must continually change what we hold in mind as we encounter new information in text. Unfortunately, though, few studies have examined the role of updating in reading comprehension using these kinds of tasks.

Why Is Working Memory Important to Reading Comprehension?

Reading comprehension requires that individuals gather ideas from text, link text ideas together in ways that make sense (and in ways consistent with the author's intention), connect those ideas to the readers' own conceptual structures

(Anderson, 1984), and then update their ever-changing mental model as they encounter new information in text (Kintsch, 1994). Further, readers combine verbal information from text with visual information in pictures, or from images they create spontaneously as they read; such dual coding supports comprehension and enriches readers' text models by enabling them to better integrate text information, but poor comprehenders are significantly less likely to spontaneously create images as they read (Hibbing & Rankin-Erickson, 2003; Sadoski, 1983, 1985, 2008; Sadoski & Paivio, 2013). When one considers what reading comprehension entails, it is not surprising that reading involves working memory. A mental **R.CCR.10** model and its structure, all of the ideas in text, one's own conceptual knowledge, and the ways that knowledge links to text information: this is quite a complicated list of things to keep in mind, all while continuing to add to the mental model under construction, which continually shifts while reading occurs.

Further, when one considers the inference making that also goes on during skilled comprehension, the complexity of memory processes is compounded. As I mentioned in Chapter 2, inference making requires that readers construct new knowledge based on (1) filling gaps in text with their own conceptual knowledge, typically called *gap-filling, knowledge-based, or elaborative inferences*, or (2) connecting ideas in text that may be separated by distance, typically called *text-connecting or text-based inferences* (Baker & Stein, 1981; Cain & Oakhill, 1999; Carnine, Kame'enui, & Woolfson, 1982; Graesser et al., 1994; see Cartwright, 2010, for a review of these inference-making processes). For example, when reading the following sentence, individuals must use their own prior knowledge **R.CCR.1** to fill in components omitted by the author.

Sadie barked furiously as the stranger climbed through the broken window.

As I tell my students, authors cannot write down everything readers need to know to understand a text. They expect us to fill in the missing pieces. So, in this sentence, you may have assumed that *Sadie is a dog* because she is barking. (This is a gap-filling inference; you used your knowledge of species-specific sounds to come up with this information.) And you also may have inferred that *the stranger is an intruder* into Sadie's home, which is why she is barking in the first place. (This is a text-connecting inference that required you to piece together the text-provided information about barking and stranger entry.) The assumption that the stranger is *entering Sadie's home* is another gap-filling inference that you make because the author provides no information about the building on which the broken window is located; you just assume that the window is part of a home because of your basic knowledge about situations in which a dog would be inside a structure with a broken window. (The broken window also could have been on a store, a church, a school, or even a car, but these are not as likely, given our everyday experiences.) These inferences place demands on your working memory. They require that you maintain text information in mind to construct a mental model of the text's meaning (storage), while using your own conceptual structures to generate new knowledge (processing), and adding that new knowledge to your continually developing mental model of the action in the text (processing). Furthermore, you must resolve ambiguity in text by choosing appropriate meanings for words, and you must remember relevant text information while discarding other, irrelevant information. And, you do these things rather effortlessly and automatically, without much conscious thought!

With respect to the RRSG (2002) framework for reading comprehension (see Figure 1.1 in Chapter 1), working memory is a reader factor that significantly affects reading comprehension and varies from person to person. Additionally, the purpose of a reading task impacts comprehension because different purposes have different working memory demands. For example, reading for details or to get information about an unfamiliar topic will place more demands on one's working memory, whereas reading for enjoyment may be much less demanding (Linderholm, 2006; Linderholm & van den Broek, 2002). Finally, regarding the RRSG framework's third dimension, working memory appears to play a greater role in comprehension of expository text than narrative text (De Beni, Borella, & Carretti, 2007), probably because expository text requires a greater degree of reliance on readers' conceptual knowledge for inference making (Best et al., 2008).

What Does Working Memory Look Like in Real Readers?

Brittany, a Student with RCD

Like many struggling comprehenders, Brittany's behavior suggests that she also has trouble with working memory. Generally, she seems to get lost in text, especially when the text is at all ambiguous, such as when she needs to link a pronoun back to the person to whom it refers. Somehow, she can't track those anaphoric references the same way your other students do. In addition, she has trouble inferring new words' meanings from context. It's as though she can't hold the relevant context in mind long enough to attach it to the word she doesn't know. Finally, with respect to integration and inference making, Brittany usually doesn't make inferences from text at all. But, when she does, they are more likely to be gap-filling inferences where she supplies information from her own conceptual structures. Unfortunately, she is not as good at noticing whether the knowledge she supplies actually fits the context of the passage. Thus, she may supply inappropriate knowledge, which contributes to her comprehension difficulties! With respect to her classroom behavior, Brittany often forgets her homework, she doesn't remember to show her parents the papers in her folder, and she's more likely than your other students to leave her belongings behind (e.g., like leaving her jacket on the playground or her lunchbox on the bus). Clearly, in her reading and everyday activities, Brittany appears to have some working memory difficulties.

Gabriela, a Good Comprehender

Now, consider Gabriela, our good comprehender. Gabriela easily infers new words' meanings from context, having no difficulty retaining and connecting the relevant contextual information with new words she encounters in text. In fact, you have noticed that Gabriela may even use new words she has learned from text, such as in conversation or by weaving them into her writing. When reading, she has no trouble tracking characters' identities, even when the text includes a number of pronominal references to characters. Further, you can count on Gabriela to make complex inferences from both narrative and expository texts, either by supplying appropriate world knowledge to fill text gaps or by connecting text elements, even when they are separated by a distance. With respect to classroom behavior, Gabriela is always on top of her assignments. You know you can count on her to submit her work on time, and she even helps remind other students of important deadlines. Gabriela has no difficulties with working memory.

What Does the Research Say?

As I noted in the beginning of this chapter, of all the cool executive skills that contribute to reading comprehension, working memory has probably received the most research attention over the last several decades. A prevailing view of the role of working memory in reading research and practice has been that of limited capacity, such that readers have limited mental space (i.e., working memory space) for processing and storing reading-related information (Just & Carpenter, 1992). You may be familiar with this idea, popularized in the 1970s by LaBerge and Samuels (1974; also see Samuels, 1979), who suggested that effortful decoding processes took up too much mental space in working memory, leaving little room for constructing meaning. Further, they argued that reading fluency (accurate, automatic decoding) was necessary to free mental space for processing meaning. This notion has become pervasive in conversations about the relation of decoding processes to reading comprehension, with reading fluency considered to be the bridge between decoding and comprehension for our students (Pikulski & Chard, 2005). Likewise, this argument even appeared in the fluency summary of the *Report of the National Reading Panel* (NRP; 2000, p. 11), which stated, "If text is read in a laborious and inefficient manner, it will be difficult for the child to remember what has been read and to relate the ideas expressed in the text to his or her background knowledge." The NRP report has influenced practice in U.S. reading instruction since 2000, with fluency instruction in the form of repeated readings of text becoming a favored intervention for improving fluency, presumably because such repetition automates decoding processes and thus frees up working memory space for processing texts' meanings (e.g., Reutzel & Hollingsworth, 1993; Ring, Barefoot, Avrit, Brown, & Black, 2013; Samuels, 1979).

This assumption, however, is troubling because fluent decoding does not always ensure that reading comprehension will occur (Applegate et al., 2009; Hicks, 2009). Take children with RCD, for example, who make up 10 to 30 % of struggling readers and demonstrate surprisingly fluent word reading abilities with comparably poor reading comprehension. (See Cartwright, 2010, for a review of research on these children.) The existence of these readers shows that for some students there is a disconnect between fluency and comprehension. Consistent with this notion, Swanson and O'Connor (2009) recently showed that fluency practice does not account for the relation of working memory to reading comprehension. Thus, something aside from fluency must be awry with these students, such as problems with executive skills.

Please note that I am not arguing that fluency instruction is not useful or effective for students, as it does foster better comprehension for many (e.g., Ring et al., 2013; Samuels, 1979); but we should be cautious in assuming that freeing mental space through fluent decoding will ensure reading comprehension for *all* students, as this is clearly not the case. We need to look a bit deeper to see other ways working memory might contribute to reading comprehension processes in our students. In other words, we need to consider *what kinds of processes need to happen in good comprehenders' working memory space* after it is freed by making word decoding fluent. The remainder of this section focuses on research that provides further insights into the various aspects of working memory's contribution to reading comprehension processes. As in prior chapters, I divide our discussion into two parts, the first focusing on research conducted from an executive skills perspective and the second focusing on research conducted from a reading perspective.

Research on Working Memory from an Executive Skills Perspective

Early studies using traditional executive skills measures of working memory in children focused on differences between children with and without specific RCD (described in Chapter 1) and yielded varied conclusions about the relation of working memory to reading comprehension, depending on the type of task that was used (Savage, Lavers, & Pillay, 2007). Therefore, in the discussion that follows, I briefly describe the features of each of the working memory tasks used in the research so that you can get an idea of the kinds of memory demands that contribute to reading comprehension as well as the variety of ways these demands can be assessed. Simple working memory tasks, for example, in which 7- to 8-year-old students are asked to recall lists of aurally presented words or visually presented pictures in exact order, do not account for the difference between good and poor comprehenders (Oakhill et al., 1986). However, 7- to 8-year-old poor comprehenders differ significantly from their peers with better comprehension on a complex digit span task (described in the assessment section, above; Yuill et al., 1989). Similarly, Stothard and Hulme (1992) tested 7- to 8-year-old students using complex working memory tasks, such as the Wechsler Intelligence Scale for Children (WISC; Wechsler, 1991) digit span subtest and a sentence span task in which students had to judge the truth or falsity of sentences while holding in mind the last word of each. Working memory on both types of measures was lower in poor comprehenders—but not significantly lower—in comparison to typically developing peers. However, their sample of children was small (only 14 poor comprehenders were tested), thus the differences between the groups of children may have reached statistical significance had more children been tested. Nation et al. (1999) tested similarly small groups of children and found that poor comprehenders performed significantly more poorly on the same type of sentence span task but not on a nonverbal, spatial span task (in which students had to locate shapes in arrays and then recall the locations of all of the shapes they had seen). Taken together, these findings suggest that 7- to 8-year-old poor comprehenders have difficulty with complex, verbal working memory tasks; that is, tasks that require simultaneous storage and processing of verbal information, which parallels the demands of reading comprehension.

The studies just described target 7- to 8-year-old children because specific reading comprehension difficulties begin to become evident around second grade, once decoding processes are relatively automatic for students (Cartwright, 2010; Chall, 1996), and specific difficulties with comprehension may contribute to late-emerging reading disabilities and the fourth-grade slump that have been observed in many students (Catts, Compton, Tomblin, & Bridges, 2012; Hirsch, 2003; Leach, Scarborough, & Rescorla, 2003). Thus, more research has been conducted on poor comprehenders around second to fourth grades. We know comparatively less about older students and adults who struggle with reading comprehension despite intact decoding abilities.

Nevertheless, when one considers the studies that involve older students, similar patterns emerge. For example, Seigneuric, Ehrlich, Oakhill, and Yuill (2000) found that working memory, assessed with verbal and numerical complex span tasks like the ones described above, predicted fourth graders' reading comprehension beyond vocabulary and decoding. More recently, Sesma and colleagues (2009) examined the role of working memory and other executive skills to reading comprehension in 9- to 15-year-old students, using arithmetic and digit span tasks that required students to read lists of numbers verbally while performing another process (calculations or recalling digits in reverse order). Working memory contributed uniquely to students' reading comprehension, even when attention, decoding, fluency, and vocabulary were controlled (Christopher et al., 2012, reported similar findings in 8- to 16-year-old students).

The same kinds of relations emerge in studies of working memory and comprehension growth across time. For example, Seigneuric and Ehrlich (2005) found that working memory contributed to reading comprehension from first to third grade, even when first-grade reading comprehension was controlled. Furthermore, in a longitudinal study over a longer period, Cain, Oakhill, and Bryant (2004) found working memory, assessed with the reading span task described earlier in this chapter, contributed to reading comprehension in students from 8 to 11 years of age, even when the contributions of word reading, verbal ability, and vocabulary were taken into account. Finally, Jerman, Reynolds, and Swanson (2012) showed working memory (assessed with a reading span task) was lower and working memory growth was slower in 7- to 17-year-old students with specific reading comprehension difficulties when compared to students with word reading difficulties and typically developing readers. Thus, there is a substantial body of evidence that complex working memory tasks that require simultaneous storage and processing of verbal information tap something important related to reading comprehension.

However, few studies have examined the relation of reading comprehension to updating in working memory, using the kind of updating task I described earlier in this chapter, in which students must listen to lists of items read very slowly and remember the final few (typically three or four) items in the list. Because they do not know when the list will end, students must track the most recently heard items, updating that list each time the assessor adds a new item to the list. This kind of working memory task parallels the kind of updating readers must do as they construct a model of a text's meaning and adjust it while continuing to encounter new information as they progress through a text. Consistent with this assumption, St. Clair-Thompson and Gathercole (2006) assessed working memory with four different complex measures (a sentence span task like the one described above, a digits backward task, and two complex nonverbal spatial span tasks) as well as two updating tasks, and performance on all measures was significantly related to students' English scores on a national assessment, which included reading, writing, spelling, and handwriting. Importantly, both complex working memory span and updating were significantly related to English outcomes in these students. Because the English scores were composites of various literacy scores, we need to be cautious in our interpretations regarding relations to reading comprehension alone. These promising findings point to the need for more work examining updating and reading comprehension.

As I noted earlier in the chapter, working memory difficulties affect more than just reading comprehension, as you might have observed in your own students. Recently Pimperton and Nation (2014) explored this possibility and discovered teachers rated 8- to 10-year-old children with RCD as having significantly more cognitive inattention problems associated with working memory than peers with better comprehension, such as forgetting things they had already learned, lacking interest in schoolwork, not reading up to par, and having difficulty with arithmetic. (The teachers were unaware of the purpose of the study; rather, they rated their students on various behaviors and then the researchers divided children into the target groups of good and poor comprehenders to compare problem behaviors.) Further, the poor comprehenders in this study who showed the most working memory-related behavior problems were significantly lower in both verbal and nonverbal complex working memory tasks, indicating that their difficulties with working memory were wide ranging. In contrast, other poor comprehenders only had weaknesses in verbal working memory, and their behaviors indicated that their working memory problems were language-specific. Along similar lines, mind-wandering behaviors, in which task-unrelated thoughts intrude into the mind while reading, partially account for the relation of reading comprehension to working memory in college students (McVay & Kane, 2012).

I should note that although we tend to notice reading comprehension problems later in elementary school (Catts et al., 2012; Hirsch, 2003; Leach et al., 2003), the relation between comprehension and working memory emerges quite early in development. Strasser and del Río (2014), for example, recently found that working memory made a significant contribution to prereaders' memory for story content, which is a prerequisite ability to reading comprehension (see Cartwright & Guajardo, 2015, for a review of work on the contributions of executive skills to prereaders' comprehension). Finally, you may not be surprised to learn that children's economic circumstances are also related to their working memory abilities, with poor children lagging behind their peers with more economic resources; however, children's memory problems differ depending on their setting, with urban poor children showing difficulty with verbal and visual–spatial working memory and rural poor children having difficulty with only visual–spatial working memory (Tine, 2014). Thus, your students' abilities may also vary, depending on your school's demographic makeup and setting.

Fortunately for readers who struggle with comprehension and working memory (and fortunately for their teachers as well) working memory can be taught (e.g., Dahlin, 2011; Melby-Lervåg, & Hulme, 2013), resulting in actual brain changes in the frontal lobes, the brain areas typically associated with executive skills (Klingberg, Forssberg, & Westerberg, 2002; Olesen, Westerberg, & Klingberg, 2004; see Chapter 1 for more on brain anatomy and executive skills). Although a recent review of research on teaching working memory suggested the positive effects of working memory instruction do not necessarily transfer to other tasks (Melby-Lervåg, & Hulme, 2013), recent studies have begun to indicate otherwise. For example, Goldin et al. (2013) taught working memory (and planning) to third graders using game-like computer tasks over 7 days, and students' working memory improved significantly; further, the effects transferred to other, unrelated executive skills tasks. However, this study did not examine transfer to academic tasks. With respect to academic tasks, Holmes, Gathercole, and Dunning (2009) showed adaptive tutoring with the Cogmed Working Memory computer program (Pearson, 2014), which began with students' initial levels of working memory abilities and stretched them to the far reaches of their competence as instruction progressed, produced significant changes in 10-year-olds' working memory and mathematical reasoning with just 35 minutes of computerized instruction per day for 20 days. Likewise, Holmes and Gathercole (2014) taught working memory using the Cogmed Working Memory Training program (Pearson, 2014) in 50 9- to 11-year-old children with lowest academic performance in comparison to peers, which resulted in significant improvements in untrained working memory tasks, English, and math performance in comparison to peers without such instruction; students' English performance included "speaking, listening, reading, and writing skills" (p. 9), which suggests students' comprehension was positively affected by the computerized instruction. Finally, in the only direct test of the effects of working memory instruction on reading comprehension that I have found, Dahlin (2011) taught third to fifth graders with attention problems with a similar computer program for 30 to 40 minutes per day for 20 to 25 days, and found significant improvements in students' reading comprehension after 5 to 6 weeks, which persisted 6 to 7 months later.

The studies just described used working memory tasks that were modeled after traditional executive skills assessments of working memory, such as verbal or spatial complex span tasks. However, after reviewing research on working memory instruction, Melby-Lervåg, and Hulme (2013) suggested domain-specific working memory tasks, that is, tasks that have demands specific to the area targeted for intervention, provide better opportunities for improvements in targeted skills. Put another way, they found that if the goal of working memory instruction is to improve reading comprehension, then working memory tasks specific to the demands of reading comprehension would be most effective for intervention. We have already suggested ways working memory might be instantiated in reading comprehension, such as holding a mental model of a text's meaning in mind (storage) while continuing to decode the words in the text (processing). But what specific aspects of meaning making might occur in good comprehenders' working memory space? As Cain, Oakhill, and Bryant (2004, p. 33) noted, "Working memory is conceptualized as the work space where integration and inference take place." And integration and inference are areas where progress has been made in better understanding the specific contributions of working memory to reading comprehension processes. Further, we have also learned that irrelevant information may interfere with poor comprehenders' construction of coherent mental models of texts' meanings while reading (e.g., Pimperton & Nation, 2010). Each of these is described in the next section.

Research on Working Memory from a Reading Perspective

Readers' working memory abilities appear to support processes that involve linking or integrating information in text. For example, resolving ambiguities in text (such as understanding a pronoun's reference when the noun to which it refers appears quite a distance away, requires that one integrate or connect stored text information with newly encountered information in text. Other processes include updating one's mental model of a text's meaning, which requires that a reader store a mental model and then make changes to that model in response to new information gleaned while continuing to read (process) the text. Finally, as discussed above, inference making requires that one recognize connections between elements of text, connect elements of text that are sometimes separated by distance, or connect elements of text with one's own knowledge in order to generate insights that the author has not explicitly expressed in the text. Recognizing the connections between sentences in text activates areas in the VLPFC, which is associated with hot and cool executive skills and simple, maintenance working memory tasks (Ferstl & von Cramon, 2001; Fletcher & Henson, 2001). The following paragraphs review research on each of these specific ways that working memory supports reading comprehension.

Resolving Ambiguities in Text

Ambiguity in text can arise for a number of reasons, such as poor grammar that makes text difficult to interpret. For example, I have a humorous plaque in my office to remind students of the importance of using proper grammar and punctuation in their writing that says the following.

LET'S EAT GRANDMA
LET'S EAT, GRANDMA
COMMAS SAVE LIVES

The first sentence, which is missing a very important punctuation mark, has an ambiguous meaning because of errors in construction. With the comma in place, readers understand that the sentence is not a call to eat one's grandparent but rather a call to that grandparent to come and eat. Let's assume that the texts that we provide our students are not ambiguous because of errors in construction. Even without such errors, there are a few ways that texts can still be ambiguous for readers.

AMBIGUOUS WORDS

First, readers may discover that words with multiple meanings—or words for which they do not yet know meanings—can produce ambiguity in text. In fact, 9- to 10-year-old poor comprehenders are significantly worse at inferring word meanings from the context of stories than peers with better comprehension, and such inference-making ability is related to complex working memory (Cain et al., 2004). Furthermore, Cain, Oakhill, and Elbro (2003) observed similar difficulties in 7- to 8-year-old children with poor comprehension skill, especially when the new words and the contextual information important for inferring meaning were separated by distance. When there is greater distance between a new vocabulary word and the contextual information necessary to define it, readers must hold the word or context in mind (storage) while continuing to read up to the point **R.CCR.1,** where the relevant counterpart appears in text (processing), then link that **R.CCR.4** new word with its meaningful context.

I should note that adults with poor reading comprehension demonstrate similar problems understanding ambiguous words. In comparison to peers with better comprehension, they are not as good at distinguishing inappropriate meanings for words with multiple possible meanings (e.g., accepting *jam* as the edible spread and rejecting *jam* as in *traffic jam*) as well as distinguishing between alternate forms of homophones (accepting *hear* and rejecting *here*). In each of these cases, the reader must keep in mind the contextual information that fosters the correct interpretation of the ambiguous word while continuing to read the text (Gernsbacher & Faust, 1991). Clearly, these simultaneous storage and processing operations draw on complex working memory.

AMBIGUOUS IDEAS

Similar issues emerge when parts of text create ambiguities in meaning. Yuill et al. (1989) compared 7- to 8-year-old good and poor comprehenders on the numerical complex working memory task described earlier in this chapter. Then the students were tested on their ability to resolve ambiguities in text. For example, readers might be surprised when reading a narrative about a student who was praised for achieving tenth place in a spelling bee. This is an ambiguous idea for readers because tenth place doesn't sound very impressive under typical circumstances. However, once readers encounter additional information in text that indicates that there were originally 250 contestants in the districtwide spelling bee, the ambiguous information makes sense: tenth place out of 250 students is pretty impressive. This kind of ambiguity resolution puts the same kinds of demands on readers as resolving ambiguous words: readers must hold the anomalous piece of information in mind (storage) while continuing to read the text (processing), and then they must locate the relevant, additional information and integrate that with the initial ambiguous reference (more processing). The poor comprehenders performed significantly more poorly on the complex working memory task. Likewise, they were worse at ambiguity resolution when the initial ambiguous statement and **R.CCR.1,** the disambiguating information were separated in text by two sentences (as **R.CCR.4** opposed to being directly adjacent to one another).

ANAPHORA

Finally, individual words or phrases also may be ambiguous because they refer to other parts of a text to ensure that early parts of text connect well to later parts of text. We call this text cohesion. For example, consider the following sentence:

> *Sally loves to go to the park with Jane because she always pushes Sally very high on the swings.*

In this sentence, the pronoun *she* refers to Jane, but readers must infer that reference. However, in typical conversation, we would probably say the following:

> *Sally loves to go to the park with Jane because she always pushes her very high on the swings.*

With two pronouns to resolve, and with the gender of all possible referents and pronouns being female, this version presents an even more difficult inferential problem for readers or listeners. Oakhill and Yuill (1986) found that 7- to 8-year-olds with poor comprehension had difficulty resolving pronouns in simple contexts, such as the first example sentence, and their difficulties were more pronounced with more complex referential relationships, such as those introduced with ambiguities of pronoun gender, as in the second example sentence.

In the preceding examples, each pronoun is an anaphoric device, or a referential device that calls attention to a previous portion of text in order to preserve text cohesion (Yuill & Oakhill, 1988). Anaphoric devices (or anaphora) come in four varieties: reference, ellipsis, substitution, and lexical (Yuill & Oakhill, 1988, p. 173); see Table 5.1 for definitions and examples of each of these. (Also see Yuill & Oakhill, 1988, for additional examples and Halliday & Hasan, 1976, for additional explanation of the role of anaphora in preserving text cohesion.) Yuill and Oakhill (1988) found that poor comprehenders were worse at resolving each of these types of anaphor, and distance between the anaphor and its referent typically compounded poor comprehenders' difficulties, especially with ellipsis. Ehrlich and colleagues found similar differences in anaphoric processing between elementary school-age, French-speaking good and poor comprehenders (Ehrlich & Remond, 1997; Ehrlich, Remond, & Tardieu, 1999; Megherbi & Ehrlich, 2005), suggesting that poor comprehenders' difficulties with anaphora seem to be pervasive, regardless of the language of text and instruction.

> *Anaphora*: referential devices that call attention to previous portions of text in order to preserve text cohesion.

R.CCR.1, R.CCR.4

Fortunately, there is some evidence that we can teach students to resolve anaphors with positive impacts on students' reading comprehension by providing them

TABLE 5.1. Definitions and Examples of Four Kinds of Anaphoric Devices That Preserve Cohesion in Text

Type	Definition	Example
Reference	Pronouns that refer a reader back to a person or object	*The rabbit nibbled lettuce and carrots, then it darted under the fence to avoid running into the farmer.* (In this sentence, the pronoun *it* refers to the rabbit.)
Substitution	A word or words that replaces another word or words	*Jason turned in the homework, and then Mary did.* (In this sentence the word *did* substitutes for the words *turned in the homework.*)
Ellipsis	Similar to substitution, except that the missing phrase is not replaced by words, much as an ellipsis (. . .) permits one to omit words in a list	*Sharon asked if Kathy's dog was really a miniature poodle, and Kathy replied, "Yes it is."* (In this example, the reader must understand that the words, *a miniature poodle,* are implied but not present in Kathy's reply.)
Lexical	When words are linked in meaningful ways but that linkage must be inferred by the reader	*Bill collected a bunch of seashells, and then he emptied his bucket so that he could build a sand castle.* (In this example the reader must understand that Bill is *collecting seashells in the bucket* even though the text doesn't explicitly state that fact.)

explicit support for working memory processes. For example, O'Connor and Klein (2004) examined three different methods for supporting anaphora resolution in high-functioning, adolescent students on the autism spectrum. Typically, students with autism show the same pattern of reading skills as students with RCD: they have age-appropriate decoding abilities with comparably poor reading comprehension (Jacobs & Richdale, 2013; O'Connor & Klein, 2004). Of the three instructional techniques tested, anaphora resolution training, which involved highlighting the anaphoric devices such as pronouns in text and then explicitly linking them with their referents, produced significant improvements in reading comprehension. However, neither cloze completion nor asking prereading questions improved students' reading comprehension performance. Baumann (1986) demonstrated similar improvements, using an explicit strategy instruction intervention with the gradual release of responsibility model in a group of typically developing third-grade students. In a series of nine lessons, Baumann (1986) taught specific types of anaphora that are commonly found in narrative texts in elementary classrooms, using terminology that students would understand: "noun substitutes, verb substitutes, and clause substitutes" (p. 75). In each lesson, consistent with the gradual release of responsibility model, Baumann (1986) provided students a purpose for the lesson (i.e., he made them aware of the goal, important for planning, as described in Chapter 2 of this book), an example, an explicit explanation, and then opportunities for guided and independent practice. After the series of nine lessons, students were able to transfer their anaphora resolution skills to other texts, including their basal readers.

In sum, readers encounter many different kinds of ambiguous information in texts that require additional processing in order to make meaning from texts. To resolve these kinds of ambiguities, readers must hold the ambiguous text element(s) in mind (storage) while continuing to read (processing); then, they must locate text information that clarifies the ambiguous text elements and use it to resolve the ambiguity (more processing). Given the storage and processing demands involved in resolving text ambiguities, it is not surprising that complex working memory is related to this important comprehension skill (Yuill et al., 1989).

Updating Representations of Texts' Meanings with Relevant (and Not Irrelevant) Information

Another specific way that working memory affects reading comprehension processes is when readers must continually update their mental model of a text's meaning while reading. Holding a mental model in mind involves storage, which is one aspect of working memory. But, as individuals continue reading the text and encounter new information relevant to the main ideas in the text, they must **R.CCR.10** add that information to their stored model, either by incorporating the new information into the model's existing structure or by changing the model so that the new information can be integrated in a way that makes sense.

These activities are processing components of working memory and are essential for skilled comprehension. However, sometimes these updating processes go awry, such as when a reader misses important information entirely, focuses on irrelevant information in text, or incorporates inappropriate background knowledge into a mental model of a text's meaning. These kinds of mistakes are often called intrusion errors because the inappropriate information intrudes upon the reader's model of a text's meaning. Intrusion errors may be related to inhibition (or a lack of inhibition), which we discuss in the next chapter. However, some evidence suggests that intrusion errors may also be due to limited activation of a reader's relevant prior knowledge or simply a lack of relevant prior knowledge (McNamara & McDaniel, 2004; McNamara & O'Reilly, 2009). I mention them here because they have a critical impact on a reader's comprehension-relevant working memory processes.

For example, De Beni and Palladino (2000) directed a group of 8-year-old good and poor comprehenders, matched on intelligence, to read a passage for a particular purpose, and then they assessed the students on their recall of relevant and irrelevant information from the text. As you might expect, the poor comprehenders recalled less relevant information than the good comprehenders overall, and they recalled fewer relevant than irrelevant ideas from the passage. These difficulties spill over into other academic areas, as well. For example, children who struggle with arithmetic word problems (which are essentially short narratives with embedded mathematical concepts) recall more irrelevant information from problems when compared to their peers who are more skilled word problem solvers (Pasolunghi, Cornoldi, & De Liberto, 1999; see Table 5.2 for a list of working-memory-related behaviors that you may observe in students who struggle with reading comprehension). So, for reading tasks, this means that as poor comprehenders are building mental models of texts' meanings, they are more inclined to incorporate inappropriate information than their peers with better comprehension. When a reader updates his or her mental model of a text's meaning with the wrong information, comprehension certainly doesn't proceed as successfully as it could!

One area of reading research that suggests ways to support poor comprehenders' construction of mental models of text with the appropriate information is work that focuses on dual coding in memory. Dual coding theory proposes that skilled thinkers and comprehenders encode information in both verbal and visual forms, and the dual nature of the mental models we construct, both verbal and visual, helps readers focus on appropriate text information, integrate text information more effectively, and dual coding strengthens memory for text content (Sadoski & Paivio, 2013). The imagery strategy, in which we ask readers to visualize the events in a narrative, is effective because it provides a second way for

TABLE 5.2. Behaviors or Characteristics You May Observe in Students Who Struggle with Working Memory

Behaviors and characteristics	Source
Recall of irrelevant information in arithmetic word problems.	Passolunghi, Cornoldi, & De Liberto (1999)
Lack of activation of conceptual knowledge relevant to a text.	McNamara & McDaniel (2004)
Recall of irrelevant information after reading a text.	De Beni & Palladino (2000)
Mind wandering.	McVay & Kane (2012)
Cognitive inattention problems, such as forgetting things they had already learned, lacking interest in schoolwork, not reading up to par, and having difficulty with arithmetic.	Pimperton & Nation (2014)
Lower socioeconomic status; few economic resources.	Tice (2014)

readers to remember text information, but poor comprehenders are less likely to spontaneously use imagery when reading (Sadoski, 1983, 1985). When readers are given concrete, visual manipulatives (Glenberg, Brown, & Levin, 2007; Rubman & Waters, 2000), are asked to draw text events (Hibbing & Rankin-Erickson, 2003; Levin, 1973; Oakhill & Patel, 1991), or are asked to create mental images (Hibbing & Rankin-Erickson, 2003; Oakhill & Patel, 1991; Pressley, 1976) to support their construction of mental models of text, their reading comprehension improves.

Just as there has been little work investigating the role of updating in reading comprehension using working memory tasks designed for that purpose, there have also been few studies investigating reading-specific updating processes. However, a recent study investigating reading-specific executive skills training indicates updating can be taught using narratives the authors describe as *changing stories* (García-Madruga et al., 2013). Changing stories involve plot sequences that require students to track information that shifts throughout the course of the narrative, such as "the order of the horses in a race [or] the state of the scoreboard during a football match" (p. 161). García-Madruga and colleagues (2013) taught third-grade students to track these kinds of changing information by asking the students to report the current state of affairs in changing stories at multiple intervals while reading. Because the text information was continually changing, the correct answers to the researchers' questions differed at each question point. Practice with this skill and other reading-specific executive skills for 50 minutes per day on 12 days over 4 weeks resulted in improvements in reading comprehension for intervention students. Of course, because the study involved instruction on multiple tasks, we cannot attribute the changes in comprehension to the changing stories instruction alone. However, of the tasks taught in that study, that particular task captures best the kinds of updating required for skilled comprehension. See Figure 5.2 for a sample story that illustrates the kind of changing story García-Madruga et al. (2013) used to teach comprehension-specific updating.

Making Inferences from Text

Finally, as noted earlier in this chapter, making inferences is another process critical to skilled reading comprehension that relies upon working memory, and poor comprehenders are less good at making inferences than their counterparts with better comprehension (Bowyer-Crane & Snowling, 2005). In fact, inference making is so important for skilled reading comprehension that Cain and Oakhill (1999) argued that inference making is a candidate cause of reading comprehension. Over a decade later, they presented evidence that inference making does, indeed, predict comprehension performance from third to sixth grades (Oakhill & Cain, 2012), suggesting that good inference-making skills produce better comprehension as children progress through school.

R.CCR.1

Field Day and the Three-Legged Race

It was Field Day at school. Katie was excited to finally get to run the three-legged race with her best friend, Morgan. They stood at the starting line waiting for the teacher to blow the whistle to signal the start of the race. Three other pairs of classmates lined up beside them: Bobby and Sam, Jenny and Ashley, and Josh and Jamal. Katie and Morgan had been practicing for weeks, and they really wanted to win first place. Mrs. Jackson, their teacher, blew the whistle, and the girls rushed across the starting line ahead of their classmates. ✎1 Katie glanced to her left as she saw Josh and Jamal shoot past her and Morgan. ✎2 The boys were quick, but Josh tripped, which slowed them down. That gave Jenny and Ashley a chance to catch up, which put them neck-and-neck with Katie and Morgan. ✎3 Bobby and Sam pulled from behind and passed the four girls, as the crowd cheered them on. Katie and Morgan could see their friends along the finish line, which made them want to win the race even more! ✎4 With a sudden burst of speed, the girls shot past the leaders and won first place. ✎5

To Assess Updating in This Changing Story:

Each ✎ symbol denotes a place where students need to stop and answer a question about the story, which indicates their ability to track and continually update information about the order of runners in the race.

✎1: Who is in the lead now? (Correct answer: Katie and Morgan)

✎2: Who is in the lead now? (Correct answer: Josh and Jamal)

✎3: Who is in the lead now? (Correct answer: no one; Jenny and Ashley are tied with Katie and Morgan)

✎4: Who is in the lead now? (Correct answer: Bobby and Sam)

✎5: Who won the race? (Correct answer: Katie and Morgan)

Bonus: Who finished in second, third, and fourth places? (Correct answer: Bobby and Sam won second place, Jenny and Ashley won third place, and Josh and Jamal came in fourth place.)

FIGURE 5.2. A sample story to illustrate the type of changing story used by García-Madruga et al. (2013) to teach updating in reading comprehension. (Such stories could also be used to assess students' abilities to track and update mental models of text information while reading.)

Inference making can be assessed in students in numerous ways. For example, Oakhill (1982) compared the inference-making ability of 7- to 8-year-old good and poor comprehenders by reading aloud pairs of sentences to the students. Then she assessed whether the students recalled information that should have been inferred from the sentences. Consider the following pair of sentences:

Shelley forgot to bring her umbrella to school.
Shelley's homework was soaked by the time she got home.

You should have inferred that it rained on Shelley (and on her homework) on the way home from school. You also may have inferred that she walked home—or that she had a very long walk outdoors from her bus stop! The good comprehenders in Oakhill's (1982) study readily made such inferences significantly more often than the poor comprehenders. Similarly, when good and poor comprehenders were asked memory questions after reading stories, Oakhill (1984) found that the good comprehenders outperformed the poor comprehenders on inferential questions (but not on literal questions), even when the story texts were made available to students. Presumably, the presence of the texts should have reduced working memory demands for students, because the students could look back at the texts to help themselves remember text information, yet this didn't make a difference for the poor comprehenders in Oakhill's study. These findings suggest something more than working memory may be involved in inference making, such as cognitive flexibility in switching back and forth between the pieces of information necessary to make an inference or the planning abilities needed to perform all the necessary steps in inference making. Consistent with this notion, Cutting, Materek, et al. (2009) found inference making, assessed with the Test of Language Competence (Wiig & Secord, 1989, as cited in Cutting, Materek, et al., 2009), was related to complex working memory, assessed with a backward digit span task, as well as to scores on the Elithorn Perceptual Maze task, which assessed planning, organization, and monitoring. However, no studies have examined the relation of cognitive flexibility to inference making.

Whether one is making a text-connecting inference or a gap-filling, elaborative inference, text information must be stored while other, relevant information is found in text or in one's conceptual knowledge, and then the various bits of information must be integrated to produce a meaningful inference. Trabasso and Magliano (1996) identified three working memory tasks that support inference making in skilled comprehenders' think-alouds while reading:

1. Activation of readers' conceptual knowledge.
2. Retention of information in working memory.
3. Recall of relevant text and conceptual information.

These three working memory tasks were important for three kinds of inferences they observed in skilled readers' think-alouds: explanatory, associative, and predictive inferences, with explanation being the primary reason observed for inference making. Pérez et al. (2014) recently found that working memory contributed to explanatory and predictive inferences, but not to associative inferences in college students. The inference you made about Shelley encountering rain on her way home from school, above, required that you draw on both text and conceptual information to explain why her homework was wet (an explanatory inference). Thus, we should remember that to support students' inference-making abilities, we must support their abilities to engage in each of these processes so that they can produce text explanations that foster comprehension.

Fortunately, inference making can be taught, and the various methods that have been successful in this regard have provided several kinds of supports to scaffold the inference-specific working memory processes that are typically lacking in poor comprehenders. As I described briefly in Chapter 2, Hansen (1981; Hansen & Pearson, 1983) taught students to connect their own experiences to story content in a two-step process that made explicit the kinds of thinking good readers do when making gap-filling, elaborative inferences from narrative texts. See below in the instructional recommendations section for more information on this technique. Their training resulted in significant improvements in reading comprehension for struggling students.

Another method that has been effective for teaching inference making is helping children identify clues to the inferences that need to be made. For example, Reutzel and Hollingsworth (1988) taught third graders to highlight key vocabulary to support inference making in narrative texts using the gradual release of responsibility model, which resulted in significant improvements in comprehension for third graders, even up to 4 weeks later. In particular, they focused on helping students identify specific kinds of inferences to support their comprehension, such as identifying the location of an event, determining the individual who initiates an action, determining the time when something occurs, and others. I will highlight more of these when we discuss instructional applications in the next section. Similarly, Yuill and Joscelyne (1988) taught inference making by providing students with short narrative texts that required inference making and were written for the purpose of the intervention. They explicitly explained to the children that the stories contained puzzles because they were missing information, and that the children would be taught to look for clues in the stories to figure out what was happening. Thus, students were aware that they were to find missing information, and they had an explicit strategy for doing so: looking for clues. Good comprehenders showed no improvements after instruction, but instruction resulted in improvements in reading comprehension for initially poor comprehenders, such that they were indistinguishable from peers with initially better comprehension. Finally, McGee and Johnson (2003) demonstrated that explicit inference instruction on narrative texts was more effective than standard comprehension instruction, which involved reading texts and answering questions. Children were taught to look for clue words, ask themselves questions, and make predictions about story content. After the intervention, 70% of the poor comprehenders in the intervention group exhibited reading comprehension performance comparable to their peers with better comprehension. Each of these approaches provided R.CCR.1, additional scaffolded support for locating and holding relevant information R.CCR.4 in working memory to support inference making.

Laing and Kamhi (2002) adopted a different approach to supporting inference making and showed that having good and poor comprehenders think aloud while reading improved their reading comprehension significantly over a condition in which they listened to stories. Thinking aloud resulted in more correct and fewer incorrect inferences, probably because the students' own language helped them regulate their working memory processes, consistent with claims that language serves self-regulatory functions that foster executive skills (Bodrova et al. 2011; Cragg & Nation, 2010). Furthermore, consistent with Trabasso and Magliano's (1996) findings with college students, good comprehenders produced more explanatory inferences than below-average readers, and explanatory inferences were related to complex verbal working memory, assessed with a reading span task.

All of the examples of inference instruction I have described thus far have focused on narrative texts. Far less is known about inference making in expository texts. As I mentioned in Chapter 2, Elbro and Buch-Iversen (2013) tested an intervention for helping sixth-grade students make gap-filling inferences, which can be easily adapted for other age groups. These scholars focused in particular on students who have relevant background knowledge but fail to connect that knowledge to the texts they are reading, which is typical of poor comprehenders. The eight-lesson intervention required that students read short (100–200 word) expository passages that required gap-filling inferences. Students were taught to use a graphic organizer that helped them visualize how the text provides some information and how students themselves must also provide some information in order for comprehension to occur. In the first lesson, some boxes in the organizer were prefilled, and students completed the portion that corresponded to contributions from their own general knowledge. By the eighth session, students were generating the connections from prior knowledge to text independently, without the graphic organizers. Students who received this inference-making intervention were compared to students who received regular reading instruction (all instruction was provided by their teachers). Intervention students improved significantly in inference making and in reading comprehension. The most exciting finding was that even though instruction occurred with expository texts alone, the effects on comprehension extended to both literal and inferential comprehension as well as comprehension of expository and narrative texts! See Figure 2.3 in Chapter 2 for examples of how one might use graphic organizers to support gap-filling inference making. In these examples, students should supply general knowledge that the poles are colder than other places on Earth in order to make an explanatory inference about the text idea that some species are moving their habitats closer to the poles. Figure 2.4 in Chapter 2 provides blank organizers for your use with your students.

How Can I Apply This Knowledge to Classroom Practice?

The first step in helping your students understand and improve their comprehension-relevant working memory is to provide explicit instruction about this important executive skill. Recall the features of the gradual release of responsibility model:

for each executive skill we need to tell our students what it is, when good readers do it, and how it helps support good readers' understanding of texts (Duffy, 2014). Further, we need to model the ways good readers' working memory skills support comprehension, begin to share responsibility for these new kinds of thinking with our students, support our students in guided practice, and finally provide opportunities for independent practice, so that the responsibility for doing the thinking about the text shifts from us to our students (Duke & Pearson, 2002; Duke et al., 2011; Pearson & Gallagher, 1983). You may introduce working memory during whole-group instruction, but the various instructional techniques designed to support students' working memory in comprehension tasks may be better suited to small-group instruction so that you can better monitor each student's progress. You can explain working memory to your students as follows:

EXPLICITLY EXPLAINING WORKING MEMORY

"Today I'm going to tell you about another thinking skill that good readers have. Good readers have really good memories. And they are good at a specific kind of memory called working memory. Working memory is that space in your head where you hold information while you're doing something because that information will help you do it better. When you're reading, working memory helps you understand texts better. It helps you connect things in texts to knowledge you already have, and it helps you connect different pieces of text together. Both of these help you better understand what you read. Let me show you what I mean with an example from *Charlotte's Web* by E. B. White (1952, p. 7). In the first chapter of the book, after her father gave her a small pig, Fern (the main human character) was on her way to school. This is what the book says next:

> By the time the bus reached school, Fern had named her pet, selecting the most beautiful name she could think of. 'Its name is Wilbur,' she whispered to herself. She was still thinking about the pig when the teacher said: 'Fern, what is the capital of Pennsylvania?' 'Wilbur,' replied Fern, dreamily. The pupils giggled. Fern blushed.

So, tell me, when the book says 'her pet,' who does 'her' refer to, and who does 'pet' refer to? [Engage students in a discussion of these words and have them explain how they know that 'her' is Fern and the 'pet' is the pig.] Now, where was Fern when the teacher asked her a question? [Students should probably respond that she is in the classroom; if they say 'school' then ask them where in school. Engage them in a discussion of how they know this.] Now, when Fern said 'Wilbur,' her classmates giggled. Why did they do this? And why did Fern blush? [Students should indicate that they thought it was funny, perhaps indicating that Harrisburg is the capital of Pennsylvania, and that Fern was embarrassed.] So, the book doesn't say 'classmates' or 'students'—it says 'pupils'—yet you knew what I meant when I asked you about Fern's classmates. And the book doesn't say that the other students thought her answer was funny, it doesn't tell you Fern was embarrassed, and it doesn't tell you the real capital of Pennsylvania, either. To answer all these questions about this little quote from *Charlotte's Web*, you used your working memory skills. You matched 'her' to Fern and 'pet' to pig, you figured out where Fern was when the teacher asked her a question, you knew that the other students (whom the author called pupils, not students) thought Fern's answer was funny, you knew Fern was embarrassed, and you knew that 'Wilbur' was not the capital of Pennsylvania! All these answers required that you hold a lot of things in your head and do things like hold bits of information from the book in mind, recall your prior knowledge (about things like pupils, Pennsylvania, giggling, and blushing), connect ideas together, and fill in ideas that weren't even in the book! Those are complicated tasks, and yet your working memory helped you do them quite easily. Sometimes, readers have more trouble, though, using their working memories to help them understand texts in this way, so we are going to learn some ways to do that more easily on every text that we read."

Given the extensive research base on working memory and reading comprehension, there are many ways to support working memory in your students. You might try the following research-based techniques to support and strengthen your students' comprehension-relevant working memory skills.

Use Think-Alouds

As we discussed in previous chapters, thinking aloud while you are teaching and explicitly reminding students of the thinking processes involved in skilled reading comprehension will help them understand how to engage in those processes necessary to support comprehension (Duffy, 2014). But, having the students think aloud themselves is just as important because it supports their working memory skills. You can:

• Remind students that good readers are good thinkers who can hold many things in their working memories to understand texts, even calling things to mind that aren't in the texts at all! Explicit reminders and questions about these thinking R.CCR.10 processes throughout the instructional day will support your students' ability to engage in these processes independently.

• Read aloud excerpts of texts and verbally express all of the things in your own working memory that enable you to understand those excerpts, such as how you make the inferences you do; connect pronouns to the appropriate referents; draw on your own prior knowledge, etc. See the example in the anaphora section below. Also see the example from *Charlotte's Web*, above.

• Have students think aloud about their own working memory processes, explaining how they know (or infer) particular things about texts, which can support and strengthen their working memory abilities (Kray & Ferdinand, 2014), increase inference making, and improve reading comprehension, especially for struggling comprehenders (Laing & Kamhi, 2002). Recall from our discussion of executive skills in Chapter 1 that executive skills are related to language abilities, and language serves self-regulatory functions, allowing children to gain increasing control over behaviors as they talk themselves through tasks (Bodrova et al., 2011; Cragg & Nation, 2010; Marcovitch et al., 2008). Once children get older, they are SL.CCR.1, less inclined to engage in the private speech characteristic of very young SL.CCR.6, children; thus, thinking aloud provides an avenue to help students engage R.CCR.10 in this important behavior that strengthens executive skills.

- Stop students periodically when they are reading and ask them what things are in their working memories that help them understand a particular text in a certain way.

Practice Working Memory Skills

To provide opportunities for students to practice their working memory skills, you can incorporate activities for this purpose into your instructional day, perhaps as daily opening activities or transitional activities.

How to Introduce Working Memory Practice

"Remember when we talked about working memory, and I showed you how you can hold many things in mind to help you understand texts? Well, we are going to practice using our working memories to make them stronger. Just like with sports or music, practice makes us better. One of the ways we can do that with working memory is to play games that make us hold things in mind while we are doing something else. Today's game is called _____." [Introduce one of the games or other activities listed below.]

- At the beginning of this chapter I described two games, the Name Game and Johnny Has an Apple in His Pocket, that require students to practice the kinds of skills involved in working memory; you can have students play these games or variations of these activities to practice working memory skills.

- You can have students practice the reading span task, using sentences such as those in Figure 5.1 and assess their reading span (i.e., the number of ending words they can recall from the sentences).

- You can generate a list of sentences, or have students generate sentences for this purpose, and require students to determine the truth or falsity of sentences while remembering the last word of each (i.e., a variation on the reading span task). Then quiz students on their memories for the last words in the lists of sentences. You could vary this activity by using lists of digits, as in a digit span task, or any of the other complex working memory tasks described earlier in this chapter.

- Using these techniques, you could assess how many items students can recall at the beginning of the academic year, and then challenge them to try to increase that number (competing with their own scores) as the school year progresses.

Practice Updating in Working Memory

When we read, we must continually update our mental model of a text's meaning as we encounter new information in text. This kind of updating is not captured in traditional complex working memory tasks. Thus, you may also want to have your students practice updating, which requires that they track information and adjust it while engaged in a task.

How to Introduce Updating Practice

"You know how we've been practicing working memory? Well, today I'm going to show you a special aspect of working memory that is really important for understanding what we read. This new skill is called updating. Updating is tricky because you have to hold some information in your head and then keep changing it as you hear new things. Let's try it. I'm going to say a list of letters slowly, and your job is to remember the last three things I say. My list is longer than three letters, so you have to pay attention and keep updating what you know about the last three items in my list. [Read aloud this list slowly: Z K R N U F.] OK, so what were the last three things I said? [They should respond: N U F.] You had to keep ZKR in your head, then change to KRN, then finally update to NUF. This is like what happens when we read; we hold information from a book in our heads and we keep adding to it or changing it as we read through the text and get new information."

- Have your students track the "last three" items in randomly arranged lists of letters (or numbers) that you read aloud slowly; have them do this mentally, updating as you read aloud, and then have them write their "last three" items on an index card to assess their updating ability. You can use lists like those in Figure 5.3 for this purpose; read them aloud at a rate of one letter every 2 seconds. To generate more lists of random letters (or numbers, or both) try this link: *www.dave-reed.com/Nifty/randSeq.html.*

- Use changing stories, such as the one in Figure 5.2, to foster and assess
R.CCR.10   updating in your students.

Teach Students How to Resolve Ambiguity in Language

There are many ways that ambiguous language places demands on readers' working memories. To introduce ambiguous language, you might say the following:

How to Introduce Ambiguous Language

"Sometimes when we read, parts of the text are confusing because we can't tell what they mean. Sometimes we don't know what words mean because they are new to us, and we have to look around in the text for clues to help us understand those words. That requires our working memories because we have to connect different pieces of text together to figure out new words. Other times, words have multiple meanings, like the word *bank*. Can anybody tell me what the two meanings of *bank* are? [Solicit responses and ask them

List Length	Random Letters
3	B H N X N S O P A
4	B W K Q P M I G J V U Y
5	S X J N X Z V P U P R Y J U Y
6	R N Z Z R G A Y Y C P H O S I X V P
7	D L L M W P E R W R Y S M R C W Q A N O I
8	T Q O L Q R M B D C H O K M V Q K C T O E Q T H
9	M W Q N Z X I E W C W R S C V G D E N G R U D Z S M Y

FIGURE 5.3. Lists of random letters to use for strengthening and assessing updating in your students.

why multiple meanings might cause trouble in understanding texts. Lead them to an appropriate response.] That's right, if we think of the wrong word meaning while reading, we may be confused about what we're reading. So, we have to use our working memories to link pieces of information from the text to things we already know about words' meanings to figure out which meanings to choose for words. For example, if I'm reading about Tom and Huck paddling downstream on a raft and encounter the word *bank*, I can use the ideas from the text about the stream and water to help me figure out **R.CCR.4** that I should choose the meaning for *bank* that refers to the sides of a body of water instead of the place that keeps money."

To teach students to resolve ambiguous language, you might do the following:

• Preread texts and identify words that may give your students trouble; plant new vocabulary in text discussions before your students read them so that the meanings will be activated in memory.

- Explicitly teach students to infer word meanings from context, thinking aloud so that they see the kinds of text clues you use to infer unfamiliar words' meanings. Teach multiple word meanings explicitly and have students distinguish between the different meanings for words in ways that require active processing of both, such as writing sentences and drawing pictures to illustrate both, or writing short narratives that incorporate both uses of the words' meanings. Consider using the following text as an example. In *Sock Monkey Goes to Hollywood* (Bell, 2003, p. 6), the text says:

> "But Sock Monkey had been very active over the years. . . . [The text shows several illustrations of Sock Monkey engaging in activities that would make one quite dirty, such as jumping into a pile of leaves, sliding into home plate, painting, and jumping in muddy puddles.] and he had never, not once in his life, ever taken a bath. Never. Now he was downright filthy."

- Your students may not have heard the word "filthy" before. Engage them in a discussion of this word, and explain the clues you used to infer that it means dirty: Sock Monkey has been very active, he has *never* taken a bath, and the pictures show many different activities that we know from personal experience cause one to be quite dirty, especially when one hasn't had a bath. Next, engage your students in a discussion of the word *downright*, which might also be unfamiliar to

W.CCR.4 them. Have your students use text clues to infer that the word could be a synonym for the words *very, completely,* or *totally.*

- Teach homonyms (words with the same spelling and different meanings) and homophones (words that sound the same but have different spellings, such as *there, their,* and *they're*) explicitly so that students are aware of the multiple meanings and spellings they may encounter in texts.

- Use read-alouds to teach ambiguous language. I listed some books in Chapter 4 that help students focus flexibly on multiple meanings of words; those can also be used to teach students how to resolve ambiguous language in text. The following additional children's books may be useful for this purpose.

  o *Parts; More Parts;* and *Even More Parts* (Arnold, 2000, 2003, 2007)
  o *How Much Can a Bare Bear Bear?* (Cleary, 2007)
  o *Miss Alaineus: A Vocabulary Disaster* (Frasier, 2000)
  o *The King Who Rained* (Gwynne, 1988)
  o *Amelia Bedelia* (Parrish, 1963)
  o *Eats, Shoots and Leaves: Why, Commas Really Do Make a Difference!* (Truss, 2006)
  o *Punctuation Takes a Vacation* (Pulver, 2004)

- Have students keep a page in their journals (or a section on the word wall) of words that have multiple meanings as well as words that sound the same but have multiple spellings; this activity will make students more aware of the existence of these words and motivate them to track those words in their reading.

• Have students write sentences, paragraphs, or journal entries that include ambiguous words, such as homonyms or anaphora, to assess their under- standing of ambiguous language.   **W.CCR.4**

Teach Anaphor Resolution

Table 5.1 lists four kinds of anaphoric devices that may pose problems for students who struggle with reading comprehension or working memory because they require that students know how to link different words or phrases across distance in text to preserve coherence in meaning. Fortunately, these can be taught! To explain anaphora, you might say the following:

How to Introduce Anaphora

"Sometimes writers use words or phrases that substitute for other parts of text to help us connect early parts of text with later ones so that they make more sense. For example, . . ."

• Explicitly teach students about the four kinds of anaphoric devices listed in Table 5.1.

• Read aloud passages of text that include anaphora, and then think aloud to demonstrate how you resolved each of them. Here is a text you could use for that purpose (also see the example from *Charlotte's Web*, above). In *The Sunsets of Miss Olivia Wiggins* (Laminack, 1998, p. 3), the text says,

> "Miss Olivia?" the nurse spoke softly. "There is a lovely sunset this after- noon. I'll move you over here where you can enjoy it." And, he pushed her   **R.CCR.1,**
> wheelchair to the west windows."   **R.CCR.4**

• You have six examples of ambiguity in this short quote, and you can explicitly describe each to your students so that they understand how you made each of these connections in your working memory:

1. The pronoun *you* refers to Miss Olivia.
2. The adverb *here* refers to the west windows mentioned later in the quote.
3. The pronoun *it* refers to the sunset.
4. The pronoun *he* refers to the nurse.
5. *He* is also ambiguous because it defies gender expectations for nurses.
6. The pronoun *her* refers to Mss Olivia.

• Following Baumann (1986), use the gradual release of responsibility model to teach specific types of anaphora that are commonly found in narrative texts in elementary classrooms, using simpler terminology that young students will readily understand: "noun substitutes, verb substitutes, and clause substitutes" (p. 75). In each lesson, provide students a purpose for the lesson (i.e., make them aware of the goal, important for planning, as described in Chapter 2 of this book), an example, an explicit explanation, and then opportunities for guided and independent practice.

• Following O'Connor and Klein (2004), teach students to highlight the anaphoric devices such as pronouns in text and then explicitly link them with their referents; checking their highlighting provides a means for assessment of their knowledge; for advanced students, you might try having them highlight different types of anaphora (from Table 5.1) with different colors or different symbols (e.g., underline, circle).

Support and Teach Inference Making

Reading comprehension relies on inference making because authors cannot write down all that readers need to know to understand texts. Thus, readers must draw on their own conceptual knowledge (one of the reasons organization is important to comprehension; see Chapter 3) or make connections between disparate text elements to achieve understanding.

R.CCR.1

How to Introduce Inference Making

"One important way our working memories help us to understand what we read is that they help us make inferences from texts. Authors can't tell us everything we need to know to understand what we read; in fact, they expect us to make connections and fill in gaps to get texts' meanings. There are two kinds of inferences we can make. One happens when we use what we already know to fill in missing information in a text. These are called gap-filling inferences. The second is when we make connections from one idea in text to another to understand the text better. Today, we are going to work on . . ."

Gap-Filling Inferences

Gap-filling inferences are like puzzles readers need to solve, using their own knowledge. However, readers can run into difficulty when they lack knowledge necessary for inference making. Most of what we know about gap-filling inferences has been examined in narrative text. The following activities can support your students' gap-filling inference making.

NARRATIVE TEXTS

• Sometimes children don't make the connections necessary for comprehension because they don't access knowledge that they already possess; ensure that students' background knowledge is sufficiently activated prior to reading a text by engaging them in a picture walk (for younger students) or a discussion of text themes, concepts, and ideas prior to reading.

- Other students may not have the relevant background knowledge necessary to support comprehension; young readers and readers from impoverished backgrounds may lack the knowledge necessary for this task. In these cases, you should provide relevant background knowledge in a class discussion or via a read-aloud to ensure students have the information they need to fill gaps in texts.

- Following Hansen (1981; Hansen & Pearson, 1983) you can teach gap-filling inference making by explicitly showing students how they can connect their lives and personal experiences to the stories that they are reading. For each lesson the teacher should select a text and engage children in interactive discussions about the students' personal experiences related to story content. Then, the next day, the teacher introduces the selected story and scaffolds students' connections of their own experiences to the stories, explicitly building on the students' specific personal experiences that they had shared in the previous lesson.

EXPOSITORY TEXTS

- Recently, Elbro and Buch-Iversen (2013) demonstrated that we can teach gap-filling inference making in expository text by showing students, using graphic organizers, how their own knowledge can fill in the missing ideas in text. Their technique improved students' comprehension of expository and narrative texts. Figure 2.4 in Chapter 2 provides blank organizers that you can use with your students to help make gap-filing inferences in both expository and narrative texts; Figure 2.3 provides an example of how this might be done, using expository texts.

Text-Connecting Inferences

Similar to the work on gap-filling inferences, most work on text-connecting inferences has been done with narrative texts. You might try one of the following research-tested techniques to help your students make the text connections necessary to support inference making.

- Following Reutzel and Hollingsworth (1988), you can have your students highlight key vocabulary to support inference making in narrative texts using the gradual release of responsibility model. In particular, over a series of lessons, they focused on helping students identify specific kinds of inferences (from Johnson & von Hoff Johnson, 1986) to support their comprehension, such as:
  - Identifying the location of an event.
  - Determining the individual who initiates an action.

- o Determining the time when something occurs.
- o Identifying a character's action.
- o Identifying an instrument that produced a result.
- o Identifying a category to which something belongs.
- o Identifying an object.
- o Determining cause–effect relations.
- o Determining the problem–solution structure in a narrative.
- o Inferring the feelings or attitudes that produce behaviors (I will say more about these kinds of inferences in Chapter 7.).

• After being taught inferences of each type, over 19 lessons, third graders' comprehension of narrative texts improved significantly and transferred to new texts.

• Following Yuill and Joscelyne (1988) and McGee and Johnson (2003), you can explain to your students that stories contain puzzles because they are missing information, and then teach them to look for clues in the stories to figure out what is happening; questions to support clue-seeking might include "Wh- questions," such as:

- o Who is doing the action?
- o What is happening?
- o Where is the story taking place?
- o When is this happening?
- o Why did it happen?
- o How did it happen?

McGee and Johnson added a prediction component to this intervention in which they used white tape to cover portions of text and had students make predictive inferences about the "missing" information; you could also use Post-it notes for this purpose.

• To incorporate writing, you might have students create pairs of sentences or short narratives that require inference making and then have students exchange their writings with peers; you can use those sentences or narratives to assess inference making in small groups.

W.CCR.2,
W.CCR.3,
W.CCR.4

Teach Students to Use Visual Information to Enhance Their Memory for Text

According to dual coding theory (Sadoski, 2008; Sadoski & Paivio, 2013), readers' abilities to construct effective, integrated models of text are enhanced when they encode information both verbally and visually. Visual supports have been taught in a number of ways.

- You can provide concrete manipulatives to support your students' abilities to imagine text content (Glenberg et al., 2007; Rubman & Waters, 2000), using dolls, flannel board characters, or paper cutouts to support visualization of action in narratives; three-dimensional models to support comprehension of science content (e.g., a model of a leaf, cell, molecule, or organ system); or maps to support understanding of historical or social events that involve geography.

- You can have your students draw pictures of text content as they read to help them encode information in both visual and verbal forms (Hibbing & Rankin-Erickson, 2003; Levin, 1973; Oakhill & Patel, 1991).

- You can teach your students to create mental images of text actions, events, and other content (Hibbing & Rankin-Erickson, 2003; Oakhill & Patel, 1991; Pressley, 1976).

What We Know and What We Still Need to Know about Working Memory

Working memory is essential for successful reading comprehension. Although popular notions of the role of working memory in reading comprehension have suggested that automatic decoding will enable successful comprehension by freeing working memory space, research suggests automatic decoding does not guarantee successful reading comprehension for many students. Many specific activities that support comprehension occur in working memory, such as resolving ambiguities, integrating information, and inference making. These can be taught with positive effects on students' reading comprehension.

These findings are encouraging, but more work is needed to provide a richer understanding of the role of working memory across text genres and the kinds of interventions that may work to improve reading-specific working memory in our students in multiple genres. For example,

- Updating tasks appears to reflect the kinds of meaning updates readers must perform to adjust their models of text meaning while they read, but we have very little research on the relation of this important skill to successful reading comprehension.

- We need much more research on ambiguity resolution, integration, and inference-making processes in informational texts. Because informational text structures vary widely and are different from those of narrative texts (see Chapter 3), we need to investigate how these processes operate in informational texts so that we can develop interventions to target these processes in our students.

- We also need more research on the role of other executive skills in inference making beyond just working memory, because even when poor comprehenders are provided the text to support inference making (and relieve memory demands), they perform more poorly on inferential comprehension questions (Oakhill, 1984).

- Finally, following the innovative work of García-Madruga et al. (2013), we need more work on reading-specific interventions to improve working memory as well as studies that tease apart the different tasks and components that support reading-specific working memory. García-Madruga and colleagues (2013) administered several reading-specific tasks to target multiple comprehension relevant executive skills in one intervention, which produced significant improvements in students' reading comprehension; thus, we cannot determine which intervention tasks target particular skills and whether any of the tasks used were more (or less) effective than the others at improving specific executive skills or reading comprehension. Additional research along these lines will go far in helping teachers implement instruction that targets the critical executive skills that underlie successful reading comprehension.

CHAPTER 6

Inhibition and Impulse Control
Resisting Distractions to Support Comprehension

Upon reading these various extracts, they not only seemed to me irrelevant, but I could perceive no mode in which any one of them could be brought to bear upon the matter at hand.

—EDGAR ALLAN POE (1899, p. 87)

Have you ever been reading a text and become distracted by a word or idea that takes you away from your central purpose for reading? Sifting through the details of a text, we must separate the wheat from the chaff, so to speak. We must decide which details are relevant and which are not, like Poe (1899) in the quote above. But texts can take us in so many directions, and it's difficult sometimes, especially for inexperienced readers, to stay on track.

Consider your students. How many times has a student been reading a text aloud and stopped to relate a tangential personal story that was sparked by a picture or word in the book? Or how many times has one of your little readers blurted out a word that shares features with the printed text but is entirely inappropriate, such as reading *tricky* as *turkey*? Perhaps you've seen your students choose behaviors during a small-group lesson (like tilting their chair backward or fiddling with objects nearby) that really aren't appropriate for the task at hand, prompting a reminder from you to "Sit like a reader." If the students we encounter are similar, these scenarios have probably played out in your classroom more times than you can count! This chapter is about the kind of behavioral and mental control necessary to suppress irrelevant responses or information so that one can focus on the task at hand. And, for us, the task at hand is reading comprehension.

Sometimes readers must resist choosing inappropriate behaviors, like blurting out a word before fully analyzing the features of the text. This kind of behavioral inhibition is often considered a hot skill, because it can have social or motivational components and consequences. Some researchers also equate this kind of inhibition with self-regulation (e.g., Liew, McTigue, Barrois, & Hughes, 2008; McClelland et al., 2007; Zhou et al., 2012). I remember a peer reading aloud in one of my classes growing up, for example, who mispronounced the first syllable of *bugle* using a short *u* sound, as in *bug* (i.e., she said "buggle"). The giggles from some classmates clearly had negative social consequences; thus, she was likely motivated to inhibit such quick, but incorrect, pronunciations in the future. Other times, readers must resist interference from irrelevant information like word meanings that don't fit the context of the current text.

R.CCR.4

In Chapter 4 we saw that the ability to consider flexibly the multiple meanings of words or phrases is sometimes helpful in comprehension, such as when a text purposefully incorporates ambiguous language. The *Amelia Bedelia* book series and jokes and riddles that rely on verbal ambiguity are examples of texts that require flexible processing of multiple word meanings. Consider the following riddle, which plays on the different meanings of the homophones *sail* and *sale*.

Q: When is a store like a ship?
A: When it has a sale.

However, in most cases, a word's second meaning might impair comprehension, such as when one thinks of a grizzly bear when reading about someone who is having to *bear* a significant burden (unless, of course, that person is actually carrying a grizzly bear). In this case, comprehension is best served when readers can suppress the irrelevant word meaning in favor of thinking about the relevant one and weaving it into their mental model of text. This mental inhibition is considered a cool executive skill. Thus, inhibition has both hot and cool components.

What Is Inhibition and How Is It Typically Assessed?

Inhibition is the ability to restrain one's normal or habitual responses as well as the ability to ignore or suppress irrelevant or distracting information, and is sometimes called *inhibitory control* or *impulse control*. As this multifaceted definition suggests, the kinds of behaviors that have commonly been called "inhibition" really represent different types of inhibitory tasks (Friedman & Miyake, 2004).

This definition highlights two aspects of inhibition processes that have been labeled *response inhibition* and *cognitive inhibition* as researchers have begun to better understand the differences between them (Arrington, Kulesz, Francis,

Fletcher, & Barnes, 2014). Response inhibition is the ability to keep oneself from engaging in a typical, habitual behavior, one that researchers call "prepotent" because the behavior has a strong prior tendency to be expressed. This is the aspect of inhibition that is more closely related to self-regulation. As experienced readers, for example, we have a tendency to automatically read printed words when we encounter them. However, in the classic Stroop Task (Stroop, 1935; also

> *Inhibition*: the ability to restrain one's normal or habitual responses as well as the ability to ignore or suppress irrelevant or distracting information; sometimes called *inhibitory control* or *impulse control*.

see MacLeod, 1991, for a review), which is used to assess response inhibition, readers must inhibit their habitual tendency to read printed words and instead name the ink colors in which color words are printed. So, for example, if the words *red, green*, and *blue* were printed in the ink colors blue, red, and green, respectively, then the correct response is incompatible with your habitual tendency to read the words. Try this one. Name the ink color of the following word:

white

Given that people typically perceive white and black as opposites, I suspect it was difficult for you to inhibit your tendency to read the word and instead name its ink color, saying "black" in response to the word *white*. You might have hesitated for a moment, and you might have even started to say *white* but then self-corrected. All of these responses are typical in this kind of response inhibition task. People take much longer and make more mistakes when they must name the ink colors in which color words are printed than when they are asked simply to read the words printed in typical black font. This task can be scored in several ways: time it takes to complete the task (i.e., faster times indicate better inhibition), uncorrected errors (i.e., more errors indicate worse inhibition), self-corrected errors (i.e., more self-corrections indicate developing inhibition), and interference score, which is calculated as the difference between color word interference performance and performance on just naming patches of color or just reading words (i.e., smaller differences indicate better inhibition).

A second kind of inhibition captured in the definition above is *cognitive inhibition* (Arrington et al., 2014), which involves the ability to suppress or ignore irrelevant or distracting information intentionally so that one can focus on the task at hand. This kind of inhibition has been studied with directed forgetting tasks, in which people are told to ignore or forget information they encounter and focus on other information instead (Wilson & Kipp, 1998). You may have heard the expression, "Pay no attention to the elephant in the room," which is an idiom that indicates the listener should ignore an obvious fact. In everyday interaction, however, it's often quite difficult to ignore something as conspicuous as an elephant in a room! (Note: this is also a wonderful idiom to use in the ambiguous language lessons I described in Chapter 4.) Similarly, it's often difficult to ignore salient but irrelevant information in text.

Response inhibition: the ability to keep oneself from engaging in a typical, habitual behavior, one that researchers call "prepotent" because the behavior has a strong prior tendency to be expressed.

Cognitive inhibition: the ability to suppress or ignore irrelevant or distracting information intentionally so that one can focus on the task at hand.

Response inhibition tasks, which involve the ability to stop or cancel a behavior, are typically associated with activity in the VLPFC, the area of the frontal lobes that is active when we engage hot or cool executive skills (Aron et al., 2004; Rubia, Smith, Brammer, & Taylor, 2003). And impairment in the VLPFC results in failure of response inhibition (Chambers et al., 2006). In contrast, cognitive inhibition tasks, which involve the ability to suppress irrelevant information, are related to activity in the right DLPFC, the area of the frontal lobes associated primarily with cool executive skills (Bunge, Ochsner, Desmond, Glover, & Gabrieli, 2001). Thus, with inhibition, the VLPFC appears to be involved in choosing an appropriate behavior for a situation, or suppressing an inappropriate behavior, whereas the DLPFC appears to be involved in maintaining a mental model of a task, such as a model of a text's meaning, and suppressing information that could interfere with that meaning model (Bunge et al., 2001). These relations make sense. To choose an appropriate behavior is often a motivated, or hot, action necessary for appropriate social functioning in many situations. Maintaining a coherent representation in mind and suppressing information that could disrupt it is typically a purely cognitive, cool task.

A familiar children's game that taps response inhibition is Simon Says. In this game, one student is given the role of "Simon" who gives directions to the remaining players to engage in particular behaviors. For example, Simon might say, "Simon says, 'Put your finger on your nose.'" And all the players must follow that direction. The tricky part is that Simon varies the instructions so that sometimes the explicit phrase "Simon says," precedes the instruction and sometimes it doesn't. When Simon doesn't say "Simon says," the players must suppress the inclination to engage in the instruction provided, such as "Put your hands on your head." If players can't suppress the behavior, they are out of the game. So, this game requires response inhibition because players must regulate their own behavior such that they follow Simon's directions when she or he says, "Simon says . . .," but suppress or cancel a behavior when Simon does not. This situation is analogous to a reading task in which a student should suppress the inclination to blurt out an inappropriate response, speak out of turn, or engage in some other habitual but inappropriate action.

An example of a game that requires cognitive inhibition is the party game, "Taboo," produced by Hasbro. Players form teams, and one person is designated the "giver," whose role is to give verbal clues to teammates who must guess target words printed on cards. The objective is for teams to guess as many words as possible in an allotted time, and the team that guesses the most words correctly wins the game. However, this game has a tricky part too. The giver is not permitted to say the target word on the card or five related, taboo words. Thus, in coming up with clues to the target word, the giver must suppress certain words that would typically come to mind and think of other, less common ones, instead. For example, if the target word is *baseball*, the taboo words might be *base, ball, bat, glove,* and *home run*. This situation is analogous to occasions when readers encounter words with multiple meanings and must suppress the more common word meaning so that they can integrate the less common, but appropriate, word meaning into their mental model of the text's meaning.

Response inhibition is assessed with a wide variety of tasks that require students to suppress habitual behaviors and engage, instead, in other behaviors. I will describe some of the most common assessments of response inhibition in this section, and then I will describe other assessments in the research review later in the chapter so that you have an idea of the variety of ways you might assess response inhibition in your students. For example, the Stroop task, described above, which involves naming the ink colors in which opposing color words are printed, is one common assessment of response inhibition. The DKEFS *Color Word Interference* subtest provides a standardized version of this task that can be used with readers from ages 8 to 89 years (Delis et al., 2001).

With prereaders or beginning readers, the Stroop task is inappropriate because it depends on the tendency of experienced readers to read printed words automatically. With younger students or struggling readers, a commonly used and reliable measure is the Day–Night task (Gerstadt, Hong, & Diamond, 1994; Simpson & Riggs, 2006), which requires students to say "night" in response to eight pictures of the sun and "day" in response to eight pictures of the moon, presented in a random order. This task is based on the assumption that young students will automatically associate the sun with day and the moon with night; thus, the task is designed to require that students suppress a habitual response. The day–night task is scored based on accuracy and speed. So, students who struggle with response inhibition will typically respond to the series of pictures more slowly, and they will make more errors when they respond to the 16 pictures than their peers with better response inhibition.

Similarly, response inhibition is sometimes assessed with tasks that require students to engage in a behavioral response that is opposite that of the assessor. For example, Locascio and colleagues (2010) used a Conflicting Motor Response task and a Contralateral Motor Response task to assess response inhibition in 10- to 14-year-olds. The conflicting task required that the students show the assessor their fist when the assessor showed them a finger, and conversely, that students show a finger when the assessor showed them a fist. In the contralateral task, the students closed their eyes and the assessor tapped them on the shoulder. When the assessor tapped the students on the right shoulder, students were required to raise the left arm, whereas when the assessor tapped the students on the left shoulder, the students had to raise the right arm. Thus, in both of these tasks, students had to inhibit a more potent response (i.e., imitating the assessor and raising the arm that was tapped, respectively) and perform actions that were opposite those responses, with the number of trials correctly performed indicating the score on both tasks. In the Locascio et al. (2010) study, each task was scored as number correct out of 48 trials.

With respect to cognitive inhibition, or the ability to suppress irrelevant information, the Flanker Task is often used with children (Thorell, Lindqvist, Bergman Nutley, Bohlin, & Klingberg, 2009) and is even featured in the NIH Toolbox Cognition Battery (Zelazo et al., 2013) as a measure of inhibition (Bauer & Zelazo, 2014). In this assessment, students are typically presented with visual displays of five arrows on a computer screen, and they are directed to pay attention to the center arrow and respond by pressing a button to indicate the direction in which the arrow is pointing. The tricky part is that in some cases, the center arrow is pointing in the same direction as the arrows surrounding (flanking) it: a congruent trial. However, in other cases, the center arrow is going in a different direction than the arrows flanking it, and students must ignore the irrelevant information (arrows pointing in a different direction) and respond by pressing a button that corresponds to the direction of the center arrow alone; this is called an incongruent trial. See Figure 6.1a for an example of a congruent trial and Figure 6.1b for

(a) Congruent Trial

(b) Incongruent Trial

FIGURE 6.1. Examples of congruent and incongruent (inhibition) trials on a Flanker Task.

an example of an incongruent trial on the Flanker Task. Adults' reading-related cognitive inhibition is typically assessed with tasks that require them to ignore words or information that they have seen previously. I will say more about such assessments in the review of research, below.

Why Is Inhibition Important to Reading Comprehension?

To comprehend texts, readers must stay on task and focus on constructing meaning. However, there are occasions when irrelevant information may intrude on meaning construction processes, such as when irrelevant word meanings are more readily accessible than more appropriate, but less common, meanings. Or text content may remind readers of irrelevant situations, experiences, or knowledge, which intrude upon a developing mental model of a text's meaning. Finally, good reading comprehension also requires that readers inhibit impulsive responses when they are reading, such as jumping to incorrect conclusions about words' identities before reading all the way through words, which impairs comprehension. And readers must engage in particular physical behaviors, such as sitting still and not squirming in their seats, which also require response inhibition. Yet struggling readers may show behavior problems that interfere with their ability to focus on reading tasks (Jorm, Share, Matthews, & MacLean, 1986; Morgan, Farkas, Tufis, & Sperling, 2008).

With respect to the RRSG (2002) framework for reading comprehension (see Figure 1.1 in Chapter 1), inhibition is certainly a reader factor. As you will see in the sections that follow, readers vary considerably in their abilities to regulate their own behavior and inhibit inappropriate responses, and they also vary considerably in their abilities to suppress or inhibit irrelevant information when constructing models of texts' meanings. Additionally, text factors are related to inhibition, because some texts require more inhibition than others. Recall from Chapter 5 that expository text places greater working memory demands on readers than narrative text (De Beni et al., 2007), probably because expository text requires a greater degree of reliance on readers' conceptual knowledge for understanding (Best et al., 2008). Because expository texts have a higher degree of unfamiliarity to students, they are more prone to interference effects when readers' background knowledge is insufficient to support their suppression of inappropriate word meanings in text (McNamara & McDaniel, 2004). I know of no studies that have examined the interaction of readers' inhibition skills with their purposes for reading (the third factor in the RAND model), or with motivation or engagement in reading tasks. Thus, more research is needed for us to understand how combinations of these factors support or detract from inhibition processes and reading comprehension.

What Does Inhibition Look Like in Real Readers?

Brittany, a Student with RCD

By now, you're quite familiar with Brittany, who has exhibited problems with executive skills and reading comprehension throughout this book. And, true to form, Brittany seems to have trouble with inhibition processes as well, which has negative impacts on her reading comprehension. For example, she seems to have difficulty engaging in the kinds of behavior regulation necessary for effective comprehension, like sitting still in her seat and resisting temptations to look around at irrelevant objects or boisterous peers rather than at her text. When reading, Brittany has trouble finding the appropriate meanings for words, often impulsively selecting the first meanings that come to mind, which certainly impairs her reading comprehension. And Brittany has trouble discarding information that seems relevant to a text's meaning early on, but is later revealed to be irrelevant as the plot develops. Brittany could benefit from some support for inhibition processes, both response inhibition and cognitive inhibition.

Gabriela, a Good Comprehender

Now consider Gabriela, who has no trouble sitting "like a reader" while engaged with a text. Things do not easily distract Gabriela while reading, such as attractive objects or rowdy peers. And she seems to have a good awareness of appropriate R.CCR.4   word meanings for texts' contexts, even when the context is pointing to a less common meaning, as is typical in expository texts.

Her success in this regard is probably related to Gabriela's rich background knowledge, reflected in her vocabulary, which supports her understanding of texts and enables her to resist interference from irrelevant information. Additionally, Gabriela's background knowledge may make her more confident in selecting appropriate meanings for ambiguous words in expository texts. Finally, Gabriela is quite good at tracking narratives with complex plots, even when they require that she backtrack and discard information that she had initially thought was useful. Gabriela seems able to resist both behavioral and cognitive interference with reading comprehension, reflecting good response inhibition and cognitive inhibition processes.

What Does the Research Say?

The relation of inhibition to reading comprehension depends upon the type of inhibition being assessed, response inhibition or cognitive inhibition, as well as the types of tasks used to assess these different varieties. And, as with other executive skills, reading-specific assessments of inhibition seem to better capture the ways that inhibition impacts reading comprehension processes. In the sections below, consistent with other chapters in this book, I review research on the relation between reading comprehension and inhibition that used executive skill-based measures of inhibition first. Then I will move on to discuss reading-specific assessments of inhibition and their relation to reading comprehension.

Research on Inhibition from an Executive Skills Perspective

Like cognitive flexibility that we discussed in Chapter 4, inhibition has received relatively little research attention in comparison to other executive skills, such as working memory. Recently, however, as interest in executive skills and their impact on academic success has increased, we have seen a surge in studies examining the impact of inhibition and other executive skills on reading comprehension. But relations of inhibition to reading have varied, depending on the type of reading task and the type of inhibition task. Because there are so many different tasks used to assess inhibition, I will describe some of the tasks used in the studies I mention below so that you get an idea of the additional ways you might assess these important executive skills in your students.

Two recent studies used the classic Stroop (1935) color word interference task, described above, to assess response inhibition and its relation to reading comprehension. Both revealed significant relations of inhibition to reading comprehension in elementary-age students (Altemeier et al., 2008; Andersson, 2008). But cognitive flexibility was a significantly better predictor of reading comprehension performance than response inhibition from the first to the fifth grades in one of those studies (Altemeier et al., 2008). Additionally, Kieffer et al. (2013) used a number–quantity adaptation of the Stroop task to eliminate the necessity for students to read printed words. In the number–quantity task, students had to count groups of X's, count groups of digits where the number of digits was congruent with the quantity indicated by the digits, and then count groups of digits when the number of digits was incongruent with the quantity indicated by the digits (see Figure 6.2). They found that response inhibition assessed with the number–quantity Stroop task made a significant contribution to reading comprehension in fourth-grade students in addition to a significant contribution of cognitive flexibility (Kieffer et al., 2013). Taken together, these studies indicate response inhibition, assessed with Stroop-type tasks, is related to reading comprehension in elementary school students. In support of this notion, response inhibition was related to both decoding and comprehension processes in a recent meta-analysis of 75 studies examining literacy skills in preschool and kindergarten (Allan, Hume, Allan, Farrington, & Lonigan, 2014), indicating response inhibition may be a good predictor of reading comprehension from an early age. However, because this research area is relatively new, we need more longitudinal work to better understand how early executive skills predict later reading comprehension.

Congruent Condition 1: Counting X's				
XXX	XXXX	XX	Correct response:	3, 4, 2
XX	XXX	X	Correct response:	2, 3, 1
Congruent Condition 2: Counting Digits				
333	22	4444	Correct response:	3, 2, 4
1	333	22	Correct response:	1, 3, 2
Incongruent Interference Condition: Counting Digits				
2	444	33	Correct response:	1, 3, 2
555	222	44	Correct response:	3, 3, 2

FIGURE 6.2. Sample items to illustrate a modified Stroop Task based on number–quantity interference.

Studies using other behavioral measures of response inhibition suggest that it is more closely related to decoding or word recognition than to reading comprehension. For example, in a study of adolescent students, Arrington et al. (2014) found differential relations of word reading and reading comprehension to the two types of inhibition we have discussed. Cognitive inhibition, assessed with a word memory task that required students to suppress the interference of previously seen words, made direct contributions to reading comprehension, whereas response inhibition had direct effects on decoding ability. In this study, response inhibition was assessed with a stop signal task that required students to press buttons in response to letters (i.e., a button on the left of a controller in response to the letter X and a button on the right in response to the letter O) unless they heard a beep immediately following the letters, indicating that they had to withhold or cancel the expected response. Similarly, Locascio et al. (2010) examined response inhibition, assessed with the Contralateral and Conflicting Motor Response tasks, described above, in students with either RCD or word-reading difficulties (WRD). Response inhibition did not contribute uniquely to reading comprehension problems (though planning did, as noted in Chapter 2), but response inhibition contributed significantly to WRD.

Consistent with these findings, preschoolers' performance on a similar behavioral measure of response inhibition was related to these young students' phonological awareness and letter knowledge (i.e., precursors to decoding ability; Blair & Razza, 2007). Response inhibition was assessed with a peg-tapping task that required children to tap twice with a wooden dowel when the assessor tapped once, and to tap once when the assessor tapped twice (Blair & Razza, 2007). Thus, the preschoolers had to resist their more typical response to imitate the assessor and perform an opposing action instead, and their performance was scored as proportion correct out of 16 trials (eight one-tap trials and eight two-tap trials, presented in a counterbalanced order). Additionally, teacher ratings of children's self-control were significantly related to phonological awareness and letter knowledge, as well as to the peg-tapping measure of response inhibition, supporting the notion that response inhibition reflects students' self-regulation abilities. Similarly, when preschoolers' response inhibition was assessed with a Head-to-Toes task that required students to perform an action opposite of the assessor's instruction (i.e., touch their heads when told to touch toes, and vice versa), response inhibition predicted students' decoding-focused skills (e.g., skills like letter knowledge and word reading) and vocabulary knowledge; furthermore, growth in response inhibition predicted growth in both decoding-focused and vocabulary skills across the pre-kindergarten year (McClelland et al., 2007). Although McClelland and colleagues (2007) assessed vocabulary, they did not assess narrative or reading comprehension; thus, we cannot draw conclusions about reading comprehension from this study.

Finally, although few longitudinal studies exist that examine the relation of inhibition to reading comprehension, Liew et al. (2008) examined the role of response inhibition, which they also describe as a component of self-regulation (also see Liew, 2012), in reading and math from first to third grades. They used the Walk a Line and Star Tracing tasks to assess inhibition. In the Walk a Line task, students walked a 2.5-inch wide, 12-foot line first without any instruction and then with instruction to walk as slowly as possible. The difference in completion times between students' line walking with and without instructions, in seconds, indicated students' self-regulatory response inhibition. Star tracing was scored in a similar fashion; students were asked to trace geometric figures (e.g., stars) with and without instructions to work as slowly as possible. Response inhibition predicted students' reading performance in third grade; however, reading was assessed with the Woodcock–Johnson III Broad Reading subscale that included letter–word identification, reading fluency, and passage comprehension. Thus, we cannot tease out the specific effects of inhibition on reading comprehension. Because two of the three scores in the reading composite were related to word reading ability, I suspect inhibition may have been more highly related to word reading skills. However, that is a question that remains for future research.

Taken together, these findings indicate response inhibition or impulse control, assessed with behavioral measures, is typically related to decoding ability rather than reading comprehension, whereas cognitive inhibition and more cognitive-based measures of response inhibition, such as the Stroop tasks, appear to be more closely related to reading comprehension. Given that reading comprehension requires us to build coherent mental models of texts' meanings, it is no surprise that the ability to inhibit or suppress irrelevant information would be related to reading comprehension. Information relevance is key to coherence in building our understanding of texts. And such inhibition plays an important role in ensuring that other executive skills can be brought to bear on comprehension processes. For example, a recent study with college students indicated mind wandering (i.e., a lack of cognitive inhibition) mediated the relation between working memory and reading comprehension in these students (McVay & Kane, 2012). Put another way, students' inability to keep themselves from thinking irrelevant thoughts while reading impacted the ways that working memory could support their reading comprehension. So, the contents of our students' working memories are only as supportive of reading comprehension as permitted by our students' inhibition skills. That makes sense, because if irrelevant information is permitted to enter into working memory, it disrupts students' attempts to construct coherent, integrated models of texts' meanings. Work reviewed in the next section provides support for this notion.

Research on Inhibition from a Reading Perspective

Studies in this section focus mainly on readers' abilities to suppress or inhibit irrelevant words or meanings in memory and reading tasks. (Memory tasks are especially relevant to reading comprehension because we must remember the meanings of texts that we read.) The ability to suppress irrelevant information is critical to reading comprehension because as we read texts we encounter many ideas. Some of these ideas are important to texts' meanings and should be retained, whereas others are not useful to our understanding of texts and must be discarded. The ability to discard, ignore, or suppress irrelevant information enables readers to build a coherent representation of texts' meanings. But good and poor comprehenders vary in the ability to do this.

R.CCR.1

For example, De Beni, Palladino, Pazzaglia, and Cornoldi (1998) assessed college-age good and poor comprehenders who were matched on logical reasoning ability with an interesting complex working memory task. Students listened to short lists of four to nine animal and nonanimal words, and they were to indicate when they heard animal words by tapping a hand on the table each time they heard an animal word. The hand tapping ensured that the students actually processed the meanings of the words. After the lists were read, the students were asked to recall the final word in each list, whether or not it was an animal word. (This task is similar to the complex working memory tasks described in Chapter 5.) The poor comprehenders recalled significantly more nonfinal animal words, indicating that task-irrelevant information for which they had just processed the meaning was intruding into their working memory and interfering with their processing of task-appropriate information. Similar findings emerged from these researchers in other groups of college students (e.g., Carretti, Cornoldi, De Beni, & Palladino, 2004; Palladino, Cornoldi, De Beni, & Pazzaglia, 2001). These studies show that poor comprehenders have trouble inhibiting or deactivating irrelevant information in working memory, which compromises their ability to construct a task-relevant mental model—an ability that is critical for successful reading comprehension.

In a similar study with elementary school children, De Beni and Palladino (2000) found the same sorts of intrusion errors on a complex working memory task in a group of 8-year-old good and poor comprehenders, matched on intelligence. The poor comprehenders recalled more inappropriate words for which they had processed the meaning (i.e., animal words that did not appear in the last position in word lists). Further, in an updating task that required 8- to 11-year-old good and poor comprehenders to remember the last three words in a list, presented orally at a rate of one word every 2 seconds, poor comprehenders recalled more formerly relevant words, showing that they had trouble deactivating information in working memory once it became irrelevant to the task (i.e., it was no longer included in the set of three most recently presented words-to-be-remembered in the updating task; see Chapter 5 for more on updating) (Carretti et al., 2005). This would be analogous to readers who are unable to ignore irrelevant information that they previously had thought was important as they were reading through a text. Similarly, elementary school-age poor comprehenders recall more formerly relevant information that is no longer useful on word memory tasks (Pimperton & Nation, 2010, in 7- to 8-year-olds) and sentence completion tasks (Cain, 2006, in 9- to 10-year-olds).

These kinds of interference effects occur when students are reading connected text, such as sentences and short passages too. For example, when fourth- to sixth-grade students encounter words with multiple meanings, also called polysemous words, in sentences, they typically interpret those words in terms of their most common meanings, even when the sentence context supports the less common meaning (e.g., interpreting *bank* as a financial institution, even when the sentence context supports the secondary meaning, the sides of a river); and this effect is especially pronounced for poor comprehenders (Mason, Kniseley, & Kendall, 1979). Similar problems suppressing inappropriate or irrelevant information occur in adult poor comprehenders too (Gernsbacher & Faust, 1991).

With respect to methods for assessing suppression in longer passages, Borella et al. (2010) used an interesting text interference task that you might adapt for use with your students. They asked 10- to 11-year olds to read short (e.g., 125–126 word) texts printed in italic font, half without and half with distracter words related to the passage, printed in nonitalic font, and interspersed throughout the texts (see Figure 6.3 for an example). Overall, students had better comprehension and read more quickly on texts without distracters, and poor comprehenders had significantly lower comprehension for the texts with distracters, indicating that they were less able to inhibit attention to the distracting words in text. This conclusion was supported by the fact that poor comprehenders also had difficulty inhibiting interference from previously seen words in a list memory task in which words from previously learned lists were recalled inappropriately for subsequent

(a) Text without Distracters

Laura was excited that it was finally autumn. She loved seeing the bright colors of changing trees. So, she decided to go for a walk to collect leaves. She found her jacket, grabbed a bag for her leaves, and walked outside. As she strolled down the side of her street, she noticed that some of the leaves seemed to be moving. When she got a little closer, she realized that there was a small animal under the leaves! Laura carefully pushed aside the colorful, leafy blanket and found a tiny, meowing kitten. Gently, Laura scooped up the kitten and placed it in her bag to keep it warm. As she walked home, Laura decided to name the kitten Autumn. Finding her friend was a wonderful surprise!

(b) Text with Distracters

Laura colors *was excited that* fall *it was* trees *finally* colors *autumn. She* leaves *loved seeing* colors *the* fall *bright* trees *colors of* fall *changing* leaves *trees.* colors *So, she decided* leaves *to* fall *go for a walk to* leaves *collect leaves. She* trees *found her* leaves *jacket,* fall *grabbed* colors *a bag for* fall *her leaves, and* leaves *walked outside. As* trees *she strolled down* colors *the side* fall *of her street, she* leaves *noticed* colors *that some* trees *of the leaves* colors *seemed* trees *to be* fall *moving. When she* trees *got a little* leaves *closer, she* colors *realized* trees *that there* fall *was a small* trees *animal* leaves *under the* colors *leaves! Laura* trees *carefully pushed* fall *aside the* leaves *colorful, leafy* colors *blanket and* fall *found a* trees *tiny, meowing* leaves *kitten. Gently,* fall *Laura scooped* trees *up the* leaves *kitten and* colors *placed it* fall *in her bag* trees *to keep it* leaves *warm. As she* colors *walked home,* fall *Laura decided* trees *to name* leaves *the kitten* colors *Autumn. Finding* fall *her friend* trees *was* leaves *a wonderful* colors *surprise!*

FIGURE 6.3. A sample passage with and without distracter items to assess students' abilities to suppress irrelevant information while reading. (Following Borella et al., 2010, four semantically related distracter words appear in the 126-word passage, 15 times each, in nonitalicized font.)

lists. However, Borella and colleagues (2010) did not find any differences in good and poor comprehenders' performance on the classic Stroop color word interference task.

Taken together, these kinds of studies indicate that our struggling comprehenders may need practice distinguishing relevant from irrelevant information in texts and in suppressing irrelevant information so that they can focus on texts' meanings. However, research in this area has not progressed to the point that we have many intervention studies indicating how we should go about teaching our students to do these things. Clearly, we need more research in this area!

We have already discussed one study in previous chapters that has attempted to teach inhibition processes alongside other executive skill processes, conducted by García-Madruga et al. (2013). Recall that these researchers used several reading-specific tasks to teach executive skills related to reading comprehension, and they suggested that a number of their tasks tapped inhibition skills, including analogies, anaphora, tracking information in changing stories (see Figure 5.1 in Chapter 5 as an example), inconsistency resolution, knowledge integration, finding the main idea, arranging sentences in order, and arranging vignettes in order. Instruction on these and other tasks produced improvements in reading comprehension for third-grade poor comprehenders. However, the teaching of several executive skills was integrated in the intervention, so we are unable to determine the precise effects of inhibition instruction alone on students' reading comprehension. Furthermore, we have no knowledge of whether direct, executive skill-based assessments of students' inhibition are related to the reading-related tasks García-Madruga et al. (2013) used to teach inhibition; thus, we cannot be certain that those tasks are actually related to students' inhibition processes. Clearly, additional research is needed in this area, too!

How Can I Apply This Knowledge to Classroom Practice?

Despite the relative newness of research on inhibition processes in reading comprehension, there are several things we may be able to do to support these processes in our students, which I describe below. As with any type of comprehension instruction, these activities should be presented to your students in ways consistent with the gradual release of responsibility model (Duke & Pearson, 2002; Duke et al., 2011; Pearson & Gallagher, 1983). That is, you should provide your students an explicit explanation of this important executive skill while modeling how it's done, involve your students in inhibition activities while sharing the responsibility for this new way of thinking, provide opportunities for your students to practice under your guidance and support, and then finally provide opportunities for independent practice. You might consider explaining inhibition as follows:

EXPLICITLY EXPLAINING INHIBITION

"We've been talking a lot about how good readers are good thinkers. Most of the time, thinking really supports our understanding of what we read. But sometimes our thinking gets in the way of understanding! Let me explain what I mean. Sometimes, when we read words that can have two meanings, we think about the wrong meaning—the one that doesn't fit in the text. When we do that, we don't understand what we read as well as we could. Other times, words might distract us, and get us thinking about things that are not related to what we are reading, like when you start thinking of your own birthday party when reading about a character's birthday. So good readers are good at ignoring things that are not relevant or important for understanding a text. The ability to ignore things that aren't important to understanding texts is called inhibition. Good readers are good at inhibition. They are not easily distracted, and they are good at focusing on important information. We are going to practice our inhibition skills today. One way that you may have done this before is when you have played Simon Says. Why do you think Simon Says is a good way to practice inhibition? What do we have to ignore when we play Simon Says? [Allow students to respond, and incorporate their responses in your explanation.] Yes, that's right! When we play Simon Says, we have to ignore all of the instructions that don't include the words 'Simon says.' There are other ways we can practice inhibition, too, and we will practice some of those today."

To help your students become more aware of, and possibly enhance, their inhibition skills, you can try the following activities.

Assess and Practice Response Inhibition

As I noted earlier in the chapter, there are many ways to assess inhibition in our students. Providing students a variety of opportunities to practice their inhibition and impulse control may help them become more aware of these skills and may also help them improve in these areas. You could use the following activities for this purpose.

Response Inhibition Tasks

Although most purely behavioral response inhibition tasks were not always related to reading comprehension in the studies reviewed above (e.g., Locascio et al., 2010), children's skill at performing these tasks in preschool was related to their comprehension skills in preschool and predicted their reading achievement at later ages (e.g., Blair & Razza, 2007). Thus, we can assume that children who did not develop skill in response inhibition in their early years might benefit from practice in those skills later. If you suspect that your students have difficulty with response inhibition that might interfere with their reading comprehension, you could try some of the following tasks. Because these tasks are active, you may want to use them as transitional activities between focused periods of study or instruction to give your students additional practice in response inhibition while also giving them opportunities to get out of their seats and move or engage in game-like activities that would seem to students to be an enjoyable diversion (not practice with an executive skill).

• The Day–Night Task (Gerstadt et al., 1994) is a classic assessment of response inhibition that can be used to assess your students' inhibition in individual or small-group settings; you might also consider an adaptation that would permit a whole-class view of students' inhibition skills, such as asking students to give a "thumbs up" in response to a sad face and a "thumbs down" in response to a happy face.

• The Peg Tapping Assessment of response inhibition involves having students perform actions that are opposite the assessor's actions (Blair & Razza, 2007); when the assessor taps once on the table, the student should tap twice; conversely, when the assessor taps twice, the student should tap once. This task is simple to administer, and the materials (two wooden dowels) are easily accessible at any home improvement or craft store; furthermore, you could even use pencils to tap on the table.

- The Head-to-Toes Task used by McClelland et al. (2007) also involves performing an action opposite to that of the assessor. In this task, students should be standing. When directed to touch their heads, students should touch their toes; and when directed to touch their toes, students should touch their heads. You should present opportunities to touch heads or toes in a random order, and students' errors indicate their levels of skill at this task, with more errors indicating less response inhibition.

- The Walk a Line Task used by Liew et al. (2008) involves having students walk a 12-foot line that is 2.5 inches wide; you could create one of these with blue painter's tape on your classroom floor. Painter's tape is widely available and is easily removed from a variety of surfaces. First, have your students walk the line quickly; then, have your students walk the line as slowly and carefully as possible. The difference in walking time for these two line walks indicates response inhibition ability, with slower walking on the second step indicating more response inhibition; additionally, you may want to count missteps too, with steps off of the line indicating less response inhibition.

- The Star Tracing Task (also used by Liew et al., 2008) involves having students trace geometric figures, most typically a star figure like the one in Figure 6.4. First, have students trace the stars without instruction. Then, instruct your students to trace the stars as slowly and carefully as possible. Like the Walk a Line Task, this task is scored by examining the difference in tracing time between the two conditions, with slower times on the second condition indicating more response inhibition; additionally, you can count the number of times your students' pencils leave the lines of the figure, with a greater number of errors indicating less response inhibition.

- The Contralateral Motor Response Task used by Locascio et al. (2010) involved tapping a student on the opposite shoulder of the desired response; that is, when the assessor tapped the student on the left shoulder, the student had to raise the right arm, and when the assessor tapped the student on the right shoulder, the student had to raise the left arm. This task is probably easier to administer individually, but you might be able to modify the task for group administration by having a group of students face you and then having them perform the action opposite that of the expected mirror image. For example, if you raise your left hand, they would be inclined to raise their right hands, because that would be the mirror image of your action; instead, students should raise their left hands, showing they can inhibit the more potent response. Several trials should be administered (Locascio et al., 2010, administered 48) with more errors indicating less response inhibition.

- Similarly, you can use the Conflicting Motor Response Task administered by Locascio et al. (2010), which involved having the students perform an action

FIGURE 6.4. A star figure you can use to administer the Star Tracing Task.

that was opposite that of the assessor; thus, when the assessor showed the child a finger, the child showed a fist, and vice versa. This task could be fairly easily administered in groups, which would give you a quick indication of students' response inhibition ability. Similar to the Contralateral Control Task, several trials should be administered, with more errors indicating less response inhibition.

Stroop Tasks

Stroop tasks have traditionally been considered response inhibition tasks (Arrington et al., 2014); however, they are more complex than tasks that involve only behavioral responses (e.g., the Peg Tapping or Walk a Line tasks that we have discussed). When we compare Stroop tasks to other, simpler behavioral inhibition tasks, it becomes clear that they involve both response and cognitive inhibition components. For example, in Stroop tasks students must inhibit their habitual behavioral response to read words or to identify a particular quantity typically associated with a digit. Additionally, at a cognitive level they must suppress one feature of complex stimuli (e.g., the underlying meaning of words or digits) and instead process a different feature of those stimuli (e.g., the color or actual quantity of digits displayed) under conflict conditions. It is this cognitive component that may make Stroop tasks more likely than other response inhibition tasks to be related to reading comprehension.

- Because the classic Stroop Color Word Interference Task is significantly related to reading comprehension (Altemeier et al., 2008; Andersson, 2008) and easily accessible online, you may consider providing your students practice with this inhibition task. Simply Google "Stroop task" and click images. You should find many examples of color words printed in ink colors that differ from the color words' identities (e.g., the word *red* printed in green ink). Additionally, you can easily create your own Stroop Task materials. Recall that the task is typically administered in three steps that should correspond to three separate displays for students.
  - First, students name patches of color.
  - Then students read color words printed in black ink.
  - Finally, students name the ink colors of color words printed in colors that conflict with the color words' identities (e.g., the word green printed in blue ink).
- You can create three different pages to present each of these steps to your students, perhaps laminating them or including them in a notebook. With practice, your students should get better at naming the ink colors on the third step, making fewer errors, and completing the task in less time than they did initially.

• Similarly, the number–quantity variation of the Stroop Task, described above (Kieffer et al., 2013), reduces the decoding demands of the classic Stroop, and it would be relatively easy to construct similar items for practice or assessment for your students (see Figure 6.2 for examples).

• Once your students understand what they are required to do with a Stroop Task, you could make laminated pages that correspond to the different steps of each of these tasks and place them at a center. Students could administer them to each other, tracking both time and errors to indicate inhibition skill; by charting these abilities over time, or in the back of a journal, you and your students can track their progress as they strengthen their inhibition skills. Keep in mind that although Stroop task performance was related to reading comprehension in prior work, no studies have examined whether teaching this type of response inhibition can improve comprehension.

Assess and Practice Cognitive Inhibition Tasks

Cognitive inhibition tasks are more closely related to reading comprehension in the research literature reviewed above. Consistent with findings by Melby-Lervåg and Hulme (2013), this is likely because the cognitive inhibition tasks typically require students to focus on comprehension-specific elements, such as determining appropriate meanings and inhibiting inappropriate meanings in lists, sentences, or passages. Based on prior research, you might try the following.

• Because Carretti et al. (2005) found inhibition errors in an updating task, you might consider using updating tasks, described in Chapter 5, to assess your students' tendencies to recall formerly relevant items; the lists of letters in Figure 5.3 could be used for this purpose, and intrusions of letters that do not appear in the set of final three letters in each list would indicate difficulty with cognitive inhibition.

• Poor comprehenders have difficulty selecting the appropriate meanings for words with multiple meanings (polysemous words; Mason et al., 1979). Thus, to provide your students opportunities to practice this skill, you can create sentences that include ambiguous words, and have your students choose the appropriate meaning and justify their choice from the sentence context.

R.CCR.1, R.CCR.4

For example, consider the following sentence: the homonym *bee* is italicized and has at least two different meanings: the more common meaning, *an insect that makes honey*, is not appropriate for this sentence, but the less common meaning, *a group of people gathered for a specific purpose* (as in a quilting bee or a spelling bee), is appropriate and can be justified by attending to sentence features such as "contest" and "he won."

After the contest was over, Steve was thrilled to learn he won the spelling *bee*.

- To generate such sentences, you may need to consult a list of homonyms and homophones; consider the list at Enchanted Learning online at this link: *www.enchantedlearning.com/english/homonyms*. You might provide possible definitions below the sentences, or you might have students look up the various definitions themselves.

- As a variation on this activity, you could ask students to generate single definitions for polysemous words to assess their perception of the most common meaning, and then have them find alternate definitions and generate sentences with the less common meanings for the words; this would expand their knowledge base, which may better equip them to resist interference from more common meanings when they encounter these words in text (McNamara & McDaniel, 2004).

- Along similar lines, because expository texts have a higher degree of unfamiliarity to students, they are more prone to interference effects when readers' background knowledge is insufficient to support their suppression of inappropriate word meanings in text (McNamara & McDaniel, 2004). Thus, you might preread expository texts to find words that would promote interference effects because students would be less familiar with the words' alternate meanings. Then, you could discuss the unfamiliar meanings before reading the text or have the students engage in activities involving the less familiar word meanings in order to support their ability to select appropriate meanings and resist interference from the more common, but inappropriate, meanings.

- You might also consider playing "Taboo," described earlier in this chapter, or a variation of it, that requires students to inhibit common words associated with the target taboo word; this might be an appropriate activity for small-group instruction that engages struggling comprehenders in inhibition of common words and meanings, favoring and motivating attention to less common meanings.

- Following the work by De Beni and colleagues (1998, 2000), you can provide your students practice focusing on relevant information and discarding irrelevant information with the Animal Word Complex Working Memory Task; for this task, you need lists of four to nine animal and nonanimal words like those in Figure 6.5. Read the lists aloud, and have your students indicate when they hear animal words by tapping a hand on the table (or desk) each time they hear an animal word (recall that the hand tapping ensures that the students actually process the meanings of the words in the lists). After the lists are read, ask your students to recall the final word in each list; number of correct words recalled indicates complex working memory, whereas number of nonfinal animal words recalled indicates students' levels of inhibition, with more words indicating weaker inhibition skills.

- Furthermore, following Borella et al. (2010), you could give your students italicized passages with and without nonitalicized, semantically related distracter words (see examples in Figure 6.3); the difference in reading speed for the two

Number of Words	List	Correct Response (Final Word to Be Recalled)	Incorrect Responses That Show Lack of Inhibition
4	Apple Cat Rabbit Flower	Flower	Cat Rabbit
5	Cow Cup Bird Chair Monkey	Monkey	Cow Bird
6	Box Snake Paper Dog Horse Book	Book	Snake Dog Horse
7	Tree Mouse Bed Worm Bear Milk Chair	Chair	Mouse Worm Bear
8	Whale House Duck Crab Pencil Spoon Lion Pear	Pear	Whale Duck Crab Lion
9	Mail Picture Hen Turtle Fork Car Rat Pig Bag	Bag	Hen Turtle Rat Pig

FIGURE 6.5. Sample lists to be used in the Animal Word Complex Working Memory Task.

kinds of passages and the difference in their levels of comprehension for each kind of passage will indicate their susceptibility to interference, with more time and poorer comprehension on distracter passages indicating less inhibition. These types of passages may also be appropriate to provide students practice in cognitive inhibition while reading.

What We Know and What We Still Need to Know about Inhibition

Inhibition appears to play a critical role in reading comprehension in elementary students and adults, and is even related to comprehension in some studies of pre-school students. Inhibition comes in two varieties: response inhibition, which is typically a hot executive skill, and cognitive inhibition, which is typically a cool executive skill. Although response inhibition tasks are sometimes related to reading comprehension, predicting later reading comprehension when assessed early in children's development, they are more closely related to success in word decoding. Relations of inhibition to reading comprehension are more likely when the inhibition tasks involve a cognitive suppression component, such as in color–word and number–quantity variations of the Stroop Task, suppressing irrelevant meanings for ambiguous words, ignoring irrelevant meanings in memory tasks, and ignoring distracters when reading passages.

However, because this research area is relatively new, we still have much more to learn about the ways inhibition supports reading comprehension.

- For example, we need more longitudinal work to better understand how early executive skills, including inhibition, predict later reading comprehension assessed independently; most of the studies of this nature use reading composites that include decoding and fluency in addition to reading comprehension, or studies don't include assessments of reading comprehension at all.

- We need to better understand how inhibition impacts reading comprehension in specific ways, developing reading-specific inhibition tasks that can be used for assessment and intervention.

- We need to know which reading-specific tasks, like those suggested by García-Madruga et al. (2013), really tap inhibition processes in our students; one way to explore this question is to examine whether performance on known measures of inhibition, such as the classic Stroop Task, correlates with performance on reading-specific tasks believed to tap inhibition, such as analogies, anaphora, tracking information in changing stories (see Figure 5.2 in Chapter 5 as an example), inconsistency resolution, knowledge integration, finding the main idea, arranging sentences in order, and arranging vignettes in order (García-Madruga et al., 2013).

- Furthermore, with respect to the RAND framework for reading comprehension, we know that inhibition is a person variable, and there is evidence that inhibition may be required for some sorts of texts (e.g., expository texts) more frequently than others; however, we know little about how inhibition relates to motivation, engagement, and reading purpose.

- Finally, and probably most important for supporting our students' reading comprehension, we need more studies of the effects of inhibition interventions on reading comprehension, from teaching classic response inhibition and Stroop performance to teaching reading-specific inhibition processes; such interventions have the potential to go far in supporting struggling comprehenders' abilities to build coherent models of texts' meanings.

CHAPTER 7

Social Understanding

The Importance of Mind Reading for Reading Comprehension

What an astonishing thing a book is. It's a flat object made from a tree
with flexible parts on which are imprinted lots of funny dark squiggles.
But one glance at it and you're inside the mind of another person, maybe
somebody dead for thousands of years. Across the millennia, an author
is speaking clearly and silently inside your head, directly to you. Writing
is perhaps the greatest of human inventions, binding together people who
never knew each other, citizens of distant epochs. Books break the shackles
of time. A book is proof that humans are capable of working magic.
— CARL SAGAN (Sagan, Druyan, & Soter, 2000)

Books really are magic in that they take us into the minds of others. We can infer
an author's purposes, beliefs, and intentions, for example, just from reading the
words he or she wrote. Good comprehenders use information about authors' purposes to better understand texts (Pressley, 2002b). However, authors' minds aren't
the only ones we encounter in texts; and, understanding authors' purposes only
takes us so far in constructing full understandings of texts. Fictional texts, in particular, take us inside the minds of characters. We learn what characters are thinking and feeling, we predict characters' actions based on their thoughts and emotional states, and we make inferences about characters' beliefs, motivations, **R.CCR.1,**
intentions, and feelings to explain why they behave in the ways that they do. **R.CCR.3**

These kinds of inferences make texts interesting and engaging because we
can relate to the thoughts and feelings of the characters, which may be why children and adults prefer social stories to other kinds of texts (Barnes, 2012; Barnes
& Bloom, 2014). Despite these preferences, though, students in the elementary
grades have significant difficulty understanding characters' internal motives
(Shannon, Kame'enui, & Baumann, 1988) and focus instead on characters' actions
(McConaughy, Fitzhenry-Coor, & Howell, 1983).

As adults, we engage in this kind of thinking on a daily basis when we speculate about the reasons for others' behavior (e.g., when we come up with reasons why others don't return our phone calls, or when we try to figure out why another person is looking for car keys in the kitchen when we know the keys were left on the table by the front door). However, we vary in our abilities to engage effectively in this kind of reasoning, even in adulthood (Miller, 2012). Moreover, transferring these skills from our daily person-to-person interactions to our reasoning about characters in texts adds an additional layer of difficulty. Readers who cannot make this leap from real life to texts, or readers who have difficulty making social inferences regardless of the context (text or actual social interaction), will have much more difficulty comprehending texts than readers who are more skilled in this area. But nuanced understandings of the events that occur in narrative texts are made possible only when readers understand the internal mental worlds of characters that motivate actions in stories (Shanahan & Shanahan, 1997).

I should note that although most research on social understanding in psychology and neuroscience has focused on individuals' understanding of others' minds, social understanding also involves the ability to think about one's own thoughts (Astington et al., 1988), otherwise known as metacognition. We have known for many years that the ability to think about one's own thoughts is important for reading comprehension because it enables readers to reflect on things like their comprehension strategy use and monitor the degree to which they understand texts (Cross & Paris, 1983; Garner, 1987; Israel et al., 2005; Keene & Zimmerman, 2007; Pearson & Gallagher, 1983). Furthermore, poor comprehenders are much less aware of their own reading processes than their peers with better comprehension (Dermitzaki et al., 2008; Jacobs & Paris, 1987; Lecce et al., 2010; Paris & Myers, 1981; Vidal-Abarca, Mañá, & Gil, 2010). However, reading research on social understanding has been a bit one-sided. Although much research has investigated the role of self-directed social understanding (i.e., metacognition) in reading comprehension, far less research has explored the role of other-directed social understanding in successful reading comprehension. We are now beginning to see that both sides are important for the comprehension process. Thus, this chapter will focus on the purposeful kinds of other-directed social understanding that support reading comprehension with specific applications to classroom reading instruction.

What Is Social Understanding and How Is It Typically Assessed?

Reasoning about our own and others' minds involves a special kind of understanding that researchers in psychology and neuroscience call *theory of mind* (see Table 1.1 in Chapter 1). Theory of mind is the ability to consider or infer one's own and others' mental and emotional states, such as thoughts, feelings, desires, motives, or intentions, and use those to make predictions and generate explanations for others' behavior. Further, like other executive skills, theory of mind develops in childhood and varies considerably in children and adults (Astington et al., 1988; Miller, 2012). Children's developing theory of mind abilities provide the foundation for the development of their metacognitive skills (Kuhn, 2000), and theory of mind is related to social competence and successful peer relations from preschool to adolescence (Bosacki & Astington, 1999; Slaughter, Dennis, & Pritchard, 2002; Watson, Nixon, Wilson, & Capage, 1999). Other terms used to describe this kind of reasoning are *social understanding* and *social imagination* (Bosacki & Astington, 1999; Lysaker et al., 2011). As I noted above, sometimes comprehension fails because students fail to make the social inferences necessary for understanding texts. In other words, they don't understand *psychological causality* (McConaughy, 1985) and make inferences about actions rather than inferences about characters' internal responses (McConaughy et al., 1983). But, as you shall see later in this chapter, this kind of reasoning can be taught, resulting in improvements in reading comprehension.

> *Social understanding*: the ability to consider or infer one's own and others' mental and emotional states, such as thoughts, feelings, desires, motives, or intentions, and use those to make predictions and generate explanations for others' behavior; also called *theory of mind* or *social imagination*.

Another aspect of social understanding that is related to theory of mind is counterfactual thinking, the ability to consider alternatives to events that have already taken place, which is usually motivated by a desire to improve on a situation (Guajardo & Turley-Ames, 2004; Guajardo et al., 2009). Counterfactual thinking and theory of mind are related, and the development of cool executive skills supports both of these aspects of social understanding (Drayton et al., 2011; Guajardo et al., 2009). When readers consider what charac-

> *Counterfactual thinking*: the ability to consider alternatives to events that have already taken place, which is usually motivated by a desire to improve on a situation.

ters could have done to change a situation in positive or negative ways, they are engaging in counterfactual thinking. For example, if a reader considers what Duncan could have done differently so that his crayons would not have quit while reading the book *The Day the Crayons Quit* by Drew Daywalt (2013), she is engaging in counterfactual thinking. Similarly, when reading an informational text on the *Titanic*, readers would be using counterfactual thinking when they consider alternative outcomes, such as the number of lives that would have been saved had the builders of the *Titanic* included enough life boats for all of the passengers aboard the ship. You can see how this kind of reasoning also involves thinking about others' thoughts, intentions, feelings, and motivations, because one must consider characters' existing motivations to suggest alternative ones. And, as you might expect, counterfactual thinking is also related to reading comprehension in children and adults (Cartwright & Guajardo, 2011; Trabasso & Bartolone, 2003).

The view of social understanding as a hot executive skill is a relatively new perspective, emerging in the last decade or so (Zelazo & Carlson, 2012; Zelazo & Müller, 2002; Zelazo et al., 2005), and is supported by a variety of evidence (see Chapter 1). For example, social understanding develops with cool executive skills (Miller & Marcovitch, 2012), and these skills predict one another in development (Blankson et al., 2013; Carlson, Claxton, & Moses, 2015; Devine & Hughes, 2014). In addition, preschoolers' ability to benefit from social understanding training depends on their levels of cool skills (Benson et al., 2013). Adjacent and overlapping brain regions in the frontal lobes serve social understanding and cool executive skills. As noted in earlier chapters, cool skills are typically associated with the DLPFC, whereas social understanding is typically associated with the OFC and the VMPFC, which have closer ties to areas of the brain that process emotion (Ardilla, 2013; Ferstl, Rinck, & von Cramon, 2005; Fletcher et al., 1995; Gallagher et al., 2000; Geraci, Surian, Ferraro, & Cantagallo, 2010; Happé et al., 1996; Shamay-Tsoory, Tomer, Berger, Goldsher, & Aharon-Peretz, 2005; Stone et al., 1998). Furthermore, both self-directed social understanding (i.e., metacognition) and other-directed social understanding activate areas in the medial prefrontal cortex (MPFC; Schmitz, Kawahara-Baccus, & Johnson, 2004; Vogeley et al., 2001). Interestingly, so does empathy, which involves understanding others' feelings by relating them to one's own (Völlm et al., 2006).

Theory of mind is usually assessed with narrative tasks that require individuals to reason about others' thoughts, beliefs, feelings, or motives. Thus, it may come as no surprise that theory of mind is related to reading comprehension, simply because narrative understanding is necessary to perform well on many theory of mind tasks! However, the relation between reading comprehension and theory of mind is not simply an artifact of using stories to assess whether individuals understand others' minds. Some theory of mind tasks do not involve narratives at all, such as the Mind in the Eyes Task, described below (Baron-Cohen, Wheelwright, Hill, Raste, & Plumb, 2001). And nonnarrative theory of mind tasks, narrative theory of mind tasks, and narrative comprehension all activate overlapping brain regions, particularly the VMPFC (Mar, 2011). In other words, understanding others' minds, even when such understanding is not assessed using stories, is significantly related to comprehension of stories because of shared executive demands that activate a frontal lobe region known for its support of hot executive function.

In children, theory of mind is usually assessed with oral narratives and visual supports, such as pictures or objects. (These practices are consistent with what we know about dual coding theory and supporting readers' construction of mental models of narratives using both visual and verbal information; see Chapter 5 for a review.) In contrast, assessments of adults' theory of mind involve reading brief narrative stories accompanied by questions that require inferences about characters' thoughts, beliefs, feelings, or motives (Bull, Phillips, & Conway, 2008). Another common assessment of adults' theory of mind involves recognition of emotions in facial expressions (Baron-Cohen et al., 2001). In the paragraphs that follow, I will describe typical assessments for children first, and then I will describe typical assessments for adults.

In the classic *unexpected contents task* that is used to assess children's theory of mind (Perner, Leekam, & Wimmer, 1987), a child is shown a box of candy and is asked what is inside. Typically, the child responds that there is candy inside. Then the assessor reveals that there is actually something different, such as a pencil, in the box. The box is closed, and the child is asked what his or her friend will think is inside the box. If the child is aware of others' thoughts and beliefs, he or she should indicate that another person would think there is candy in the box. However, young children consistently fail this task and say that another person will think there is a pencil in the box! That is, young children attribute their own thoughts to others, rather than understanding how others' thoughts may be different from their own.

This kind of error can be quite problematic in story comprehension because characters' thoughts, feelings, or beliefs rarely match our own, yet they are often critically important to understanding characters' actions. This highlights the executive component of social understanding that is essential to skilled reading comprehension. Readers must be able to reflect on their own thoughts, feelings, and motivations, and be able to set them aside and separate them from the thoughts, feelings, and motivations of others in order to use the information about others' minds to make inferences about others' behaviors. In other words, skilled reading comprehension requires the ability to coordinate one's own and others' perspectives (e.g., I know there is a pencil in the box, but my friend will think there is candy in the box). And, as you might expect, the flexible coordination of social information is related to cognitive flexibility, which requires similar kinds of mental coordination in cool tasks (Devine & Hughes, 2014; Guajardo et al., 2009).

A second task that is commonly used to assess children's theory of mind is the classic *false belief task* (Wimmer & Perner, 1983). In this task, children are presented a scenario in which a character has a mistaken belief about the location of an object, and they are shown dolls to support their understanding of the scenario. First, the children are introduced to a doll, Maxi, and his mother (also a doll), and then they hear a narrative like the one that follows, supported by movements of the dolls in and out of the scene.

"Maxi and his mother come home from the store with some chocolate and place it into a cupboard (location A). Then, Maxi goes out to play. His mother uses the chocolate to bake a cake, and she puts it into a drawer (location B). Mom leaves, and then Maxi comes back inside and wants to eat some chocolate."

After children hear and view the scenario, they are asked, *"Where will Maxi look for the chocolate?"* To answer this question correctly, children must set aside their own knowledge of the true location of the chocolate (the drawer, location B) and respond that Maxi will look in the location where he last saw the chocolate (the cupboard, location A). But even 6- to 8-year-old children do not consistently get this question correct, even though they remember the chocolate's original location, indicating that their mistakes are not working memory failures. Rather, the children are not yet able to infer a character's thoughts or beliefs and predict the character's action based on those inferences (Wimmer & Perner, 1983).

Typically developing adults, adolescents, and older elementary children have little difficulty with these simple scenarios. Thus, more complex theory of mind tasks must be used to assess older children's and adults' abilities to infer others' mental states. Short, written narratives with questions that require inferences about others' motives, thoughts, or feelings are one typical assessment of theory of mind for individuals beyond preschool and early elementary ages, and these are sometimes supported with pictures (Bull et al., 2008; Fletcher et al., 1995; Happé, 1994; Sullivan, Zaitchik, & Tager-Flusberg, 1994). A typical, short narrative in one of these tasks might look like the one that follows:.

> "Kendra bought Shannon a book about dinosaurs for her birthday. Many people came to Shannon's birthday party, and she received several different books. A few weeks later, Kendra was at Shannon's house for a visit. Kendra spilled juice all over the dinosaur book and said, 'Oh, no! I've ruined your book!' Shannon said, 'That's okay. I didn't like that book anyway. Somebody gave it to me for my birthday.' Why did Shannon say that?"
>
> a. She was questioning Kendra's choice of gifts.
> b. So Kendra wouldn't feel bad about spilling juice on the book.
> c. Shannon couldn't remember that Kendra gave her the book.
> d. She was glad the book was ruined.

The correct answer to the question about Shannon's thoughts is option c. Students who have difficulty inferring others' mental states or feelings might choose one of the distracter items, rather than the item that best characterizes an inference based on social understanding. Another theory of mind task that is commonly used with adults is the Mind in the Eyes Task (Baron-Cohen et al., 2001) that requires individuals to make inferences about others' feelings simply by looking at pictures of eyes that reflect various emotional expressions; individuals respond by choosing one best answer from four possible options.

I should note that individuals on the autism spectrum typically have difficulty with theory of mind tasks; in fact, difficulty with social understanding is a defining trait for these individuals (Baron-Cohen et al., 2001; Happé, 1994). Not surprisingly, individuals with autism also have difficulty with reading comprehension, particularly with social texts (Brown, Oram-Cardy, & Johnson, 2013; Jacobs & Richdale, 2013). And, although children and adults prefer social stories (Barnes, 2012; Barnes & Bloom, 2014), individuals with autism prefer nonsocial texts (Barnes, 2012). Furthermore, social understanding is a significant predictor of reading comprehension in children with autism, even when oral language and word reading abilities are controlled (Ricketts, Jones, Happé, & Charman, 2013).

With respect to games that involve this particular executive skill, the card game Old Maid requires good social understanding for successful performance. This game can be played with specially designed decks of cards or a standard deck of 52 cards with one queen removed. For the sake of this example, let's assume that the queen of clubs was removed, leaving the queen of spades as the Old Maid. Players are dealt all of the cards in the deck, and each player discards pairs of matching cards (e.g., red fives, black threes, etc.). The object of this game is to discard all cards without being left with the "Old Maid" card in one's hand. The players who are able to discard all of their cards and avoid the Old Maid are safe, whereas the player who is left with the Old Maid loses the game. Once players discard all of their matched pairs, they take turns drawing single cards from other players' hands, typically proceeding in a clockwise direction around the group. Players discard any matched pairs acquired by drawing cards from others' hands. Social understanding comes into play particularly for the player holding the Old Maid card. Because the object is to rid oneself of the card as quickly as possible, the player holding the Old Maid must mask his or her true feelings, which is often difficult for younger players who grin or giggle when another player unknowingly reaches for the Old Maid. Other players, on the other hand, must be adept at inferring the Old Maid holder's true feelings or intentions, which enables them to avoid drawing that card and losing the game.

Along similar lines, the classic children's game Hide and Seek requires that hiders understand the perspectives of seekers and use that information to conceal their location and deceive the seekers. I have enjoyed watching my 4-year-old's understanding of this game develop across the past year. At first, he had no idea that I could see him or hear him and use that information to find him. So, like many preschoolers, he would hide in ways that left parts of his body exposed, or he would move or make noises (like giggling) that led me directly to his location. He has gradually learned that he needs to conceal all of his body parts from my view and stay very still so that I don't detect motion. And recently, he has achieved the insight that he should be very quiet so that I don't hear him and locate him by sound. However, he still hides in exactly the same location every time he hides, so he doesn't quite understand that I can use information from our last game to find him in this one. I'm eager to see when that insight finally emerges!

Why Is Social Understanding Important to Reading Comprehension?

As is clear from the preceding discussion, inferences about characters' mental states, such as their emotions, beliefs, thoughts, and intentions, are essential for successful reading comprehension. Additionally, our reasoning about characters in texts often involves more than just thinking about others' thoughts or feelings and how those internal states motivate others' behaviors. Sometimes we must think about the thoughts of characters that are also making inferences about other characters' thoughts. Consider the picture book *The Duckling Gets a Cookie!?* (Willems, 2012). In this story, there are two characters: a duckling and a pigeon. The duckling, who is perceived by the pigeon as a rival, asks for—and receives—a cookie (with nuts). The pigeon proceeds to berate the duckling because the pigeon wrongly assumes that the duckling intends to keep the cookie for herself; readers familiar with this character from other stories understand that the pigeon assumes the duckling will behave in the same selfish manner that characterizes the pigeon's typical behaviors in other stories. The reader and the pigeon learn, however, that the duckling intends to give the cookie to the pigeon, whose behavior changes dramatically because he wrongly assumes the duckling actually has altruistic motives. In a humorous plot twist, the reader finally discovers that the duckling actually wanted to give the cookie away because it contained nuts, which she didn't like, so that she could ask for a cookie without nuts for herself! Thus, to comprehend this story, the reader must understand the pigeon's multiple mistaken assumptions and the duckling's actual internal motivation that remains unknown to the pigeon. In other words, to understand the humor in the story, the reader must think about the pigeon's thinking about the duckling's thoughts, about which the pigeon remains in the dark. Other theory of mind tasks have been developed to assess this kind of thinking about characters' thoughts about others' thinking; these are called second-order theory of mind tasks and are more difficult than the tasks described above (Sullivan et al., 1994). Recent evidence indicates second-order theory of mind is significantly related to reading comprehension in elementary students (Cartwright & Guajardo, 2011).

Donahue (2013) describes this important skill as perspective taking: readers must take perspectives of characters, which sometimes requires the understanding that characters may also be taking others' perspectives too. Bruner and colleagues suggested that reading comprehension requires that readers think about texts in terms of two levels that he called landscapes: the landscape of action and the landscape of consciousness (Bruner, 1988, 1990; Feldman, Bruner, Renderer, & Spitzer, 1996). In other words, when we read narrative texts, there is more to think about than just observable actions or character behaviors; we also have to infer thoughts, feelings, and intentions; infer effects of those internal states on characters' behaviors; and then integrate the two levels of understanding to produce a more nuanced understanding of text. As you might expect, Astington (1990; also see Pelletier & Astington, 2004; Riggio & Cassidy, 2009) found that children are not able to do this until they have a well-developed theory of mind.

Like other executive skills, the development of social understanding is related to oral language development. For example, oral language skill is related to both theory of mind understanding (e.g., Astington & Jenkins, 1999) and counterfactual reasoning ability (Beck, Riggs, & Gorniak, 2009; Drayton et al., 2011; Guajardo et al., 2009; Guajardo, Petersen, & Marshall, 2013). Additionally, mothers' language to 4- to 6-year-old children, which supports children's language development, predicts children's memory for the false portions of statements about false beliefs (Farrant, Maybery, & Fletcher, 2012). For example, in the sentence *Jamal thinks his ball is in the closet*, a child would have to remember the false statement that characterizes Jamal's belief that the ball is in the closet when the child knows that the ball was actually left outside. This is a critical component of theory of mind understanding, and Farrant and colleagues have shown that mothers' language to children supports this understanding. By analogy, when read- **R.CCR.1** ing, students must understand and remember many things that may be inconsistent with their own thoughts, feelings, motivations, knowledge, or intentions, but our students' abilities to do so often depend on their levels of social understanding.

In a nutshell, social understanding supports inference making. We already talked about inference making in Chapter 5 when we discussed the role of working memory in supporting gap-filling and text-connecting inferences. Sometimes readers need to fill gaps or connect text elements that involve nonsocial information. Other times, though, readers must make inferences about the contents of characters' minds: the invisible, internal states of characters, like thoughts, feelings, motivations, intentions, or beliefs. Understanding these social bases for inferences requires more than just working memory; these kinds of inferences require social understanding, which makes them more difficult for students who do not have well-developed social understanding abilities. Inference-making ability differentiates good from poor comprehenders, even in very young children (Stahl, 2014); and even prereaders' inferences about characters' goals, actions, and mental states predict their narrative comprehension (Tompkins, Guo, & Justice, 2013).

Thus, with respect to the RRSG (2002) framework for reading comprehension, social understanding is clearly a reader characteristic that influences reading comprehension processes in important ways. Additionally, social understanding is also a text feature, because texts vary with respect to the amount of mental and emotional language they contain; in other words, texts vary with respect to the amount of social inferences they require for successful reading comprehension (Barnes, 2012; Dyer, Shatz, & Watson, 2002; Dyer-Seymour, Shatz, Wellman, & Saito, 2004). Little work has been conducted to examine whether reading purpose relates to social understanding. However, we can assume that if an individual is reading to get information about setting, for example, that purpose requires fewer social inferences. However, if an individual is reading to understand the sequence of events in a story, understanding characters' internal motivations will play a greater role in comprehension processes. Finally, I speculate that understanding authors' purposes in writing texts may also be supported by social understanding abilities. After all, to understand an author's purpose, one must be able to take the perspective of the author or read the author's mind. To date, though, research has yet to examine this relation.

What Does Social Understanding Look Like in Real Readers?

Brittany, a Student with RCD

As we have seen in previous chapters, Brittany seems to have difficulty with executive skills, and her executive skill difficulties undermine her abilities to get meaning from text. Social understanding is no exception. Brittany has difficulty inferring why characters do the things that they do. As we have seen in previous chapters, her retellings of stories often miss key details and lack organization. Furthermore, consistent with her difficulties with social understanding, Brittany's retellings of stories focus on actions and events rather than the underlying, internal reasons for characters' actions. When you assess your students' social understanding, Brittany seems to have a hard time taking other students' perspectives; and her narration of the events in a wordless picture book sound more like a running commentary on a string of events rather than a coherent narrative that is held together by the underlying motives, thoughts, and feelings of the characters depicted on the book's pages. When you track Brittany's language in her retellings and conversations about books, you find that she uses very few words that refer to mental or emotional states. Beyond her text processing, Brittany also seems to have poor peer relations. She doesn't seem to understand others' perspectives, she doesn't have a good sense of the appropriate ways to interact with peers, and peers' responses are often lost on Brittany; it's as though she doesn't understand the effects of her actions on others. When you talk with her about her choices that resulted in negative peer reactions, she is unable to generate alternative actions that could have produced a different, more positive result. Thus, Brittany's processing of text and her interactions with peers point to an underlying difficulty with social understanding. She could benefit from additional support in this area.

Gabriela, a Good Comprehender

Now consider Gabriela, who is one of your star comprehenders. She has no difficulty identifying characters' motives, feelings, or thoughts, and she draws on these internal states to explain characters' actions in her conversations about and retellings of texts. Gabriela's retellings are peppered with vocabulary words that describe internal mental and emotional states, words like *think, know, guess, feel*, and *want*. In fact, in her daily conversations you have noticed that she uses these words more frequently than many of her peers. (We will say more about these kinds of words later in the chapter.) Although Gabriela notes actions and events in stories and can identify story structures, she has no difficulty making more abstract inferences about characters' internal motivations for their actions, providing her a deeper understanding of texts than peers like Brittany who focus on actions and events alone.

R.CCR.3

Finally, in a broader sense, you have noticed that Gabriela has excellent peer relations. She is able to interpret peers' responses, recognize peers' feelings, and show empathy for peers who are upset. Her behavior, language, and responses to text clearly indicate that Gabriela has excellent social understanding.

What Does the Research Say?

As I have noted previously, the role of social understanding in reading comprehension has received little research attention in comparison to other, cool executive skills. But the research that has been done to date is exciting and suggests that we can, indeed, support and teach this important aspect of our students' hot executive functioning with positive effects on their reading comprehension. As in other chapters, I will begin by reviewing research conducted from an executive skills perspective and then move on to discuss research conducted from a reading perspective. I will conclude the chapter with applications of this work for classroom practice and suggestions for future research.

Research on Social Understanding from an Executive Skills Perspective

Narratives provide a context for learning about and thinking about characters' minds. Because narrative comprehension provides many opportunities to practice making inferences about others' minds, researchers have investigated the connection between the two in children and adults. For example, Kim and Phillips (2014) recently found that preschoolers' theory of mind, inhibition, and monitoring skills predicted narrative comprehension beyond age and verbal ability. However, this relation is affected by text features, as recently demonstrated by Ronfard and Harris (2013) who explored the relation of social understanding to comprehension in the context of a familiar children's story: Little Red Riding Hood. I enjoyed the title to this article, *When Will Little Red Riding Hood Become Scared?*, which indicates these researchers' focus. They found that 4- to 6-year-olds were better at attributing correct mental states to Red Riding Hood when asked what she was feeling earlier in the story, when she was far from her grandma's house rather than when she was closer to it; that is, they found that more distance in the narrative produced better attributions about characters' minds. Additionally, they found that emotion attributions were harder for children than understanding what Red Riding Hood knew (or didn't know). Furthermore, other findings suggest that from preschool to second grade children are better at attributing mental and emotional states with simpler stories that include fewer characters and events (Sullivan et al., 1994). Thus, we should consider text features when we design lessons to support children's understanding of characters' internal mental and emotional reactions.

We should be careful, however, to ensure that children have the opportunity to construct mental and emotional inferences from text themselves. When kinder-

R.CCR.3 garten children were provided mental and emotional language and inferences in storybooks explicitly and compared to a group that had to construct such inferences themselves (i.e., because they were presented implicitly), the implicit group was significantly better at explaining social inferences than their peers who had received explicit information about characters' mental and emotional states (Peskin & Astington, 2004).

In other words, consistent with what is known about successful comprehension strategies instruction (Brown, 2008), children must do the thinking about social inferences themselves, rather than having teachers do the thinking for them. But they are not able to make such internal attributions until they have fairly well developed theory of mind understanding (Astington, 1990; Pelletier & Astington, 2004; Riggio & Cassidy, 2009). Consistent with this notion, theory of mind understanding is significantly related to preschoolers' narrative comprehension and predicts preschoolers' responsiveness to comprehension intervention (Cartwright et al., 2014).

These findings suggest children's abilities to make internal attributions about characters develop slowly across childhood. Parent storybook reading with children that includes discussion of mental states of characters promotes these kinds of inferences (Adrián, Clemente, & Villanueva, 2007; Adrián, Clemente, Villanueva, & Rieffe, 2005; Ruffman, Slade, & Crowe, 2002) and results in richer retellings from preschool children, providing evidence of better narrative comprehension (Aram et al., 2013). And children's use of mental state language in such

SL.CCR.2 contexts is also related to the development of their social understanding (Symons, Peterson, Slaughter, Roche, & Doyle, 2005). Finally, mothers' provision of causal explanations of mental and emotional states of characters in storybook reading contexts is associated with 3- to 6-year-olds' theory of mind competence, and children on the autism spectrum benefit particularly from such explanations that involve emotional content (Slaughter, Peterson, & Mackintosh, 2007).

Indeed, children as young as 5 years of age will construct emotional inferences about protagonists' internal states in stories and movies spontaneously, an ability that improves across childhood into adulthood (Diergarten & Nieding, in press). In an examination of the development of narrative competence and social understanding across the transition from kindergarten to first grade, Gamannossi and Pinto (2014) also found that children's understanding of deception in narratives increased with age, and they suggested that narrative comprehension might actually influence children's understanding of others' minds. Consistent with this notion, Mar, Tackett, and Moore (2010) observed that 4- to 6-year olds' exposure to storybooks and movies (but not television) predicted their social understanding. Further, Guajardo and Watson (2002) discovered that 3- and 4-year-old children's social understanding could be improved through intentional discussions of characters' internal mental and emotional states in the context of storybook reading. In their study such discussions promoted significant improvements in social understanding for children after 1 week, which persisted up to 4 weeks later! Thus, we can teach even very young children to better understand the mental worlds **SL.CCR.1** of characters in stories, producing improvements in their social understanding.

Adults are more likely than children to refer to characters' psychological goals in explanations of story content, and the tendency to make mental state attributions for characters' behaviors by referring to beliefs and emotions increases with age from 5 years to adulthood; however, children are more likely to attribute characters' antisocial rather than prosocial actions to internal causes (Lovett & Pillow, 2010). Despite these findings, even adults vary in social understanding. And adults who read more fiction, which involves more practice thinking about characters' mental states, have higher levels of social understanding (Kidd & Castano, 2013).

Furthermore, adults' processing of characters' internal mental and emotional states activate the same areas in the frontal lobes (i.e., the MPFC), regardless of whether the narratives are presented in textual or nonverbal, cartoon formats (Gallagher et al., 2000). Further, when adults are tasked with detecting narrative inconsistencies in the meaning construction process, social inconsistencies are processed in the MPFC, and chronological inconsistencies are processed elsewhere (Ferstl et al., 2005). Similarly, stories that require adults to make inferences about characters' mental and emotional states activate the MPFC, whereas stories that require inferences about physical, nonsocial information do not (Fletcher et al., 1995). Taken together, these findings indicate social inferences have a special status that supports, and is supported by reading of fictional texts and possi- **R.CCR.7** bly expository texts that involve character interactions. Research from a reading perspective also supports this conclusion, as you will find in the next section.

Research on Social Understanding from a Reading Perspective

Only recently have reading researchers begun to focus on the important role of social inference making in the development of narrative and reading comprehension. For example, Tompkins and colleagues (2013) recently found that prereaders' inferences about characters' goals, actions, and mental states predicted their narrative comprehension. And Lysaker and Miller (2013) observed that social understanding is evident, even in children's comprehension of wordless picture books. Stahl (2014) recently highlighted the important status of inferences about characters' internal states for the development of prekindergarten and kindergarten students' comprehension. However, she also noted that these kinds of inferences are less common for children in this age group, who focus instead on characters' actions; thus, she suggests we should make concerted efforts to provide explicit instruction in social inference making (Stahl, 2014). We will return to this idea in the next section on classroom applications.

R.CCR.1,
R.CCR.3

In older children, Shannon et al. (1988) found that 7- to 11-year-old students were not able to make inferences about the internal motivations for characters' actions in stories unless the motives were stated explicitly. Along similar lines, 9- to 11-year-olds do not typically include internal motivations in their retellings of stories (Carnine et al.,1982; McConaughy et al., 1983). Despite these findings, we know that social understanding can be taught, resulting in improvements to students' narrative and text comprehension; studies that have done so will be described below.

As I noted earlier in the chapter, counterfactual thinking is another important aspect of social understanding that is related to the development of reading comprehension. Recall that counterfactual thinking involves generating alternatives to the current state of affairs, typically to improve upon a situation. For example, after spilling coffee across the desk, ruining several items in the process, we typically come up with various alternative scenarios that would have prevented this unpleasant occurrence. Likewise, when reading, we may come up with potential alternatives to the current situation as we predict or make inferences about story events. I know of only one study that has examined the relation of counterfactual reasoning to the development of reading comprehension in children, which I conducted with my colleague Nicole Guajardo (Cartwright & Guajardo, 2011; Guajardo & Cartwright, 2015). We found a significant relation between preschoolers' counterfactual reasoning and their reading comprehension in third grade, even when decoding ability, theory of mind, vocabulary, working memory, and cognitive flexibility were controlled. We also found that third-grade theory of mind, assessed with a more complex task (Sullivan et al., 1994) predicted third-grade reading comprehension beyond decoding ability, vocabulary, working memory, and cognitive flexibility. These findings suggest counterfactual thinking plays an important role in the development of reading comprehension, but additional research is necessary to confirm this finding and evaluate implications for practice. Finally, I should note that a recent study with adults suggests adult readers are sensitive to counterfactual information in narratives (de Vega, Urrutia, & Riffo, 2007), but more work is needed to understand the precise relation between counterfactual thinking and reading comprehension across the lifespan.

A few recent intervention studies have demonstrated the effectiveness of teaching social understanding for improving reading comprehension. For example, Stahl (2014) described using video narratives or picture books to help prereaders better understand the role of characters' internal states in the action of stories. She suggests discussing the psychological causes of characters' problems in the stories, discussing characters' internal goals, motivations for actions, and reactions to concluding events in stories. Class discussions of this nature can support prereaders' beginning understandings of the role of social understanding in stories (Stahl, 2014). Similarly, Lysaker et al. (2011; also see Lysaker & Tonge, 2013) engaged second to third graders in relationally oriented reading instruction that involved similar discussions of the psychological causes of characters' actions, which fostered improvements in social understanding and reading comprehension in these students.

R.CCR.1,
R.CCR.3,
R.CCR.7,
SL.CCR.1,
SL.CCR.2

Other researchers have used story mapping procedures, similar to the ones I described in Chapter 3 that involve adding information about characters' internal motivations to readers' conceptions of the structures of stories. For example, Emery (1996) engaged 9- to 11-year-old students in a three-step procedure that involved adding character perspectives to story maps, resulting in improved comprehension. Shanahan and Shanahan (1997) described a comparable method for teaching students to analyze effects of internal states on characters' actions, and comparing different characters' perspectives on the same actions and events in stories (e.g., comparing the wolf's perspective and the pigs' perspectives on the actions and events in *The Three Little Pigs*), using Character Perspective Charts, which resulted in improved comprehension.

R.CCR.2,
R.CCR.3,
R.CCR.5

Finally, in research with older students, Carnine, Stevens, Clements, and Kame'enui (1982) showed that facilitative questions to increase focus on psychological causes in stories, as well as practice identifying such causes with explicit feedback, enhanced fourth- to sixth-grade readers' abilities to consider characters' motives and improved their reading comprehension.

How Can I Apply This Knowledge to Classroom Practice?

As with all of the instructional practices described in this book, and just as you would with any process important for reading comprehension, you should introduce social understanding to your students in ways that are consistent with the gradual release of responsibility model (Duffy, 2014; Duke & Pearson, 2002; Duke et al., 2011; Pearson & Gallagher, 1983). That is, you should provide your students an explicit explanation of social understanding while modeling how good readers use this information to understand text, involve your students in activities that involve social understanding while sharing the responsibility for this new way of thinking, provide opportunities for your students to practice under your guidance and support, and then finally provide opportunities for independent practice applying social understanding in a variety of texts. You might consider explaining social understanding as follows:

EXPLICITLY EXPLAINING SOCIAL UNDERSTANDING

"You know how we have been talking about different ways that good readers think? Well, today we are going to learn about another one, and this is really important for helping you understand stories. Good readers are really good at thinking about why characters do the things they do, because good readers think about what characters might be thinking or feeling! You might say that good readers are good 'mind readers.' They read characters' minds! When we read about characters, we read about the actions that they take, but that is only part of the story. Figuring out *why* characters do what they do is really important to truly understanding what is going on in books. The trouble is, authors don't always tell us everything about why characters do the things they do. Instead, they want us to figure those things out; they want us to make inferences and fill in the gaps in the text with what we know about thoughts and feelings. Sometimes, we can figure out what a character is thinking, what a character knows or doesn't know, what a character is feeling, how a character reacts, or what a character might want to happen in a story (i.e., their motivations or intentions). Thoughts and feelings are invisible things in stories, but they are very powerful, because they are the real reasons why characters do the things that they do. Today we're going to practice reading characters' minds so we can understand stories better."

You might want to provide an example to your students using a simple text at first, because research suggests simpler stories with fewer characters and events are easier for students when they are learning to infer characters' mental states (Sullivan et al., 1994). Picture books are often terrific resources for beginning to talk about characters' thoughts and feelings (Dyer et al., 2000; Dyer-Seymour et al., 2004; Lysaker et al., 2011). Earlier in the chapter I described one that can support your students' understanding of characters' false beliefs, *The Duckling Gets a Cookie!?* (Willems, 2012), which is one of the most difficult theory of mind concepts for young children (Wellman & Liu, 2004). In this text, which I described earlier in the chapter, the pigeon's thoughts and feelings affect his actions in the story. For example, he is envious of the duckling because the duckling has a cookie, and he does not. And the pigeon also has mistaken beliefs about what the duckling is going to do with the cookie. (The pigeon thinks the duckling is going to eat the cookie herself and not share it.) The pigeon's feelings of envy and his mistaken belief about what the duckling will do cause the pigeon's subsequent actions and reactions. (He becomes angry, and then he engages in some angry behaviors, like shouting at the duckling.) You can use simple texts such as this one to help your students look for clues to characters' beliefs and feelings. Have your students explain why the pigeon thinks what he does and feels what he does, drawing on clues in the text to justify their responses. These kinds of text discussions foster student attention to and understanding of characters' minds. The research reviewed in this chapter suggests several things you can do to teach and assess social understanding to foster deeper understanding of texts in your students. You might try some of the following suggestions to infuse these concepts into your instruction.

Consider Text Types and Features

When you are selecting texts to teach social understanding, remember that some texts will be easier for your students to use for social inference making.

- As demonstrated by Ronfard and Harris (2013), emotion attributions were harder for children than understanding what characters knew or didn't know. Thus, character knowledge may be a better starting point for discussions of this type than characters' feelings, so choose texts that provide opportunities to discuss characters' differences in knowledge or beliefs and how those will affect characters' behaviors. Then move on to more difficult concepts, such as emotions.

- Additionally, they found that the more distance in a story's narrative between the character's action and your questions about the character's thoughts and feelings, the easier it will be for your students to make mental and emotional state attributions (Ronfard & Harris, 2013). Thus, when engaging your students in discussions of mental state concepts in texts, be aware of the timing of R.CCR.1, your questions with respect to the storyline to give your students their best R.CCR.3 opportunities to understand the effects of social understanding on characters' actions.

- Furthermore, as noted above, children are better at attributing mental and emotional states with simpler stories that include fewer characters and events (Sullivan et al., 1994). Thus, you may wish to begin with simple texts or picture books when you design lessons to support children's understanding of characters' internal mental and emotional reactions and their effects on actions in stories. As I noted previously, Mo Willems books are popular picture books that have limited numbers of characters and props, and many are written in a graphic novel style with plentiful opportunities for discussing characters' mental and emotional states and motivations. See Table 7.1 for a list of books you can use for this purpose.

- Lysaker and Miller (2013) used wordless picture books to teach social understanding because the lack of printed text means that students must offer their own interpretations of, and will be more likely to offer mental state and emotional

TABLE 7.1. Simple Picture Books That Afford Opportunities for Discussing Social Understanding

Title	Author	Publication year (publisher)
Don't Let the Pigeon Drive the Bus!	Mo Willems	2003 (Hyperion)
The Pigeon Finds a Hot Dog!	Mo Willems	2004 (Hyperion)
Knuffle Bunny	Mo Willems	2004 (Hyperion)
Don't Let the Pigeon Stay Up Late!	Mo Willems	2006 (Hyperion)
Knuffle Bunny Too	Mo Willems	2007 (Hyperion)
I Will Surprise My Friend	Mo Willems	2008 (Hyperion)
Knuffle Bunny Free	Mo Willems	2010 (Hyperion)
Can I Play, Too?	Mo Willems	2010 (Hyperion)
The Duckling Gets a Cookie!?	Mo Willems	2012 (Hyperion)
A Big Guy Took My Ball!	Mo Willems	2013 (Hyperion)
That Is Not a Good Idea!	Mo Willems	2013 (Hyperion)

explanations for, characters' actions; that is, the lack of printed text means that there are no text-based explanations for characters' actions—everything must be constructed by the reader. These kinds of texts are therefore ideal for teaching and assessing students' awareness of the contents of characters' minds. Some wordless picture books you might use for this purpose are listed in Table 7.2.

R.CCR.7

• Comics or graphic novels, even those without words, provide another type of text that can be used to teach and assess social inference making in your students (Gallagher et al., 2000). Like wordless picture books, these graphic formats may provide a useful way to help students focus on aspects of social understanding without the additional demands of decoding impacting their thinking about characters' interactions.

• Movies provide another medium that offers opportunities to discuss characters' mental and emotional states (Mar et al., 2010; Stahl, 2014). You might consider showing video clips from students' favorite films to pique interest in reading favorite characters' minds. Then help your students transfer the newfound skill to reading.

Don't Forget about Counterfactual Thinking

We are just beginning to learn how counterfactual thinking relates to the development of reading comprehension in children (Cartwright & Guajardo, 2011;

TABLE 7.2. Wordless Picture Books You Can Use to Assess and Teach Social Understanding

Title	Author	Publication year (publisher)
The Snowman	Raymond Briggs	1978 (Random House Books for Young Readers)
Pancakes for Breakfast	Tomie dePaola	1978 (HMH Books for Young Readers)
A Boy, a Dog, and a Frog	Mercer Mayer	2003 (Dial)
Frog, Where Are You?	Mercer Mayer	2003 (Dial)
The Flower Man	Mark Ludy	2005 (Scribble and Sons)
Flotsam	David Wiesner	2006 (Clarion Books)
The Adventures of Polo	Regis Faller	2006 (Roaring Book Press)
Rainstorm	Barbara Lehman	2007 (HMH Books for Young Readers)
Chalk	Bill Thomson	2010 (Two Lions)
A Ball for Daisy	Chris Raschka	2011 (Schwartz & Wade)
Where's Walrus	Stephen Savage	2011 (Scholastic Press)
The Boy and the Airplane	Mark Pett	2013 (Simon & Schuster Books for Young Readers)
Flora and the Flamingo	Molly Idle	2013 (Chronicle Books)
Flora and the Penguin	Molly Idle	2014 (Chronicle Books)
Out of the Blue	Allison Jay	2014 (Barefoot Books)

Guajardo & Cartwright, 2015), and we have known for a bit longer that this kind of thinking is related to reading comprehension in adults (Trabasso & Bartolone, 2003). Recall that counterfactual thinking involves generating alternative outcomes to events, usually to make a situation better (Guajardo & Turley-Ames, 2004). However, sometimes we might engage in counterfactual thinking to make ourselves feel better about something, and in those cases we generate alternatives that are worse than the current situation. For example, one evening my dog reached up onto my desk at home and began gnawing at the corner of a pile of my students' papers. I was certainly not happy about the situation and hoped that my students might find the teeth marks (and missing pieces) humorous when I returned their papers. In order to make myself feel better, I remember telling a colleague, "Well, at least he only ate the corners. I can still grade them. He could have devoured the entire stack of papers!" In that case, I was considering an alternative that was worse than the current situation to make myself feel better about what had happened. Either way, counterfactual thinking is related to the development of reading comprehension in children and adults.

Why might this particular kind of social understanding be related to reading comprehension? We don't know exactly, but I speculate that it may be because reading itself involves thinking about alternatives to one's current reality. That is, the things we read in books are typically unrelated to our own current circumstances, so we must hold in mind models of text meaning that are different from what we know to be the case in the real world. Additionally, when we predict what will happen in stories, revise our predictions, and make new ones, we are considering alternatives to the current state of affairs in our mental model of the action in a story. So, how might you incorporate counterfactual thinking into instruction? I know of no studies that have done so, but there are several things you may try that are likely to foster your students' abilities to engage in counterfactual thinking.

- When discussing stories in whole- or small-group contexts, explain to your students that good readers are good at thinking about ways things could be different from how they really are in stories or in real life. Have your students come up **SL.CCR.1** with alternate endings to stories and discuss them in whole- or small-group contexts.

- You might use this as a reader response activity. After reading a text to your students, have them each come up with an alternate ending, which they can write or draw, depending on their age and skill level, and that they subsequently share with their small group or the whole class. Each student will thus get prac- **W.CCR.3,** tice coming up with an alternative ending, and all students will benefit from **W.CCR.4** hearing several different alternate endings shared by their peers.

- In daily conversations with your students, you can relate stories of your personal experiences that could have turned out differently if you had chosen a different path (e.g., my students' papers might not have been eaten if I had kept them in my bag instead of putting them on my desk). Have your students come up with suggested alternative actions that you can take in future, similar circumstances.

- Introduce the concept of counterfactual thinking in small-group instruction, model how you might engage in this kind of thinking using your own experiences as examples, and then have your students generate examples from their own lives that would have turned out differently if they had made different choices.

- Have students write about personal events in their journals and **W.CCR.3,** then suggest multiple ways that the outcomes for the events could have been **W.CCR.4** different, either for the better or for worse.

- Use daily classroom events as teachable moments to model counterfactual thinking for your students. For example, when a student forgets to push in his chair and another person trips over it, you can ask what the student could have done to keep the other person from tripping. There are many opportunities throughout the day to consider alternatives to reality. Highlight these for your students.

Practice, Practice, Practice

Just as comprehension strategies instruction requires much independent practice in text discussions so that students can transfer the strategies to a variety of texts (Brown, 2008), learning to apply social understanding to making inferences about characters in texts requires the same kinds of interactive discussions over and over again. These kinds of discussions provide an audible example of the kinds of thinking that go on in good comprehenders' heads; and, because characters' internal mental, emotional, and motivational states are not typically readily visible to us in words or illustrations in text, these discussions provide one of the only ways students can access these important, but invisible, causal elements of text (Cartwright, 2010; Duffy, 2014).

- Even in prekindergarten and kindergarten children, explicit instruction in social inference making with interactive text discussions can support students' developing narrative comprehension (Stahl, 2014).

- Social understanding comes with its own specialized vocabulary. Interactive discussions with students about characters' thoughts, feelings, and motivations provide many opportunities for you to introduce the vocabulary essential for effective social understanding. When students engage in regular discussions of the internal states of characters in books, they begin to incorporate mental state terms into their own lexicons, permitting them to more easily transfer inferences based on social understanding to new texts (Symons et al., 2005).

R.CCR.4

- Additionally, as with any specialized vocabulary, the words specific to social understanding can be taught intentionally. See Table 7.3 for examples of mental state terms that you can use with your students; these are divided into three types: words that reflect thinking processes, words that reflect motivations, and words that reflect feelings.

  o Introduce these words to your students in vocabulary lessons, on your word wall, and in your conversations; make students aware, daily, of the role of mental and emotional states in individuals' behavior in texts, in your classroom, and in their own lives.
  o Saturate your discussions of texts with these words.
  o Have students use these words in their written responses to books.
  o Use this list to take anecdotal notes during text discussions in small-group instruction to denote when and whether students use these terms. If they don't, you may need to do more to help infuse these words into your students' speaking, writing, reading, and thinking vocabularies so that their developing social reasoning skills become just another facet of the way they think about texts.

TABLE 7.3. Examples of Mental and Emotional State Words

Type of words	Examples
Cognition *Refer to thinking*	believe, bet, dream, figure, forget, guess, have an idea, imagine, know, pretend, remember, suppose, think, trick, understand, wonder
Motivation *Refer to desires*	desire, hope, like, love, miss, need, want, wish *(includes negative references as well, such as don't want, etc.)*
Emotion *Refer to feelings*	afraid, angry, bad, bored, cry, frustrated, good, happy, hate, hopeful, like, love, mad, pleased, sad, worried *(includes negative references as well, such as not happy, unhappy, etc.)*

• Text discussions and written responses to texts should use *causal language* to describe the connection of characters' internal states to events in stories. For example, when I was recently reading my son *The Duckling Gets a Cookie!?* (Willems, 2012), he asked why the pigeon made the statement he did on the first page of the book (where the pigeon indicated displeasure with the book's title); I asked my son why *he* thought the pigeon said that, and he replied, "Because, he wants the cookie . . . and he wants to drive the bus, and he wants a hot dog!" He used causal explanatory connections from the pigeon's desires to the pigeon's actions, and he connected to two other books in which the pigeon had similar motivations (see Table 7.1)! Model this causal reasoning explicitly, and help your students make explicit causal statements that incorporate the mental state terms in Table 7.3 to facilitate their understanding of the various ways that internal states cause actions.

R.CCR.1,
R.CCR.3

• Keep in mind that students, especially younger elementary students, find it easier to attribute antisocial actions to internal features of characters, whereas prosocial behaviors are more difficult for students to connect to internal causes (Lovett & Pillow, 2010). It's as though young students assume appropriate behaviors occur because they are "supposed to" or because everyone is expected to follow the rules for appropriate behavior; that is, in young students' minds, appropriate behaviors occur because of external causes, and inappropriate behaviors occur because of internal causes. Thus, you might consider beginning with texts that capitalize on this tendency; teach social understanding of antisocial actions first, and then use those instances to help students transfer those skills to a greater variety of situations.

• Remember that Peskin and Astington (2004) showed that children had better social understanding after reading texts when they had to construct their own interpretations of text and make mental state inferences themselves instead of having the mental and emotional state explanations supplied for them in stories. That is, as with other aspects of comprehension instruction, students need to construct their own knowledge and do their own thinking (e.g., Brown, 2008; Duffy, 2014). Students' active engagement in making social inferences will promote learning and transfer to new situations and texts in ways that teacher provision of those inferences and thoughts for students will not.

- Finally, keep in mind that social understanding can be taught explicitly. Guajardo and Watson (2002), Lysaker and colleagues (2011; also see Lysaker & Tonge, 2013), and Stahl (2014) have provided evidence that social understanding can be taught in the context of intentional text discussions designed for that purpose; Guajardo and Watson showed that these gains in understanding persist for up to 4 weeks after lessons occur. To craft intentional discussions of this nature, you can discuss

  o The fact that authors do not tell us how characters' thoughts and feelings cause actions, so we have to read characters' minds to understand stories.
  o The psychological causes of characters' problems in stories.
  o Characters' internal goals, desires, thoughts, or feelings.
  o The motivations for specific actions (such as my brief discussion with my son about the pigeon's utterance on the first page of a book, described above).
  o Characters' reactions to initiating and concluding events in stories.

- Sometimes, students need extra supports for understanding how characters' internal reactions have causal effects in narratives. Two studies have demonstrated the utility of adding characters' internal states to story maps so that students have a visual support for recognizing the causal role of internal states in stories (Emery, 1996; Shanahan & Shanahan, 1997). To do this, you can use the story map provided in Chapter 3 (Figure 3.9) and have students add information about a R.CCR.3, character's internal states to each of the components of the map to highlight R.CCR.5, internal causes and reactions that tie story components together (beginning R.CCR.6 event, response/goal, attempts, outcome, reaction).

- As students become more proficient at analyzing internal, social causes in stories, you can help them engage in deeper levels of analysis by comparing multiple characters' perspectives within the same story (Shanahan & Shanahan, 1997), using story maps like the one in Figure 3.9 that you complete in parallel from different characters' perspectives (e.g., one from the shark's perspective and one from the fishes' perspectives in the story *The Three Little Fish and the Big Bad Shark* [Geist, 2007]); see Figure 7.1 for a parallel map you can use for this purpose, adapted from Figure 3.9.

- Carnine, Stevens, et al. (1982) compared two methods of helping fourth- to sixth-grade students identify characters' motives in simple and complex stories that described situations in which one character tricked another. Key to these stories was that there was an apparent motive, described explicitly, that was created

Story: _____

Character 1: _____ Character 2: _____

Setting 1: _____ Setting 2: _____

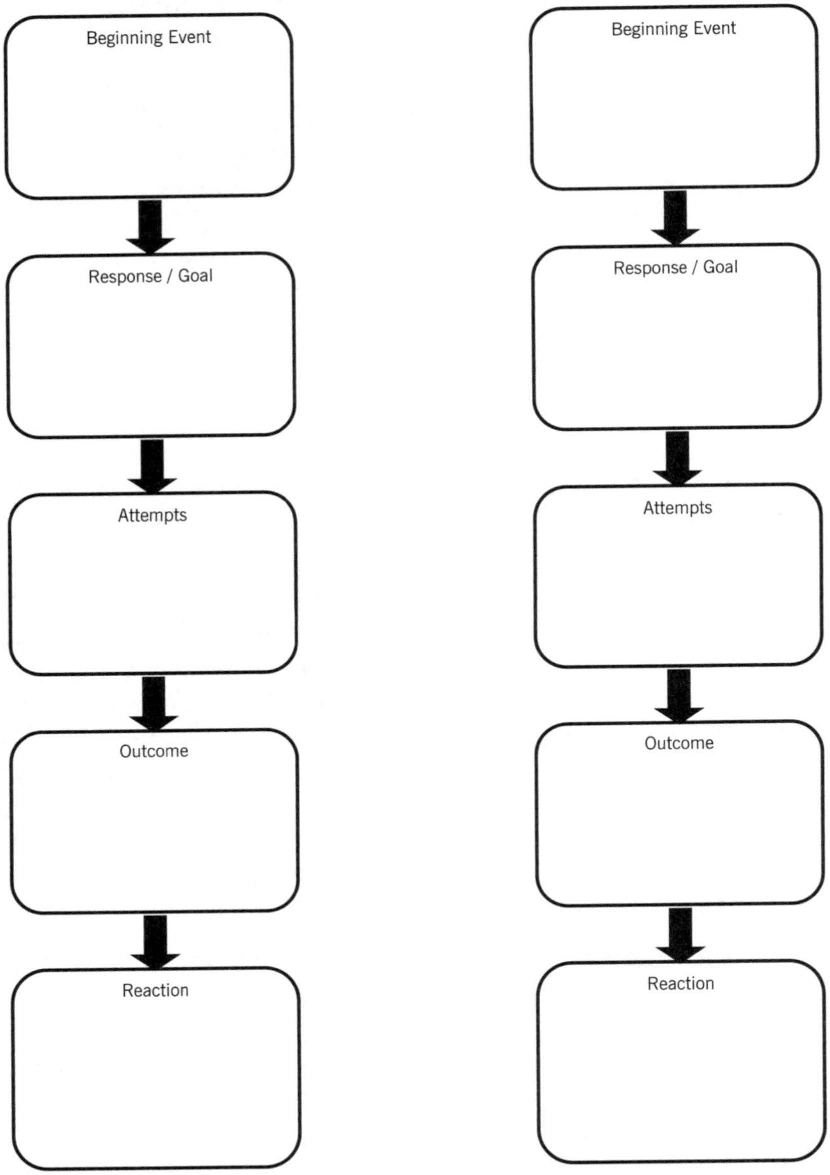

| Beginning Event | Beginning Event |

| Response / Goal | Response / Goal |

| Attempts | Attempts |

| Outcome | Outcome |

| Reaction | Reaction |

FIGURE 7.1. Mapping stories from multiple perspectives.

to induce a false belief in another story character, and there was a true, underlying motive that was implied. Carnine, Stevens, et al. (1982) showed that providing students practice identifying underlying motives with explicit feedback was just as effective as asking a series of facilitative questions to increase focus on psychological causes in stories; both methods enhanced fourth- to sixth-grade readers' abilities to consider characters' motives and improved their reading comprehension. The practice with feedback method was far less time-consuming for teachers who used the following method to support students' understanding of and ability to infer characters' motives. They asked students to describe the underlying character motives in stories and then provided feedback about completeness of students' responses. If students' responses were complete, they werve told, "Very good. That was a very complete answer." However, if their responses were incorrect or not complete, the teacher (researcher) modeled a correct inference about characters' motivations, beginning with the following phrase, "The real reason is . . . " (Carnine, Stevens, et al., 1982, p. 186). To use this method with your students, you need multiple examples of stories with underlying character motives that must be inferred so that you have enough examples to model for students and then provide them practice with new texts.

• Remember that your students' abilities to make inferences based on characters' internal states is going to be contingent on their own levels of social understanding or theory of mind (Astington, 1990; Pelletier & Astington, 2004; Riggio & Cassidy, 2009). Thus, you may want to assess your students' levels of social understanding, using procedures suggested in the next section.

Assessing Social Understanding

You may find that your students vary considerably in social understanding, and so you may decide to assess baseline levels of social understanding to help you group your students for instruction or to identify students who could benefit from some explicit instruction in using mental and emotional state information for better understanding texts. The following are some ways you might incorporate social understanding assessment into your classroom routines.

• The classic unexpected contents assessment of social understanding (Perner et al., 1987), which is probably most appropriate for early elementary students, can be easily adapted to assess your own students' theory of mind. Find any closed container that students would recognize (e.g., a crayon box, a juice box, a cereal box, or a box of crackers), and replace its contents with something surprising. I have assessed theory of mind in preschoolers, for example, using a candy box that contained a pink plastic pig! This assessment should be conducted individually.

Present the box to your student and ask what he or she thinks is inside. (The student should answer with the typical contents of the container; thus, if you use a crayon box, your student should think crayons are inside.) Then show your student the surprising contents of the box (e.g., you can use rubber bands, pencils, stickers, or anything else you have on hand), close the box again, and ask your student, "If I show _____ [name of the student's classmate] this box, what will he or she think is inside?" If your student is able to think about others' thoughts, he or she will say that the classmate will think there are crayons inside. If your student has difficulty thinking about others' thoughts, he or she may say that the classmate will say what is really in the box (whatever surprising contents you had hidden inside and just revealed to your student). Incorrect responses on this task may indicate the need for more practice inferring others' mental states.

• Other ways to assess your students' social understanding are to have your students describe reasons for characters' behaviors while reading texts that you have prescreened for explainable social themes. Keep in mind those text features that facilitate such explanations for students who are learning this skill (e.g., antisocial actions, thoughts, or beliefs instead of emotions, and distance between questions and actions in texts; see above). Small-group instruction is an ideal context for this type of informal assessment. Your students' explanations will give you insights into their abilities to infer characters' thoughts, feelings, and beliefs. Anecdotal notes will help you determine which students may need additional assessment and instruction to support their use of social understanding to better understand texts. You could also print the list of mental state vocabulary in Table 7.3 and mark the words your students use in their explanations during small-group instruction.

• For an individual, text-based assessment, you might have a student "read" a wordless picture book to you, such as one of the books listed in Table 7.2, and note your students' use of the mental state words listed in Table 7.3. This could be a useful progress monitoring assessment at various times during the academic year. Separated by several weeks, your students' explanations for the same text (or even different texts) will give you a window into the extent to which your students understand and use information about characters' internal motivations when comprehending stories.

What We Know and What We Still Need to Know about Social Understanding

Although social understanding is relatively new to the discussion of executive skills, evidence clearly indicates that social understanding, like other executive skills, is an important frontal lobe function, and social understanding activates frontal lobe areas associated with executive functioning that also overlap with those areas recruited by narrative comprehension. Furthermore, we know that social understanding is related to metacognition, oral language development, narrative comprehension, and reading comprehension. Knowledge of characters' thoughts, beliefs, feelings, and motivations enables readers to understand texts at a deeper level because they can make inferences about the internal causes of characters' actions in stories. Further, we know that reading fictional and narrative texts can facilitate social understanding in typically developing children and adults who prefer social stories to nonsocial ones. Individuals on the autism spectrum, however, have difficulty with social understanding; and they have difficulty with reading comprehension, especially with social texts, which may be why they prefer nonsocial texts.

We know that narrative texts provide many opportunities for students to learn and practice the mental and emotional state vocabulary words that are essential to skilled social understanding. And, regarding text features, researchers have demonstrated that simple picture books and wordless picture books are excellent texts to use to begin teaching social understanding. Students who are learning this important executive skill may understand characters' internal motivations better in texts that describe antisocial actions or situations when thoughts and beliefs, rather than feelings, are the driving forces behind characters' behaviors. Thus, texts that include these features may be better starting points for discussions of social understanding with your students. Finally, we also know that counterfactual thinking, another aspect of social understanding, is related to reading comprehension in children and adults. However, we know very little else about how and why that relation exists. Clearly more work is needed in this area.

Because the relation of various aspects of social understanding to reading is such a new research area in the fields of reading and executive skills, many questions remain to provide a fuller understanding of how these skills are related and how social understanding should be incorporated into effective comprehension instruction programs. The following list suggests starting points for filling these gaps:

- We need to know how social understanding is related to reading comprehension across the lifespan, whether it can be taught in struggling adult learners, and whether the few studies that have shown social understanding can be taught to children can be replicated with additional ages and grade levels.

- Although we have some evidence, we really know little about what texts are more or less effective in teaching social understanding. Certainly fictional narratives would be most amenable to this kind of instruction, but what about expository texts that describe human events and actions? History and social studies courses inevitably include information about human actions and reactions, but very little work has examined the relations of social understanding to the comprehension of these kinds of texts. As mentioned in Chapter 3, Gaskins and colleagues (2013) are doing some innovative work looking at action cycles in social studies and history courses at Benchmark School, a school for struggling readers in Media, Pennsylvania; they taught students to focus on the ways that human needs and reactions motivate human actions and produce historical or social changes, which improved students' comprehension of social studies and history texts. Such instruction is based in social understanding, but we need more studies of this nature with expository texts.

• We need additional work on social-understanding interventions that can be implemented with various ages and grade levels, and in varied instructional contexts. The studies that have been conducted to date have yielded promising results, but we need to know more about how to facilitate this important kind of executive skill in our students.

• As noted previously, no work has examined whether social understanding is related to readers' understanding of authors' purposes for writing texts. Social understanding may be an important underlying cognitive ability that supports readers' understanding of authors' purposes, which should, in turn, support reading comprehension.

• Finally, we need to know more about why counterfactual thinking is related to reading comprehension in children and adults, whether it can be taught, and, if it can be taught, whether such instruction will also improve reading comprehension.

Linking the New with the Old

How Are Familiar Comprehension Skills and Strategies Related to Executive Skills?

Re-vision—the act of looking back, of seeing with fresh eyes, of entering an old text from a new critical direction.
—ADRIENNE RICH (1972, p. 18)

Education is the great conversion process under which abstract knowledge becomes useful and productive activity. It is something that need never stop. No matter how old we become, we can acquire knowledge and use it. We can gather wisdom and profit from it. We can grow and progress and improve—and, in the process, strengthen the lives of those within our circle of influence.
—GORDON B. HINCKLEY (2009, pp. 69–70)

As you've read through the chapters in this book, you have probably made connections to your existing knowledge of effective comprehension instruction. In Chapter 2, for example, we talked about predicting, a strategy that has enjoyed a prominent place in professional texts on reading comprehension instruction (e.g., Block & Duffy, 2008; Duke et al., 2011; Keene & Zimmerman, 2007) and in the numerous basal reader series many schools use to guide elementary literacy instruction. (See Dewitz et al., 2009, for a review of the strategies typically included in basal reader series.) You've probably wondered too how familiar concepts, such as metacognition and comprehension strategies, fit into the bigger picture of executive skills that we have been discussing in this book. As the quotes at the beginning of this chapter suggest, this brief epilogue is intended to help you re-vision your thinking about the processes involved in skilled reading comprehension and effective comprehension instruction in a way that connects your existing knowledge with the new ideas you've encountered in this book. In so doing, the students, parents, teachers, and coaches with whom you work—that is, those within your circle of influence—will benefit from your new understandings about the thinking processes that underlie skilled reading comprehension.

Metacognition and Self-Regulated Learning

For decades, we have understood that the primary goal in effective instruction is to teach "students how to do things the way smart people do things" (Pressley & Gaskins, 2006, p. 106) by equipping them with the cognitive skills and strategies necessary to direct or regulate their own learning toward successful ends, because these are the behaviors we observe in successful learners (Zimmerman, 1990). With respect to reading comprehension in particular, we have known for some time that expert comprehenders are active, regulate their own comprehension processes, and use particular strategies to ensure their comprehension goals are met (Pressley & Afflerbach, 1995; Pressley & Lundeberg, 2008; Wyatt et al., 1993). Additionally, evidence has shown that when we teach students to become metacognitively aware of their comprehension processes and equip them with the specific cognitive strategies known to support skilled reading comprehension, our students' reading comprehension improves (Brown, Pressley, Van Meter, & Schuder, 1996; Brown, 2008; Duffy, Roehler, & Herrmann, 1988; Pressley et al., 1989). Thus, best practices in reading comprehension instruction have involved helping our students become self-regulated learners who are aware of the mental processes they use to comprehend texts and who are able to engage intentionally in particular cognitive activities to promote their own learning, such as using comprehension strategies to facilitate their understanding of texts (Block & Pressley, 2002; Israel et al., 2005; Keene & Zimmerman, 2007; Pressley, 2002b).

Metacognition is an aspect of *social understanding* that we discussed in Chapter 7. We learned in that chapter that it is no coincidence that metacognition and comprehension are related: they activate overlapping areas in the frontal lobes of the brain (Mar, 2011; Schmitz et al., 2004; Vogeley et al., 2001). As I noted in Chapter 1, *our executive skills are what we use to engage in self-regulated, goal-directed behavior in any area of life, from planning and executing a trip to the grocery store to reading and understanding a complex journal article.* You may have inferred that executive skills are the mental processes that underlie self-regulated learning. The fact that skilled comprehenders demonstrate a high degree of self-regulation and metacognitive awareness of their reading processes is evidence that they have high levels of executive skills that they can employ to reach their comprehension goals. In short, executive skills drive and support metacognitively aware, self-regulated reading comprehension.

Comprehension Strategies

Comprehension strategies are probably the most familiar and widely popularized aspects of comprehension instruction over the last few decades. Because skilled comprehenders regularly employ a small set of cognitive strategies to achieve their comprehension goals (Pressley & Afflerbach, 1995; Pressley & Lundeberg, 2008; Wyatt et al., 1993), and teaching this set of strategies results in significant improvements in comprehension for struggling students (Brown et al., 1996; Brown, 2008; Duffy et al., 1988; Pressley et al., 1989), we have seen a steep rise in the popularity of comprehension strategies instruction in professional texts for teachers (e.g., Harvey & Goudvis, 2007; Keene & Zimmerman, 2007) and in elementary classrooms. For the past decade, at least, I have not been able to walk into any elementary classroom without seeing at least one wall chart devoted to reminding students to use their comprehension strategies. And, as noted above, comprehension strategies instruction has made its way into the various basal reader series typically used by elementary schools to guide literacy instruction (DeWitz et al., 2009).

Skilled comprehenders employ particular cognitive strategies as part of their plan to understand a text (see Chapter 2) to ensure that they achieve their comprehension goals (Pressley & Afflerbach, 1995; Wyatt et al., 1993), and they do so flexibly, shifting focus as needed to ensure they understand what they read (Pressley & Lundeberg, 2008). The flexibility with which skilled comprehenders select and shift between their various cognitive strategies involves the kind of *cognitive flexibility* described in Chapter 4. Such flexible strategy use provides evidence that readers are, indeed, deliberately guiding their learning to particular ends; that is, flexible, deliberate strategy use is evidence of the operation of executive skills. Indeed, strategic reading comprehension and learning from text are associated with activity in the frontal lobes in regions typically associated with executive skills (Moss et al., 2011; Moss et al., 2013; see Baker et al., 2014, for a review). In the following paragraphs I describe how each of the most common comprehension strategies relates to the executive skills presented in this book (Brown, 2008; Keene & Zimmerman, 2007; Pressley, 2002b; Pressley & Gaskins, 2006).

Connecting to Prior Knowledge

One of the first strategies we teach our students is to make connections to their own prior knowledge, or schemas, because such connections facilitate reading comprehension (Anderson, 1984; Anderson & Pearson, 1984). In fact, struggling comprehenders benefit from explicit instruction in this strategy, resulting in significant increases in their reading comprehension (Hansen, 1981; Hansen & Pearson, 1983). We discussed this strategy in the context of *planning* (Chapter 2) because one of the key ways that skilled comprehenders prepare to read texts is to check their prior knowledge to see what they already know abut the topic of a text. In addition, as we discussed in Chapter 5, as skilled comprehenders construct mental models of texts' meanings in *working memory* (Kintsch, 1994), they draw on prior knowledge to make inferences that fill gaps in the text (Baker & Stein, 1981; Elbro & Buch-Iversen, 2013; Oakhill & Cain, 1999).

Self-Questioning

Not only do skilled comprehenders draw on prior knowledge when approaching a new text, they also ask themselves questions about the text, which aids them in their goal-directed search for meaning as they read (Afflerbach & Pressley, 1995; Brown, 2008; Pressley, 2002b). Like making connections to prior knowledge, self-questioning is an essential component of *planning* to understand a text (Chapter 2), and continuing to seek answers to one's self-directed questions while reading is essential to maintaining and updating that plan in *working memory* (Chapter 5).

Predicting

Making predictions involves using one's prior knowledge along with clues from text to make hypotheses about text content (Brown, 2008; Pressley, 2002b). As part of the *planning* process for comprehension (Chapter 2), predictions often arise from self-questioning as potential answers to a readers' questions about a text prior to reading. Predicting also continues to occur throughout the reading process as readers construct and update mental models of text meaning in *working memory* as they progress through texts (Chapter 5).

Using Text Structure

When *planning* to understand a text, skilled comprehenders also preview and use text structure to help themselves *organize* text information in *working memory* as they construct models of text meaning while reading (Afflerbach & Pressley, 1995; Pressley & Gaskins, 2006; Pressley & Lundeberg, 2008). Additionally, teaching text structures improves students' comprehension of narrative and expository texts (Williams, 2003, 2005). Awareness and use of text structure are important aspects of readers' *organizational* processes that we discussed in Chapter 3; readers who are able to recognize and extract information about text structure when they read have significantly better reading comprehension than readers who are not aware of structure or cannot use that information as they attempt to construct models of text meaning.

Visualizing

We have known that visualizing, otherwise known as mental imagery, is a tremendously effective strategy for helping readers remember information from texts since the 1970s (e.g., Levin, 1973; Pressley, 1976). And it is no surprise that skilled comprehenders also visualize text content to help themselves make sense of text (Pressley & Afflerbach, 1995). As we discussed in Chapter 5, according to dual coding theory, when skilled readers build models of text meaning in *working memory*, they do so in multiple ways: verbally and visually (Sadoski, 2008; Sadoski & Paivio, 2013). Encoding text information in multiple ways strengthens readers' memory for and understanding of text content. But struggling comprehenders often fail to make the kinds of mental images necessary to support comprehension (Sadoski, 1983, 1985). Fortunately, when they are taught to process both verbal and visual information when reading, consistent with dual coding models of text comprehension, their comprehension improves (Levin, 1973; Pressley, 1976).

Making Inferences

Inference making occurs in *working memory* (see Chapter 5) and comes in at least two varieties. Readers make text-based or text-connecting inferences that require integration of multiple bits of information from text, and, as mentioned above, readers make gap-filling inferences that require them to supply information from their own prior knowledge that is missing from texts (Baker & Stein, 1981; Cain & Oakhill, 1999; Elbro & Buch-Iversen, 2013; Graesser et al., 1994). These inference-making processes also require that readers be able to suppress irrelevant information in *working memory*, a critical aspect of *inhibition*, which we discussed briefly in Chapter 5 and again in Chapter 6, in order to construct appropriate inferences that are relevant to a text's meaning.

Sometimes inferences require that readers think about and supply basic world knowledge that is nonsocial in nature. Other times, however, inferences require that readers understand the internal mental, motivational, or emotional states of characters in order to comprehend and predict characters' actions in texts. But these inferences are often more difficult for younger and struggling readers, who make inferences about actions rather than inferences about characters' internal responses (McConaughy, 1985; McConaughy et al., 1983). Fortunately, we can teach students as young as kindergarteners to make inferences based on characters' internal states, resulting in improvements in reading comprehension (Carnine et al., 1982; Lysaker et al., 2011; Stahl, 2014). Social inferences like these are more difficult than nonsocial inferences because they require that readers also rely on *social understanding*, a hot executive skill, which we discussed in Chapter 7, that is essential for skilled reading comprehension.

Summarizing

Finally, we also know that skilled comprehenders are able to produce good summaries of texts that they read, which preserve most important aspects of meaning of longer texts (Brown, 2008; Pressley, 2002b; Pressley & Afflerbach, 1995). According to Levin and Hanten (2005, p. 84), "to extract the 'gist' or meaning from connected language (e.g., summarization), executive functions are needed to prioritize the importance of information and inhibit irrelevant details, and working memory [is needed] to hold information in storage during transformation." Prioritization of the importance of information draws on readers' *organizational skills* (Chapter 3), inhibition of irrelevant details draws on readers' *inhibition* processes (Chapter 6), holding text information in mind while transforming one's more detailed representation to a summary requires *complex working memory* skill (Chapter 5) and *cognitive flexibility* (Chapter 4) is probably necessary to switch back and forth between one's more detailed representation of a text's meaning and the summary under construction. Most of the research in this area has focused on readers' inabilities to construct summaries after brain injury, finding that working memory and inhibition processes are both related to summarization ability (Chapman et al., 2006; Gamino, Chapman, & Cook, 2009; Hanten et al., 2004); however, more research is needed to understand the relation of various executive skills to noninjured, skilled readers' summarization abilities.

How Might All of These Processes Work Together in Reading Comprehension?

Before Reading

When skilled comprehenders pick up a new text, they approach the reading task very deliberately, with a *plan* to understand the text for a particular purpose. To prepare to understand a text, skilled comprehenders preview the text, *making connections* to their own prior knowledge about the topic of the text, *asking themselves questions* about what they might encounter in the text, and *making predictions* about what they expect to discover as they read. Moreover, they *preview the text's structure*, because they are aware that knowledge of text structure will help them *organize* incoming information as they read and support their own construction of a model of the text's meaning in *working memory*. Thus, even when *planning* for comprehension before reading begins, skilled comprehenders display remarkable *cognitive flexibility, shifting* between thoughts of their own prior knowledge, asking questions, making predictions, and previewing text structure, all while maintaining focus on their primary goal for understanding the text.

During Reading

As they begin to read, skilled comprehenders rely on their high levels of *cognitive flexibility* to manage decoding processes while building a coherent model of text meaning in *working memory*, continuing to *draw on their prior knowledge* to understand the ideas and words they encounter and to make gap-filling *inferences* when necessary. These activities require that skilled comprehenders *flexibly juggle* multiple kinds of information as they read, such as letter–sound information recruited in decoding processes, information about text and language organization, word meanings and their links to prior knowledge, *visualization* of actions and events in the text, text-based *inference* and integration processes, information and inferences about characters' internal mental worlds that recruit *social understanding* processes, and *updating* the ever-evolving model of text meaning under construction in *working memory* as these processes continue. Skilled comprehenders also draw on their *inhibition* processes while reading to suppress irrelevant information in the text, ignore other distractions in the environment, and to refrain from engaging in habitual behaviors that would not support reading comprehension, such as looking at their phones or checking social media. Skilled comprehenders are able to manage *flexibly* all of these processes while they identify the most important features of text to *construct summaries* that will support comprehension and memory for text content during reading and after reading has concluded. Summarization necessarily requires maintenance of relevant information in *working memory, inhibition* of attention to irrelevant or tangential information, and the *cognitive flexibility* necessary to switch back and forth between the more detailed model of the text's meaning and the summary of the essential portions of the text.

After Reading

Finally, even after they finish reading a text, skilled comprehenders continue to reflect on text content, *connecting* the new information they have learned to their existing knowledge structures in ways that capitalize on their existing conceptual *organization, flexibly shifting* and adjusting their own knowledge structures as necessary in response to the new information gleaned from text. In addition, skilled comprehenders draw conclusions about the *questions* and *predictions* that guided their *planning* and processing of the text, and they evaluate the extent to which they were successful in implementing their *plan* to reach particular comprehension goals. These postreading activities necessarily recruit *working memory* as skilled readers reflect on their *summary* of text information; call their own *prior knowledge, predictions,* and *questions* to mind; revise knowledge structures as necessary; and evaluate the extent to which their comprehension goals were met.

Concluding Thoughts

Skilled reading comprehension is like an intricate piece of music in which skilled comprehenders masterfully and purposefully weave together the most complex mental processes available to human minds. I close with a snippet from the quote with which I opened Chapter 1. Skilled reading comprehension reflects "the most intricate workings of the human mind, as well as . . . the most remarkable specific performance that civilization has learned in all its history" (Huey, 1908, p. 6). After reading this text, my hope is that you better understand executive skills and what they look like in young readers, and that you come away from your reading of this text with an understanding of why executive skills are essential to successful reading comprehension and comprehension instruction, knowledge of executive skills-based reading comprehension intervention strategies you can try with your students, and a sense of what we know now and what we need to know in order to take best advantage of what the neurosciences have to offer for helping our students develop into active, purposeful, thinking readers.

APPENDIX A. Rubric for Assessing Executive Skills in Observations of Your Students' Reading Behavior

Executive skill	High level	Low level
Planning	Before beginning a reading task, student assesses his or her existing knowledge about the text's topic and sets a goal for reading; student previews text and notes structure and organizational signals; student connects to prior knowledge, asks questions about the text, and makes predictions about what he or she will discover when reading; after setting a goal, checking prior knowledge, and previewing the text, student begins reading with a goal in mind and is clearly aware of processes and strategies that will support his or her progress toward that goal.	Student is not aware that he or she can engage in behaviors to support understanding before beginning to read a text; doesn't appear to approach text with any clear plan in mind; when beginning a reading task, student just picks up the text and begins reading on the first page without previewing the text; doesn't link new information to existing knowledge prior to reading; doesn't pay attention to the organizational features that highlight important points in the text, such as bolded glossary terms, headings and subheadings, diagrams, and labels; student seems to lack a clear goal and/or awareness of processes he or she could use to reach an assigned reading goal.
Organization	Student is aware of language structure, producing and understanding complex and correctly formed sentences, in speaking, reading, and writing; has a clear sense of narrative structure, as evidenced by well-organized retellings of stories that preserve causal relationships between story elements; writing preserves narrative structure, as well; student is aware of the organization of his or her conceptual knowledge, making connections from prior knowledge to new concepts encountered in text; student is aware of the organizational cues in expository text, using features like headings, bolded words, diagrams, and labels; and student has an awareness of the different kinds of expository text structures and can use them to get information from texts.	Student is less aware of proper word order and sentence structure than peers, as evidenced in production of sentences in speaking and writing, and in understanding of sentences in listening and reading; student's narrative writing and retellings of stories lack coherent structure, indicating a lack of awareness of narrative structure; when reading expository text, student doesn't seem to pay attention to the organizational features that highlight important points in the text, such as bolded glossary terms, headings and subheadings, diagrams, and labels; student seems to lack awareness that organizational features of expository text can facilitate comprehension or could help him or her connect new information in text to existing knowledge structures; student seems to lack awareness of the various expository text structures and fails to use them to support comprehension.

Executive skill	High level	Low level
Cognitive flexibility	Student is a skilled decoder whose fluency and comprehension are appropriate for grade level; student can coordinate word-level processing with meaning construction and can easily read aloud a story and then retell it, preserving the causal chain of events and remembering details critical to the plot; student makes connections across texts, flexibly considering how information in a current text relates to other texts he or she has read and integrating information across texts when appropriate; student easily grasps humor based on multiple word meanings (e.g., riddles), comprehends metaphors, idioms, and figurative language, and is able to select appropriate word meanings that fit text contexts; student has no difficulty changing focus and transitioning between tasks during the school day.	Student has appropriate decoding skills for grade level (or even above-grade-level decoding skills) with good fluency, but reading comprehension is low; student gets "stuck" on particular interpretations of text and can't change perspective to incorporate new ideas; student has difficulty with words with multiple meanings, such as jokes and riddles based on verbal ambiguity, metaphors, idioms, or figurative language; student has difficulty connecting or integrating information across passages or texts; student doesn't seem to transition between tasks very well during the school day; student can have trouble switching perspectives or focus when necessary to ensure understanding or to follow the routines of the school day.
Working memory	Student easily infers new words' meanings from context, having no difficulty retaining and connecting the relevant contextual information with new words encountered in text; student remembers and uses new words in conversation or writing; when reading, student has no trouble tracking characters' identities, even when the text includes a number of pronominal references to characters; student can make complex inferences from both narrative and expository texts, either by supplying appropriate world knowledge to fill text gaps or by connecting text elements, even when they are separated by a distance; student is always on top of assignments, remembers homework, submits work on time, and is able to keep up with belongings.	Student has difficulty inferring new words' meanings from context and cannot seem to hold the relevant context in mind long enough to attach it to unknown words; student seems to get lost in text, especially when the text is ambiguous, and does not track anaphoric references as well as peers; with respect to integration and inference making, student usually doesn't make inferences from text; student's attempts at inference making are more likely to be gap-filling inferences, but student may not notice whether the knowledge supplied actually fits the context of the passage; with respect to classroom behavior, student often forgets homework, doesn't remember to return forms or share forms/information with parents when required; student is more likely than peers to leave belongings behind.

Executive skill	High level	Low level
Inhibition	Student has no difficulty sitting "like a reader" while engaged with a text; student is not easily distracted while reading with such things as attractive objects or rowdy peers nearby; student has good awareness of appropriate word meanings for texts' contexts, even when the context is pointing to a less common meaning, as is typical in expository texts (i.e., student can inhibit inappropriate word meanings); student can resist interference from irrelevant information and is confident in selecting appropriate meanings for ambiguous words in expository texts; student is good at tracking narratives with complex plots, even when they require that the student discard information that had originally seemed useful; student can resist both behavioral and cognitive interference to support reading comprehension and stay on task.	Student has difficulty engaging in the kinds of behavior regulation necessary for effective comprehension, like sitting still and resisting temptations to look around at irrelevant objects or boisterous peers rather than at the text; student has trouble finding the appropriate meanings for words in reading, writing, and speaking, often impulsively selecting the first meanings that come to mind; student also has trouble discarding information that seems relevant to a text's meaning early on, but is later revealed to be irrelevant as the plot develops and may become fixated on irrelevant information; student has difficulty resisting both behavioral and cognitive interference in order to support reading comprehension and has difficulty staying on task.
Social understanding	Student has no difficulty identifying characters' motives, feelings, or thoughts, and draws on these internal states to explain characters' actions in conversations about and retellings of information in texts; retellings are peppered with vocabulary words that describe internal mental and emotional states, words like *think, know, guess, feel*, and *want* (see Table 7.3); in daily conversations, student seems to use these words more frequently than peers; student notes actions and events in stories and can identify story structures, and student has no difficulty making more abstract inferences about characters' internal motivations for their actions, providing a deeper understanding of texts than peers; in a broader sense, student has excellent peer relations, is able to interpret peers' responses, recognizes peers' feelings, and shows empathy for peers who are upset.	Student has difficulty inferring why characters do the things that they do and student's retellings of stories often miss key details and lack organization; student's retellings of stories focus on actions and events rather than the underlying, internal reasons for characters' actions, and sound more like a running commentary on a string of events rather than a coherent narrative that is held together by the underlying motives, thoughts, and feelings of the characters; student uses few words that refer to internal mental and emotional states (see Table 7.3) in retellings and conversations about books; in a broader sense, student has poor peer relations, doesn't seem to understand others' perspectives, doesn't have a good sense of the appropriate ways to interact with peers, and peers' responses are often lost on him or her; student may not understand or be aware of the effects of his or her actions on others and is unable to generate alternative actions that could have produced a different, more positive result from peers.

APPENDIX B. List of Games That Require Behaviors Related to the Executive Skills Described in This Book

Executive skill	Game(s)[a]	Executive demands
Planning	*Checkers* Chess Connect Four Pick Up Stix Rubik's Cube Jenga	Each of these requires consideration of multistep reasoning, in which (1) successive steps are contingent on performance on earlier steps or (2) each move requires imagining impacts on multiple other pieces or players (e.g., in Jenga), in order to produce successful performance.
Organization	*Twenty Questions* *I Spy* Scattergories Apples to Apples Rummy Poker	Card games, such as rummy and poker, require awareness of different ways to organize subsets of cards (i.e., according to suit and/or value). Twenty Questions, I Spy, Scattergories, and Apples to Apples require awareness of conceptual organization.
Cognitive flexibility	*Set* *Uno* Sorting Stones Riddles	Set and Uno require players to attend to, and switch between, multiple features of cards at the same time (e.g., color, number, etc.). Sorting Stones are a children's educational toy that can be sorted by shape and color and can be used to teach switching. Riddles require flexible attention to, and ability to switch between, multiple meanings of words.
Working memory	*Johnny has an Apple in His Pocket* *The Name Game* Memory Go Fish Five Little Monkeys Simon	Johnny has an Apple in his pocket and The Name Game require that students hold information in mind (storage) while coming up with appropriate responses for their turn (processing) and updating the stored information with each successive student's turn (updating). Memory and Go Fish require students to remember the locations of cards in an array or in others' hands (storage) while also engaging in appropriate moves on their turns (processing). The Five Little Monkeys and other counting rhymes require students to remember where they are in the reverse counting sequence (storage) while engaging in the singing/saying of the rhyme (processing). Simon, an electronic game that involves repetition of ever-increasing numbers of tones, taps and likely strengthens students' simple working memory span.

[a]Games for which executive demands are described in text are denoted with *italics*.

Executive skill	Game(s)	Executive demands
Inhibition	*Simon Says* Red Light Green Light Head and Shoulders, Knees and Toes BINGO Song *Taboo* Mad Gab	Simon Says; Red Light, Green Light; Head and Shoulders, Knees and Toes, and the BINGO song require response inhibition because students must refrain from responding in particular ways. Taboo and Mad Gab require cognitive inhibition because players must suppress interference from certain kinds of information (taboo words in Taboo and word meanings in Mad Gab) to be successful.
Social understanding	*Old Maid* *Hide and Seek* Poker	Old Maid, Hide and Seek, and poker all require players to be aware of others' thoughts, perceptions, and emotions, and they require that players be aware of their own behavior in order to conceal information from others.

Children's Literature Cited

Arnold, T. (2000). *Parts*. New York: Dial Books for Young Readers.

Arnold, T. (2003). *More parts*. New York: Dial Books for Young Readers.

Arnold, T. (2007). *Even more parts*. New York: Dial Books for Young Readers.

Barretta, G. (2007). *Dear deer*. New York: Holt.

Bell, C. (2003). *Sock Monkey goes to Hollywood: A star is bathed*. Cambridge, MA: Candlewick Press.

Bloom, B. (1999). *Wolf*. New York: Orchard Books.

Cleary, B. P. (2007). *How much can a bare bear bear?* Minneapolis, MN: Millbrook Press.

Daywalt, D. (2013). *The day the crayons quit*. New York: Philomel.

Frasier, D. (2007). *Miss Alaineus: The vocabulary disaster*. New York: Houghton Mifflin.

Geist, W. (2007). *The three little fish and the big bad shark*. New York: Scholastic Books.

Gwynne, F. (1988a). *A little pigeon toad*. New York: Aladdin Paperbacks.

Gwynne, F. (1988b). *The king who rained*. New York: Aladdin Paperbacks.

Hughes, C. D. (2012). *National Geographic little kids first big book of space*. Washington, DC: National Geographic Books.

Kenah, K. (2014). *Ferry tail*. Ann Arbor, MI: Sleeping Bear Press.

Laminack, L. L. (1998). *The sunsets of Miss Olivia Wiggins*. Atlanta, GA: Peachtree Press.

Loewen, N. (2011). *You're toast and other metaphors*. North Mankato, MN: Picture Window Books.

MacAulay, K., & Kalman, B. (2005). *Reptiles of all kinds*. New York: Crabtree.

Parrish, H. (2003). *Amelia Bedelia, bookworm*. New York: Scholastic Books.

Parrish, P. (1963). *Amelia Bedelia*. New York: Harper Collins.

Piper, W. (1976). *The little engine that could*. New York: Platt & Munk.

Pulver, R. (2004). *Punctuation takes a vacation*. New York: Holiday House.

Rabe, T. (2009). *There's no place like space! All about our solar system* (from The Cat in the Hat's Learning Library). New York: Random House.

Scieszka, J. (1996). *The true story of the three little pigs*. New York: Puffin Books.

Terban, M. (2007a). *Eight ate: A feast of homonym riddles.* New York: Houghton Mifflin.

Terban, M. (2007b). *In a pickle and other funny idioms.* New York: G. P. Putnam's Sons.

Truss, L. (2006). *Eats, shoots and leaves: Why, commas really do make a difference!* New York: G. P. Putnam's Sons.

Viorst, J. (1972). *Alexander and the terrible, horrible, no good, very bad day.* New York: Aladdin Paperbacks.

White, E. B. (1952). *Charlotte's web.* New York: Harper Collins.

Willems, M. (2007). *There is a bird on your head!* New York: Hyperion Books for Children.

Willems, M. (2012). *The duckling gets a cookie!?* New York: Hyperion Books for Children.

Willems, M. (2013). *A big guy took my ball!* New York: Hyperion Books for Children.

References

Aaron, P. G., Joshi, M., & Williams, K. A. (1999). Not all reading disabilities are alike. *Journal of Learning Disabilities, 32,* 120–137.

Adams, M. J., & Collins, A. (1977). *A schema-theoretic view of reading* (Technical Report No. 32). Cambridge, MA: Bolt, Beranek, & Newman.

Adrián, J. E., Clemente, R. A., & Villanueva, L. (2007). Mothers' use of cognitive state verbs in picture-book reading and the development of children's understanding of mind: A longitudinal study. *Child Development, 78*(4), 1052–1067.

Adrian, J. E., Clemente, R. A., Villanueva, L., & Rieffe, C. (2005). Parent–child picture-book reading, mothers' mental state language and children's theory of mind. *Journal of Child Language, 32*(3), 673–686.

Akhondi, M., Malayeri, F. A., & Samad, A. A. (2011). How to teach expository text structure to facilitate reading comprehension. *The Reading Teacher, 64*(5), 368–372.

Alarcón-Rubio, Sánchez-Medina, J. A., & Prieto-García, J. R. (2014). Executive function and verbal self-regulation in childhood: Developmental linkages between partially internalized private speech and cognitive flexibility. *Early Childhood Research Quarterly, 29,* 95–105.

Allan, N. P., Hume, L. E., Allan, D. M., Farrington, A. L., & Lonigan, C. J. (2014). Relations between inhibitory control and the development of academic skills in preschool and kindergarten: A meta-analysis. *Developmental Psychology, 50*(10), 2368–2379.

Allan, N. P., & Lonigan, C. J. (2011). Examining the dimensionality of effortful control in preschool children and its relation to academic and socio-emotional indicators. *Developmental Psychology, 47,* 905–915.

Altemeier, L. E., Abbott, R. D., & Berninger, V. W. (2008). Executive functions for reading and writing in typical literacy development and dyslexia. *Journal of Clinical and Experimental Neuropsychology, 30,* 588–606.

Altemeier, L. E, Jones, J., Abbott, R. D., & Berninger, V. W. (2006). Writing readers and reading writers: Note taking and report writing in third and fifth graders. *Developmental Neuropsychology, 29,* 161–173.

245

Alzheimer's Association & Centers for Disease Control and Prevention. (2013). *The Healthy Brain Initiative: The public health road map for state and national partnerships, 2013–2018*. Chicago: Alzheimer's Association. Retrieved from *www.cdc.gov/aging/pdf/2013-healthy-brain-initiative.pdf*.

Amso, D., & Casey, B. J. (2006). Beyond what develops when: Neuroimaging may inform how cognition changes with development. *Current Directions in Psychological Science, 15*, 24–29.

Anderson, P. (2002). Assessment and development of executive function (EF) during childhood. *Child Neuropsychology, 8*, 71–82.

Anderson, R. C. (1984). Role of the reader's schema in comprehension, learning, and memory. In R. C. Anderson, J. Osborn, & R. J. Tierney (Eds.), *Learning to read in American schools: Basal readers and content texts* (pp. 243–257). Hillsdale, NJ: Erlbaum.

Anderson, R. C., & Pearson, P. D. (1984). A schema-theoretic view of basic processes in reading comprehension. In P. D. Pearson, R. Barr, M. L. Kamil, & P. Mosenthal (Eds.), *Handbook of reading research* (pp. 255–291). New York: Longman.

Anderson, T. H., & Armbruster, B. B. (1984). Content area textbooks. In R. C. Anderson, J. Osborn, & R. J. Tierney (Eds.), *Learning to read in American schools: Basal readers and content texts* (pp. 193–226). Hillsdale, NJ: Erlbaum.

Anderson, V. A., Anderson, P., Northam, E., Jacobs, R., & Catroppa, C. (2001). Development of executive functions through late childhood and adolescence in an Australian sample. *Developmental Neuropsychology, 20*, 385–406.

Anderson, V. A., & Spencer-Smith, M. (2013). Children's frontal lobes: No longer silent? In D. T. Stuss & R. T. Knight (Eds.), *Principles of frontal lobe function* (2nd ed., pp. 118–134). New York: Oxford University Press.

Andersson, U. (2008). Working memory as a predictor of written arithmetical skills in children: The importance of central executive functions. *British Journal of Educational Psychology, 78*(2), 181–203.

Applegate, M. D., Applegate, A. J., & Modla, V. (2009). "She's my best reader; she just can't comprehend": Studying the relationship between fluency and comprehension. *The Reading Teacher, 62*, 512–521.

Aram, D., Fine, Y., & Ziv, M. (2013). Enhancing parent–child shared book reading interactions: Promoting references to the book's plot and socio-cognitive themes. *Early Childhood Research Quarterly, 28*, 111–122.

Ardilla, A. (2013). Development of metacognitive and emotional executive functions in children. *Applied Neuropsychology Child, 2*, 82–87.

Armbruster, B. B., Anderson, T. H., & Ostertag, J. (1987). Does text structure/summarization instruction facilitate learning from expository text? *Reading Research Quarterly, 22*, 331–346.

Armbruster, B. B., & Armstrong, J. O. (1993). Locating information in text: A focus on children in the elementary grades. *Contemporary Educational Psychology, 18*, 139–161.

Aron, A. R., Robbins, T. W., & Poldrack, R. A. (2004). Inhibition and the right inferior frontal cortex. *Trends in Cognitive Sciences, 8*, 170–177.

Arrington, C. N., Kulesz, P. A., Francis, D. J., Fletcher, J. M., & Barnes, M. A. (2014). The contribution of attentional control and working memory to reading comprehension and decoding. *Scientific Studies of Reading, 18*, 325–346.

Astington, J. W. (1990). Narrative and the child's theory of mind. In B. K. Britton & A. D. Pellegrini (Eds.), *Narrative thought and narrative language* (pp. 151–171). Hillsdale, NJ: Erlbaum.

Astington, J. W., Harris, P. L., & Olson, D. R. (1988). *Developing theories of mind*. New York: Cambridge University Press.

Astington, J. W., & Jenkins, J. M. (1999). A longitudinal study of the relation between language and theory-of-mind development. *Developmental Psychology, 35*, 1311–1320.

Baker, L., & Stein, N. (1981). The development of prose comprehension skills. In C. M. Santa & B. L. Hayes (Eds.), *Children's prose comprehension: Research and practice* (pp. 7–43). Newark, DE: International Reading Association.

Baker, L., Zeliger-Kandasamy, A., & DeWyngaert, L. U. (2014). Neuroimaging evidence of comprehension monitoring. *Psihologijske Teme, 23,* 167–187.

Barkley, R. A. (1997). Behavioral inhibition, sustained attention, and executive functions: Constructing a unifying theory of ADHD. *Psychological Bulletin, 121,* 65–94.

Barkley, R. A. (2012). *Executive functions: What they are, how they work, and why they evolved.* New York: Guilford Press.

Barnes, J. L. (2012). Fiction, imagination, and social cognition: Insights from autism. *Poetics, 40*(4), 299–316.

Barnes, J. L., & Bloom, P. (2014). Children's preference for social stories. *Developmental Psychology, 50*(2), 498.

Baron-Cohen, S., Wheelwright, S., Hill, J., Raste, Y., & Plumb, I. (2001). The "Reading the Mind in the Eyes" test revised version: A study with normal adults, and adults with Asperger syndrome or high-functioning autism. *Journal of Child Psychology and Psychiatry, 42*(2), 241–251.

Barquero, L. A., Davis, N., & Cutting, L. E. (2014). Neuroimaging of reading intervention: A systematic review and activation likelihood estimate meta-analysis. *PLoS ONE, 9*(1), e88638.

Bauer, P. J., & Zelazo, P. D. (2014). The National Institutes of Health Toolbox for the assessment of neurological and behavioral function: A tool for developmental science. *Child Development Perspectives, 8*(3), 119–124.

Baumann, J. F. (1986). Teaching third-grade students to comprehend anaphoric relationships: The application of a direct instruction model. *Reading Research Quarterly, 21,* 70–90.

Beck, S. R., Riggs, K. J., & Gorniak, S. L. (2009). Relating developments in children's counterfactual thinking and executive functions. *Thinking and Reasoning, 15,* 337–354.

Bell, M. A. (2012). A psychobiological perspective on working memory performance at 8 months of age. *Child Development, 83,* 251–265.

Benasich, A. A., & Tallal, P. (2002). Infant discrimination of rapid auditory cues predicts later language impairment. *Behavioural Brain Research, 136,* 31–49.

Benson, J. E., Sabbagh, M. A., Carlson, S. M., & Zelazo, P. D. (2013). Individual differences in executive functioning predict improvement from theory-of-mind training. *Developmental Psychology, 49,* 1615–1627

Benton, A. L., Elithorn, A., Fogel, M. L., & Kerr, M. (1963). A perceptual maze test sensitive to brain damage. *Journal of Neurology, Neurosurgery, and Psychiatry, 26*(6), 540–544.

Berg, E. A. (1948). A simple objective technique for measuring flexibility in thinking. *Journal of General Psychology, 39,* 15–22.

Berlin, L., Bohlin, G., & Rydell, A. (2003). Relations between inhibition, executive functioning, and ADHD symptoms: A longitudinal study from age 5 to 8 ½ years. *Child Neuropsychology, 9,* 255–266.

Best, J. R., & Miller, P. H. (2010). A developmental perspective on executive function. *Child Development, 81,* 1641–1660.

Best, J. R., Miller, P. H., & Jones, L. L. (2009). Executive functions after age 5: Changes and correlates. *Developmental Review, 29,* 180–200.

Best, J. R., Miller, P. H., & Naglieri, J. A. (2011). Relations between executive function and academic achievement from ages 5 to 17 in a large, representative national sample. *Learning and Individual Differences, 21,* 327–336.

Best, R. M., Floyd, R. G., & McNamara, D. S. (2008). Differential competencies contributing to children's comprehension of narrative and expository texts. *Reading Psychology, 29,* 137–164.

Bhide, A., Power, A., & Goswami, U. (2013). A rhythmic musical intervention for poor readers:

A comparison of efficacy with a letter-based intervention. *Mind, Brain, and Education,* 7, 113–123.

Bialystok, E., & Niccols, A. (1989). Children's control over attention to phonological and semantic properties of words. *Journal of Psycholinguistic Research, 18,* 369–387.

Bigler, R. S., & Liben, L. S. (1992). Cognitive mechanisms in children's gender stereotyping: Theoretical and educational implications of a cognitive-based intervention. *Child Development, 63,* 1351–1363.

Bigler, R. S., & Liben, L. S. (1993). A cognitive-developmental approach to racial stereotyping and reconstructive memory in Euro-American children. *Child Development, 64,* 1507–1518.

Bjorklund, D. (2012). *Children's thinking: Cognitive development and individual differences* (5th ed.). Belmont, CA: Wadsworth.

Blair, C., Knipe, H., Cummings, E., Baker, D. P., Gamson, D., Eslinger, P., et al. (2007). A developmental neuroscience approach to the study of school readiness. In R. Pianta, M. J. Cox, & K. L. Snow (Eds.), *School readiness and the transition to kindergarten in the era of accountability* (pp. 149–174). Baltimore, MD: Brookes.

Blair, C., Raver, C. C., Berry, D. J., & Family Life Project Investigators. (2014). Two approaches to estimating the effect of parenting on the development of executive function in early childhood. *Developmental Psychology, 50,* 554–563.

Blair, C., & Razza, R. P. (2007). Relating effortful control, executive function, and false belief understanding to emerging math and literacy ability in kindergarten. *Child Development, 78,* 647–663.

Blakemore, S., & Choudhury, S. (2006). Development of the adolescent brain: Implications for executive function and social cognition. *Journal of Child Psychology and Psychiatry, 47,* 296–312.

Blankson, A. N., O'Brien, M., Leerkes, E. M., Marcovitch, S., Calkins, S. D., & Weaver, J. M. (2013). Developmental dynamics of emotion and cognition processes in preschoolers. *Child Development, 84,* 346–360.

Blaye, A., & Chevalier, N. (2011). The role of goal representation in preschoolers' flexibility and inhibition. *Journal of Experimental Child Psychology, 108,* 469–483.

Block, C. C., & Duffy, G. G. (2008). Research on teaching comprehension: Where we've been and where we're going. In C. C. Block & S. R. Parris (Eds.), *Comprehension instruction: Research-based best practices* (2nd ed., pp. 19–37). New York: Guilford Press.

Block, C. C., & Pressley, M. (Eds.). (2002). *Comprehension instruction: Research-based best practices.* New York: Guilford Press.

Bock, A., Cartwright, K. B., Gonzalez, C., O'Brien, S., Robinson, M. F., Schmerold, K., et al. (2015). The role of cognitive flexibility in pattern understanding. *Journal of Education and Human Development, 4,* 19–25.

Bock, A. M., Gallaway, K. C., & Hund, A. M. (2014). Specifying links between executive functioning and theory of mind during middle childhood: Cognitive flexibility predicts social understanding. *Journal of Cognition and Development,* published online April 3, 2014.

Bodrova, E., Leong, D. J., & Akhutina, T. V. (2011). When everything new is well-forgotten old: Vygotsky/Luria insights in the development of executive functions. *New Directions for Child and Adolescent Development, 133,* 11–28.

Borella, E., Carretti, B., & Pelegrina, S. (2010). The specific role of inhibition in reading comprehension in good and poor comprehenders. *Journal of Learning Disabilities, 43,* 541–552.

Bosacki, S., & Astington, J. W. (1999). Theory of mind in preadolescence: Relations between social understanding and social competence. *Social Development, 8*(2), 237–255.

Bowyer-Crane, C., & Snowling, M. J. (2005). Assessing children's inference generation: What do tests of reading comprehension measure? *British Journal of Educational Psychology, 75,* 189–201.

Britton, B. K., & Glynn, S. M. (Eds.). (1987). *Executive control processes in reading.* Hillsdale, NJ: Erlbaum.

Brock, L. L., Rimm-Kaufman, S. E., Nathanson, L., & Grimm, K. J. (2009). The contributions of "hot" and "cool" executive function to children's academic achievement, learning-related behaviors, and engagement in kindergarten. *Early Childhood Research Quarterly, 24,* 337–349.

Brown, H. M., Oram-Cardy, J., & Johnson, A. (2013). A meta-analysis of the reading comprehension skills of individuals on the autism spectrum. *Journal of Autism and Developmental Disorders, 43*(4), 932–955.

Brown, R. (2008). The road not yet taken: A transactional strategies approach to comprehension instruction. *The Reading Teacher, 61,* 538–547.

Brown, R., Pressley, M., Van Meter, P., & Schuder, T. (1996). A quasi-experimental validation of transactional strategies instruction with low-achieving second-grade readers. *Journal of Educational Psychology, 88*(1), 18.

Bruner, J. (1988). *Actual minds, possible worlds.* Cambridge, MA: Harvard University Press.

Bruner, J. (1990). *Acts of meaning.* Cambridge, MA: Harvard University Press.

Bull, R., Espy, K. A., & Wiebe, S. A. (2008). Short-term memory, working memory, and executive functioning in preschoolers: Longitudinal predictors of mathematical achievement at age 7 years. *Developmental Neuropsychology, 33,* 205–228.

Bull, R., Phillips, L. H., & Conway, C. A. (2008). The role of control functions in mentalizing: Dual-task studies of theory of mind and executive function. *Cognition, 107*(2), 663–672.

Buly, M. R., & Valencia, S. (2002). Below the bar: Profiles of students who fail state reading assessments. *Educational Evaluation and Policy Analysis, 24,* 219–239.

Bunge, S. A., Ochsner, K. N., Desmond, J. E., Glover, G. H., & Gabrieli, J. D. (2001). Prefrontal regions involved in keeping information in and out of mind. *Brain, 124,* 2074–2086.

Bunge, S. A., & Wright, S. B. (2007). Neurodevelopmental changes in working memory and cognitive control. *Current Opinion in Neurobiology, 17,* 243–250.

Cain, K. (1996). Story knowledge and comprehension skill. In C. Cornoldi & J. Oakhill (Eds.), *Reading comprehension difficulties: Processes and intervention* (pp. 167–192). Hillsdale, NJ: Erlbaum.

Cain, K. (2003). Text comprehension and its relation to coherence and cohesion in children's fictional narratives. *British Journal of Developmental Psychology, 21,* 335–351.

Cain, K. (2006). Individual differences in children's memory and reading comprehension: An investigation of semantic and inhibitory deficits. *Memory, 14,* 553–569.

Cain, K., & Oakhill, J. (1996). The nature of the relationship between comprehension skill and the ability to tell a story. *British Journal of Developmental Psychology, 14,* 187–201.

Cain, K., & Oakhill, J. V. (1999). Inference making ability and its relation to comprehension failure. *Reading and Writing, 11,* 489–503.

Cain, K., Oakhill, J., & Bryant, P. (2004). Children's reading comprehension ability: Concurrent prediction by working memory, verbal ability, and component skills. *Journal of Educational Psychology, 96,* 31–42.

Cain, K., Oakhill, J. V., & Elbro, C. (2003). The ability to learn new word meanings from context by school-age children with and without language comprehension difficulties. *Journal of Child Language, 30,* 681–694.

Cain, K., Oakhill, J., & Lemmon, K. (2004). Individual differences in the inference of word meanings from context: The influence of reading comprehension, vocabulary knowledge, and memory capacity. *Journal of Educational Psychology, 96,* 671–681.

Cain, K., Oakhill, J., & Lemmon, K. (2005). The relation between children's reading comprehension level and their comprehension of idioms. *Journal of Experimental Child Psychology, 90*(1), 65–87.

Carlson, S. M., Claxton, L. J., & Moses, L. J. (2015). The relation between executive function and theory of mind is more than skin deep. *Journal of Cognition and Development, 16,* 186–197.

Carlson, S. M., Moses, L. J., & Claxton, L. J. (2004). Individual differences in executive functioning and theory of mind: An investigation of inhibitory control and planning ability. *Journal of Experimental Child Psychology, 87,* 299–319.

Carnine, D. W., Kame'enui, E. J., & Woolfson, N. (1982). Training of textual dimensions related to text-based inferences. *Journal of Literacy Research, 14*(3), 335–340.

Carnine, D. W., Stevens, C., Clements, J., & Kame'enui, E. J. (1982). Effects of facilitative questions and practice on intermediate students' understanding of character motives. *Journal of Literacy Research, 14*(2), 179–190.

Carpenter, G. A., & Grossberg, S. (1987). A massively parallel architecture for a self-organizing neural pattern recognition machine. *Computer Vision, Graphics, and Image Processing, 37,* 54–115.

Carr, E. M., Dewitz, P., & Patberg, J. P. (1983). The effect of inference training on children's comprehension of expository text. *Journal of Literacy Research, 15*(3), 1–18.

Carretti, B., Borella, E., Cornoldi, C., & De Beni, R. (2009). Role of working memory in explaining the performance of individuals with specific reading comprehension deficits: A meta-analysis. *Learning and Individual Differences, 19,* 246–251.

Carretti, B., Cornoldi, C., De Beni, R., & Palladino, P. (2004). What happens to information to be suppressed in working-memory tasks?: Short and long term effects. *Quarterly Journal of Experimental Psychology Section A, 57,* 1059–1084.

Carretti, B., Cornoldi, C., De Beni, R., & Romanó, M. (2005). Updating in working memory: A comparison of good and poor comprehenders. *Journal of Experimental Child Psychology, 91,* 45–66.

Cartwright, K. B. (1997). *The role of multiple classification skill in children's early skilled reading.* Unpublished doctoral dissertation, University of Arkansas.

Cartwright, K. B. (2002). Cognitive development and reading: The relation of reading-specific multiple classification skill to reading comprehension in elementary school children. *Journal of Educational Psychology, 94,* 56–63.

Cartwright, K. B. (2005, December). *The role of flexibility in moderating effects of vocabulary on children's reading comprehension.* Paper presented at the annual meeting of the Literacy Research Association (formerly the National Reading Conference), Miami, FL.

Cartwright, K. B. (2006). Fostering flexibility and comprehension in elementary students. *The Reading Teacher, 59,* 628–634.

Cartwright, K. B. (2007). The contribution of graphophonological–semantic flexibility to reading comprehension in college students: Implications for a less simple view of reading. *Journal of Literacy Research, 39,* 173–193.

Cartwright, K. B. (Ed.). (2008). *Literacy processes: Cognitive flexibility in learning and teaching.* New York: Guilford Press.

Cartwright, K. B. (2009). The role of cognitive flexibility in reading comprehension: Past, present, and future. In S. E. Israel & G. Duffy (Eds.), *Handbook of research on reading comprehension* (pp. 115–139). New York: Routledge.

Cartwright, K. B. (2010). *Word callers: Small-group and one-to-one interventions for children who "read" but don't comprehend.* Portsmouth, NH: Heinemann.

Cartwright, K. B. (2011, April). *The development of graphophonological–semantic cognitive flexibility: Insights from children's mistakes.* Paper invited for a symposium on Executive Control and Complex Cognition at the Biennial Meeting of the Society for Research in Child Development, Montreal, Canada.

Cartwright, K. B. (2012). *Insights from cognitive neuroscience: The importance of executive function for early reading development and education* [Special issue on neuroscience perspectives]. *Early Education and Development, 23,* 24–36.

Cartwright, K. B. (2015). Executive function and reading comprehension: The critical role of cognitive flexibility. In S. R. Parris & K. Headley (Eds.), *Comprehension instruction: Research-based best practices* (3rd ed., pp. 56–71). New York: Guilford Press.

Cartwright, K. B., & Coppage, E. A. (2009, December). *Cognitive profiles of word callers: Cognitive flexibility, vocabulary, and word identification in elementary school-aged good and poor comprehenders.* Paper presented at the 59th annual meeting of the Literacy Research Association (formerly the National Reading Conference), Albuquerque, NM.

Cartwright, K. B., Coppage, E. A., Guiffré, H., & Strube, L. (2008, July). *A comparison of metacognitive skills and cognitive flexibility in good and poor comprehenders.* Poster presented at the annual meeting of the Society for the Scientific Study of Reading, Asheville, NC.

Cartwright, K. B., DeBruin-Parecki, A., Vaughn, S., Badalis, J., & Orelski, J. (2014, July). *The role of theory of mind and executive skills in preschoolers' expressive vocabulary, narrative comprehension, and response to comprehension intervention.* Poster presented at Head Start's 12th National Research Conference on Early Childhood, Washington, DC.

Cartwright, K. B., & DeWyngaert, L. U. (2014, December). *The contribution of EF and motivation to reading comprehension in former elementary students with good and poor reading comprehension.* Paper presented at the annual meeting of the Literacy Research Association, Marco Island, FL.

Cartwright, K. B., & Guajardo, N. R. (2011, March). *A longitudinal study of the role of theory of mind in elementary students' metacognition and reading comprehension.* Poster presented at the biennial meeting of the Society for Research in Child Development, Montreal, Canada.

Cartwright, K. B. & Guajardo, N. R. (2015). The role of hot and cool executive functions in pre-reader comprehension. In A. DeBruin-Parecki, A. van Kleeck, & S. Gear (Eds.), *Developing early comprehension: Laying the foundation for reading success* (pp. 151–177). Baltimore, MD: Brookes.

Cartwright, K. B., Guiffré, H., Bock, A., & Coppage, E. A. (2011, October). *Effects of executive function training on reading comprehension and cognitive flexibility in second to fifth grade struggling readers.* Poster presented at the biennial meeting of the Cognitive Development Society, Philadelphia, PA.

Cartwright, K. B., Isaac, M., & Dandy, K. (2006). The development of reading-specific representational flexibility: A cross-sectional comparison of second graders, fourth graders, and college students. In A. V. Mittel (Ed.), *Focus on educational psychology* (pp. 173–194). New York: Nova Science.

Cartwright, K. B., Lane, A. B., & Singleton, T. S. (2012, December). *Effects of an executive skills intervention for reading comprehension in an RTI framework.* Paper presented at the annual meeting of the Literacy Research Association, San Diego, CA.

Cartwright, K. B., Marshall, T. R., Dandy, K., & Isaac, M. C. (2010). The development of graphophonological–semantic cognitive flexibility and its contribution to reading comprehension in beginning readers. *Journal of Cognition and Development, 11,* 61–85.

Catts, H. W., Compton, D., Tomblin, J. B., & Bridges, M. S. (2012). Prevalence and nature of late-emerging poor readers. *Journal of Educational Psychology, 104,* 166.

Catts, H. W., Hogan, T. P., & Fey, M. E. (2003). Subgrouping poor readers on the basis of individual differences in reading-related abilities. *Journal of Learning Disabilities, 36,* 151–164.

Centre for Evaluation and Monitoring. (2014). *PIPS baseline—Assessment.* Accessed June 8, 2014, at *www.cem.org/pips-baseline/assessment.*

Chall, J. S. (1996). *Stages of reading development* (2nd ed.). Fort Worth, TX: Harcourt Brace.

Chambers, C., Bellgrove, M., Stokes, M., Henderson, T., Garavan, H., Robertson, I., et al. (2006). Executive "brake failure" following deactivation of human frontal lobe. *Journal of Cognitive Neuroscience, 18,* 444–455.

Chang, K. E., Sung, Y. T., & Chen, I. D. (2002). The effect of concept mapping to enhance text comprehension and summarization. *Journal of Experimental Education, 71*(1), 5–23.

Chapman, S. B., Gamino, J. F., Cook, L. G., Hanten, G., Li, X., & Levin, H. S. (2006). Impaired discourse gist and working memory in children after brain injury. *Brain and Language, 97*(2), 178–188.

Chase, M., Son, E. H., & Steiner, S. (2014). Sequencing and graphic novels with primary-grade students. *The Reading Teacher, 67*, 435–443.

Chevalier, N., James, T. D., Wiebe, S. A., Nelson, J. M., & Espy, K. A. (2014). Contribution of reactive and proactive control to children's working memory performance: Insight from item recall durations in response sequence planning. *Developmental Psychology, 50*, 1999–2008.

Chevalier, N., Sheffield, T. D., Nelson, J. M., Clark, C. A. C., Wiebe, S. A., & Espy, K. A. (2012). Underpinnings of the costs of flexibility in preschool children: The roles of inhibition and working memory. *Developmental Neuropsychology, 37*, 99–118.

Chik, P. P. M., Ho, C. S. H., Yeung, P. S., Chan, D. W. O., Chung, K. K. H., Luan, H., et al. (2012). Syntactic skills in sentence reading comprehension among Chinese elementary school children. *Reading and Writing, 25*(3), 679–699.

Christopher, M. E., Miyake, A., Keenan, J. M., Pennington, B., DeFries, J. C., Wadsworth, S. J., et al. (2012). Predicting word reading and comprehension with executive function and speed measures across development: A latent variable analysis. *Journal of Experimental Psychology: General, 141*, 470–488.

Clark, C. A. C., Pritchard, V. E., & Woodward, L. J. (2010). Preschool executive functioning abilities predict early mathematics achievement. *Developmental Psychology, 46*, 1176–1191.

Clay, M. M. (2001). *Change over time in children's literacy development.* Portsmouth, NH: Heinemann Educational Books.

Cleary, B. T. (2012). *A-B-A-B-A A book of pattern play.* Minneapolis, MN: Mills Press Trade.

Colé, P., Duncan, L. G., & Blaye, A. (2014). Cognitive flexibility predicts early reading skills. *Frontiers in Psychology: Cognitive Science, 5*(565), 1–8.

Collins, A. M., & Loftus, E. F. (1975). A spreading-activation theory of semantic processing. *Psychological Review, 82*, 407–428.

Common Core State Standards Initiative. (2014). *Common Core State Standards Initiative: Preparing America's students for college and career.* Retrieved March 30, 2014, from *www.corestandards.org.*

Conners, F. A. (2009). Attentional control and the simple view of reading. *Reading and Writing, 22*, 591–613.

Cragg, L., & Chevalier, N. (2012). The processes underlying flexibility in childhood. *Quarterly Journal of Experimental Psychology, 65*, 209–232.

Cragg, L., & Nation, K. (2010). Language and the development of cognitive control. *Topics in Cognitive Science, 2*, 631–642.

Crook, S. R., & Evans, G. W. (2014). The role of planning skills in the income-achievement gap. *Child Development, 85*, 405–411.

Cross, D. R., & Paris, S. G. (1988). Developmental and instructional analyses of children's metacognition and reading comprehension. *Journal of Educational Psychology, 80*(2), 131.

Cuevas, K., & Bell, M. A. (2014). Infant attention and early childhood executive function. *Child Development, 85*, 397–404.

Cuevas, K., Deater-Deckard, K., Kim-Spoon, J., Watson, A. J., Morasch, K. C., & Bell, M. A. (2014). What's mom got to do with it?: Contributions of maternal executive function and caregiving to the development of executive function across early childhood. *Developmental Science, 17*, 224–238.

Cutting, L. E., Clements-Stephens, A., Pugh, K. R., Burns, S., Cao, A., Pekar, J. J., et al. (2013). Not all reading disabilities are dyslexia: Distinct neurobiology of specific comprehension deficits. *Brain Connectivity, 3,* 199–211.

Cutting, L. E., Eason, S. H., Young, K. M., & Alberstadt, A. L. (2009). Reading comprehension: Cognition and neuroimaging. In K. Pugh and P. McCardle (Eds.), *How children learn to read: Current issues and new directions in the integration of cognition, neurobiology, and genetics of reading and dyslexia research and practice* (pp. 195–213). New York: Psychology Press.

Cutting, L. E., Materek, A., Cole, C. A. S., Levine, T. M., & Mahone, E. M. (2009). Effects of fluency, oral language, and executive function on reading comprehension performance. *Annals of Dyslexia, 59,* 34–54.

Dahlin, K. I. E. (2011). Effects of working memory training on reading in children with special needs. *Reading and Writing, 24,* 479–491.

Daneman, M., & Carpenter, P. A. (1980). Individual differences in working memory and reading. *Journal of Verbal Learning and Verbal Behavior, 19,* 450–466.

Das-Smaal, E. A., de Jong, P. F., & Koopmans, J. R. (1993). Working memory, attentional regulation and the Star Counting Test. *Personality and Individual Differences, 14*(6), 815–824.

Davey, B., & McBride, S. (1986). Effects of question-generation training on reading comprehension. *Journal of Educational Psychology, 78,* 256.

Davidson, M. C., Amso, D., Anderson, L. C., & Diamond, A. (2006). Development of cognitive control and executive functions from 4 to 13 years: Evidence from manipulations of memory, inhibition, and task switching. *Neuropsychologia, 44,* 2037–2078.

Dawson, P., & Guare, R. (2003). *Executive skills in children and adolescents: A practical guide to assessment and intervention.* New York: Guilford Press.

Dawson, P., & Guare, R. (2009). *Smart but scattered: The revolutionary "executive skills" approach to helping kids reach their potential.* New York: Guilford Press.

Dawson, P., & Guare, R. (2010). *Executive skills in children and adolescents: A practical guide to assessment and intervention* (2nd ed.). New York: Guilford Press.

Dawson, P., & Guare, R. (2012). *Coaching students with executive skill deficits.* New York: Guilford Press.

Daywalt, D. (2013). *The day the crayons quit.* New York: Philomel Books.

De Beni, R., Borella, E., & Carretti, B. (2007). Reading comprehension in aging: The role of working memory and metacomprehension. *Aging, Neuropsychology, and Cognition, 14*(2), 189–212.

De Beni, R., & Palladino, P. (2000). Intrusion errors in working memory tasks: Are they related to reading comprehension ability? *Learning and Individual Differences, 12,* 131–143.

De Beni, R., Palladino, P., Pazzaglia, F., & Cornoldi, C. (1998). Increases in intrusion errors and working memory deficit of poor comprehenders. *Quarterly Journal of Experimental Psychology: Section A, 51,* 305–320.

De Jong, P. F., & Das-Smaal, E. A. (1990). The Star Counting Test: An attention test for children. *Personality and Individual Differences, 11*(6), 597–604.

De Jong, P. F., & Das-Smaal, E. A. (1995). Attention and intelligence: The validity of the Star Counting Test. *Journal of Educational Psychology, 87*(1), 80–92.

Delis, D. C., Kaplan, E., & Kramer, J. H. (2001). *Delis–Kaplan executive function system.* San Antonio, TX: Pearson Education.

Dermitzaki, I. (2005). Preliminary investigation of relations between young students' self-regulatory strategies and their metacognitive experiences. *Psychological Reports, 97,* 759–768.

Dermitzaki, I., Andreou, G., & Paraskeva, V. (2008). High and low reading comprehension achievers' strategic behaviors and their relation to performance in a reading comprehension situation. *Reading Psychology, 29,* 471–492.

De Vega, M., Urrutia, M., & Riffo, B. (2007). Canceling updating in the comprehension of counterfactuals embedded in narratives. *Memory and Cognition, 35*, 1410–1421.

Devine, R. T., & Hughes, C. (2014). Relations between false belief understanding and executive function in early childhood: A meta-analysis. *Child Development, 85*, 1777–1794.

Dewitz, P., Carr, E. M., & Patberg, J. P. (1987). Effects of inference training on comprehension and comprehension monitoring. *Reading Research Quarterly, 22*, 99–121.

Dewitz, P., & Dewitz, P. K. (2003). They can read the words, but they can't understand: Refining comprehension assessment. *The Reading Teacher, 56*, 422–435.

Dewitz, P., Jones, J., & Leahy, S. (2009). Comprehension strategy instruction in core reading programs. *Reading Research Quarterly, 44*, 102–126.

Diamond, A. (2013). Executive functions. *Annual Review of Psychology, 64*, 135–168.

Diamond, A., & Kirkham, N. (2005). Not quite as grown-up as we like to think: Parallels between cognition in childhood and adulthood. *Psychological Science, 16*(4), 291–297.

Diergarten, A. K., & Nieding, G. (in press). Children's and adults' ability to build online emotional inferences during comprehension of audiovisual and auditory texts. *Journal of Cognition and Development.*

DiStefano, P., Noe, M., & Valencia, S. (1981). Measurement of the effects of purpose and passage difficulty on reading flexibility. *Journal of Educational Psychology, 73*, 602–606.

Dolch, E. W. (1960). *Teaching primary reading* (3rd ed.). Champaign, IL: Garrard Press.

Domnauer, T. (2012). *Patterns and sequence: Stick kids workbook.* Cypress, CA: Creative Teaching Press.

Donahue, M. L. (2013). Perspective-taking and reading comprehension of narratives: Lessons learned from "The Bean." In C. A. Stone, E. R. Silliman, B. J. Ehren, & G. P. Wallach (Eds.), *Handbook of language and literacy: Development and disorders* (2nd ed.). New York: Guilford Press.

Doyle, A. C. (1986). *Sherlock Holmes: The complete novels and stories* (Vol. 1). New York: Bantam Books.

Drayton, S., Turley-Ames, K. J., & Guajardo, N. R. (2011). Counterfactual thinking and false belief: The role of executive function. *Journal of Experimental Child Psychology, 108*, 532–548.

Dreher, M. J. (1992). Searching for information in textbooks. *Journal of Reading, 35*, 364–371.

Dreher, M. J. (1993). Reading to locate information: Societal and educational perspectives. *Contemporary Educational Psychology, 18*, 129–138.

Dreher, M. J., & Brown, R. F. (1993). Planning prompts and indexed terms in textbook search tasks. *Journal of Educational Psychology, 85*(4), 662–669.

Dreher, M. J., & Guthrie, J. T. (1990). Cognitive processes in textbook chapter search tasks. *Reading Research Quarterly, 25*, 323–339.

Dreher, M. J., & Sammons, R. B. (1994). Fifth graders' search for information in a textbook. *Journal of Literacy Research, 26*(3), 301–314.

Duffy, G. G. (2014). *Explaining reading: A resource for explicit teaching of the Common Core Standards* (3rd ed.). New York: Guilford Press.

Duffy, G. G., Roehler, L. R., & Herrmann, B. A. (1988). Modeling mental processes helps poor readers become strategic readers. *The Reading Teacher, 41*, 762–767.

Duke, N. K. (2000). 3.6 minutes per day: The scarcity of informational texts in first grade. *Reading Research Quarterly, 35*(2), 202–224.

Duke, N. K., Cartwright, K. B., & Hilden, K. (2014). Difficulties with reading comprehension. In C. A. Stone, E. R. Silliman, B. J. Ehren, & G. P. Wallach (Eds.), *Handbook of language and literacy: Development and disorders* (2nd ed., pp. 451–468). New York: Guilford Press.

Duke, N. K., Norman, R. R., Roberts, K. L., Martin, N. M., Knight, J. A., Morsink, P. M., et al. (2013). Beyond concepts of print: Development of concepts of graphics in text, preK to grade 3. *Research in the Teaching of English, 48*, 175–203.

Duke, N. K., & Pearson, P. D. (2002). Effective practices for developing reading comprehension.

In S. J. Samuels & A. E. Farstrup (Eds.), *What research has to say about reading instruction* (3rd ed., pp. 205–242). Newark, DE: International Reading Association.

Duke, N. K., Pearson, P. D., Strachan, S. L., & Billman, A. K. (2011). Essential elements of fostering and teaching reading comprehension. In S. J. Samuels & A. E. Farstrup (Eds.), *What research has to say about reading instruction* (4th ed., pp. 51–93). Newark, DE: International Reading Association.

Durkin, D. (1978). What classroom observations reveal about reading comprehension instruction. *Reading Research Quarterly, 14*, 481–533.

Dyer, J. R., Shatz, M., & Wellman, H. M. (2000). Young children's storybooks as a source of mental state information. *Cognitive Development, 15*(1), 17–37.

Dyer-Seymour, J. R., Shatz, M., Wellman, H. M., & Saito, M. T. (2004). Mental state expressions in U.S. and Japanese children's books. *International Journal of Behavioral Development, 28*(6), 546–552.

Dymock, S. (2007). Comprehension strategy instruction: Teaching narrative text structure awareness. *The Reading Teacher, 61*(2), 161–167.

Eason, S. H. & Cutting, L. E. (2009). Examining sources of poor comprehension in older poor readers. In R. K. Wagner, C. Schatschneider, & C. Phythian-Sence (Eds.), *Beyond decoding: The behavioral and biological foundations of reading comprehension* (pp. 263–283). New York: Guilford Press.

Ehrlich, M. F., & Remond, M. (1997). Skilled and less skilled comprehenders: French children's processing of anaphoric devices in written texts. *British Journal of Developmental Psychology, 15*, 291–309.

Ehrlich, M. F., Remond, M., & Tardieu, H. (1999). Processing of anaphoric devices in young skilled and less skilled comprehenders: Differences in metacognitive monitoring. *Reading and Writing, 11*, 29–63.

Elbro, C., & Buch-Iversen, I. (2013). Activation of background knowledge for inference making: Effects on reading comprehension. *Scientific Studies of Reading, 17*(6), 435–452.

Emery, D. W. (1996). Helping readers comprehend stories from the characters' perspectives. *The Reading Teacher, 49*, 534–541.

Englert, C. S., & Thomas, C. C. (1987). Sensitivity to text structure in reading and writing: A comparison between learning disabled and non-learning disabled students. *Learning Disability Quarterly, 10*, 93–105.

Eslinger, P. J., Biddle, K., Pennington, B., & Page, R. B. (1999). Cognitive and behavioral development up to 4 years after early right frontal lobe lesion. *Developmental Neuropsychology, 15*, 157–191.

Eslinger, P. J., & Grattan, L. M. (1993). Frontal lobe and frontal-striatal substrates for different forms of human cognitive flexibility. *Neuropsychologia, 31*(1), 17–28.

Fabricius, W. V. (1988). The development of forward search planning in preschoolers. *Child Development, 59*, 1473–1488.

Fagot, B. I., & Gauvain, M. (1997). Mother–child problem solving: Continuity through the early childhood years. *Developmental Psychology, 33*, 480–488.

Farrant, B. M., Maybery, M. T., & Fletcher, J. (2012). Language, cognitive flexibility, and explicit false belief understanding: Longitudinal analysis in typical development and specific language impairment. *Child Development, 83*(1), 223–235.

Fay-Stammbach, T., Hawes, D. J., & Meredith, P. (2014). Parenting influences on executive function in early childhood: A review. *Child Development Perspectives*.

Feldman, C. F., Bruner, J., Renderer, B., & Spitzer, S. (1990). Narrative comprehension. In B. K. Britton & A. D. Pellegrini (Eds.), *Narrative thought and narrative language* (pp. 1–78). Hillsdale, NJ: Erlbaum.

Ferstl, E., Rinck, M., & von Cramon, D. (2005). Emotional and temporal aspects of situation model processing during text comprehension: An event-related fMRI study. *Journal of Cognitive Neuroscience, 17*, 724–739.

Ferstl, E. C., & von Cramon, D. Y. (2001). The role of coherence and cohesion in text comprehension: An event-related fMRI study. *Cognitive Brain Research, 11*(3), 325–340.

Fisher, D., Frey, N., & Lapp, D. (2008). Shared readings: Modeling comprehension, vocabulary, text structures, and text features for older readers. *The Reading Teacher, 61*, 548–556.

Fitzgerald, F. S. (1964). *The crack up.* New York: New Directions.

Fitzgerald, J., & Spiegel, D. L. (1983). Enhancing children's reading comprehension through instruction in narrative structure. *Journal of Literacy Research, 15*, 1–17.

Fletcher, P. C., Happé, F., Frith, U., Baker, S. C., Dolan, R. J., Frackowiak, R. S., & Frith, C. D. (1995). Other minds in the brain: A functional imaging study of "theory of mind" in story comprehension. *Cognition, 57*(2), 109–128.

Fletcher, P. C., & Henson, R. N. A. (2001). Frontal lobes and human memory insights from functional neuroimaging. *Brain, 124*, 849–881.

Friedman, N. P., & Miyake, A. (2004). The relations among inhibition and interference control functions: A latent-variable analysis. *Journal of Experimental Psychology: General, 133*, 101–135.

Friedman, N. P., Miyake, A., Robinson, J. L., & Hewitt, J. K. (2011). Developmental trajectories in toddlers' self-restraint predict individual differences in executive functions 14 years later: A behavioral genetic analysis. *Developmental Psychology, 47*, 1410–1430.

Fry, E. B., & Kress, J. E. (2012). *The reading teacher's book of lists.* San Francisco: Wiley.

Frye, D., Zelazo, P. D., & Palfai, T. (1995). Theory of mind and rule-based reasoning. *Cognitive Development, 10*, 483–527.

Fuchs, D., & Fuchs, L. S. (2009). Responsiveness to intervention: Multilevel assessment and instruction as early intervention and disability identification. *The Reading Teacher, 63*, 250–252.

Fuchs, D., Fuchs, L. S., & Vaughn, S. (2008). *Response to intervention: A framework for reading educators.* Newark, DE: International Reading Association.

Fuchs, L. S., Fuchs, D., & Deno, S. L. (1985). Importance of goal ambitiousness and goal mastery to student achievement. *Exceptional Children, 52*, 63–71.

Fuchs, L. S., & Vaughn, S. (2012). Responsiveness-to-intervention: A decade later. *Journal of Learning Disabilities, 45*, 195–203.

Fuhs, M. W., & Day, J. D. (2011). Verbal ability and executive functioning development in preschoolers at Head Start. *Developmental Psychology, 47*, 404–416.

Fuhs, M. W., Nesbitt, K. T., Farran, D. C., & Dong, N. (2014). Longitudinal associations between executive functioning and academic skills across content areas. *Developmental Psychology,* Advance online publication at *http://dx.doi.org/10.1037/a0036633.*

Gaa, J. P. (1973). Effects of individual goal-setting conferences on achievement, attitudes, and goal-setting behavior. *Journal of Experimental Education, 42*, 22–28.

Gaa, J. P. (1979). The effects of individual goal-setting conferences on academic achievement and modification of locus of control orientation. *Psychology in the Schools, 16*, 591–597.

Gallagher, H. L., Happé, F., Brunswick, N., Fletcher, P. C., Frith, U., & Frith, C. D. (2000). Reading the mind in cartoons and stories: An fMRI study of "theory of mind" in verbal and nonverbal tasks. *Neuropsychologia, 38*(1), 11–21.

Gamannossi, B. A., & Pinto, G. (2014). Theory of mind and language of mind in narratives: Developmental trends from kindergarten to primary school. *First Language, 34*, 262–272.

Gamino, J. F., Chapman, S. B., & Cook, L. G. (2009). Strategic learning in youth with traumatic brain injury: Evidence for stall in higher-order cognition. *Topics in Language Disorders, 29*(3), 224–235.

Ganske, K. (2006). *Word sorts and more: Sound, pattern, and meaning explorations.* New York: Guilford Press.

García-Madruga, J. A., Elosúa, M. R., Gil, L., Gómez-Veiga, Vila, J. O., Orjales, I., et al. (2013). Reading comprehension and working memory's executive processes: An intervention study in primary school students. *Reading Research Quarterly, 48*, 155–174.

Garon, N., Bryson, S. E., & Smith, I. M. (2008). Executive function in preschoolers: A review using an integrative framework. *Psychological Bulletin, 134*, 31–60.

Garner, R. (1987). *Metacognition and reading comprehension.* New York: Ablex.

Gaskins, I. W., Satlow, E., & Pressley, M. (2007). Executive control of reading comprehension in the elementary school. In L. Meltzer (Ed.), *Executive function in education: From theory to practice* (pp. 194–215). New York: Guilford Press.

Gaskins, R. W., & Gaskins, I. W. (1997). Creating readers who read for meaning and love to read: The Benchmark School reading program. In S. A. Stahl & D. A. Hayes (Eds.), *Instructional models in reading* (pp. 131–159). Mahwah, NJ: Erlbaum.

Gaskins, R. W., Nehring, A., & Solic, K. (2013, December). *How would that change the context?: The effects of a conceptually based framework on the depth of thinking of struggling readers during literature discussions.* Paper presented at the annual meeting of the Literacy Research Association, Dallas, TX.

Gathercole, S. E., Pickering, S. J., Ambridge, B., & Wearing, H. (2004). The structure of working memory from 4 to 15 years of age. *Developmental Psychology, 40*, 177–190.

Gaux, C., & Gombert, J. E. (1999). Implicit and explicit syntactic knowledge and reading in pre-adolescents. *British Journal of Developmental Psychology, 17*, 169–188.

Geraci, A., Surian, L., Ferraro, M., & Cantagallo, A. (2010). Theory of mind in patients with ventromedial or dorsolateral prefrontal lesions following traumatic brain injury. *Brain Injury, 24*, 978–987.

Gergen, K. (2000). *The saturated self: Dilemmas of identity in contemporary life.* New York: Basic Books.

Gernsbacher, M. A., & Faust, M. E. (1991). The mechanism of suppression: A component of general comprehension skill. *Journal of Experimental Psychology: Learning, Memory, and Cognition, 17*, 245–262.

Gernsbacher, M. A., & Robertson, R. R. (1995). Reading skill and suppression revisited. *Psychological Science, 6*, 165–169.

Gershberg, F. B., & Shimamura, A. P. (1995). Impaired use of organizational strategies in free recall following frontal lobe damage. *Neuropsychologia, 33*(10), 1305–1333.

Gerstadt, C. L., Hong, Y. J., & Diamond, A. (1994). The relationship between cognition and action: Performance of children 3½–7 years old on a Stroop-like day–night test. *Cognition, 53*, 129–153.

Gersten, R., Fuchs, L. S., Williams, J. P., & Baker, S. (2001). Teaching reading comprehension strategies to students with learning disabilities. *Review of Educational Research, 71*, 279–320.

Gillet, J. W., & Richards, H. C. (1979). Reading comprehension test performance and hierarchical classification. *Journal of Literacy Research, 11*, 381–385.

Glenberg, A. M., Brown, M., & Levin, J. R. (2007). Enhancing comprehension in small reading groups using a manipulation strategy. *Contemporary Educational Psychology, 32*(3), 389–399.

Goldin, A. P., Segretin, M. S., Hermida, M. J., Paz, L., Lipina, S. J., & Sigman, M. (2013). Training planning and working memory in third graders. *Mind, Brain, and Education, 7*, 136–146.

Goldstein, S., & Naglieri, J. A. (Eds.). (2014). *Handbook of executive functioning.* New York: Springer.

Gotgay, N., Giedd, J. N., Lusk, L., Hayashi, K. M., Greenstein, D., Vaituzis, C., et al. (2004). Dynamic mapping of human cortical development during childhood through early adulthood. *Proceedings of the National Academy of Science, 101*, 8174–8179.

Graesser, A. C., Singer, M., & Trabasso, T. (1994). Constructing inferences during narrative text comprehension. *Psychological Review, 101*, 371–395.

Graham, L., & Wong, B. Y. (1993). Comparing two modes of teaching a question-answering strategy for enhancing reading comprehension: Didactic and self-instructional training. *Journal of Learning Disabilities, 26*, 270–279.

Grattan, L. M., Bloomer, R. H., Archambault, F. X., & Eslinger, P. J. (1994). Cognitive flexibility and empathy after frontal lobe lesion. *Cognitive and Behavioral Neurology, 7*(4), 251–259.

Griffin, J. A., & Friedman, S. L. (2007). *NICHD Study of Early Childcare and Youth Development.* Washington, DC: National Institutes of Health.

Guajardo, N. R., & Cartwright, K. B. (2015). *A longitudinal study of the role of false belief understanding in elementary students' reading awareness and reading comprehension.* Manuscript in preparation.

Guajardo, N. R., Parker, J., & Turley-Ames, K. J. (2009). Associations among false belief understanding, counterfactual reasoning, and executive function. *British Journal of Developmental Psychology, 27,* 681–702.

Guajardo, N. R., Petersen, R., & Marshall, T. R. (2013). The roles of explanation and feedback in false belief understanding: A microgenetic analysis. *Journal of Genetic Psychology, 174,* 225–252.

Guajardo, N. R., & Turley-Ames, K. J. (2004). Preschoolers' generation of different types of counterfactual statements and theory of mind understanding. *Cognitive Development, 19,* 53–80.

Guajardo, N. R., & Watson, A. C. (2002). Narrative discourse and theory of mind development. *Journal of Genetic Psychology, 163,* 305–325.

Guare, R. (2014). Context in the development of executive functions in children. *Applied Neuropsychology: Child,* published online February 25, 2014.

Guare, R., Dawson, P., & Guare, C. (2013). *Smart but scattered teens: The "executive skills" program for helping teens reach their potential.* New York: Guilford Press.

Guastello, E. F., Beasley, T. M., & Sinatra, R. C. (2000). Concept mapping effects on science content comprehension of low-achieving inner-city seventh graders. *Remedial and Special Education, 21*(6), 356–364.

Guo, Y., Roehrig, A. D., & Williams, R. S. (2011). The relation of morphological awareness and syntactic awareness to adults' reading comprehension: Is vocabulary knowledge a mediating variable? *Journal of Literacy Research, 43,* 159–183.

Gurney, D., Gersten, R., Dimino, J., & Carnine, D. (1990). Story grammar: Effective literature instruction for high school students with learning disabilities. *Journal of Learning Disabilities, 23*(6), 335–342.

Hall, K. M., & Sabey, B. L. (2007). Focus on the facts: Using informational texts effectively in early elementary classrooms. *Early Childhood Education Journal, 35,* 261–268.

Hall, K. M., Sabey, B. L., & McClellan, M. (2005). Expository text comprehension: Helping primary-grade teachers use expository texts to full advantage. *Reading Psychology, 26*(3), 211–234.

Halliday, M., & Hasan, R. (1976). *Cohesion in English.* New York: Longman.

Hansen, J. (1981). The effects of inference training and practice on young children's reading comprehension. *Reading Research Quarterly, 16,* 391–417.

Hansen, J., & Pearson, P. D. (1983). An instructional study: Improving the inferential comprehension of good and poor fourth-grade readers. *Journal of Educational Psychology, 75,* 821–829.

Hanten, G., Chapman, S. B., Gamino, J. F., Zhang, L., Benton, S. B., Stallings-Roberson, G., et al. (2004). Verbal selective learning after traumatic brain injury in children. *Annals of Neurology, 56*(6), 847–853.

Happé, F. G. (1994). An advanced test of theory of mind: Understanding of story characters' thoughts and feelings by able autistic, mentally handicapped, and normal children and adults. *Journal of Autism and Developmental Disorders, 24*(2), 129–154.

Happé, F. G., Ehlers, S., Fletcher, P., Frith, U., Johansson, M., Gillberg, C., et al. (1996). "Theory of mind" in the brain: Evidence from a PET scan study of Asperger syndrome. *NeuroReport, 8*(1), 197–201.

Harvey, S., & Goudvis, A. (2007). *Strategies that work: Teaching comprehension for understanding and engagement.* Portland, ME: Stenhouse.

Henderson, L., Snowling, M., & Clarke, P. (2013). Accessing, integrating, and inhibiting word meaning in poor comprehenders. *Scientific Studies of Reading, 17,* 177–198.

Hendricks, C., Pasnak, R., Willson-Quayle, A., Trueblood, L., Malabonga, V., & Ciancio, D. (1999). Effects of instruction in sequencing and class inclusion for first graders. *Genetic, Social, and General Psychology Monographs, 125,* 297–312.

Hendricks, C., Trueblood, L., & Pasnak, R. (2006). Effects of teaching patterning to 1st-graders. *Journal of Research in Childhood Education, 21,* 79–89.

Hessels-Schlatter, C. (2010). Development of a theoretical framework and practical application of games in fostering cognitive and metacognitive skills. *Journal of Cognitive Education and Psychology, 9,* 116–138.

Hibbing, A. N., & Rankin-Erickson, J. L. (2003). A picture is worth a thousand words: Using visual images to improve comprehension for middle school struggling readers. *The Reading Teacher, 56,* 758–770.

Hicks, C. P. (2009). A lesson on reading fluency learned from The Tortoise and the Hare. *The Reading Teacher, 63,* 319–323.

Hinckley, G. B. (2009). *Standing for something: 10 neglected virtues that will heal our hearts and homes.* New York: Random House.

Hirsch, E. D. (2003). Reading comprehension requires knowledge—of words and the world. *American Educator, 27,* 10–13.

Hoehl, S., Reid, V., Mooney, J., & Striano, T. (2008). What are you looking at?: Infants' neural processing of an adult's object-directed eye gaze. *Developmental Science, 11,* 10–16.

Holmes, J., & Gathercole, S. E. (2014). Taking working memory training from the laboratory into schools. *Educational Psychology, 34,* 440–450.

Holmes, J., Gathercole, S. E., & Dunning, D. L. (2009). Adaptive training leads to sustained enhancement of poor working memory in children. *Developmental Science, 12,* F9–F15.

Hong-Nam, K., Leavell, A. G., & Maher, S. (2014). The relationships among reported strategy use, metacognitive awareness, and reading achievement of high school students. *Reading Psychology,* published online June 20, 2014,

Hongwanishkul, D., Happaney, K. R., Lee, W. S. C., & Zelazo, P. D. (2005). Assessment of hot and cool executive function in young children: Age-related changes and individual differences. *Developmental Neuropsychology, 28,* 617–644.

Hua, A. N., & Keenan, J. M. (2014). The role of text memory in inferencing and in comprehension deficits. *Scientific Studies of Reading, 18,* 415–431.

Huey, E. B. (1908). *The psychology and pedagogy of reading.* New York: Macmillan.

Hughes, C. (1998). Executive function in preschoolers: Links with theory of mind and verbal ability. *British Journal of Developmental Psychology, 16,* 233–253.

Hughes, C., & Ensor, R. (2007). Executive function and theory of mind: Predictive relations from ages 2 to 4. *Developmental Psychology, 43,* 1447–1459.

Huizinga, M., Dolan, C. V., & van der Molen, M. W. (2006). Age-related change in executive function: Developmental trends and a latent variable analysis. *Neuropsychologia, 44,* 2017–2036.

Hutto, D. D. (2007). The narrative practice hypothesis: Origins and applications of folk psychology. *Royal Institute of Philosophy Supplement, 60,* 43–68.

Idol, L. (1987). Group story mapping: A comprehension strategy for both skilled and unskilled readers. *Journal of Learning Disabilities, 20,* 196–205.

Idol, L., & Croll, V. J. (1987). Story-mapping training as a means of improving reading comprehension. *Learning Disability Quarterly, 10,* 214–229.

Inhelder, B., & Piaget, J. (1964). *The early growth of logic in the child* (E. A. Lunzer & D. Papert, Trans.). New York: Humanities Press.

Insel, T. R., Landis, S. C., & Collins, F. S. (2013). The NIH brain initiative. *Science, 340*(6133), 687–688.

Israel, S. E., Block, C. C., Kinnucan-Welsch, K., & Bauserman, K. (2005). *Metacognition in literacy learning: Theory, assessment, instruction, and professional development.* Mahwah, NJ: Erlbaum.

Jacobs, D. W., & Richdale, A. L. (2013). Predicting literacy in children with a high-functioning autism spectrum disorder. *Research in Developmental Disabilities, 34,* 2379–2390.

Jacobs, J. E., & Paris, S. G. (1987). Children's metacognition about reading: Issues in definition, measurement, and instruction. *Educational Psychologist, 22*(3–4), 255–278.

Jacques, S., & Zelazo, P. D. (2005). On the possible roots of cognitive flexibility. In B. Homer & C. S. Tamis-LeMonda (Eds.), *The development of social cognition and communication* (pp. 53–81). Mahwah, NJ: Erlbaum.

Jerman, O., Reynolds, C., & Swanson, H. L. (2012). Does growth in working memory span or executive processes predict growth in reading and math in children with reading disabilities? *Learning Disability Quarterly, 35*(3), 144–157.

Johnson, D. D., Pittelman, S. D., & Heimlich, J. E. (1986). Semantic mapping. *The Reading Teacher, 39,* 778–783.

Johnson, D. D., & von Hoff Johnson, B. (1986). Highlighting vocabulary in inferential comprehension instruction. *Journal of Reading, 29,* 622–625.

Johnson, L., Graham, S., & Harris, K. R. (1997). The effects of goal setting and self-instruction on learning a reading comprehension strategy: A study of students with learning disabilities. *Journal of Learning Disabilities, 30,* 80–91.

Johnson, M. H. (2011). *Developmental cognitive neuroscience* (3rd ed.). Malden, MA: Wiley-Blackwell.

Joint Legislative Audit and Review Commission (2011). *Strategies to promote third grade reading performance in Virginia.* Retrieved June 11, 2014 from *http://jlarc.virginia.gov/Reports/Rpt418.pdf.*

Jorm, A. F., Share, D. L., Matthews, R., & Maclean, R. (1986). Behaviour problems in specific reading retarded and general reading backward children: A longitudinal study. *Journal of Child Psychology and Psychiatry, 27,* 33–43.

Just, M. A., & Carpenter, P. A. (1992). A capacity theory of comprehension: Individual differences in working memory. *Psychological Review, 99,* 122–149.

Kane, M. J., & Engle, R. W. (2002). The role of prefrontal cortex in working-memory capacity, executive attention, and general fluid intelligence: An individual-differences perspective. *Psychonomic Bulletin and Review, 9,* 637–671.

Kara, S. (2013). The role explicit teaching of signals play on reading comprehension. *TEM Journal: Technology, Education, Management, Informatics, 2,* 28–34.

Kardash, C. M., & Noel, L. K. (2000). How organizational signals, need for cognition, and verbal ability affect text recall and recognition. *Contemporary Educational Psychology, 25,* 317–331.

Karnath, H. O., Wallesch, C. W., & Zimmermann, P. (1991). Mental planning and anticipatory processes with acute and chronic frontal lobe lesions: A comparison of maze performance in routine and non-routine situations. *Neuropsychologia, 29*(4), 271–290.

Katzir, T., & Paré-Blagoev, J. (2006). Applying cognitive neuroscience research to education: The case of literacy. *Educational Psychologist, 41,* 53–74.

Kaufman, C. (2010). *Executive function in the classroom: Practical strategies for improving performance and enhancing skills for all students.* Baltimore, MD: Brookes.

Keene, E. O., & Zimmermann, S. (2007). *Mosaic of thought: The power of comprehension strategy instruction.* Portsmouth, NH: Heinemann.

Kendeou, P., & van den Broek, P. (2007). The effects of prior knowledge and text structure on comprehension processes during reading of scientific texts. *Memory and Cognition, 35,* 1567–1577.

Kidd, D. C., & Castano, E. (2013). Reading literary fiction improves theory of mind. *Science, 342*(6156), 377–380.

Kidd, J. K., Carlson, A. G., Gadzichowski, K. M., Boyer, C. E., Gallington, D. A., & Pasnak, R. (2013). Effects of patterning instruction on the academic achievement of 1st-grade children. *Journal of Research in Childhood Education, 27*, 224–238.

Kidd, J. K., Pasnak, R., Gadzichowski, K. M., Gallington, D. A., McKnight, P., Boyer, C. E., & Carlson, A. (2014). Instructing first-grade children on patterning improves reading and mathematics. *Early Education and Development, 25*, 134–151.

Kieffer, M. J., Vukovic, R. K., & Berry, D. (2013). Roles of attention shifting and inhibitory control in fourth-grade reading comprehension. *Reading Research Quarterly, 38*, 333–348.

Kim, A. H., Vaughn, S., Wanzek, J., & Wei, S. (2004). Graphic organizers and their effects on the reading comprehension of students with LD: A synthesis of research. *Journal of Learning Disabilities, 37*, 105–118.

Kim, S. H., Han, D. H., Lee, Y. S., Kim, B. N., Cheong, J. H., & Han, S. H. (2014). Baduk (the Game of Go) improved cognitive function and brain activity in children with attention deficit hyperactivity disorder. *Psychiatry Investigation, 11*, 143–151.

Kim, Y. S., & Phillips, B. (2014). Cognitive correlates of listening comprehension. *Reading Research Quarterly, 49*, 269–281.

Kintsch, W. (1994). Text comprehension, memory, and learning. *American Psychologist, 49*, 294–303.

Kirsch, I. S., & Guthrie, J. T. (1984). Adult reading practices for work and leisure. *Adult Education Quarterly, 34*, 213–232.

Klahr, D., & Robinson, M. (1981). Formal assessment of problem solving and planning processes in preschool children. *Cognitive Psychology, 13*, 113–148.

Klingberg, T., Forssberg, H., & Westerberg, H. (2002). Increased brain activity in frontal and parietal cortex underlies the development of visuospatial working memory capacity during childhood. *Journal of Cognitive Neuroscience, 14*, 1–10.

Klingner, J. K., & Vaughn, S. (1999). Promoting reading comprehension, content learning, and English acquisition though Collaborative Strategic Reading (CSR). *The Reading Teacher, 52*, 738–747.

Knightly, L. M., Jun, S., Oh, J. S., & Au, T. K. (2003). Production benefits of childhood overhearing. *Journal of the Acoustical Society of America, 114*, 465–474.

Korkman, M., Kirk, U., & Kemp, S. (1998). *NEPSY: A developmental neuropsychological assessment*. San Antonio, TX: Psychological Corporation.

Kray, J., & Ferdinand, N. K. (2013). How to improve cognitive control in development during childhood: Potentials and limits of cognitive interventions. *Child Development Perspectives, 7*, 121–125.

Kuhn, D. (2000). Metacognitive development. *Current Directions in Psychological Science, 9*(5), 178–181.

Kulman, R., Stoner, G., Ruffolo, L., Marshall, S., Slater, J., Dyl, A., et al. (2010). Teaching executive functions, self-management, and ethical decision-making through popular videogame play. In K. Schrier & D. Gibson (Eds.), *Designing games for ethics: Models, techniques and frameworks* (pp. 193–207). Hershey, NY: Information Science Reference.

LaBerge, D., & Samuels, S. J. (1974). Toward a theory of automatic information processing in reading. *Cognitive Psychology, 6*, 293–323.

Laing, S. P., & Kamhi, A. G. (2002). The use of think-aloud protocols to compare inferencing abilities in average and below-average readers. *Journal of Learning Disabilities, 35*, 437–448.

Larner, A. (2009). Neuropsychology of board games puzzles and quizzes. *Advances in Clinical Neuroscience and Rehabilitation, 9*(5), 42.

Laski, E. V., & Siegler, R. S. (2014). Learning from number board games: You learn what you encode. *Developmental Psychology, 50,* 853–864.

Leach, J. M., Scarborough, H. S., & Rescorla, L. (2003). Late-emerging reading disabilities. *Journal of Educational Psychology, 95,* 211–224.

Lecce, S., Zocchi, S., Pagnin, A., Palladino, P., & Taumoepeau, M. (2010). Reading minds: The relation between children's mental state knowledge and their metaknowledge about reading. *Child Development, 81,* 1876–1893.

Lee, K., Bull, R., & Ho, R. M. H. (2013). Developmental changes in executive functioning. *Child Development, 84,* 1933–1953.

Lemarié, J., Lorch Jr, R. F., Eyrolle, H., & Virbel, J. (2008). SARA: A text-based and reader-based theory of signaling. *Educational Psychologist, 43*(1), 27–48.

Levin, H. S., & Hanten, G. (2005). Executive functions after traumatic brain injury in children. *Pediatric Neurology, 33*(2), 79–93.

Levin, J. R. (1973). Inducing comprehension in poor readers: A test of a recent model. *Journal of Educational Psychology, 65,* 19–24.

Levorato, M. C., Roch, M., & Nesi, B. (2007). A longitudinal study of idiom and text comprehension. *Journal of Child Language, 34,* 473–494.

Library of Congress. (2000). *Project on the decade of the brain.* Washington, DC: Library of Congress. Accessed at *www.loc.gov/loc/brain.*

Liew, J. (2012). Effortful control, executive functions, and education: Bringing self-regulatory and social-emotional competencies to the table. *Child Development Perspectives, 6,* 105–111.

Liew, J., McTigue, E. M., Barrois, L., & Hughes, J. N. (2008). Adaptive and effortful control and academic self-efficacy beliefs on achievement: A longitudinal study of 1st through 3rd graders. *Early Childhood Research Quarterly, 23,* 515–526.

Linderholm, T. (2006). Reading with purpose. *Journal of College Reading and Learning, 36,* 70–80.

Linderholm, T., & van den Broek, P. (2002). The effects of reading purpose and working memory capacity on the processing of expository text. *Journal of Educational Psychology, 94,* 778–784.

Locascio, G., Mahone, E. M., Eason, S. H., & Cutting, L. E. (2010). Executive dysfunction among children with reading comprehension deficits. *Journal of Learning Disabilities, 43,* 441–454.

Lorch Jr, R. F. (1989). Text-signaling devices and their effects on reading and memory processes. *Educational Psychology Review, 1,* 209–234.

Lorch, R., Lemarié, J., & Grant, R. (2011). Signaling hierarchical and sequential organization in expository text. *Scientific Studies of Reading, 15,* 267–284.

Lorch Jr, R. F., & Lorch, E. P. (1996). Effects of organizational signals on free recall of expository text. *Journal of Educational Psychology, 88,* 38–48.

Lovett, S. B., & Pillow, B. H. (2010). Age-related changes in children's and adults' explanations of interpersonal actions. *Journal of Genetic Psychology, 171,* 139–167.

Lundblom, E. E., & Woods, J. J. (2012). Working in the classroom improving idiom comprehension through classwide peer tutoring. *Communication Disorders Quarterly, 33*(4), 202–219.

Lysaker, J. T., & Miller, A. (2013). Engaging social imagination: The developmental work of wordless book reading. *Journal of Early Childhood Literacy, 13*(2), 147–174.

Lysaker, J., & Tonge, C. (2013). Learning to understand others through relationally oriented reading. *The Reading Teacher, 66*(8), 632–641.

Lysaker, J. T., Tonge, C., Gauson, D., & Miller, A. (2011). Reading and social imagination: What relationally oriented reading instruction can do for children. *Reading Psychology, 32,* 520–566.

MacLeod, C. M. (1991). Half a century of research on the Stroop effect: An integrative review. *Psychological Bulletin, 109,* 163–203.

Mahapatra, S., Das, J. P., Stack-Cutler, H., & Parrila, R. (2010). Remediating reading comprehension difficulties: A cognitive processing approach. *Reading Psychology, 31*(5), 428–453.

Mandler, J. M., & DeForest, M. (1979). Is there more than one way to recall a story? *Child Development, 50,* 886–889.

Mandler, J. M., & Goodman, M. S. (1982). On the psychological validity of story structure. *Journal of Verbal Learning and Verbal Behavior, 21,* 507–523.

Mandler, J. M., & Johnson, N. S. (1977). Remembrance of things parsed: Story structure and recall. *Cognitive Psychology, 9,* 111–151.

Mar, R. A. (2011). The neural bases of social cognition and story comprehension. *Annual Review of Psychology, 62,* 103–134.

Mar, R. A., Tackett, J. L., & Moore, C. (2010). Exposure to media and theory-of-mind development in preschoolers. *Cognitive Development, 25*(1), 69–78.

Marcovitch, S., Jacques, S., Boseovski, J. J., & Zelazo, P. D. (2008). Self-reflection and the cognitive control of behavior: Implications for learning. *Mind, Brain, and Education, 2,* 136–141.

Mason, J. M., Kniseley, E., & Kendall, J. (1979). Effects of polysemous words on sentence comprehension. *Reading Research Quarterly, 15,* 49–65.

Mason, R. A., & Just, M. A. (2007). Lexical ambiguity in sentence comprehension. *Brain Research, 1146,* 115–127.

Mather, P. W. (1985). Test review: Nelson Reading Skills Test. *Journal of Reading, 29,* 238–242.

Mazzocco, M. M. M., & Kover, S. T. (2007). A longitudinal assessment of executive function skills and their association with math performance. *Child Neuropsychology, 13,* 18–45.

McClelland, M. M., Cameron, C. E., Connor, C. M., Farris, C. L., Jewkes, A. M., & Morrison, F. J. (2007). Links between behavioral regulation and preschoolers' literacy, vocabulary, and math skills. *Developmental Psychology, 43,* 947–959.

McCloskey, G., Perkins, L. A., & Van Divner, B. (2009). *Assessment and intervention for executive function difficulties.* New York: Routledge.

McConaughy, S. H. (1985). Good and poor readers' comprehension of story structure across different input and output modalities. *Reading Research Quarterly, 22,* 219–232.

McConaughy, S. H., Fitzhenry-Coor, I., & Howell, D. C. (1983). Developmental differences in schemata for story comprehension. In K. E. Nelson (Ed.), *Children's language* (Vol. 4, pp. 385–421). Hillsdale, NJ: Erlbaum.

McGee, A., & Johnson, H. (2003). The effect of inference training on skilled and less skilled comprehenders. *Educational Psychology, 23,* 49–59.

McGill-Franzen, A., & Allington, R. L. (Eds.). (2011). *Handbook of reading disability research.* New York: Routledge.

McLean, J. F., & Hitch, G. J. (1999). Working memory impairments in children with specific arithmetic learning disabilities. *Journal of Experimental Child Psychology, 74,* 240–260.

McNamara, D. S., & McDaniel, M. A. (2004). Suppressing irrelevant information: Knowledge activation or inhibition? *Journal of Experimental Psychology: Learning, Memory, and Cognition, 30,* 465–482.

McNamara, D. S., & O'Reilly, T. (2009). Theories of comprehension skill: Knowledge and strategies versus capacity and suppression. *Advances in Psychology Research* (Vol. 62, pp. 113–136). Hauppauge, NY: Nova Science.

McVay, J. C., & Kane, M. J. (2012). Why does working memory capacity predict variation in reading comprehension?: On the influence of mind wandering and executive attention. *Journal of Experimental Psychology: General, 141,* 302–320.

Medin, D. L., Goldstone, R. L., & Gentner, D. (1993). Respects for similarity. *Psychological Review, 100*, 254–278.

Medin, D. L., & Schaffer, M. M. (1978). Context theory of classification learning. *Psychological Review, 85*, 207–238.

Megherbi, H., & Ehrlich, M. F. (2005). Language impairment in less skilled comprehenders: The on-line processing of anaphoric pronouns in a listening situation. *Reading and Writing, 18*, 715–753.

Melby-Lervåg, M., & Hulme, C. (2013). Is working memory training effective?: A meta-analytic review. *Developmental Psychology, 49*, 270–291.

Meltzer, L. (Ed.). (2007). *Executive function in education: From theory to practice.* New York: Guilford Press.

Meltzer, L. (2010). *Promoting executive function in the classroom.* New York: Guilford Press.

Meltzoff, A. N., Kuhl, P. K., Movellan, J., & Sejnowski, T. J. (2009). Foundations for a new science of learning. *Science, 325*, 284–288.

Meyer, B. J. F., Brandt, D. M., & Bluth, G. J. (1980). Use of top-level structure in text: Key for reading comprehension of ninth-grade students. *Reading Research Quarterly, 16*, 72–103.

Meyer, B. J. F., & Freedle, R. O. (1984). Effects of discourse type on recall. *American Educational Research Journal, 21*, 121–143.

Meyer, B. J. F., & Poon, L. W. (2001). Effects of structure strategy training and signaling on recall of text. *Journal of Educational Psychology, 93*, 141–159.

Miller, S. A. (2012). *Theory of mind: Beyond the preschool years.* New York: Psychology Press.

Miller, S. E., & Marcovitch, S. (2012). How theory of mind and executive function co-develop. *Review of Philosophical Psychology, 3*, 597–625.

Mills, C. B., Diehl, V. A., Birkmire, D. P., & Mou, L. C. (1995). Reading procedural texts: Effects of purpose for reading and predictions of reading comprehension models. *Discourse Processes, 20*, 79–107.

Miyake, A., Friedman, N. P., Emerson, M. J., Witzki, A. H., & Howerter, A. (2000). The unity and diversity of executive functions and their contributions to complex "frontal lobe" tasks: A latent variable analysis. *Cognitive Psychology, 41*, 49–100.

Mokhtari, K., & Niederhauser, D. S. (2010, December). *The contributions of vocabulary knowledge and syntactic awareness to 5th grade students' reading comprehension.* Paper presented at the 60th annual meeting of the Literacy Research Association, Fort Worth, TX.

Mokhtari, K., & Thompson, H. B. (2006). How problems of reading fluency and comprehension are related to difficulties in syntactic awareness skills among fifth graders. *Literacy Research and Instruction, 46*(1), 73–94.

Montague, M., Maddux, C. D., & Dereshiwsky, M. I. (1990). Story grammar and comprehension and production of narrative prose by students with learning disabilities. *Journal of Learning Disabilities, 23*(3), 190–197.

Montgomery, D. E., & Koeltzow, T. E. (2010). A review of the day–night task: The Stroop paradigm and interference control in young children. *Developmental Review, 30*, 308–330.

Moore, M., & Wade, B. (1998). Reading and comprehension: A longitudinal study of ex-Reading Recovery students. *Educational Studies, 24*, 195–203.

Morasch, K. C., & Bell, M. A. (2011). The role of inhibitory control in behavioral and physiological expressions of toddler executive function. *Journal of Experimental Child Psychology, 108*, 593–606.

Morgan, P. L., Farkas, G., Tufis, P. A., & Sperling, R. A. (2008). Are reading and behavior problems risk factors for each other? *Journal of Learning Disabilities, 41*, 417–436.

Morris, R. G., Ahmed, S., Syed, G. M., & Toone, B. K. (1993). Neural correlates of planning ability: Frontal lobe activation during the Tower of London Test. *Neuropsychologia, 31*(12), 1367–1378.

Morrow, L. M. (1985). Retelling stories: A strategy for improving young children's comprehension, concept of story structure, and oral language complexity. *Elementary School Journal, 85,* 647–661.

Moss, J., Schunn, C. D., Schneider, W., & McNamara, D. S. (2013). The nature of mind wandering during reading varies with the cognitive control demands of the reading strategy. *Brain Research, 1539,* 48–60.

Moss, J., Schunn, C. D., Schneider, W., McNamara, D. S., & VanLehn, K. (2011). The neural correlates of strategic reading comprehension: Cognitive control and discourse comprehension. *NeuroImage, 58,* 675–686.

Nation, K., Adams, J. W., Bowyer-Crane, C. A., & Snowling, M. J. (1999). Working memory deficits in poor comprehenders reflect underlying language impairments. *Journal of Experimental Child Psychology, 73,* 139–158.

Nation, K., Cocksey, J., Taylor, J. S. H., & Bishop, D. V. M. (2010). A longitudinal investigation of early reading and language skills in children with poor reading comprehension. *Journal of Child Psychology and Psychiatry, 51,* 1031–1039.

Nation, K. & Snowling, M. J. (1999). Developmental differences in sensitivity to semantic relations among good and poor comprehenders: Evidence from semantic priming. *Cognition, 70,* B1–B13.

Nation, K., & Snowling, M. J. (2000). Factors influencing syntactic awareness skills in normal readers and poor comprehenders. *Applied Psycholinguistics, 21,* 229–241.

Nation, K., & Snowling, M. J. (2004). Beyond phonological skills: Broader language skills contribute to the development of reading. *Journal of Research in Reading, 27,* 342–356.

National Reading Panel (U.S.). (2000). *Report of the National Reading Panel: Teaching children to read: An evidence-based assessment of the scientific research literature on reading and its implications for reading instruction.* Bethesda, MD: National Institute of Child Health and Human Development, National Institutes of Health.

Nesbit, J. C., & Adesope, O. O. (2006). Learning with concept and knowledge maps: A meta-analysis. *Review of Educational Research, 76*(3), 413–448.

Ness, M. K. (2008). Supporting secondary readers: When teachers provide the "what," not the "how." *American Secondary Education, 37,* 80–95.

Ness, M. K. (2009). Reading comprehension strategies in secondary content area classrooms: Teacher use of and attitudes towards reading comprehension instruction. *Reading Horizons, 49,* 143–166.

Ness, M. K. (2011a). Explicit reading comprehension instruction in elementary classrooms: Teacher use of reading comprehension strategies. *Journal of Research in Childhood Education, 25,* 98–117.

Ness, M. K. (2011b). Teachers' use of and attitudes toward informational text in K–5 classrooms. *Reading Psychology, 32,* 28–53.

Oakhill, J. (1982). Constructive processes in skilled and less skilled comprehenders' memory for sentences. *British Journal of Psychology, 73,* 13–20.

Oakhill, J. (1984). Inferential and memory skills in children's comprehension of stories. *British Journal of Educational Psychology, 54,* 31–39.

Oakhill, J. V., & Cain, K. (2012). The precursors of reading ability in young readers: Evidence from a four-year longitudinal study. *Scientific Studies of Reading, 16,* 91–121.

Oakhill, J. V., Hartt, J., & Samols, D. (2005). Levels of comprehension monitoring and working memory in good and poor comprehenders. *Reading and Writing, 18,* 657–686.

Oakhill, J. V., & Patel, S. (1991). Can imagery training help children who have comprehension problems? *Journal of Research in Reading, 14*(2), 106–115.

Oakhill, J. V., & Yuill, N. (1986). Pronoun resolution in skilled and less-skilled comprehenders: Effects of memory load and inferential complexity. *Language and Speech, 29,* 25–37.

Oakhill, J. V., & Yuill, N. (1996). Higher order factors in comprehension disability: Processes and remediation. In C. Cornoldi & J. Oakhill (Eds.), *Reading comprehension difficulties: Processes and intervention* (pp. 69–92). Mahwah, NJ: Erlbaum.

Oakhill, J. V., Yuill, N., & Parkin, A. (1986). On the nature of the difference between skilled and less-skilled comprehenders. *Journal of Research in Reading, 9,* 80–91.

O'Connor, I. M., & Klein, P. D. (2004). Exploration of strategies for facilitating the reading comprehension of high-functioning students with autism spectrum disorders. *Journal of Autism and Developmental Disorders, 34,* 115–127.

Olesen, P. J., Westerberg, H., & Klingberg, T. (2004). Increased prefrontal and parietal activity after training of working memory. *Nature Neuroscience, 7,* 75–79.

Oliver, K. (2009). An investigation of concept mapping to improve the reading comprehension of science texts. *Journal of Science Education and Technology, 18*(5), 402–414.

Otero, T. M., & Barker, L. A. (2014). The frontal lobes and executive functioning. In S. Goldstein & J. A. Naglieri (Eds.), *Handbook of executive functioning* (pp. 29–44). New York: Springer.

Owen, A. M., Downes, J. J., Sahakian, B. J., Polkey, C. E., & Robbins, T. W. (1990). Planning and spatial working memory following frontal lobe lesions in man. *Neuropsychologia, 28*(10), 1021–1034.

Ozonoff, S., Pennington, B. F., & Rogers, S. J. (1991). Executive function deficits in high-functioning autistic individuals: Relationship to theory of mind. *Journal of Child Psychology and Psychiatry, 32,* 1081–1105.

Palinscar, A. S., & Brown, A. L. (1984). Reciprocal teaching of comprehension-fostering and comprehension-monitoring activities. *Cognition and Instruction, 1,* 117–175.

Palincsar, A. S., & Brown, A. L. (1986). Interactive teaching to promote independent learning from text. *The Reading Teacher, 39,* 771–777.

Palladino, P., Cornoldi, C., De Beni, R., & Pazzaglia, F. (2001). Working memory and updating processes in reading comprehension. *Memory and Cognition, 29,* 344–354.

Paris, S. G., Cross, D. R., & Lipson, M. Y. (1984). Informed strategies for learning: A program to improve children's reading awareness and comprehension. *Journal of Educational Psychology, 76,* 1239–1252.

Paris, S. G., & Jacobs, J. E. (1984). The benefits of informed instruction for children's reading awareness and comprehension skills. *Child Development, 55,* 2083–2093.

Paris, S. G., & Myers, M. (1981). Comprehension monitoring, memory, and study strategies of good and poor readers. *Journal of Literacy Research, 13*(1), 5–22.

Pasnak, R., Madden, S. E., Malabonga, V. A., Holt, R., & Martin, J. W. (1996). Persistence of gains from instruction in classification, seriation, and conservation. *Journal of Educational Research, 90*(2), 87–92.

Pasolunghi, M. C., Cornoldi, C., & De Liberto, S. (1999). Working memory and intrusions of irrelevant information in a group of specific poor problem solvers. *Memory and Cognition, 27,* 779–790.

PBS Kids. (2014). "Super Why" theme song. Retrieved on June 11, 2014, from *http://pbskids. org/superwhy/#/game/jukebox.*

Pearson (2014). Cogmed working memory training. Retrieved on August 30, 2014, from *www. cogmed.com.*

Pearson Education (2014). The Wechsler Intelligence Scale for Children. Retrieved on July 9, 2014, from *www.pearsonclinical.com/psychology/products/100000310/wechsler-intelligence-scale-for-children-fourth-edition-wisc-iv.html#tab-details.*

Pearson, P. D., & Gallagher, M. C. (1983). The instruction of reading comprehension. *Contemporary Educational Psychology, 8,* 317–344.

Pearson, P. D., Hansen, J., & Gordon, C. (1979). The effect of background knowledge on young children's comprehension of explicit and implicit information. *Journal of Literacy Research, 11,* 201–209.

Pelletier, J., & Astington, J. W. (2004). Action, consciousness, and theory of mind: Children's ability to coordinate story characters' actions and thoughts. *Early Education and Development, 15,* 5–22.

Pellicano, E. (2007). Links between theory of mind and executive function in young children with autism: Clues to developmental primacy. *Developmental Psychology, 43,* 974–990.

Pérez, A. I., Paolieri, D., Macizo, P., & Bajo, T. (2014). The role of working memory in inferential sentence comprehension. *Cognitive Processing, 15,* 405–413.

Perner, J., & Lang, B. (1999). Development of theory of mind and executive control. *Trends in Cognitive Sciences, 3,* 337–344.

Perner, J., Leekam, S. R., & Wimmer, H. (1987). Three-year-olds' difficulty with false belief: The case for a conceptual deficit. *British Journal of Developmental Psychology, 5*(2), 125–137.

Perner, J., Ruffman, T., & Leekam, S. R. (1994). Theory of mind is contagious: You can catch it from your siblings. *Child Development, 65,* 1228–1238.

Peskin, J., & Astington, J. W. (2004). The effects of adding metacognitive language to story texts. *Cognitive Development, 19*(2), 253–273.

Peterson, E., & Welsh, M. C. (2014). The development of hot and cool executive functions in childhood and adolescence: Are we getting warmer? In S. Goldstein & J. A. Naglieri (Eds.), *Handbook of executive functioning* (pp. 45–68). New York: Springer.

Piaget, J., & Inhelder, B. (1969). *The psychology of the child* (H. Weaver, Trans.). New York: Basic Books. (Original work published 1966)

Pikulski, J. J., & Chard, D. J. (2005). Fluency: Bridge between decoding and reading comprehension. *The Reading Teacher, 58*(6), 510–519.

Pillow, B. H., & Lovett, S. B. (1998). "He forgot": Young children's use of cognitive explanations for another person's mistakes. *Merrill–Palmer Quarterly, 44,* 378–403.

Pimperton, H., & Nation, K. (2010). Suppressing irrelevant information from working memory: Evidence for domain-specific deficits in poor comprehenders. *Journal of Memory and Language, 62,* 380–391.

Pimperton, H., & Nation, K. (2014). Poor comprehenders in the classroom: Teacher ratings of behavior in children with poor reading comprehension and its relationship with individual differences in working memory. *Journal of Learning Disabilities, 47,* 199–207.

Pinnell, G. S., Fried, M. D., & Estice, R. M. (1990). Reading Recovery: Learning how to make a difference. *The Reading Teacher, 43,* 282–295.

Poe, E. A. (1899). *The mystery of Marie Rogêt.* New York: Fenno.

Prabhakaran, V., Narayanan, K., Zhao, Z., & Gabrieli, J. D. E. (2000). Integration of diverse information in working memory within the frontal lobe. *Nature Neuroscience, 3*(1), 85–90.

Prencipe, A., Kesek, A., Cohen, J., Lamm, C., Lewis, M. D., & Zelazo, P. D. (2011). Development of hot and cool executive function during the transition to adolescence. *Journal of Experimental Child Psychology, 108,* 621–637.

Pressley, G. M. (1976). Mental imagery helps eight-year-olds remember what they read. *Journal of Educational Psychology, 68,* 355–359.

Pressley, M. (2002a). Comprehension strategies instruction: A turn-of-the-century status report. In C. C. Block & M. Pressley (Eds.), *Comprehension instruction: Research-based best practices* (pp. 11–27). New York: Guilford Press.

Pressley, M. (2002b). Metacognition and self-regulated comprehension. In A. E. Farstrup & S. J. Samuels (Eds.), *What research has to say about reading instruction* (pp. 291–309). Newark, DE: International Reading Association.

Pressley, M., & Afflerbach, P. (1995). *Verbal protocols of reading: The nature of constructively reading.* Hillsdale, NJ: Erlbaum.

Pressley, M., & Allington, R. L. (2014). *Reading instruction that works: The case for balanced teaching* (4th ed.). New York: Guilford Press.

Pressley, M., & Gaskins, I. W. (2006). Metacognitively competent reading comprehension is constructively responsive reading: How can such reading be developed in students? *Metacognition and Learning, 1*(1), 99–113.

Pressley, M., Johnson, C. J., Symons, S., McGoldrick, J. A., & Kurita, J. A. (1989). Strategies that improve children's memory and comprehension of text. *Elementary School Journal, 90*, 3–32.

Pressley, M., & Lundeberg, M. (2008). An invitation to study professionals reading professional-level texts: A window on exceptionally complex, flexible reading. In K. B. Cartwright (Ed.), *Literacy processes: Cognitive flexibility in learning and teaching* (pp. 165–187). New York: Guilford Press.

Pressley, M., Wharton-McDonald, R., Mistretta-Hampston, J., & Echevarria, M. (1998). Literacy instruction in 10 fourth- and fifth-grade classrooms in upstate New York. *Scientific Studies of Reading, 2*, 159–194.

Priebe, S. J., Keenan, J. M., & Miller, A. C. (2012). How prior knowledge affects word identification and comprehension. *Reading and Writing, 25*, 131–149.

Pulvermüller, F., & Knoblauch, A. (2009). Discrete combinatorial circuits emerging in neural networks: A mechanism for rules of grammar in the human brain? *Neural Networks, 22*, 161–172.

Putnam, S. P., & Rothbart, M. K. (2006). Development of short and very short forms of the Children's Behavior Questionnaire. *Journal of Personality Assessment, 87*, 102–112.

Quillian, M. R. (1967). Word concepts: A theory and simulation of some basic semantic capabilities. *Behavioral Science, 12*, 410–430.

Ramscar, M., Dye, M., Gustafson, J. W., & Klein, J. (2013). Dual routes to cognitive flexibility: Learning and response-conflict resolution in the dimensional change card sort task. *Child Development, 84*, 1308–1323.

RAND Reading Study Group. (2002). *Reading for understanding: Toward an R&D program in reading comprehension.* Santa Monica, CA: Author.

Raver, C. C., Blair, C., Willoughby, M., & The Family Life Project Key Investigators. (2013). Poverty as a predictor of 4-year-olds' executive function: New perspectives on models of differential susceptibility. *Developmental Psychology, 49*, 292–304.

Reading Rockets. (2014). Story maps. Retrieved on July 24, 2014, from *www.readingrockets.org/strategies/story_maps.*

Recht, D. R., & Leslie, L. (1988). Effect of prior knowledge on good and poor readers' memory of text. *Journal of Educational Psychology, 80*, 16–20.

Reuter-Lorenz, P. A., Jonides, J., Smith, E. E., Hartley, A., Miller, A., Marshuetz, C., et al. (2000). Age differences in the frontal lateralization of verbal and spatial working memory revealed by PET. *Journal of Cognitive Neuroscience, 12*, 174–187.

Reutzel, D. R., & Hollingsworth, P. M. (1988). Highlighting key vocabulary: A generative-reciprocal procedure for teaching selected inference types. *Reading Research Quarterly, 23*, 358–378.

Reutzel, D. R., & Hollingsworth, P. M. (1993). Effects of fluency training on second graders' reading comprehension. *Journal of Educational Research, 86*, 325–331.

Reutzel, R., Read, S., & Fawson, P. (2009). Using information trade books as models for teaching expository text structure to improve children's reading comprehension: An action research project. *Journal of Reading Education, 35*, 31–38.

Reynolds, C. R., & Voress, J. (2007). *Test of Memory and Learning* (TOMAL-2). Austin, TX: PRO-ED.

Rhoades, B. L., Greenberg, M. T., Lanza, S. T., & Blair, C. (2011). Demographic and familial predictors of early executive function development: Contribution of a person-centered perspective. *Journal of Experimental Child Psychology, 108*, 638–662.

Rich, A. (1972). When we dead awaken: Writing as re-vision. *College English, 34*, 18–30.

Ricketts, J., Jones, C. R., Happé, F., & Charman, T. (2013). Reading comprehension in autism spectrum disorders: The role of oral language and social functioning. *Journal of Autism and Developmental Disorders, 43*(4), 807–816.

Ricketts, J., Sperring, R., & Nation, K. (2014). Educational attainment in poor comprehenders. *Frontiers in Psychology: Cognitive Science, 5*(Article 445), 1–11.

Riggio, M. M., & Cassidy, K. W. (2009). Preschoolers' processing of false beliefs within the context of picture book reading. *Early Education and Development, 20*(6), 992–1015.

Ring, J. J., Barefoot, L. C., Avrit, K. J., Brown, S. A., & Black, J. L. (2013). Reading fluency instruction for students at risk for reading failure. *Remedial and Special Education, 34,* 102–112.

Roberts, K. L., Norman, R. R., Duke, N. K., Morsink, P., Martin, N. M., & Knight, J. A. (2013). Diagrams, timelines, and tables—oh, my! Fostering graphical literacy. *The Reading Teacher, 67,* 12–23.

Roese, N. J. (1997). Counterfactual thinking. *Psychological Bulletin, 121,* 133–148.

Roid, G. H., Miller, L. J., Pomplun, M., & Koch, C. (2013). *Leiter International Performance Scale.* Wood Dale, IL: Stoelting.

Ronfard, S., & Harris, P. L. (2014). When will Little Red Riding Hood become scared?: Children's attribution of mental states to a story character. *Developmental Psychology, 50*(1), 283–292.

Roth, F. P., & Spekman, N. J. (1994). Oral story production in adults with learning disabilities. In R. L. Bloom, L. K. Obler, S. De Santi, & J. S. Ehrlich (Eds.), *Discourse analysis and applications: Studies in adult clinical populations* (pp. 131–148). Hillsdale, NJ: Erlbaum.

Rubia, K., Smith, A. B., Brammer, M. J., & Taylor, E. (2003). Right inferior prefrontal cortex mediates response inhibition while mesial prefrontal cortex is responsible for error detection. *NeuroImage, 20,* 351–358.

Rubman, C. N., & Waters, H. S. (2000). A, B seeing: The role of constructive processes in children's comprehension monitoring. *Journal of Educational Psychology, 92*(3), 503–514.

Rudnick, M., Sterritt, G. M., & Flax, M. (1967). Auditory and visual rhythm perception and reading ability. *Child Development, 38,* 581–587.

Rueda, M. R., Posner, M. I., & Rothbart, M. K. (2005). The development of executive attention: Contributions to the emergence of self-regulation. *Developmental Neuropsychology, 28,* 573–594.

Ruffman, T., Perner, J., Naito, M., Parkin, L., & Clements, W. (1998). Older (but not younger) siblings facilitate false belief understanding. *Developmental Psychology, 34,* 161–174.

Ruffman, T., Slade, L., & Crowe, E. (2002). The relation between children's and mothers' mental state language and theory-of-mind understanding. *Child Development, 73*(3), 734–751.

Sadoski, M. (1983). An exploratory study of the relationships between reported imagery and the comprehension and recall of a story. *Reading Research Quarterly, 19,* 110–123.

Sadoski, M. (1985). Commentary: The natural use of imagery in story comprehension and recall: Replication and extension. *Reading Research Quarterly, 20,* 658–667.

Sadoski, M. (2008). Dual coding theory: Reading comprehension and beyond. In C. C. Block & S. R. Parris (Eds.), *Comprehension instruction: Research-based best practices* (2nd ed., pp. 38–49). New York: Guilford Press.

Sadoski, M., & Paivio, A. (2013). *Imagery and text: A dual coding theory of reading and writing.* New York: Routledge.

Sagan, C., Druyan, A., & Soter, S. (Writers). (2000). Episode 11: The persistence of memory. In A. Malone (Producer and Director), *Cosmos: A personal journey.* Studio City, CA: Cosmos Studios.

Samuels, S. J. (1979). The method of repeated readings. *The Reading Teacher, 32,* 403–408.

Savage, R., Lavers, N., & Pillay, V. (2007). Working memory and reading difficulties: What we know and what we don't know about the relationship. *Educational Psychology Review, 19*(2), 185–221.

Saxe, R., Schulz, L. E., & Jiang, Y. V. (2006). Reading minds versus following rules: Dissociating theory of mind and executive control in the brain. *Social Neuroscience, 1,* 284–298.

Schmitz, T. W., Kawahara-Baccus, T. N., & Johnson, S. C. (2004). Metacognitive evaluation, self-relevance, and the right prefrontal cortex. *NeuroImage, 22*(2), 941–947.

Schneider, W. E., Schumann-Hengsteler, R. E., & Sodian, B. E. (2005). *Young children's cognitive development: Interrelationships among executive functioning, working memory, verbal ability, and theory of mind.* Mahwah, NJ: Erlbaum.

Scholastic, Inc. (2010). *Scholastic teacher's friend: Patterns learning mats.* New York: Author.

Schunk, D. H., & Rice, J. M. (1989). Learning goals and children's reading comprehension. *Journal of Reading Behavior, 21,* 279–293.

Schunk, D. H., & Rice, J. M. (1991). Learning goals and progress feedback during reading comprehension instruction. *Journal of Reading Behavior, 23,* 351–364.

Seigneuric, A., & Ehrlich, M. F. (2005). Contribution of working memory capacity to children's reading comprehension: A longitudinal investigation. *Reading and Writing, 18,* 617–656.

Seigneuric, A., Ehrlich, M. F., Oakhill, J. V., & Yuill, N. M. (2000). Working memory resources and children's reading comprehension. *Reading and Writing, 13,* 81–103.

Sénéchal, M., & LeFevre, J. (2002). Parental involvement in the development of children's reading skill: A five-year longitudinal study. *Child Development, 73,* 445–460.

Sesma, H. W., Mahone, E. M., Levine, T., Eason, S. H., & Cutting, L. E. (2009). The contribution of executive skills to reading comprehension. *Child Neuropsychology, 15,* 232–246.

Shallice, T. (1982). Specific impairments of planning. *Philosophical Transactions of the Royal Society of London, Part B, 298,* 199–209.

Shamay-Tsoory, S. G., Tomer, R., Berger, B. D., Goldsher, D., & Aharon-Peretz, J. (2005). Impaired "affective theory of mind" is associated with right ventromedial prefrontal damage. *Cognitive and Behavioral Neurology, 18,* 55–67.

Shanahan, T., & Shanahan, S. (1997). Character perspective charting: Helping children to develop a more complete conception of story. *The Reading Teacher, 50,* 668–677.

Shankweiler, D., Lundquist, E., Katz, L., Stuebing, K. K., Fletcher, J. M., Brady, S., et al. (1999). Comprehension and decoding: Patterns of association in children with reading difficulties. *Scientific Studies of Reading, 3,* 69–94.

Shannon, P., Kame'enui, E. J., & Baumann, J. F. (1988). An investigation of children's ability to comprehend character motives. *American Educational Research Journal, 25*(3), 441–462.

Shiotsu, T., & Weir, C. J. (2007). The relative significance of syntactic knowledge and vocabulary breadth in the prediction of reading comprehension test performance. *Language Testing, 24*(1), 99–128.

Short, E. J., & Ryan, E. B. (1984). Metacognitive differences between skilled and less skilled readers: Remediating deficits through story grammar and attribution training. *Journal of Educational Psychology, 76,* 225–235.

Simon, H. A. (1975). The functional equivalence of problem solving skills. *Cognitive Psychology, 7,* 268–288.

Simpson, A., & Riggs, K. J. (2006). Conditions under which children experience inhibitory difficulty with a "button-press" go/no-go task. *Journal of Experimental Child Psychology, 94,* 18–26.

Slaughter, V., Dennis, M. J., & Pritchard, M. (2002). Theory of mind and peer acceptance in preschool children. *British Journal of Developmental Psychology, 20*(4), 545–564.

Slaughter, V., Peterson, C. C., & Mackintosh, E. (2007). Mind what mother says: Narrative input and theory of mind in typical children and those on the autism spectrum. *Child Development, 78*(3), 839–858.

Smith, H. K. (1967). The responses of good and poor readers when asked to read for different purposes. *Reading Research Quarterly, 3,* 53––83.

Solanto, M. V. (2013) *Cognitive-behavioral therapy for adult ADHD: Targeting executive dysfunction.* New York: Guilford Press.

Sowell, E. R., Thompson, P. M., Leonard, C. M., Welcome, S. E., Kan, E., & Toga, A. W.

(2004). Longitudinal mapping of cortical thickness and brain growth in normal children. *Journal of Neuroscience, 24,* 8223–8231.

Spiegel, D. L., & Fitzgerald, J. (1986). Improving reading comprehension through instruction about story parts. *The Reading Teacher, 39,* 676–682.

Spyridakis, J. H., & Standal, T. C. (1987). Signals in expository prose: Effects on reading comprehension. *Reading Research Quarterly, 22,* 285–298.

Stahl, K. A. D. (2014). Fostering inference generation with emergent and novice readers. *The Reading Teacher, 67*(5), 384–388.

St Clair-Thompson, H. L., & Gathercole, S. E. (2006). Executive functions and achievements in school: Shifting, updating, inhibition, and working memory. *Quarterly Journal of Experimental Psychology, 59,* 745–759.

Stein, N. L., & Glenn, C. G. (1975). *An analysis of story comprehension in elementary school children.* (Report No. PS 008 544). Retrieved from ERIC database (ED 121 474). St. Louis, MO: Washington University.

Sterritt, G. M., & Rudnick, M. (1966). Auditory and visual rhythm perception in relation to reading ability in fourth grade boys. *Perceptual and Motor Skills, 22,* 859–864.

Stevens, R. J., Van Meter, P., & Warcholak, N. D. (2010). The effects of explicitly teaching story structure to primary grade children. *Journal of Literacy Research, 42,* 159–198.

Stone, C. A., Silliman, E. R., Ehren, B. J., & Wallach, G. P. (Eds.). (2014). *Handbook of language and literacy: Development and disorders* (2nd ed.). New York: Guilford Press.

Stone, V. E., Baron-Cohen, S., & Knight, R. T. (1998). Frontal lobe contributions to theory of mind. *Journal of Cognitive Neuroscience, 10,* 640–656.

Stothard, S. E., & Hulme, C. (1992). Reading comprehension difficulties in children: The role of language comprehension and working memory skills. *Reading and Writing: An Interdisciplinary Journal, 4,* 245–256.

Strasser, K., & del Río, F. (2014). The role of comprehension monitoring, theory of mind, and vocabulary depth in predicting story comprehension and recall of kindergarten children. *Reading Research Quarterly, 49,* 169–187.

Stroop, J. R. (1935). Studies of interference in serial verbal reactions. *Journal of Experimental Psychology, 18*(6), 643–62.

Stuss, D. T., Alexander, M. P., Palumbo, C. L., Buckle, L., Sayer, L., & Pogue, J. (1994). Organizational strategies with unilateral or bilateral frontal lobe injury in word learning tasks. *Neuropsychology, 8,* 355–373.

Sullivan, K., Zaitchik, D., & Tager-Flusberg, H. (1994). Preschoolers can attribute second-order beliefs. *Developmental Psychology, 30*(3), 395–402.

Swan, P. (2003). *Patterns in mathematics, grades 3–6: Investigating patterns in number relationships.* Rowley, MA: Didax Educational Resources.

Swanson, H. L., Howard, C. B., & Saez, L. (2006). Do different components of working memory underlie different subgroups of reading disabilities? *Journal of Learning Disabilities, 39,* 252–269.

Swanson, H. L., & O'Connor, R. (2009). The role of working memory and fluency practice on reading comprehension of students who are dysfluent readers. *Journal of Learning Disabilities, 42,* 548–575.

Symons, D. K., Peterson, C. C., Slaughter, V., Roche, J., & Doyle, E. (2005). Theory of mind and mental state discourse during book reading and story-telling tasks. *British Journal of Developmental Psychology, 23*(1), 81–102.

Tallal, P. (2004). Improving language and literacy is a matter of time. *Nature Reviews Neuroscience, 5,* 721–728.

Tallal, P., & Gaab, N. (2006). Dynamic auditory processing, musical experience and language development. *Trends in Neurosciences, 29,* 382–390.

Taylor, B. M. (1982). Text structure and children's comprehension and memory for expository material. *Journal of Educational Psychology, 74,* 323–340.

Taylor, H. B., Anthony, J. L., Aghara, R., Smith, K. E., & Landry, S. H. (2008). The interaction of early maternal responsiveness and children's cognitive abilities on later decoding and reading comprehension skills. *Early Education and Development, 19*, 188–207.

Taylor, M. B., & Williams, J. P. (1983). Comprehension of learning-disabled readers: Task and text variations. *Journal of Educational Psychology, 75*, 743–751.

Thorell, L. B., Lindqvist, S., Bergman Nutley, S., Bohlin, G., & Klingberg, T. (2009). Training and transfer effects of executive functions in preschool children. *Developmental Science, 12*, 106–113.

Tine, M. (2014). Working memory differences between children living in rural and urban poverty. *Journal of Cognition and Development, 15*, 599–613.

Toll, S. W. M., Van der Ven, S. H. G., Kroesbergen, E. H., & Van Luit, J. E. H. (2011). Executive functions as predictors of math learning disabilities. *Journal of Learning Disabilities, 44*, 521–532.

Tompkins, V., Guo, Y., & Justice, L. M. (2013). Inference generation, story comprehension, and language skills in the preschool years. *Reading and Writing, 26*, 403–429.

Tong, X., Tong, X., Shu, H., Chan, S., & McBride-Chang, C. (2014). Discourse-level reading comprehension in Chinese children: What is the role of syntactic awareness? *Journal of Research in Reading, 37*(S1), S48–S70.

Torppa, M., Tolvanen, A., Poikkeus, A., Eklund, K., Lerkkanen, M., Leskinen, E., et al. (2007). Reading development subtypes and their early characteristics. *Annals of Dyslexia, 57*, 3–32.

Trabasso, T., & Bartolone, J. (2003). Story understanding and counterfactual reasoning. *Journal of Experimental Psychology: Learning, Memory and Cognition, 29*, 904–923.

Trabasso, T., & Magliano, J. P. (1996). Conscious understanding during comprehension. *Discourse Processes, 21*, 255–287.

Trabasso, T., Stein, N. L., & Johnson, L. R. (1981). Children's knowledge of events: A causal analysis of story structure. *Psychology of Learning and Motivation, 15*, 237–282.

Tyrrell, D. S. (1980). *The development of sequencing abilities in good and poor readers.* Unpublished doctoral dissertation, Cornell University, Ithaca, NY.

Unsworth, N., & Engle, R. W. (2008). Speed and accuracy of accessing information in working memory: An individual differences investigation of focus switching. *Journal of Experimental Psychology: Learning, Memory, and Cognition, 34*, 616–630.

Ursache, A., Blair, C., Stifter, C., Voegtline, K., & The Family Life Project Investigators. (2013). Emotional reactivity and regulation in infancy interact to predict executive functioning in early childhood. *Developmental Psychology, 49*, 127–137.

van den Broek, P. (1989). Causal reasoning and inference making in judging the importance of story statements. *Child Development, 60*, 286–297.

van der Sluis, S., de Jong, P. F., & van der Leij, A. (2007). Executive functioning in children, and its relations with reasoning, reading, and arithmetic. *Intelligence, 35*, 427–449.

Vidal-Abarca, E., Mañá, A., & Gil, L. (2010). Individual differences for self-regulating task-oriented reading activities. *Journal of Educational Psychology, 102*, 817–826.

Vogeley, K., Bussfeld, P., Newen, A., Herrmann, S., Happé, F., Falkai, P., et al. (2001). Mind reading: Neural mechanisms of theory of mind and self-perspective. *NeuroImage, 14*(1), 170–181.

Völlm, B. A., Taylor, A. N., Richardson, P., Corcoran, R., Stirling, J., McKie, S., et al. (2006). Neuronal correlates of theory of mind and empathy: A functional magnetic resonance imaging study in a nonverbal task. *NeuroImage, 29*(1), 90–98.

Wagner, R. K., & Sternberg, R. J. (1987). Executive control in reading comprehension. In B. K. Britton & S. M. Glynn (Eds.), *Executive control processes in reading* (pp. 1–21). Hillsdale, NJ: Erlbaum.

Walker, C. M., Gopnik, A., & Ganea, P. A. (2015). Learning to learn from stories: Children's developing sensitivity to the causal structure of fictional worlds. *Child Development, 86*, 310–318.

Watson, A. C., Nixon, C. L., Wilson, A., & Capage, L. (1999). Social interaction skills and theory of mind in young children. *Developmental Psychology, 35*, 386–391.

Watson, A. J. (1979). Multiple seriation and learning to read. *Australian Journal of Education, 23*(2), 171–180.

Weaver, P. A. (1979). Improving reading comprehension: Effects of sentence organization instruction. *Reading Research Quarterly, 15*, 129–146.

Weaver, P. A., & Dickinson, D. K. (1982). Scratching below the surface structure: Exploring the usefulness of story grammars. *Discourse Processes, 5*(3–4), 225–243.

Webster, L., & Ammon, P. (1994). Linking written language to cognitive development: Reading, writing, and concrete operations. *Research in the Teaching of English, 28*, 89–109.

Wechsler, D. (1991). *WISC-III: Wechsler Intelligence Scale for Children.* San Antonio, TX: Psychological Corporation.

Wellman, H. M., & Liu, D. (2004). Scaling of theory-of-mind tasks. *Child Development, 75*, 523–541.

Welsh, M. C. (1991). Rule-guided behavior and self-monitoring on the Tower of Hanoi disk-transfer task. *Cognitive Development, 6*, 59–76.

Welsh, M. C., & Huizinga, M. (2005). Tower of Hanoi disk-transfer task: Influences of strategy knowledge and learning on performance. *Learning and Individual Differences, 15*, 283–298.

Wenner, J. (2004). Preschoolers' comprehension of goal structure in narratives. *Memory, 12*(2), 193–202.

Werker, J. F., & Tees, R. C. (1984). Cross-language speech perception: Evidence for perceptual reorganization during the first year of life. *Infant Behavior and Development, 7*, 49–63.

White, S., Chen, J., & Forsyth, B. (2010). Reading-related literacy activities of American adults: Time spent, task types, and cognitive skills used. *Journal of Literacy Research, 42*, 276–307.

White House Press Release (2013, April 2). *Fact sheet: BRAIN initiative.* Office of the Press Secretary. Accessed at *www.whitehouse.gov/the-press-office/2013/04/02/fact-sheet-brain-initiative.*

Wijekumar, K. K., Meyer, B. J., & Lei, P. (2012). Large-scale randomized controlled trial with 4th graders using intelligent tutoring of the structure strategy to improve nonfiction reading comprehension. *Educational Technology Research and Development, 60*, 987–1013.

Williams, J. P. (2003). Teaching text structure to improve reading comprehension. In H. L. Swanson, K. R. Harris, & S. Graham (Eds.), *Handbook of learning disabilities* (pp. 293–305). New York: Guilford Press.

Williams, J. P. (2005). Instruction in reading comprehension for primary-grade students: A focus on text structure. *Journal of Special Education, 39*, 6–18.

Williams, J. P., Lauer, K. D., Hall, K. M., Lord, K. M., Gugga, S. S., Bak, S. J., et al. (2002). Teaching elementary school students to identify story themes. *Journal of Educational Psychology, 94*, 235–248.

Williams, J. P., Pollini, S., Nubla-Kung, A. M., Snyder, A. E., Garcia, A., Ordynans, J. G., et al. (2014). An intervention to improve comprehension of cause/effect through expository text structure instruction. *Journal of Educational Psychology, 106*, 1–17.

Williams, J. P., Stafford, K. B., Lauer, K. D., Hall, K. M., & Pollini, S. (2009). Embedding reading comprehension training in content-area instruction. *Journal of Educational Psychology, 101*, 1–20.

Wilson, S. P., & Kipp, K. (1998). The development of efficient inhibition: Evidence from directed-forgetting tasks. *Developmental Review, 18*, 86–123.

Wimmer, H., & Perner, J. (1983). Beliefs about beliefs: Representation and constraining function of wrong beliefs in young children's understanding of deception. *Cognition, 13*(1), 103–128.

Wolf, M. (1986). Rapid alternating stimulus naming in the developmental dyslexias. *Brain and Language, 27,* 360–379.

Wolman, C., van den Broek, P., & Lorch, R. F. (1997). Effects of causal structure on immediate and delayed story recall by children with mild mental retardation, children with learning disabilities, and children without disabilities. *Journal of Special Education, 30,* 439–455.

Wong, B. Y., & Jones, W. (1982). Increasing metacomprehension in learning disabled and normally achieving students through self-questioning training. *Learning Disability Quarterly, 5,* 228–240.

Wong, B. Y., & Wilson, M. (1984). Investigating awareness of and teaching passage organization in learning disabled children. *Journal of Learning Disabilities, 17*(8), 477–482.

Woodcock, R. W., Johnson, M. B., & Mather, N. (1989). *Woodcock–Johnson Psycho-Educational Battery—Revised.* Allen, TX: DLM Teaching Resources.

Wyatt, D., Pressley, M., El-Dinary, P. B., Stein, S., Evans, P., & Brown, R. (1993). Comprehension strategies, worth and credibility monitoring, and evaluations: Cold and hot cognition when experts read professional texts that are important to them. *Learning and Individual Differences, 5,* 49–72.

Yan, R. & Yu, G. (2006). Cognitive flexibility of reading-disabled children: Development and characteristics. *Chinese Journal of Clinical Psychology, 14*(1), 33–35.

Yeniad, N., Malda, M., Mesman, J., van IJzendoorn, M. H., Emmen, R. A. G., & Prevoo, M. J. L. (2014). Cognitive flexibility children across the transition to school: A longitudinal study. *Cognitive Development, 31,* 35–47.

Yeniad, N., Malda, M., Mesman, J., van IJzendoorn, M. H., & Pieper, S. (2013). Shifting ability predicts math and reading performance in children: A meta-analytical study. *Learning and Individual Differences, 23,* 1–9.

Yuill, N. (1996). A funny thing happened on the way to the classroom: Jokes, riddles, and metalinguistic awareness in understanding and improving poor comprehension in children. In C. Cornoldi & J. Oakhill (Eds.), *Reading comprehension difficulties: Processes and intervention* (pp. 193–220). Mahwah, NJ: Erlbaum.

Yuill, N. (2007). Visiting joke city: How can talking about jokes foster metalinguistic awareness in poor comprehenders? In D. S. McNamara (Ed.), *Reading comprehension strategies: Theories, interventions and technologies* (pp. 325–345). Mahwah, NJ: Erlbaum.

Yuill, N. (2009). The relation between ambiguity understanding and metalinguistic discussion of joking riddles in good and poor comprehenders: Potential for intervention and possible processes of change. *First Language, 29,* 65–79.

Yuill, N., & Joscelyne, T. (1988). Effect of organizational cues and strategies on good and poor comprehenders' story understanding. *Journal of Educational Psychology, 80,* 152–158.

Yuill, N., Kerawalla, L., Pearce, D., Luckin, R., & Harris, A. (2008). Using technology to teach flexibility through peer discussion. In K. B. Cartwright (Ed.), *Literacy processes: Cognitive flexibility in learning and teaching* (pp. 320–341). New York: Guilford Press.

Yuill, N., & Oakhill, J. (1988). Understanding of anaphoric relations in skilled and less skilled comprehenders. *British Journal of Psychology, 79,* 173–186.

Yuill, N., & Oakhill. J. (1991). *Children's problems in text comprehension.* Cambridge, UK: Cambridge University Press.

Yuill, N., Oakhill, J., & Parkin, A. (1989). Working memory, comprehension ability and the resolution of text anomaly. *British Journal of Psychology, 80,* 351–361.

Zampini, L., Suttora, C., D'Odorico, L., & Zanchi, P. (2013). Sequential reasoning and listening text comprehension in preschool children. *European Journal of Developmental Psychology, 10,* 563–579.

Zelazo, P. D. (2006). The dimensional change card sort (DCCS): A method of assessing executive function in children. *Nature Protocols, 1,* 297–301.

Zelazo, P. D. (2013, November). *Executive function and the developing brain: Implications for education.* Presentation for the Annual Meeting of the Association of Metropolitan

School Districts, St. Paul, MN. Video available at *www.youtube.com/watch?v=r2-j7pqO-foU; presentation slides available at www.amsd.org/wp-content/uploads/2013/09/Zelazo_AMSD_7_Nov_13.pdf.*

Zelazo, P. D., Anderson, J. E., Richler, J., Wallner-Allen, K., Beaumont, J. L., & Weintraub, S. (2013). NIH Toolbox Cognition Battery (CB): Measuring executive function and attention. *Monographs of the Society for Research in Child Development, 78*(4), 1–172.

Zelazo, P. D., & Carlson, S. M. (2012). Hot and cool executive function in childhood and adolescence: Development and plasticity. *Child Development Perspectives, 6*, 354–360.

Zelazo, P. D., & Müller, U. (2002). Executive function in typical and atypical development. In U. Goswami (Ed.), *Blackwell handbook of childhood cognitive development* (pp. 445–469). Malden, MA: Blackwell.

Zelazo, P. D., Müller, U., Frye, D., & Marcovitch, S. (2003). The development of executive function in early childhood. *Monographs of the Society for Research in Child Development, 68*(3), 1–155.

Zelazo, P. D., Qu, L., & Müller, U. (2005). Hot and cool aspects of executive function: Relations in early development. In W. Schneider, R. Schumann-Hengsteler, & B. Sodian (Eds.), *Young children's cognitive development* (pp. 71–93). Mahwah, NJ: Erlbaum.

Zhou, Q., Chen, S. H., & Main, A. (2012). Commonalities and differences in the research on children's effortful control and executive function: A call for an integrated model of self-regulation. *Child Development Perspectives, 6*, 112–121.

Zimmerman, B. J. (1990). Self-regulated learning and academic achievement: An overview. *Educational Psychologist, 25*(1), 3–17.

Zipke, M. (2007). The role of metalinguistic awareness in the reading comprehension of sixth and seventh graders. *Reading Psychology, 28*(4), 375–396.

Zipke, M. (2008). Teaching metalinguistic awareness and reading comprehension with riddles. *The Reading Teacher, 62*(2), 128–137.

Zipke, M., Ehri, L. C., & Cairns, H. S. (2009). Using semantic ambiguity instruction to improve third graders' metalinguistic awareness and reading comprehension: An experimental study. *Reading Research Quarterly, 44*, 300–321.

Index